ZAGATSURVEY®

2006

SAN FRANCISCO BAY AREA RESTAURANTS

Local Editor: Meesha Halm

Editor: Caren Campbell

Published and distributed by
ZAGAT SURVEY, LLC
4 Columbus Circle
New York, New York 10019
Tel: 212 977 6000
E-mail: sanfran@zagat.com
Web site: www.zagat.com

Acknowledgments

We thank Erika Adams, Antonia Allegra, Heidi Cusick, Nel and Charles Ellwein, Jon, Olive and Jude Fox, Leroy and Esther Meshel, Steven Shukow, Karen Solomon and Sharron Wood. We are also grateful to our assistant editor, Victoria Elmacioglu, and editorial assistant, Josh Rogers, as well as the following members of our staff: Reni Chin, Larry Cohn, Schuyler Frazier, Jeff Freier, Natalie Lebert, Mike Liao, Dave Makulec, Robert Poole, Thomas Sheehan, Joshua Siegel, Carla Spartos, Erinn Stivala and Sharon Yates.

Contents

About This Survey

Here are the results of our *2006 San Francisco Bay Area Restaurant Survey,* covering 943 restaurants as tested, and tasted, by 6,871 local restaurant-goers.

This marks the 26th year that Zagat Survey has reported on the shared experiences of diners like you and our 20th anniversary in SF. What started in 1979 as a hobby involving 200 of our friends rating local NYC restaurants has come a long way. Today we have over 250,000 active surveyors and now cover entertaining, golf, hotels, resorts, spas, movies, music, nightlife, shopping and tourist attractions. All of these guides are based on consumer surveys. Our guides are also available on PDAs, cell phones and by subscription at zagat.com, where you can vote and shop as well.

By regularly surveying large numbers of avid customers, we hope to have achieved a uniquely current and reliable guide. This year's participants dined out an average of 3.2 times per week, meaning this guide is based on roughly 1.15 million meals. Of these 6,800 plus surveyors, 47% are women, 53% men; the breakdown by age is 13% in their 20s; 31%, 30s; 19%, 40s; 21%, 50s; and 16%, 60s or above. Our editors have synopsized our surveyors' opinions, with their comments shown in quotation marks. We sincerely thank each of these people; this book is really "theirs."

We are especially grateful to our longtime San Francisco editor, Meesha Halm, who is both a Bay Area restaurant critic and a cookbook author.

To help guide our readers to San Francisco's best meals and best buys, we have prepared a number of lists. For the overall Bay Area, see Most Popular (page 9), Top Ratings (pages 10–15) and Best Buys (page 16). Top ratings broken down by region can be found at the beginning of each section. In addition, we have provided 44 handy indexes.

To vote in any of our upcoming *Surveys,* just register at zagat.com. Each participant will receive a free copy of the resulting guide (or a comparable reward). Your comments and even criticisms of this guide are also solicited. There is always room for improvement with your help. Just contact us at sanfran@zagat.com.

New York, NY
September 27, 2005

Nina and Tim Zagat

What's New

After a rough couple of years, the San Francisco restaurant scene is once more alive and cooking. One-third of surveyors report that they dine out more than they did two years ago, while overall our voters eat out or take out more than half their meals in a given week. Factor in all the flash, foam and fanfare that typify this year's newcomers, and it's clear why Golden Gaters are telling restaurateurs, in the words of their celluloid governor, "I'll be back."

Hot Spots: Perhaps no restaurant embodies the return of swank supping more than Myth, where Sean O'Brien (once Gary Danko's right-hand man) is making magic in surveyors' favorite neighborhood for dining, Downtown; in that same section, Scott Howard (of Marin's Fork) plans to open an eponymous New American this fall. In areas south of Market Street, it looks like dot-com-era déjà vu all over again at hip haunts like Jack Falstaff, La Suite, Oola and Zuppa. Still to come are Ame, a New American from Terra's Hiro Sone at the soon-to-open St. Regis Hotel, and a high-end Mexican, Tres Agaves.

Tired of Tapas? Another batch of global small-plates providers – Louka, Luella, Picco and Stomp, among others – attests to chefs' continuing affection for *petits plats,* though surveyors seem less enthralled. Only 48% said they like the tapas trend, while only about 27% feel small-plate dining offers a better value than traditional dining. Maybe cost-conscious consumers have discovered, as Winston Churchill might have said, "never has so much been owed by so many for so little."

Northern Lights: Despite rising gas prices, 23% of respondents say they'd gladly drive over an hour for a good dinner, which bodes well for wine-country neophytes Cyrus, Press and Restaurant Budo and Yountville's forthcoming Redd from Richard Reddington (ex Auberge du Soleil). Meanwhile, in-town diners are in luck now that the French Laundry Trickle-Down Effect has shown up in the city proper: Former employees of Thomas Keller are heading up Masa's and the new U Street Lounge.

Keeping Tabs: Sixty percent of respondents say they're shelling out more for meals this year, with the average dinner costing $35.52 (up 5.2% from last year). That's 11.1% higher than the U.S. norm – not too surprising, since after all SF's food is anything but ordinary.

San Francisco, CA
September 27, 2005

Meesha Halm

Ratings & Symbols

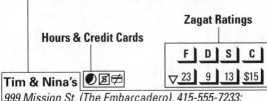

Name, Address, Phone Number & Web Site

Zagat Ratings

Hours & Credit Cards

F	D	S	C
▽ 23	9	13	$15

Tim & Nina's ◐ ⌧ ⊄

999 Mission St. (The Embarcadero), 415-555-7233;
www.zagat.com

Open "more or less when they feel like it", this bit
of unembellished Embarcadero ectoplasm excels at
seafood with an Asian-Argentinean-Albanian twist; the
staff seems "fresh off the boat", and while the view of
the garbage barges is "a drag", no one balks at the
bottom-feeder prices.

Review, with surveyors' comments in quotes

Top Spots: Places with the highest overall ratings, popularity
and importance are listed in BLOCK CAPITAL LETTERS.

Hours: ◐ serves after 11 PM
⌧ closed on Sunday

Credit Cards: ⊄ no credit cards accepted

Ratings are on a scale of **0** to **30. Cost (C)** reflects our
surveyors' estimate of the price of dinner with one
drink and tip.

F	Food	D	Decor	S	Service	C	Cost
23		9		13		$15	

0–9	poor to fair	**20–25** very good to excellent
10–15	fair to good	**26–30** extraordinary to perfection
16–19	good to very good	▽ low response/less reliable

For newcomers or survey write-ins listed without ratings,
the price range is indicated as follows:

I	$25 and below	**E**	$41 to $65
M	$26 to $40	**VE**	$66 or more

Most Popular

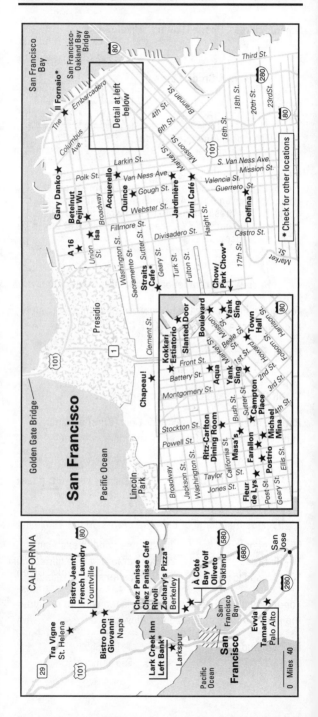

subscribe to zagat.com

Most Popular

Each of our surveyors has been asked to name his or her five favorite Bay Area restaurants. The following list reflects their choices. Places outside of San Francisco are marked as follows: E=East of SF; N=North; and S=South. When a restaurant has locations both inside and outside the city limits, we include the notation SF as well.

1. Gary Danko
2. Boulevard
3. French Laundry/N
4. Slanted Door
5. Chez Panisse Café/E
6. Chez Panisse/E
7. Aqua
8. Delfina
9. Zuni Café
10. Farallon
11. Evvia/S
12. Jardinière
13. Michael Mina
14. Fleur de Lys
15. Zachary's Pizza/E
16. Bistro Jeanty/N
17. Kokkari Estiatorio
18. Straits Cafe/S/SF
19. Chapeau!
20. Masa's
21. A 16
22. Tamarine/S
23. Campton Place
24. Left Bank/E/N/S
25. Rivoli/E
26. Town Hall
27. À Côté/E
28. Il Fornaio/E/N/S/SF
29. Bistro Don Giovanni/N
30. Oliveto/E
31. Tra Vigne/N
32. Postrio
33. Ritz-Carlton Din. Rm.
34. Betelnut Pejiu Wu
35. Yank Sing
36. Chow/Park Chow/E/SF
37. Bay Wolf/E
38. Lark Creek Inn/N
39. Acquerello
40. Quince

It's obvious that many of the restaurants on the above list are among the San Francisco area's most expensive, but if popularity were calibrated to price, we suspect that a number of other restaurants would join the above ranks. Given the fact that both our surveyors and readers love to discover dining bargains, we have added a list of 80 Best Buys and restaurants offering bargain prix fixe menus on pages 16–18. These are restaurants that give real quality at extremely reasonable prices.

Top Ratings Overall

Excluding places with low voting, unless indicated by a ▽.

Top Food

29 Gary Danko
28 French Laundry/N
    Manresa/S
    Erna's Elderberry Hse./E
    Sushi Ran/N
    Masa's
    Farmhouse Inn/N
27 Fleur de Lys
    La Folie
    Sierra Mar/S
    Michael Mina
    Chez Panisse Café/E
    Cafe La Haye/N
    Marché/S
    Rivoli/E
    Chapeau!
    Le Papillon/S*
    Chez Panisse/E
    Terra/N
    Hana Japanese/N

    Boulevard
    Marinus/S
    La Toque/N
    Fork/N
    Ritz-Carlton Din. Rm.
    Kabuto
    Quince
26 Aqua
    Campton Place
    Jardinière
    Acquerello
    Delfina
    Cole's Chop House/N
    Tartine Bakery
    Lalime's/E
    Bistro Jeanty/N
    Cafe Gibraltar/S
    House
    Pearl Oyster Bar/E
    CAFÉ KATi

By Cuisine

American (New)
29 Gary Danko
28 French Laundry/N
27 Michael Mina
    Terra/N
    Boulevard

American (Traditional)
26 Lark Creek Inn/N
23 Buckeye Roadhouse/N
22 Liberty Cafe
    Lark Creek/E
    BIX

Bakeries
26 Tartine Bakery
25 Mama's Wash. Sq.
24 Downtown Bakery/N
    Gayle's Bakery/S
23 Boulange de Cole/Polk

Barbecue
25 Foothill Cafe/N
24 Bo's Barbecue/E
23 Brother's Korean
    Brother-in-Law BBQ
    Buckeye Roadhouse/N

Cajun/Creole/Southern
23 Brother-in-Law BBQ
20 Everett & Jones BBQ/E
    Kate's Kitchen
18 PJ's Oyster Bed
17 Elite Cafe

Californian
28 Erna's Elderberry Hse./E
    Farmhouse Inn/N
27 Sierra Mar/S
    Chez Panisse Café/E
    Cafe La Haye/N

Chinese
25 Ton Kiang
    Yank Sing
24 Jai Yun▽
    Koi Palace/S
    Tommy Toy's

Continental
23 El Paseo/N
    Chantilly/S
    Anton & Michel/S
21 Maddalena's/S
20 Shadowbrook/S

---

* Indicates a tie with restaurant above

Top Food

Dim Sum
25 Ton Kiang
 Yank Sing
24 Koi Palace/S
22 Fook Yuen Seafood/S
 Harbor Village

Eclectic
26 Willi's Wine Bar/N
24 Celadon/N
 Va de Vi/E
 Firefly
23 Willow Wood Mkt./N

French
27 Fleur de Lys
 La Folie
 Le Papillon/S
 La Toque/N
25 Cafe Jaqueline

French (Bistro)
27 Chapeau!
26 Bistro Jeanty/N
25 Fringale
 Bouchon/N
24 Chez Papa Bistrot

French (New)
28 Manresa/S
 Masa's
27 Marché/S
 Marinus/S
 Ritz-Carlton Din. Rm.

Fusion
26 House
 CAFÉ KATi
24 Silks
 Eos Rest./Wine Bar
 Flying Fish Grill/S

Hamburgers
21 Taylor's Automatic/N/SF
20 Mo's
 Burger Joint/S/SF
19 Barney's/E/N/SF
18 Balboa Cafe/E/SF

Indian/Pakistani
25 Amber India/S
24 Vik's Chaat Corner/E
23 Indian Oven
 Ajanta/E
 Shalimar/E/SF

Italian
27 Quince
26 Acquerello
 Delfina
25 Oliveto/E
 Dopo/E

Japanese
28 Sushi Ran/N
27 Hana Japanese/N
 Kabuto
25 Kirala/E
24 O Chamé/E

Latin American
24 Limón
23 Charanga
 Fonda Solana/E
 Fresca
22 El Raigon

Mediterranean
27 Chez Panisse Café/E
 Rivoli/E
 Chez Panisse/E
26 Campton Place
 Lalime's/E

Mexican
24 La Taqueria/S/SF
23 Taqueria Can-Cun
 Doña Tomás/E
 Pancho Villa/S/SF
22 Maya

Middle Eastern
24 Helmand, The
22 Dish Dash/S
 Truly Mediterranean
 Maykadeh▽
20 La Méditerranée/E/SF

Pizza
25 Tommaso's
 Zachary's Pizza/E
 Pizzetta 211
24 Postrio
 Pazzia

Seafood
26 Aqua
 Pearl Oyster Bar/E
 Swan Oyster Depot
25 Hog Island Oyster
 Willi's Seafood/N

Top Food

Spanish/Basque
25 Piperade
23 Bocadillos
22 Zarzuela
21 B44
20 Iberia/S

Steakhouses
26 Cole's Chop House/N
24 Harris'
   House of Prime Rib
23 Anzu
   Ruth's Chris Steak

Tapas (Latin)
24 Zuzu/N
23 Bocadillos
   Charanga
   César/E
19 Cha Cha Cha

Thai
25 Thep Phanom
24 Soi Four/E
   Manora's
23 Marnee
   Basil

Vegetarian
28 French Laundry/N
27 Fleur de Lys
24 Millennium
23 Greens
19 Geranium

Vietnamese
25 Tamarine/S
   Slanted Door
23 Thanh Long
   Crustacean
   Three Seasons/E/S/SF

By Special Feature

Breakfast
26 Tartine Bakery
25 Dottie's True Blue
   Oliveto Cafe/E
   Mama's Wash. Sq.
24 Gayle's Bakery/S

Brunch
28 Erna's Elderberry Hse./E
26 Campton Place
   Lark Creek Inn/N
   John Ash & Co./N
24 Navio/S

Child-Friendly
25 Yank Sing
21 Taylor's Automatic/N/SF
   Picante Cocina/E
19 Barney's/E/N/SF
15 Pasta Pomodoro/E/S/SF

Hotel Dining
28 Masa's
   Hotel Vintage Ct.
   Farmhouse Inn/N
   Farmhouse Inn
27 Sierra Mar/S
   Post Ranch Inn
   Michael Mina
   Westin St. Francis
   Hana Japanese/N
   Doubletree Plaza

Late Night
25 Bouchon/N
24 Zuni Café
23 Brother's Korean
   Taqueria Can-Cun
   Fonda Solana/E

Newcomers/Rated
27 Cyrus/N▽
26 Rest. Budo/N▽
24 Myth▽
   Jack Falstaff
22 La Suite

Newcomers/Unrated
   Coco 500
   Pizzeria Delfina
   Press/N
   Winterland
   Zuppa

People-Watching
27 Boulevard
26 Jardinière
24 Zuni Café
   Jack Falstaff
22 Spago Palo Alto/S

Small Plates
27 Fork/N
26 Pearl Oyster Bar/E
   Willi's Wine Bar/N
25 Tamarine/S
   Isa

Top Food

Tasting Menu

29 Gary Danko
28 French Laundry/N
   Manresa/S
   Masa's
27 Michael Mina

Trendy

24 Myth
   Jack Falstaff
   Town Hall
20 Oola
19 Frisson

Wine Bar

24 Eos Rest./Wine Bar
23 A 16
   César/E
22 bacar
17 Nectar Wine Lounge

Winning Wine Lists

27 Michael Mina
26 Fifth Floor
24 PlumpJack Cafe/E/SF
23 Rubicon
22 bacar

Worth a Trip

28 French Laundry/N
   Yountville
   Erna's Elderberry Hse./E
   Oakhurst
   Farmhouse Inn/N
   Forestville
27 Sierra Mar/S
   Big Sur
   Chez Panisse/E
   Berkeley

Top Decor

29 Sierra Mar/S
28 Garden Court
Ahwahnee Din. Rm./E
Pacific's Edge/S
Auberge du Soleil/N
27 Ana Mandara
Farallon
Gary Danko
Erna's Elderberry Hse./E
Navio/S
Fleur de Lys
Ritz-Carlton Din. Rm.
26 Jardinière
Marinus/S
Shadowbrook/S
Seasons
Domaine Chandon/N
French Laundry/N
Wente Vineyards/E
Silks

25 Myth
John Ash & Co./N
BIX
Madrona Manor/N
Campton Place
Bing Crosby's/E
Martini House/N
Lark Creek Inn/N
Fifth Floor
Farmhouse Inn/N
Ozumo*
Sutro's at Cliff Hse.*
Tonga Room
Boulevard
Roy's Pebble Beach/S
Grand Cafe
Kokkari Estiatorio
Aqua
Asia de Cuba
Masa's

Outdoors

Alexander Valley/N
Angèle/N
Auberge du Soleil/N
Barndiva/N
Bay Wolf/E
B44
Bistro Aix
Brix/N
Casanova/S
Chez Spencer
Domaine Chandon/N
Doña Tomás/E
Enrico's Sidewalk

Foreign Cinema
Hurley's/N
Isa
Jack Falstaff
Lark Creek Inn/N
Martini House/N
Pinot Blanc/N
Plouf
Rest. Budo/N▽
Ritz-Carlton Terrace
Sea Salt/E
Tra Vigne/N
Wente Vineyards/E

Romance

Acquerello
Applewood Inn/N
Auberge du Soleil/N
Aziza
Cafe Jacqueline
Casanova/S
Chez Panisse/E
Chez Spencer
Cyrus/N
El Paseo/N
Erna's Elderberry Hse./E
Fleur de Lys
Jardinière

Julius' Castle
Khan Toke
La Forêt/S
L'Auberge Carmel/S
Le Papillon/S
Madrona Manor/N
Manka's Inverness/N
Marinus/S
Martini House/N
Ritz-Carlton Din. Rm.
Sierra Mar/S
Tallula
Venticello

Rooms

Ahwahnee Din. Rm./E
Ana Mandara
Aqua
Asia de Cuba
BIX
Boulevard
Cetrella Bistro/S
Evvia/S
Farallon
Frisson
Garden Court
Grand Cafe
Jardinière
Jeanty at Jack's

Kokkari Estiatorio
La Suite
Le Colonial
Martini House/N
Masa's
Michael Mina
Myth
Pinot Blanc/N
Poggio/N
Rest. Budo/N
Ritz-Carlton Din. Rm.
St. Orres/N
Tallula
Tartare

Views

Ahwanee Din. Rm./E
Albion River Inn/N
Angèle/N
Auberge du Soleil/N
Beach Chalet
Bella Vista/S
Brix/N
Caprice/N
Carnelian Room
Cliff House Bistro
Greens
Guaymas/N
Jordan's/E

Julius' Castle
Ledford House/N
Navio/S
Nepenthe/S
Pacific's Edge/S
Poggio/N
Roy's Pebble Beach/S
Scoma's/N/SF
Sierra Mar/S
Slanted Door
Sutro's at Cliff Hse.
Waterfront
Wente Vineyards/E

Top Service

28 Gary Danko
Erna's Elderberry Hse./E
Ritz-Carlton Din. Rm.
27 French Laundry/N
Marinus/S
Masa's
Farmhouse Inn/N
26 Sierra Mar/S
Chapeau!
La Toque/N
Fleur de Lys
Seasons
Acquerello
Michael Mina
Albona Rist.
Campton Place
Le Papillon/S
Chez Panisse/E
25 Silks
Ritz-Carlton Terrace

Manresa/S
La Folie
Marché aux Fleurs/N
Terra/N
Fifth Floor
Chez TJ/S
La Forêt/S
Aqua
Rivoli/E
Lark Creek Inn/N
Auberge du Soleil/N
Quince
Chez Panisse Café/E
Marché/S
24 Boulevard
Jardinière
Cafe Beaujolais/N
Cafe La Haye/N
Tartare
Wente Vineyards/E

Best Buys

Top Bangs for the Buck

1. Saigon Sandwiches
2. Caspers Hot Dogs/E
3. Taqueria Can-Cun
4. Rosamunde Grill
5. El Balazo
6. Downtown Bakery/N
7. Cactus Taqueria/E
8. Pancho Villa/S/SF
9. Jay's Cheesesteak
10. Burger Joint/S/SF
11. La Cumbre Taqueria/S/SF
12. La Taqueria/S/SF
13. Red's Java House
14. Nick's Crispy Tacos
15. Truly Mediterranean
16. Tartine Bakery
17. Boulange Cole/Polk
18. Joe's Taco Lounge/N
19. Picante Cocina/E
20. Kate's Kitchen
21. Vik's Chaat Corner/E
22. Tacubaya/E
23. Fenton's Creamery/E
24. Dottie's True Blue
25. Asqew Grill/E/SF
26. Jimtown Store/N
27. Pork Store Café
28. Chloe's Cafe
29. Bette's Oceanview/E
30. Mama's Royal Cafe/E
31. Café Fanny/E
32. Juan's Place/E
33. Frjtz Fries
34. Pacific Catch
35. Barney's/E/N/SF
36. Lovejoy's Tea Rm.
37. Taylor's Automatic/N/SF*
38. King of Thai
39. Axum Cafe
40. Citrus Club

Other Good Values

A La Turca
A 16
Baker St. Bistro
Bendean/E
Blue Jay Cafe
Bocadillos
Boulette's Larder
Burma Super Star
Canteen
César/E
Chapeau!
Charanga
Chow/Park Chow
Citizen Thai
Coco 500
Dopo/E
Firefly
Giordano Bros.
Goood Frikin' Chicken
Helmand, The
Hyde St. Bistro
jZcool/S
Le Charm Bistro
Luna Park
Oola
Osha Thai Noodles
Pakwan/E/SF
Pesce
Pizzaiolo/E
Pizzeria Delfina
Pizzeria Picco/N
Pizzetta 211
Powell's Place
Shabu-Sen
Shalimar/E/SF
So
Ti Couz
Tommaso's
Zatar/E
Zuppa

Prix Fixe Bargains
(Dinner for $30 & Under)

Ajanta/E 15.00
Alamo Square 12.50
Alfred's Steak 30.00
Axum Cafe 12.00
Baker St. Bistro 14.50
Bendean/E 13.00
Bistro Liaison/E 28.00
Bistro Ralph/N 22.00
Cetrella Bistro/S 24.95
Chez Panisse Café/E 28.00
Christophe/N 22.00
Cozmo's Corner 28.00
Della Santina's/N 30.00
Firefly 30.00
Gayle's Bakery/S 10.95
Gaylord India/S/SF 27.95
girl & the fig/N 28.00
Le Charm Bistro 28.00
Left Bank/E/N/S 30.00
Mandarin 30.00
Market/N 29.95
MarketBar 30.00
Matterhorn Swiss 15.00
Maya 29.95
Mecca 29.95
Moose's 29.95
Pinot Blanc/N 28.00
Rist. Bacco 25.00
rnm 25.00
Sanraku 22.50
South Park Cafe 29.95
Three Seasons/E/S/SF 29.95
Tita's hale 'aina 10.95
Town's End 13.50
Tratt. La Siciliana/E 25.00
Watercress 20.00
Yabbies Coastal 25.00
Zazie 17.50

Prix Fixe Bargains
(Lunch for $28 & Under)

Absinthe $21.95
Anjou $16.00
BIX $21.95
Café Marcella/S. $19.95
Chez Panisse Café/E $26.00
girl & the fig/N $28.00
Grand Cafe $24.95
Hurley's/N $15.00
Left Bank/E/N/S $20.00
Lovejoy's Tea Rm. $15.95
Market/N $14.95
MarketBar $23.00
Moose's $16.95
Scoma's/N/SF $21.50

City of San Francisco

Top Ratings in SF Proper

Excluding places with low voting, unless indicated by a ▽.

Top Food

29	Gary Danko		Tartine Bakery
28	Masa's		House
27	Fleur de Lys		CAFÉ KATi
	La Folie		Swan Oyster Depot
	Michael Mina		Frascati
	Chapeau!		Fifth Floor
	Boulevard	**25**	Dottie's True Blue
	Ritz-Carlton Din. Rm.		Tommaso's
	Kabuto		Cafe Jacqueline
	Quince		Hog Island Oyster
26	Aqua		Piperade
	Campton Place		Chez Spencer
	Jardinière		Ton Kiang
	Acquerello		Isa
	Delfina		Slanted Door

By Cuisine

American (New)
- **29** Gary Danko
- **27** Michael Mina
-     Boulevard
- **25** Dottie's True Blue
- **24** Postrio

American (Traditional)
- **25** Mama's Wash. Sq.
- **24** Rosamunde Grill
- **22** Liberty Cafe
-     BIX
-     Miss Millie's

Bakeries
- **26** Tartine Bakery
- **23** Boulange Cole/Polk
- **21** Citizen Cake
- **20** Town's End
- **18** Il Fornaio

Californian
- **26** Jardinière
- **24** Hawthorne Lane
-     PlumpJack Cafe
-     Jack Falstaff
- **23** Rubicon

Chinese
- **25** Ton Kiang
-     Yank Sing
- **24** Jai Yun▽
-     Tommy Toy's
- **23** R & G Lounge

French
- **27** Fleur de Lys
-     La Folie
- **25** Cafe Jacqueline
-     Chez Spencer
-     Isa

French (Bistro)
- **27** Chapeau!
- **25** Fringale
- **24** Clémentine
-     Chez Papa Bistrot
- **23** Jeanty at Jack's

French (New)
- **28** Masa's
- **27** Ritz-Carlton Din. Rm.
- **26** Fifth Floor
- **25** Tartare
- **23** Rubicon

Fusion
26 House
CAFÉ KATi
24 Silks
Eos Rest./Wine Bar
22 SUMI

Hamburgers
21 Taylor's Automatic
20 Mo's
Burger Joint
19 Barney's
18 Balboa Cafe

Indian/Pakistani
23 Indian Oven
Shalimar
Pakwan
20 Tallula
19 Gaylord India

Italian
27 Quince
26 Acquerello
24 Sociale
Antica Trattoria
23 Tratt. Contadina

Japanese
27 Kabuto
25 Maki
24 Kyo-Ya
Ozumo
Ebisu

Latin American
24 Limón
23 Charanga
Fresca
22 El Raigon
21 Espetus Churrascaria

Mediterranean
26 Campton Place
Frascati
25 Kokkari Estiatorio
24 Cortez
Zuni Café

Mexican
24 La Taqueria
23 Taqueria Can-Cun
Pancho Villa
22 Maya
21 Nick's Crispy Tacos

Middle Eastern
24 Helmand, The
22 Truly Mediterranean
Maykadeh∇
21 A La Turca∇
17 Kan Zaman

Pizza
25 Tommaso's
Pizzetta 211
24 Postrio
Pazzia
23 Pauline's Pizza

Seafood
26 Aqua
Swan Oyster Depot
25 Hog Island Oyster
24 Farallon
Pesce

Spanish/Basque
25 Piperade
23 Bocadillos
22 Zarzuela
21 B44
18 Iluna Basque

Steakhouses
24 Harris'
House of Prime Rib
23 Anzu
Ruth's Chris
Morton's

Tapas (Latin)
23 Bocadillos
Charanga
22 Zarzuela
20 Ramblas
19 Cha Cha Cha

Thai
25 Thep Phanom
24 Manora's
23 Marnee
Basil
22 Koh Samui

Vietnamese
25 Slanted Door
23 Thanh Long
Crustacean
Three Seasons
22 Ana Mandara

Top Food

By Special Feature

Breakfast
26 Tartine Bakery
25 Dottie's True Blue
   Mama's Wash. Sq.
23 Boulange Cole/Polk
21 Chloe's Cafe

Brunch
26 Campton Place
25 Ton Kiang
   Yank Sing
24 Zuni Café
22 Ella's

Child-Friendly
25 Yank Sing
21 Taylor's Automatic
19 Barney's
15 Pasta Pomodoro
13 Mel's Drive-In

Hotel Dining
28 Masa's
   Hotel Vintage Ct.
27 Michael Mina
   Westin St. Francis
   Ritz-Carlton Din. Rm.
   Ritz-Carlton Hotel
26 Campton Place
   Campton Place Hotel
   Fifth Floor
   Hotel Palomar

Late Night
24 Zuni Café
22 Scala's Bistro
20 Brazen Head
   Globe
   Absinthe

Newcomers/Rated
24 Myth
   Jack Falstaff
22 La Suite
21 C&L Steakhouse
20 Oola

Newcomers/Unrated
Canteen
Coco 500
Pizzeria Delfina
Winterland
Zuppa

Outdoor Seating
25 Isa
24 Sociale
23 Ritz-Carlton Terrace
22 La Suite
21 Foreign Cinema

People-Watching
27 Boulevard
26 Jardinière
24 Zuni Café
   Postrio
   Town Hall

Power Scenes
27 Michael Mina
   Boulevard
26 Aqua
23 Rubicon
21 One Market

Romance
29 Gary Danko
27 Fleur de Lys
25 Cafe Jacqueline
24 Aziza
23 Venticello

Small Plates
25 Isa
24 Cortez
   Eos Rest./Wine Bar
   Pesce
23 Chez Nous

Tasting Menus
29 Gary Danko
28 Masa's
27 Fleur de Lys
   Michael Mina
   Ritz-Carlton Din. Rm.

Trendy
24 Myth
   Jack Falstaff
23 A 16
20 Oola
19 Frisson

Winning Wine Lists
27 Michael Mina
26 Fifth Floor
24 PlumpJack Cafe
23 Rubicon
22 bacar

By Location

Castro/Noe Valley
24 Firefly
Incanto
Deep Sushi
23 Rist. Bacco
22 Miss Millie's

Chinatown
23 R & G Lounge
21 Great Eastern
Hunan Home's
House of Nanking
20 Yuet Lee

Cow Hollow/Marina
25 Isa
24 PlumpJack Cafe
23 Greens
Three Seasons
A 16

Downtown
28 Masa's
27 Michael Mina
26 Aqua
Campton Place
25 Piperade

Embarcadero
27 Boulevard
25 Hog Island Oyster
Slanted Door
24 Ozumo
22 La Suite

Fisherman's Wharf
29 Gary Danko
22 Grandeho Kamekyo
Ana Mandara
21 Mandarin
Scoma's

Haight-Ashbury/Cole Valley
24 Eos Rest./Wine Bar
23 Boulange Cole/Polk
22 Grandeho Kamekyo
21 Zazie
20 Pork Store Café

Hayes Valley/Civic Center
26 Jardinière
24 Zuni Café
22 Hayes St. Grill
21 Suppenküche
Citizen Cake

Lower Haight
25 Thep Phanom Thai
24 Rosamunde Grill
23 Indian Oven
rnm
21 Axum Cafe

Mission
26 Delfina
Tartine Bakery
25 Chez Spencer
24 La Taqueria
Limón

Nob Hill/Russian Hill
27 Fleur de Lys
La Folie
Ritz-Carlton Din. Rm.
26 Acquerello
Swan Oyster Depot

North Beach
26 House
25 Tommaso's
Cafe Jacqueline
Mama's Wash. Sq.
24 Helmand, The

Pacific Heights/Japantown
27 Quince
26 CAFÉ KATi
25 Maki
23 Chez Nous
22 Eliza's

Richmond
27 Chapeau!
Kabuto
25 Ton Kiang
Pizzetta 211
24 Clémentine

SoMa
26 Fifth Floor
25 Fringale
24 Pazzia
Hawthorne Lane
Jack Falstaff

Sunset/West Portal
24 Burma Super Star
Ebisu
23 Thanh Long
Marnee Thai
21 Chou Chou

Top Decor

28 Garden Court
27 Ana Mandara
   Farallon
   Gary Danko
   Fleur de Lys
   Ritz-Carlton Din. Rm.
26 Jardinière
   Seasons
   Silks
25 Myth

BIX
Campton Place
Fifth Floor
Ozumo
Sutro's at Cliff Hse.*
Tonga Room
Boulevard
Grand Cafe
Kokkari Estiatorio
Aqua

Top Service

28 Gary Danko
   Ritz-Carlton Din. Rm.
27 Masa's
26 Chapeau!
   Fleur de Lys
   Seasons
   Acquerello
   Michael Mina
   Albona Rist.
   Campton Place

25 Silks
   Ritz-Carlton Terrace
   La Folie
   Fifth Floor
   Aqua
   Quince
24 Boulevard
   Jardinière
   Tartare
23 Clémentine

Top Bangs for the Buck

1. Saigon Sandwiches
2. Taqueria Can-Cun
3. Rosamunde Grill
4. El Balazo
5. Pancho Villa
6. Jay's Cheesesteak
7. Burger Joint
8. La Cumbre Taqueria
9. La Taqueria
10. Red's Java House

11. Nick's Crispy Tacos
12. Truly Mediterranean
13. Tartine Bakery
14. Boulange Cole/Polk
15. Kate's Kitchen
16. Dottie's True Blue
17. Asqew Grill
18. Pork Store Café
19. Chloe's Cafe
20. Frjtz Fries

Other Good Values

A 16
Baker St. Bistro
Bocadillos
Burma Super Star
Chapeau!
Charanga
Chow/Park Chow
Firefly
Helmand, The
Hyde St. Bistro

Le Charm Bistro
L'Osteria del Forno
Luna Park
Osha Thai Noodles
Pakwan
Pesce
Pizzetta 211
Shalimar
Ti Couz
Tommaso's

City of San Francisco

	F	D	S	C

Absinthe ◑   20 23 19 $41

398 Hayes St. (Gough St.), 415-551-1590;
www.absinthe.com

Punsters perceive "the spirits of Lautrec and Degas" in
this French-Med brasserie whose "sexy", "swanky" belle
epoque "bordello" vibe attracts Hayes Valley "hipsters" and
the "theaterland" crowd; fans favor the "solid", "authentic"
cuisine (brunch is "divine") and the *très charmant* vintage
cocktails", but foes feel service is often "slow" and
"condescending" and suggest proprietors "change the
name to Abstain"; P.S. no "green fairy" here, but the wine
"tome" lists 700 labels.

Ace Wasabi's   21 15 17 $31

3339 Steiner St. (bet. Chestnut & Lombard Sts.), 415-567-4903

"Ten years" after its founding, this "rock 'n' roll sushi
spot" and Marina "meat market" is still stuffed with
"twentysomethings" "reliving frat memories" while "hot
waiters" deliver "super-fresh" sashimi and "Americanized"
"fun-house rolls"; granted, it's "claustrophobic" and "loud",
the waits are "interminable" and "better" Japanese
restaurants "abound", but the "Ken and Barbie yuppie set"
are "too busy" with their "carb-friendly creations" to notice;
P.S. bingo winners get "$20 off your bill."

Acme Chophouse   20 19 18 $47

24 Willie Mays Plaza (bet. King & 3rd Sts.), 415-644-0240;
www.acmechophouse.com

Though Traci Des Jardins' "convenient" South Beach
"stadium spot" is "crammed" "when the Giants play", the
"casual" "meat haven" morphs into a "real restaurant"
with "better service on non-game days"; carnivores
happily "rub elbows" with pro athletes while gnawing on
"big, juicy", "organic" chops paired with wines from a
"comprehensive" cellar; alas, some say, "like so many things
associated with sports" it's "vastly overpriced."

ACQUERELLO ⊠   26 23 26 $67

1722 Sacramento St. (bet. Polk St. & Van Ness Ave.),
415-567-5432; www.acquerello.com

"If you want to impress" – or even "propose" – do it at this
"blessedly quiet" "haute Italian" "in a converted church"
just off Van Ness; the "exquisite" cuisine is "decadent"
and the "solicitous service" is downright "impeccable", so
even if the "'edgy' dot-com crowd" doesn't exactly adore
the "elderly-meets-'80s" decor, others declare it drips with

"old-world elegance" and deem an evening here a "sublime dining experience" with the "prices to prove it."

Alamo Square   21 19 19 $26
803 Fillmore St. (bet. Fulton & Grove Sts.), 415-440-2828
You'll get a "square meal" and a "square deal" at this "chic little" French seafood bistro in a "not-so-chic" part of the Western Addition; the fin fare is "fresh" (if perhaps "unexciting": "pick a fish, pick a sauce, pick a side") and the staff is "charming", plus the place's $12.50 midweek "prix fixe" dinners, "no-corkage Wednesday nights" and free parking lot elicit a round of applause.

A La Turca   ∇ 21 9 17 $17
869 Geary St. (Larkin St.), 415-345-1011
"Don't let the sketchy neighborhood", "slow service" and "divey decor" deter you from seeking out this small slice of "Istanbul on Geary" urge young Turks who frequent this "refreshingly different" "bare-bones diner" in the Tenderloin; the payoff is fare that's "gutsy" and "sometimes great" ("wonderful meze", "excellent lamb dishes") – and "the price is right", no haggling required.

ALBONA RISTORANTE   24 17 26 $40
ISTRIANO 🖫
545 Francisco St. (bet. Mason & Taylor Sts.), 415-441-1040
For a "homey" yet "fabulous" evening, nothing compares to this "strange little" North Beach "gem" run by "gregarious" chef-owner Bruno Viscovi; he expounds on the "excellent", "offbeat Istrian offerings" – think Italian with "Croatian and Eastern European flair" – in a "loquacious" style that comes off as "great entertainment" or "badgering" depending on your mood and desire for peace.

Alegrias, Food From Spain   19 14 18 $30
2018 Lombard St. (Webster St.), 415-929-8888
At this "quiet", "family-run" Marina spot, "classic tapas" (not "newfangled small plates"), "delicious sangria" and "bread to sop up" the "amazing sauces" have "sparked" many a "love affair with Spanish cuisine"; "reasonable" prices and staffers who "go out of their way" keep the Iberian infatuation in force, though "dated" decor has some aesthetes less than *alegre*.

Alfred's Steak House 🖫   19 18 19 $46
659 Merchant St. (bet. Kearny & Montgomery Sts.),
415-781-7058; www.alfredssteakhouse.com
"If you like liquor, leather and ladies", then this Downtown institution with "big red booths" is "your steakhouse" – "aged beef" hangs in the hallway, Caesar salads are "made tableside" and "delicious artery-hardening sides" come à la carte; a dip in the Food score and increasingly "churlish" service suggest it's "on a downhill slope", but if you're lubricated by a "monster martini, maybe you won't notice."

Alice's　　20｜15｜18｜$19
1599 Sanchez St. (29th St.), 415-282-8999

"You can get anything you want – except bad food" at this "always busy", "cheerful" Noe Valley Chinese; granted, the "excellent use" of "fresh local ingredients in traditional dishes" is "not totally authentic" and the "pushy" waiters "rush you out the door", but all agree the chow is "tasty", "fast" and "a great value" ("lunch plates are a steal").

Alioto's　　16｜15｜16｜$37
8 Fisherman's Wharf (bet. Jefferson & Taylor Sts.), 415-673-0183;
www.aliotos.com

"Out-of-towners from Iowa will be impressed" – especially "if you pick up the bill" – at this "granddaddy of the Wharf area" where you can keep an eye on the frolicking "sea lions in the Bay"; the "old-school waiters", "cheesy ambiance" and "touristy" Italian fin fare aren't "all they're cracked up to be" but if you "stick to simple dishes" like Dungeness crab "you should do well."

Americano　　–｜–｜–｜M
Hotel Vitale, 8 Mission St. (The Embarcadero), 415-278-3777;
www.americanorestaurant.com

This flagship restaurant in the new Hotel Vitale gets plenty of zing from its Embarcadero location and the playful Cal-Italian cuisine of chef Paul Arenstam (ex Grand Cafe), whose produce-driven dishes include a pizza 'margarita' topped with jalapeños, nopales and lime; the serene dining room, circular cocktail lounge and patio with aromatherapy garden all offer views of the Bay.

Amici's East Coast Pizzeria　　20｜12｜16｜$18
216 King St. (3rd St.), 415-546-6666
2033 Union St. (Buchanan St.), 415-885-4500
www.amicis.com

Though grumpy Gothamites grumble "if you don't sell slices you ain't no East Coast pizzeria", "even Jersey pizza snobs" go for this "family-friendly" local chain's "terrific", "flavorful" pies, "blistered, crispy crusts" with "West Coast toppings" (oy, "soy mozzarella") at "NYC prices"; "no-frills" interiors and "uneven service", however, have many *amici* "speed-dialing" for "lightning-fast delivery"; N.B. branches throughout the Bay Area.

ANA MANDARA　　22｜27｜21｜$45
Ghirardelli Sq., 891 Beach St. (Polk St.), 415-771-6800;
www.anamandara.com

At this "sumptuous", "movie-set" Fisherman's Wharfer you can "escape" to a "starry night in colonial Vietnam", where "the politics were all wrong but the food was fabulous"; the "flavor-rich" New French–Indochinese entrees are "authentic" and "imaginative" (but portions are "so small"), while service ranges from "accommodating" to "rough";

P.S. the upstairs lounge is said to be a "happening scene" for "cocktails, finger food" and live jazz on weekends.

Andalu   21 19 18 $35
3198 16th St. (Guerrero St.), 415-621-2211; www.andalusf.com
"You may have been to a zillion" *petits-plats* places but devotees declare you'll "find some things to make you smile" at this "cavernous" "yuppie" fave in the Mission; Eclectic eats showing "influences as varied as Latin America and the Deep South" match up with "excellent" half-bottles and "wacky soju cocktails"; servers may be "smiling" or "snotty", however, and the unsated sigh "when they say 'small plates', they mean it": "two people, $150, left hungry."

Angkor Borei   ▽ 20 10 20 $19
3471 Mission St. (Cortland Ave.), 415-550-8417; www.cambodiankitchen.com
"Don't let the outside" of this unassuming Bernal Heights Cambodian "fool you"; inside, staffers are "all smiles" as they serve up "roll-your-own lettuce cup concoctions" and other "flavorful", "reasonably priced" traditional dishes "adapted for local produce" (including vegetarian-friendly "fake-meat options"); if the, um, "unpretentious" decor doesn't appeal, they also deliver throughout the city.

Angkor Wat ⊠   21 17 20 $25
4217 Geary Blvd. (bet. 6th & 7th Aves.), 415-221-7887
Wat's not to like about this Inner Richmond Cambodian "gem" ask admirers who adore the dishes' "outstanding flavors" ("my date wanted to bathe in" her soup) – but not the "small portions"; still, it's "always fun" on "weekends" when the "authentic" dancers perform, and even without the show it's a "happy place" since the owner bestows "long-stem roses and silk scarves" on "lucky celebrants."

Anjou ⊠   23 18 21 $40
44 Campton Pl. (bet. Post & Sutter Sts.), 415-392-5373; www.anjou-sf.com
If this "charming little" Downtown bistro that's "down an alley off Union Square" and run by "*le chef* and *madame*" doesn't feel "French enough for you" – what with "the waiters' lovely accents", the "straightforward" cookery and the "cheek-by-jowl seating" – then nothing will; *les amis* advise "ignore the '70s fern-bar decor" for the sake of a "great pre-theater" or "post-shopping meal" that "won't break the bank" (especially the $16 "two-course lunch").

Antica Trattoria   23 19 21 $35
2400 Polk St. (Union St.), 415-928-5797
Food-loving Freuds figure "a person would be crazy to eat in North Beach" amid the tourists "when they could come" to this "reasonably priced" "sleeper" in Russian Hill for "*delizioso*" "rustic Northern Italian" *cucina* plus a "well-

thought-out" list of regional wines; there's "not much to look at except" the "helpful waiters", which is just fine by "affluent" regulars who appreciate how the "austere feeling and small size" "keep out the riffraff."

Anzu
23　19　20　$46

Hotel Nikko, 222 Mason St. (O'Farrell St.), 415-394-1100; www.restaurantanzu.com

With "excellent beef" and "exquisite sushi" prepared anzu like it, the Hotel Nikko's "gracious" Asian steakhouse draws "Japanese tourists and businessmen" who venerate chef "Takahashi-san", "finicky" eaters "pleased" by the "amazing" Sunday jazz brunch and the staff's "attention to detail", and show-goers glad to dine within "walking distance" of the Downtown theaters; only a few fuss about "stale" ambiance and "pricey" yet "small servings."

Aperto
20　15　19　$29

1434 18th St. (Connecticut St.), 415-252-1625

"Amid raucous competition on Potrero Hill", this "homey" "standby" is "what you want in a neighborhood Italian": "uncomplicated", "tasty" eats and "friendly service" at "decent prices"; if it's "not worth driving across town" for, that suits the locals who "hope this stays hidden" so that "you can always get in"; N.B. no reservations.

AQUA
26　25　25　$69

252 California St. (bet. Battery & Front Sts.), 415-956-9662; www.aqua-sf.com

"Under Laurent Manrique", this "sophisticated" Downtown Cal-French has continued to serve "splendid meals from the sea" plus "superb" "interpretations of foie gras", paired with wines from an "excellent" list; "meticulous" servers minister to a "chic clientele (celebs included)" that's "packed like sardines" in the "elegant, contemporary" dining room; a few fear this "frenetic" "fish house" is "drowning in foo-foo", but most folks come ready and willing to "turn up the hearing aid" and "break the bank."

A. Sabella's
19　19　20　$37

2766 Taylor St. (Jefferson St.), 415-771-6775; www.asabellas.com

"One of the few places to get a real meal" on Fisherman's Wharf, this "slightly kitschy" docksider is a place self-respecting "locals can take out-of-town guests" for the de rigueur SF treat – simply prepared "fresh seafood" – along with "old-fashioned service" and picture-postcard "views of the Bay"; crabby contrarians, however, snap this fishery is a "tourist trap if ever there was one."'

Asia de Cuba
20　25　19　$53

Clift Hotel, 495 Geary St. (Taylor St.), 415-929-2300; www.clifthotel.com

At this "star-spotting" "spin-off" in Downtown's Clift Hotel surveyors say sitting down to "creative" Asian–Nuevo

Latino fare is "like eating in a nightclub", what with Philippe Starck's "Alice in Wonderland" interiors, "super-dark" "mood lighting", "deafening house music", "full-of-attitude" staffers and the "rich and the restless" "showing off midriffs and spike heels"; still, if you're aiming to "impress" someone or "get out of the doghouse", this is a "stylish" place to "party, party, party."

AsiaSF   17 | 19 | 21 | $37

201 Ninth St. (Howard St.), 415-255-2742; www.asiasf.com
"Only in SF or one of the weirder parts of Bangkok" can you find a "crossdressing" "waiter/waitress" outfitted "as Beyoncé" who will show off her "powerful vocals and sexy booty" and then serve you "surprisingly good" Asian fusion small plates and "potent" cocktails; this "high-energy" SoMa gender-bender may be "rowdy and low-rent" but it's "fun for both your X and Y chromosomes", so go "at least once" – "with an open mind and lots of cash."

A 16   23 | 19 | 18 | $38

2355 Chestnut St. (bet. Divisadero & Scott Sts.), 415-771-2216; www.a16sf.com
Expect "a 16-person line" out the door of this ultra-trendy, "minimalist" Marina vino venue where "the young and the privileged" chow down on "hold-onto-your-taste buds" Neapolitan cuisine ("impeccable", "crispy, blistered pizza") along with "brilliant" Italian wines; when the dining room is "packed" and "mind-numbingly" "noisy", though, the staff gets "harried", and an "underwhelmed" minority grumbles "all the hype has gone to the owners' heads."

Asqew Grill   19 | 12 | 14 | $13

3583 16th St. (Market St.), 415-626-3040
1607 Haight St. (Clayton St.), 415-701-9301
3348 Steiner St. (Chestnut St.), 415-931-9201
www.asqewgrill.com
"Dr. Atkins would be proud" of these "skewer-slingers" – their California-style "healthy, tasty" and "varied" meat and veggie kebabs that can be "mixed and matched" with "innovative" "salads and starches" to create "clever multiethnic combos"; given the "fast-food prices" and the brisk pace, "don't expect much in the way of decor or service" but it's "terrific" for those who just want a "quick bite"; N.B. there's a branch in the East Bay.

Axum Cafe   21 | 8 | 15 | $14

698 Haight St. (Pierce St.), 415-252-7912; www.axumcafe.com
"Vegetarians, adventure seekers and starving students" who aren't "afraid to get their hands dirty" flock to this "always packed", "zero-atmosphere" Lower Haighter where "delicious" Ethiopian "finger food" "eaten family-style with injera" seems to "magically appear within seconds" and disappear just as fast; most regulars will recommend

you "skip the wine" ("it's no Two-Buck Chuck") in favor of "pitchers of beer" – just ask 'em.

Azie   22 | 22 | 19 | $44 |
826 Folsom St. (bet. 4th & 5th Sts.), 415-538-0918; www.restaurantlulu.com
"Sometimes Asian fusion works, sometimes it doesn't", but this "sexy", stylish SoMa Asian–New French manages "more hits than misses"; "steady" staffers serve "inventive", "exotic" cuisine "decorated with color and style" and a "broad" selection of wines (600 labels); "go with a sizable group" to "sample more dishes" or sit *à deux* in a curtained booth and "smooch with your sweetheart."

Aziza   24 | 23 | 20 | $40 |
5800 Geary Blvd. (22nd Ave.), 415-752-2222; www.aziza-sf.com
Given the "casbah ambiance" of this Outer Richmonder, fans lack only "a camel and a hookah" to feel like they're in Marrakech, thanks to "rich" "updated Moroccan cuisine" that "opens new doors in your life" and "friendly" servers who "treat you like royalty"; weekend belly dancers may either "enhance" the meal or "play havoc with your digestion", depending on your taste, but all agree that the five-course tasting menu is a "fabulous bargain."

bacar   22 | 23 | 21 | $48 |
448 Brannan St. (bet. 3rd & 4th Sts.), 415-904-4100; www.bacarsf.com
"Aging gracefully", this SoMa "survivor" combines live jazz, a "stellar" "wine list the size of *War and Peace*", "top-quality" Med–New American "bites" and a "staff that knows its stuff" to make this "gorgeous" "loftlike setting" "one of the city's coolest big-room scenes"; be sure to "designate a driver" because "it's all about the opportunity to taste without the bottle splurge"; N.B. lunch served on Fridays.

Baker Street Bistro   20 | 15 | 19 | $28 |
2953 Baker St. (bet. Greenwich & Lombard Sts.), 415-931-1475
You don't need to be Sherlock Holmes to figure out why this "unbelievably cramped" yet "quaint" Marina hang is so popular; it feels like an "out-of-the-way bistro in Paris" where "seductive accents abound" and the specialty du jour is "old-fashioned French dishes" "served competently" at "not-too-fussy prices" (check out the "bargain" prix fixe); "sit at the sidewalk tables for a quieter" meal.

Balboa Cafe   18 | 18 | 18 | $31 |
3199 Fillmore St. (Greenwich St.), 415-921-3944; www.plumpjack.com
Gavin Newsom may well show up at this Traditional American "old boys'" "watering hole" in Cow Hollow ("think oak and Tiffany glass") where cocktailers "sip Bloody Marys" or tipple off of the "amazing" wine list ("if it ain't on the list, they have a store across the street");

unfortunately the "mating rituals" in the "meat-market" bar might "infringe on your dinner"; P.S. Squaw Valley's "slopeside" location caters to the "après-ski crowd."

Bambuddha Lounge ⊠   18 | 22 | 16 | $33
Phoenix Hotel, 601 Eddy St. (bet. Larkin & Polk Sts.), 415-885-5088; www.bambuddhalounge.com
The Zen "temple-meets-motel atmosphere" of this "über-cool" venue in the Tenderloin's Phoenix Hotel attracts "twentysomethings" who nibble on "inventive" Southeast Asian eats or sip cocktails at the "poolside bar" – if you can transcend the "withering gazes of the wannabe hipsters" and the imperfections of the just-"ok" service.

Baraka   22 | 20 | 19 | $39
288 Connecticut St. (18th St.), 415-255-0387; www.barakasf.net
Sure, there's "hype" surrounding this "dark, sultry Morocco-inspired date spot" on Potrero Hill, but the fact is this 44-seater pleases patrons who want to drink "plenty of sangria" and share "simply delicious" French-Med "small and large plates"; the frugal fret "you're paying" for that "fake" North African ambiance and slam "hard-selling" staffers, but all agree it's a "fun" "alternative" to the usual places.

Barney's Gourmet Hamburgers   19 | 12 | 14 | $14
3344 Steiner St. (bet. Chestnut & Lombard Sts.), 415-563-0307
4138 24th St. (Castro St.), 415-282-7770
www.barneyshamburgers.com
Burger biters "have a cow" about this "no-fuss" local chain specializing in "anything you can imagine between a bun" ("plenty of meatless options") "overflowing" with "generous and inventive toppings", plus "addictive curly fries" and "milkshakes that ease any pain"; though decor and service are "barely passable", most branches do offer "great" outdoor seating; N.B. additional locations East and South of SF.

Basil Thai Restaurant & Bar   23 | 17 | 19 | $25
1175 Folsom St. (bet. 7th & 8th Sts.), 415-552-8999; www.basilthai.com
"Nice Thai" josh SoMa "business people" and other savvy sorts who regularly "eat in or take out" from this "under-the-radar" Bangkok boîte; its "piquant", "prettied-up" "nouveau" Siamese eats and "streamlined surroundings" make it "very hip", so even though "slow service" may Thai you up, you "gotta love" a "consistent performer" where "you can always count on getting a table."

Beach Chalet Brewery   13 | 21 | 12 | $27
1000 Great Hwy. (bet. Fulton St. & Lincoln Way), 415-386-8439; www.beachchalet.com
"Location, location, location" is the lure of this seaside suds spot where "more tourists than locals" flock for "excellent microbrews" and "splendid views" of "surfers and kite-

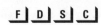
fliers on Ocean Beach"; critics beach about "anemic service" and "lackluster" New American pub grub but admit the "don't-miss museum" (with WPA frescoes that "rival Coit Tower's") and "live music" are some compensation.

Bella Trattoria
21 | 17 | 21 | $29

3854 Geary Blvd. (3rd Ave.), 415-221-0305; www.bellatrattoria.com
Inner Richmonders "hate to vote" for this "incarnation of the movie *Big Night*" because they fear it "might get too busy"; still, with its "reasonably priced", "flawlessly prepared" Southern Italian *cucina,* "comfortable" dining room and "warm", "pampering waiters" ("what flirts!"), it's hard to keep this "staple" a secret; N.B. no lunch on weekends.

BETELNUT PEJIU WU
22 | 22 | 17 | $33

2030 Union St. (Buchanan St.), 415-929-8855; www.betelnutrestaurant.com
"Is it worth" waiting "an eternity" for a table at this "noisy and overtrendy" Cow Hollow "scene" where "young business jerks and their trophies" "pile in" "day and night"?; "hell yeah" retort regulars, citing its "innovative", "spicy" Pan-Asian plates served by staffers who "look like they're from *90210*" amid "bamboo-and-ceiling-fan" dining areas that "transport you to the East."

B44
21 | 18 | 18 | $36

44 Belden Pl. (bet. Bush & Pine Sts.), 415-986-6287; www.b44sf.com
"You might as well be in Barcelona" at this Downtowner crammed with "Europeans" who "rhapsodize over" the "awesome" paellas and other "tasty Catalan cuisine"; "though you have to squint at the menu and converse by yelling", the "intriguing" wines (perhaps "the best Spanish list in NorCal"), "movie-set ambiance" and "sexy" (though often "snotty") staffers "really capture the Med spirit", particularly when you dine alfresco in the alley.

Big 4
21 | 24 | 23 | $54

Huntington Hotel, 1075 California St. (Taylor St.), 415-771-1140; www.big4restaurant.com
There's big formality at the Huntington Hotel's "genteel" homage to a quartet of "19th-century railroad tycoons", where Nob Hill nabobs come when they're "in the mood to dress up", since the dining room and piano bar are "the *ne plus ultra* of old-world clubbiness"; the "attentive" servers present "innovative" New American cuisine (including "esoteric" eats like "ostrich, bison, kudu") and a "fine" Cali-centered 350-label wine list, so it's particularly nice to be "old money" "when the check comes."

Biscuits and Blues
16 | 14 | 16 | $25

401 Mason St. (Geary St.), 415-292-2583
This legendary SF nightclub, which has been cooking up live blues and Southern-inspired munchies since 1995,

has opened a full-service restaurant upstairs; founder and consulting chef Regina Charboneau has crafted a casual menu reflecting her Mississippi roots – expect a variety of jambalayas, gumbos and her famous fried chicken.

Bistro Aix   22 | 18 | 21 | $35 |

3340 Steiner St. (bet. Chestnut & Lombard Sts.), 415-202-0100; www.bistroaix.com

"At the risk of ruining a great secret", frugal Francophiles 'fess up this "unpretentious" Marina bistro is their "go-to spot" for "delicious" Cal-Gallic fare that's neither "budget-breaking" nor particularly "mind-blowing"; however, it "can get noisy" so plenty prefer the "charming" heated patio where "twinkling white lights" and a "Van Gogh–style mural of the SF skyline" aix-entuate the positive.

Bistro Boudin ⊅   _ | _ | _ | I |

160 Jefferson St. (near Pier 43½), 415-928-1849; www.boudinbakery.com

You'll find this bistro and bar with waterfront views on the second floor of Boudin at The Wharf, the 26,000-sq.-ft. flagship of San Francisco's original sourdough bakery (it also houses a bread museum, gourmet market and casual cafe); the affordable menu features that famed dough in myriad forms, including pizza baked in a rustic brick oven that provides the room's focal point.

Bistro Clovis   20 | 16 | 19 | $35 |

1596 Market St. (Franklin St.), 415-864-0231

"Since more than doubling its size" and taking on "new decor", this relatively "undiscovered" French bistro on "Rue de Market" in Hayes Valley feels like a "European retreat"; slow-food "classics" are proffered "at a reasonable price" by an "authentically" Gallic staff; oenophiles "love the [oft-changing] wine sampler" showcasing regional *vins,* but if you want something to suck down something stronger you're out of luck.

BIX   22 | 25 | 22 | $50 |

56 Gold St. (bet. Montgomery & Sansome Sts.), 415-433-6300; www.bixrestaurant.com

"It's all about" the "cocktails, baby" at this "nostalgic", "visually arresting" '30s-style Downtown "supper club"; this "cooler-than-cool" bi-level lounge is perennially "packed" with "yuppies in heat" who groove to "wonderful" nightly jazz and swill "the best martinis in town"; "gracious" staffers get "high marks" as well for their handling of the "luxe" Franco-American cuisine; N.B. lunch on Fridays only.

Blanca Cafe ●⊠   _ | _ | _ | I |

1441 Grant Ave. (Green St.), 415-291-9944; www.blancacafe.com

Modeled after the owner's favorite cafe in Malaga, this Iberian wine bar in North Beach exudes a welcoming vibe as warming as a glass of Rioja; stewards behind the dark-

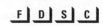
wood bar pour vinos from Spain (plus a few from California to appease the natives) that can be paired with cheeses, cured olives and a domestic variety of *jamon* similar to that from the famed pigs of Andalusia.

Blowfish Sushi To Die For   20 | 21 | 16 | $37

2170 Bryant St. (20th St.), 415-285-3848; www.blowfishsushi.com
"If you can survive" the "pounding music" and "seizure-inducing anime" at this "insanely noisy" "techno-themed" Japanese in the Mission, "twentysomethings" promise you're in for "divine" "fusion apps", "wacky rolls" and "dangerous" sake drinks proffered by "servers with great body art"; meanwhile "purists horrified by the disco sushi" "blow this place off", warning "you might die of starvation while waiting for service"; P.S. there's a branch South of SF as well.

Blue Jay Cafe   ▽ 18 | 13 | 13 | $19

919 Divisadero St. (McAllister St.), 415-447-6066
Western Addition locals "slip in" to this Dixie-inspired "Technicolor dream" for "Southern comforts" of the culinary sort – and if the soul food won't "fool any Tuscaloosa transplants", at least it goes for "half the price" others charge; tip: "go when the DJ spins" R&B since "desultory service" makes this "an experience to be enjoyed slowly."

Blue Plate, The ⊠   22 | 17 | 19 | $34

3218 Mission St. (29th St.), 415-282-6777; www.blueplatesf.com
"Young foodies" and "nostalgic hippies" "wander down" from Bernal Heights to this "hipster-grunge" "hangout" for "$1 cans of Olympia beer" and "imaginative" twists on "hearty" "Middle American" standards; true, "not everyone will appreciate" the "funky" digs, the "snarky" staffers or the "deafening" music (which can be avoided on the "heavenly patio"), but "it works very well in this neighborhood."

Blupointe ⊠   – | – | – | M

239 Kearny St. (bet. Bush & Sutter Sts.), 415-986-4450; www.blupointesf.com
This petite bivalve bar and lounge with Franco-Asian flair is the latest boîte to be anchored Downtown; although there are plenty of offerings from the land (including wood-oven pizzas), it's well-priced seafood that's the pointe – from the mother-of-pearl-topped raw bar's offerings to the specialty, steamed clams or mussels *avec frites,* served with sauces such as Thai red curry.

Bocadillos ⊠   23 | 19 | 20 | $31

710 Montgomery St. (Washington St.), 415-982-2622; www.bocasf.com
"Piperade's younger brother" specializes in "big flavors in small packages", namely "inventive riffs" on "traditional" Iberian tapas (including the namesake sandwiches) along with "unusual wines" from Spain and the Basque region;

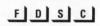
with "no reservations", the "small", "Euroficd" Downtown boîte ends up "packed tighter than the sardines they serve here" as a "post-work" crowd collects at the counters or the "communal seating in the center of the dining room."

Bodega Bistro   ▽ 24 | 12 | 18 | $19

607 Larkin St. (Eddy St.), 415-921-1218
Despite its name, there's nothing Hispanic about this Tenderloin sleeper, a Vietnamese joint named for beef, lamb and chicken (*bo, de, ga*); supporters savor some of SF's "best pho" and "refreshing papaya salad" for a "fraction of the cost" charged at more "famous" venues while the "owner and staff work hard" to ensure "patrons are happy"; the decor may be unimpressive, but this spot's still "more upscale" than its divey neighbors "near the new Asian Art Museum."

Boulange de Cole/de Polk ⊅   23 | 15 | 14 | $14

1000 Cole St. (Parnassus St.), 415-242-2442
2310 Polk St. (Green St.), 415-345-1107
With servers who "have the ennui nailed", it's easy to "pretend you're in a Parisian cafe" at these twin bakeries in Russian Hill and Cole Valley where Gallic gourmands "indulge their taste buds" with "sinful" (if "overpriced") "crusty croissants, creamy coffee" and other "street food" from *la belle France*; it's "even better" if you "grab one of the outside tables" for breakfast, lunch or a snack.

Boulette's Larder   – | – | – | M

1 Ferry Bldg. Mktpl. (bet. Market & Washington Sts.), 415-399-1155; www.bouletteslarder.com
Nestled in the Ferry Building on the Embarcadero, this New American gourmet market is primarily known for its ever-changing inventory of take-out goodies; however, savvy foodies settle in at the 10-person communal board for table service at breakfast and lunchtime (plus beignets on Sunday) – at one end of the store they can see the cooks working at the large stoves, at the other they can gaze out at the Bay and Bay Bridge.

BOULEVARD   27 | 25 | 24 | $60

Audiffred Bldg., 1 Mission St. (Steuart St.), 415-543-6084; www.boulevardrestaurant.com
"No restaurant symbolizes SF better" than this French–New American on the Embarcadero; "the hustle and bustle", "magnificent Bay Bridge views" and "gorgeous belle epoque" interior "make it an exciting place to dine", while staffers provide "flawless service" ("like perfectly matched skaters in an Olympic ice dance"); better yet, Nancy Oakes' "gutsy", "dynamic" gastronomy – complemented by a "killer wine list" – remains "fabulously consistent"; sure, it's "hard to get reservations" and it's "pricey, but aren't you worth it?"

Brandy Ho's   20 | 11 | 16 | $21

217 Columbus Ave. (bet. Broadway St. & Pacific Ave.),
415-788-7527; www.brandyhos.com

For Chinese food that's "hotter than Hades" fire-eaters
flock to this "funky" Chinatown "dive" where they "sit at
the counter and gape in awe" at the "cooks cranking out
dishes in giant woks", then dig in to "authentic" Hunan
specialties ("unrivaled fried dumplings"); staffers "can be
abrupt" but the "delivery service is great."

Brazen Head, The ◑⇗   20 | 19 | 20 | $34

3166 Buchanan St. (Greenwich St.), 415-921-7600;
www.brazenheadsf.com

"Despite no sign", "no cards" and "no reservations", this
Cow Hollow "king of incognito dining" is "popular with
chefs" and other "grateful" late-nighters who "tuck away"
in the "dim", "clubby" interior; if there's "nothing inventive"
on the "hearty" American pub menu (best bet: "excellent
pepper steak"), who cares when the "superb bartender"
"always remembers your favorite drink"?

Brindisi Cucina di Mare ☒   ▽ 21 | 18 | 18 | $35

88 Belden Pl. (Pine St.), 415-593-8000;
www.brindisicucina.com

This "cute" Italian "gives its neighbors" in Downtown's
French enclave "a run for their money", offering "melt-in-
your-mouth" seafood from the Adriatic coast in a "comfy"
(if "cramped") frescoed dining room; "it's easy to go for
lunch and find yourself still there at dinnertime", but is that
because it's so "inviting" to eat alfresco and "people-watch"
or because the service can turn it into an "all-day affair"?

Brother-in-Law's Bar-B-Que   23 | 4 | 13 | $15

705 Divisadero St. (Grove St.), 415-931-7427

'Cue-linarians confirm this "no-frills" "take-out" Southern
"BBQ joint" in the Western Addition is "right up there with
its East Bay competitors" ("if I were a pig, this is where I
would want to be basted and served up on a bun") and
what's more, "you can smell" the "smoky goodness"
"all the way down Divisadero"; though "it has parking",
given the "grungy" storefront digs, you might as well "keep
the car running."

Brother's Korean Restaurant   23 | 7 | 14 | $23

4014 Geary Blvd. (bet. 4th & 5th Aves.), 415-668-2028
4128 Geary Blvd. (bet. 5th & 6th Aves.), 415-387-7991 ◑

If you want to know "where all the Koreans go to eat", look
no further than this "bare-bones", "fluorescent-lit" pair of
"DIY" "tabletop BBQ" joints in the Inner Richmond run by
"gracious" twin brothers; even "after midnight" you can "get
off on your pyromania" grilling up meat while the harried
staff stages a "parade of condiments" and "freebies" –
just be ready to "smell like a smoked pig for days."

Buca di Beppo   13 | 16 | 16 | $24 |
855 Howard St. (bet. 4th & 5th Sts.), 415-543-7673;
www.bucadibeppo.com
See review in South of San Francisco Directory.

Burger Joint   20 | 13 | 16 | $11 |
700 Haight St. (Pierce St.), 415-864-3833
807 Valencia St. (19th St.), 415-824-3494 ⊘
The name may be generic but these "bright", "clean" patty
purveyors in the Lower Haight and Mission (and SFO) put
an undeniably SF stamp on their eats – "succulent", "eco-
friendly" hot dogs and "Niman Ranch burgers" plus shakes
containing locally made ice cream, all sold by "hipster"
kids to "post–*Fast Food Nation*" "conscious carnivores";
also geographically apt are the "eye-popping" prices.

Burma Super Star   24 | 14 | 18 | $21 |
309 Clement St. (4th Ave.), 415-387-2147;
www.burmasuperstar.com
Superstar indeed, swoon the "tribes of followers" who crave
this Inner Richmond Himalayan hideaway's "exciting"
Burmese fare, "a mix 'n' match of Indian, Thai and Chinese"
("flavor-packed", "distinctive" curries, "salads and noodle
dishes") served by a "conscientious" staff; less stellar
are the "small", "down-home" dining room and "no-
reservations policy" resulting in "excruciating waits."

Butler & The Chef Cafe, The ⌧   ▽ 19 | 19 | 17 | $18 |
155A South Park St. (bet. 2nd & 3rd Sts.), 415-896-2075;
www.oralpleasureinc.com
Dishing up "a little slice of France" on SoMa's "own South
Park", this gourmet Gallic "dot-bomb survivor" (now under
new management) is still a "favorite lunch spot" of tech
types who flock to the petite bistro to "eat quiche" and "be
happy"; "everything is authentic", including the "antique
furniture" and the "staff with an attitude"; N.B. no dinner.

butterfly embarcadero   19 | 21 | 17 | $39 |
(fka butterfly)
Pier 33 (Bay St.), 415-864-8999; www.butterflysf.com
It's hard to imagine how "dining on Cal-Asian cuisine" in a
"stunning setting" overlooking the Bay "could be anything
but magnificent", but this "spacious" supper club on the
Embarcadero still isn't soaring as high as it might; fans fete
the "creative" food's "architectural presentations" and
the "great" jazz, but foes frown that the "noise can make
you crazy" and service "needs to improve" as well.

Cafe Bastille ⌧   18 | 16 | 17 | $30 |
22 Belden Pl. (bet. Bush & Pine Sts.), 415-986-5673;
www.cafebastille.com
With "French voices in the air", "tables only inches apart"
and "authentically inefficient waiters", this "intimate

bistro" enables you to "imagine you are eating your frites in the Marais" instead of Downtown's Belden Place; though its "tasty" Gallic cuisine is nothing revolutionary, *amis* advise *allez* to the alley for "magical" alfresco dining; P.S. the Bastille Day bash is "a must."

Café Claude   18 | 18 | 16 | $27 |
7 Claude Ln. (bet. Grant Ave. & Kearny St.), 415-392-3515; www.cafeclaude.com
This "quaint *poche*-sized" Downtown bistro "feels like a discovery" say surveyors who spend "leisurely" weekend evenings listening to "good-caliber" live jazz (sans cover) and avow the "atmosphere and food couldn't be more Parisian" – down to the alfresco tables, "slow-moving staff" and "hectic", "cramped quarters"; meanwhile a few cynics are "convinced everyone's French accent is fake."

Cafe Divine   – | – | – | I |
1600 Stockton St. (Union St.), 415-986-3414
To err is human, but to snack on panini whilst sipping espresso divine, or so suggests the name of this corner cafe in North Beach located in the gracious '20s-era Dante Building; amid high ceilings and cathedral windows that allow the sun to stream in, the kitchen cranks out a limited menu of sandwiches, salads and whimsically named pizzas such as the Inferno and Purgatorio.

Cafe Jacqueline   25 | 18 | 18 | $48 |
1454 Grant Ave. (bet. Green & Union Sts.), 415-981-5565
It's "all soufflés, all the time" at this North Beach veteran turning out "light-as-air" "masterpieces" for sharing in its candlelit confines (a "fabulous date place"); the "epic" dinner takes "forever" ("I could have laid the eggs myself"), but you'll see why if you "visit the kitchen" for a peep at Madame Jacqueline and her "farmload" of *oeufs*; puff daddies (and mommies) have less patience for the "waiter who imitates stereotypical French-brasserie service."

CAFÉ KATI   26 | 18 | 23 | $46 |
1963 Sutter St. (bet. Fillmore & Webster Sts.), 415-775-7313; www.cafekati.com
Even after "15-plus years", "personable" Asian-fusion pioneer Kirk Webber keeps this now-ubiquitous blend from "looking tired"; supporters state this "intimate" (read: "cramped") Japantown "gem" "could move Downtown and double the prices" and "people would still flood in" for Webber's "delectable works of art", "impressive" wines and "staff that cares."

Cafe Lo Cubano ◗   ▽ 16 | 20 | 15 | $14 |
3401 California St. (Laurel St.), 415-831-4672; www.cafelocubano.com
In Presidio Heights, an area "already suffering caffeine jitters", this new "casual Latin" cafe "sets itself apart"

with its "chic '60s" "loungey feel"; the "authentic pressed
Cuban sandwiches" and café con leche are "a dream", but
early visitors vituperate it's all "served at the languorous
pace of a hot Havana afternoon."

Café Tiramisu ⊠   20 | 16 | 18 | $35 |
28 Belden Pl. (bet. Bush & Pine Sts.), 415-421-7044;
www.cafetiramisu.com
"Step off Bush Street" and into Italy at this "picturesque"
Downtowner where "hunky owners" deliver "homemade
pastas" and "don't-miss desserts" (tiramisu, anyone?) to
patrons paying "prices that'd make the Venetians blush";
it's best to sit outside, because indoors the tables are "so
close together you are almost on your neighbor's lap."

Caffe Centro ⊠   ∇ 20 | 14 | 16 | $15 |
102 South Park St. (bet. 2nd & 3rd Sts.), 415-882-1500;
www.caffecentro.com
"Trade sharp elbows with the all-too-hip" at this "tiny",
"out-of-the-way cafe" that's been a "long-term South Park
favorite" in SoMa since the high-flying dot-com days, but
forget about "snagging a seat" inside – instead, "grab"
your "great" but "overpriced" panino and "sit in the park
across the street" for some "people-watching."

Caffe Delle Stelle   16 | 13 | 16 | $28 |
395 Hayes St. (Gough St.), 415-252-1110
If not exactly a star, this "hectic" Hayes Valley "standby"
still "gets the job done" for the "opera/symphony crowd on
a budget"; a kitchen that "doesn't try to be too creative"
doles out "solid" Tuscan "standards" "fast" and at a
"reasonable cost" along with free "pitchers of bubbly
water"; even so, longtimers lament this once-"kitschy"
trattoria now feels "dusty and exhausted."

Caffe Macaroni ⊠⇗   19 | 14 | 21 | $27 |
59 Columbus Ave. (Jackson St.), 415-956-9737;
www.caffemacaroni.com
The decor "doesn't look like much" ("ignore the pasta on
the walls and ceiling"), but *amici* seeking the "real deal"
insist this North Beach Italian's "original", "fresh" *cucina*
is "better than most" offered in the area; what the "quaint"
quarters lack in elbow room ("upstairs the ceiling is barely
6-ft. high") is made up for by wildly "entertaining" waiters
who "make Roberto Benigni look sedate."

Caffè Museo   17 | 15 | 11 | $18 |
San Francisco Museum of Modern Art, 151 Third St.
(bet. Howard & Mission Sts.), 415-357-4500;
www.caffemuseo.com
Even if its food isn't exactly a "masterpiece", SFMOMA's
perennially packed concession in SoMa "probably gets
more traffic than the museum itself" thanks to "healthy",
"tasty" Italian-Med panini and salads that can be enjoyed at

"cheery sidewalk tables"; critics paint it as an "overpriced", "glorified cafeteria" yet those who need a "respite from touring the galleries" exhibit plenty of interest.

CAMPTON PLACE   26 25 26 $70
Campton Place Hotel, 340 Stockton St. (bet. Post & Sutter Sts.), 415-955-5555; www.camptonplace.com
This "luxe" Downtowner near Union Square may be "calm" and "sumptuously decorated" in the traditional "damask-tablecloth mode", but be prepared to be "blown away" "visually and gastronomically" by chef Daniel Humm, who keeps the place humming with "sublime" French-Med "foamy food" ("each course a concentrated marvel") presented with "formality and efficiency"; still, a few faultfinders cite "breathtaking prices" for "tiny portions."

C & L Steakhouse   ▽ 21 21 21 $60
1250 Jones St. (Clay St.), 415-771-5400; www.cl-steak.com
"Not your classic steakhouse", this "chichi" new "high-end" beef parlor atop "Snob Hill" sets itself apart from its touristy chain brethren via a clever culinary conceit from exec chef Laurent Manrique (Aqua): "you travel the U.S." with a mix 'n' match selection of "representative" meats and "artery-killing" sides "offered by city"; unfortunately, like the peripatetic menu, the "friendly" servers can sometimes be "all over the place."

Canteen   _ _ _ I
Commodore Hotel, 817 Sutter St. (Jones St.), 415-928-8870
A rowboat-size restaurant in Downtown's Commodore Hotel, this joint consists of a dinerlike setup with a counter and some booths, but nobody seems to mind squeezing in for the 'creative neoclassical' dinner menu from chef Dennis Leary (ex Rubicon) that's awash in seasonal Californian flavors; N.B. Wednesday's $32 three-course prix fixe is a don't-miss.

Carnelian Room   16 24 20 $55
Bank of America Ctr., 555 California St., 52nd fl. (bet. Kearny & Montgomery Sts.), 415-433-7500
"Tourists", "power-lunchers" and "even some locals" just can't resist that "drop-dead view"; it "excuses" "tired" decor, "polished" but "lukewarm" service and "overpriced", "mediocre" American food, but "good luck" when fog obscures the panorama – "a local maxim" holds that "the higher the restaurant, the worse the food" and, well, this place is "52 stories" up; N.B. a post-*Survey* remodeling and menu retooling may outdate the Food and Decor scores.

Catch   18 20 18 $33
2362 Market St. (bet. Castro & 16th Sts.), 415-431-5000; www.catchsf.com
To "land a catch of the gustatory or gentlemanly sort", the "velvet Mafia" comes to this "upscale" seafooder; enjoy

the former – "well-prepared, fresh fish" – in a "sleek, modern interior" with "classy" live piano nightly, or reel in the latter from the "indoor/outdoor" patio overlooking an "endless parade of Castro hotties"; still, critics crab about "unremarkable" fare ("they should change the name to Mrs. Paul's") and snap "throw this one back."

Cha Am Thai   20 | 14 | 17 | $19 |
Museum Parc, 701 Folsom St. (3rd St.), 415-546-9711;
www.chaamthaisf.com
In the face of intense "competition", this humble SoMa Thai remains a "neighborhood standby" for fare that "hits the spot" (but "won't kill your budget"), including "mild dishes for the uninitiated palate"; its location's convenient to "Yerba Buena Gardens, SFMOMA" or Moscone; P.S. the Berkeley branch is "a hop and a skip" from the "UC campus" (tip: "sit on the charming porch" with its "treehouse" feel).

Cha Cha Cha   19 | 16 | 15 | $24 |
1801 Haight St. (Shrader St.), 415-386-5758
2327 Mission St. (bet. 19th & 20th Sts.), 415-648-0504
www.cha3.com
"Originator of the tapas trend", this "kitsch-tastic" Haight Street haunt and its pubby Mission sibling still crank out "explosively flavorful" Pan-Caribbean small plates for revelers going "ga ga ga" in these "impossibly noisy" boîtes; "expect to wait" "a million years" for a table, and due to "slow service" you may well wait some more before eating, so "keep yourself occupied" with a glass of the "where'd-my-feet-go? sangria."

CHAPEAU!   27 | 18 | 26 | $44 |
1408 Clement St. (15th Ave.), 415-750-9787
"Hats off" to Philippe Gardelle, the "hardest-working" restaurateur in San Francisco, "who cooks, works the dining room, acts as sommelier and choreographs the staff" at his "humble" Inner Richmond "sardine can"; servers who work "with Parisian perfection" proffer "spectacular" bistro classics (the prix fixe dinners are "a great value") plus an "affordable" wine list that "encourages adventurousness"; as you leave, ladies get a "kiss on the cheek from the charming proprietor" himself.

Charanga ⌧   23 | 18 | 20 | $26 |
2351 Mission St. (bet. 19th & 20th Sts.), 415-282-1813;
www.charangasf.com
"Festive, colorful and fun", this "quaint", wallet-friendly "Mission gem" creates "delightful and delectable" Pan-Latin–Caribbean small plates; although you'll "wait up to an hour for a table", the vibe is so "casual" and "laid-back" you may "want to pull up a chair and invite" the "friendly" staffers to share some "delicious yuca frita" and a pitcher of the signature sangria.

Chaya Brasserie   22 | 22 | 20 | $47 |
132 The Embarcadero (bet. Howard & Mission Sts.),
415-777-8688; www.thechaya.com
"Is it Japanese? is it French? don't worry", just be happy you
can "dine well" on "delicate" fusion fare "and still watch
the waistline" at this "polished", "sexy" LA "immigrant" on
the Embarcadero; sushi samplers fuel salarymen at lunch
and the bar's "lively" at happy hour, so even if the staff is
a mite "impressed with itself", overall it's an "extremely
enjoyable experience – until you get the check."

Cheesecake Factory, The   16 | 16 | 15 | $25 |
Macy's, 251 Geary St., 8th fl. (bet. Powell & Stockton Sts.),
415-391-4444; www.thecheesecakefactory.com
In this foodie metropolis where "chains are a sin", famished
families are a bit "embarrassed" to admit they "really,
really like" this ornate yet "kind of cheesy" factory, and not
just for its "magnificent view of Union Square"; given the
perennial "crowds" you'll "wait for eons" before sitting
down to "gargantuan", "unfinishable" portions of "standard
American fare" (tip: "eat dessert first"); N.B. a location in
San Jose has special parking spaces designated for takeout.

Chenery Park   22 | 18 | 22 | $36 |
683 Chenery St. (Diamond St.), 415-337-8537;
www.chenerypark.com
"Glen Park's only high-end" eatery "does the neighborhood
proud" – this New American run by former Boulevardiers
provides "comfort food with class" and an "excellent" Cal-
centric wine list in a "relaxed atmosphere"; albeit a tad
"cramped" (particularly on Tuesday's "well-received Kids'
Night"), it's "just what the doctor ordered" "for families who
miss eating out" at the "big-name" destinations Downtown.

Chez Maman   22 | 14 | 19 | $23 |
1453 18th St. (bet. Connecticut & Missouri Sts.), 415-824-7166
"Grab a seat at the bar" (that's all there is, besides "two
tiny tables") and tuck into the "*magnifique* burgers", steak
frites and crêpes at this "Mrs." to Chez Papa, a Potrero Hill
shoebox serving a "scaled-down" yet still "genuinely" Gallic
bistro menu; as you eat you'll be "face-to-face" with "your
neighbor" and the one "hardworking French dude who
serves the whole place"; N.B. ratings apply only to the
18th Street location; other branches were slated to open
in fall 2005.

Chez Nous   23 | 16 | 19 | $34 |
1911 Fillmore St. (bet. Bush & Pine Sts.), 415-441-8044
"The gods of little plates are smiling" and so will you at Pac
Heights' pioneer *petit plats* palace due to "impeccable"
Med munchies; the "young, attractive and tattooed" staff
often gets "jammed" in the "noisy" room, but if you're
"savoring delicious wine" and "sharing" snacks with

friends, a "joyous evening is guaranteed"; P.S. reservations are now accepted but "rush hour" still "resembles a yuppie version of the line for *Star Wars.*"

Chez Papa Bistrot　　　24 17 20 $40

1401 18th St. (Missouri St.), 415-255-0387; www.chezpapasf.com
"If you can stand the close quarters", this "tightly packed" Potrero Hill nook is a "charming" translation of a Parisian bistro sans the "cigarette smoke"; while some "question the authenticity" (but not the "attitude") of the French-accented staff, none can doubt the "perfectly prepared Provençal" plates, "wonderful assortment of wines" or "hip vibe" sustained "late into the evening."

Chez Spencer ⊠　　　25 20 22 $51

82 14th St. (Folsom & Harrison Sts.), 415-864-2191
"Park your car, lock the doors", "ask for the chef's tasting menu and let 'er rip" at this haute (or is that "haughty"?) haunt "hidden among the warehouses" in the Mission; its "simple, modern", "impeccable" and "expensive" French cuisine is presented with "such care", but a dip in the Decor score suggests that the "well-heeled crowd" digs the "charming" garden patio more than the "industrial-chic" "converted-garage" interiors.

Chloe's Cafe ⊅　　　21 11 17 $15

1399 Church St. (26th St.), 415-648-4116
"The only thing more likely to get me up early on a Saturday is being lit on fire" rave Noe Valley noshers who nibble on the "incredible" pancakes and "fluffy omelets" "jammed with fresh ingredients" at this Traditional American "niche player for breakfast"; if you arrive on the later side, plan to wait "on the curb with everyone else" as there is "barely enough room" inside for the staff.

Chou Chou Patisserie　　　21 17 21 $34
Artisanale & French Bistro

400 Dewey St. (Woodside Ave.), 415-242-0960;
www.chouchousf.com
As "French as it gets" – with requisite accented waiters and "little elbow room" – this is just one of SF's many "charming bistros" but it's a revelation for Forest Hill residents who "couldn't ask for a better neighborhood restaurant"; the "Provençal potted pies" and other "hearty" "comfort foods" are "lulus", but what takes the cake are the "sumptuous" dessert tarts – "the best" this side of Paris, where the owner runs another patisserie.

CHOW/PARK CHOW　　　19 15 17 $21

215 Church St. (bet. 15th & Market Sts.), 415-552-2469
1240 Ninth Ave. (bet. Irving & Lincoln Sts.), 415-665-9912
This "king of comfort food" New American chainlet (with outposts in the Castro, Inner Sunset and East Bay) proffers a "dependable" melting-pot menu with enough "fresh,

organic" ingredients "to suit foodies"; the "homey" haunts are "no-brainers" for cost-conscious couples and families with kids, but note that though the staff is "attentive, bordering on efficient", service nevertheless "can be slow."

Circolo ⊠   18   21   17 $43
500 Florida St. (Mariposa St.), 415-553-8560; www.circolosf.com
"First impressions are great" at this Mission newcomer with "trendy" bamboo-and-rock-garden decor, a "tapas-ish" Nuevo Latino fusion menu and a lively lounge serving "sexy lychee gimlets"; "later" visits, though, have even Circolo friends fretting – they suggest "turning on the lights" so patrons could figure out if it's "Peruvian or Asian", "nightclub or fine-dining experience"; just don't bother asking the staffers, who "know nothing about anything."

Citizen Cake/Cupcake   21   17   18 $31
399 Grove St. (Gough St.), 415-861-2228; www.citizencake.com
Virgin Megastore, 2 Stockton St., 3rd fl. (Market St.),
415-399-1565; www.citizencupcake.com
Hayes Valley's mod "pastry paradise" offers plenty of "extremely good" Cal entrees – but "sugar junkies" prefer to "skip dinner" in favor of a "naughty treat from the cases" ("an outrageous way to pull in some calories before the ballet"); putting up with waiters who may be a tad too sweet on themselves is less of a cakewalk; P.S. the more casual "Cup", overlooking Union Square, features "faboo panini" and a "candy-store vibe."

Citizen Thai and The Monkey   _   _   _   I
1268 Grant Ave. (Vallejo St.), 415-364-0008; www.citizenthai.com
Diners more in the mood for red curry than red sauce will delight at the debut of this inexpensive Siamese duo in North Beach; Citizen Thai offers a bi-level Buddhist-temple-like setting for enjoying Southeast Asian small plates with a California twist; the adjacent Monkey (a reference to SoMa sibling Koh Samui & The Monkey) is a noodle bar cranking out inexpensive Bangkok street food canteen-style and a bar pouring beer, wine and cocktails.

Citrus Club   18   13   16 $15
1790 Haight St. (Shrader St.), 415-387-6366
Haight Street's "hippest noodle house" "keeps packing 'em in" for "wildly economical" "big-ass bowls" of udon, soba and soup; phos fret the "pedestrian" Pan-Asian provender "lacks authenticity" (it's "mostly vegan or vegetarian") and "doesn't taste as exciting as it smells", but for "members of this club" the "filling" fare and "decent drinks" make it "great before a night out."

Clémentine ⊠   24   20   23 $41
126 Clement St. (bet. 2nd & 3rd Aves.), 415-387-0408
"When you need your Paris fix" this "gem" on Clement Street ("where you'd never expect such a charming little

bistro") is a "real find"; although "noisy with the chatter of Richmond yuppies", this "darling" destination allows you to have a "pleasant meal without breaking the bank", thanks in part to "warm" owners and servers whose "French accents make the good" Gallic "classics" seem even "better than they are."

Cliff House Bistro　　　16 | 22 | 16 | $35
1090 Point Lobos Ave. (Geary St.), 415-386-3330;
www.cliffhouse.com
"If you can't get a table downstairs" at Sutro's to "watch the crashing waves", this "decent" cliff-sider at the Outer Richmond's Point Lobos qualifies as a "close second", especially after its $18 million makeover – though nostalgics mourn the shift from "elegant", "Old San Francisco" interiors to a "modern, cold", "steel-and-blond-wood" decor; ok, the California-style seafood is "uneven" and "service is slow", but given these "stunning views" "who's in a hurry anyway?"

Coco 500 🖫　　　– | – | – | M
500 Brannan St. (4th St.), 415-543-2222;
www.coco500.com
Loretta Keller has morphed Bizou, her longtime SoMa spot, into a more casual affair, trading the white tablecloths for hardwood tops, a community table and a larger bar; the menu is still Cal-Med (signatures such as the beef cheeks will be frequent specials), but diners can now create their own multiple-course meals.

Colibrí Mexican Bistro　　　21 | 20 | 19 | $35
438 Geary St. (bet. Mason & Taylor Sts.), 415-440-2737;
www.colibrimexicanbistro.com
This new "upscale Mexican" serves "sophisticated" re-creations of the classics ("rich and well-spiced sauces", "phenomenal grilled cactus that's all tickle and no prickle"); "service slows down" when the Downtown cantina fills up, but given its "all-day dining" and a "festive late-night bar" pouring more than 100 tequilas, amigos aver it's the "perfect spot after shopping or before the theater."

Cortez　　　24 | 24 | 21 | $46
Adagio Hotel, 550 Geary St. (Taylor St.), 415-292-6360;
www.cortezrestaurant.com
"It's all about small plates" at this "swanky" Adagio Hotel boîte Downtown where a "lithe, model-esque crowd" sashays into the "Calder-meets-Mondrian" surroundings (with "hoops and colored plastic balls hanging around") for "meticulously fashioned" Mediterranean "morsels" and "creative cocktails" – eats and drinks that may be "served in shot glasses" by a "knowledgeable staff"; meanwhile, given the "small portions", tabulations "don't sneak up, they jump up."

Cosmopolitan ☒   20 | 21 | 20 | $42 |
Rincon Ctr., 121 Spear St. (bet. Howard & Mission Sts.),
415-543-4001; www.thecosmopolitancafe.com
Although this SoMa "sleeper" is ideal for "strong cocktails"
and "generous happy-hour plates", "no one but the lunch
crowd has noticed" that the "delicious" New American fare
is "great for dinners" as well; indeed, if you can "get past
the sea of secretaries" and "yuppies" at the "perpetually
overcrowded" bar, you'll "discover a grand", "metropolitan"
dining room staffed by an "attentive" crew.

Cote Sud ☒   20 | 17 | 18 | $36 |
4238 18th St. (Diamond St.), 415-255-6565; www.cotesudsf.com
Castrolites "in on the secret" that $25 buys a "homestyle"
three-course French meal ("cassoulet good enough to
justify the angioplasty cost") consider this "low-key"
second-story Provençal bistro a cote above; though the
"funkily laid-out" "auberge-style" Victorian is *un peu petit*,
it does have a "romantic" covered balcony – so it's sad
that service by the "fresh-off-the-boat staff" is "spotty" (or
maybe just "snobby").

Cozmo's Corner Grill   17 | 17 | 15 | $31 |
2001 Chestnut St. (Fillmore St.), 415-351-0175;
www.cozmoscorner.com
"Attractive but auditorially abrasive when crowded", this
bar for "aroused singles" "that's also a restaurant" is a
"typical Marina pickup joint"; proponents praise the "eye
candy", the signature "Cozmos, of course" and often
"creative" New American eats; critics counter "I don't
know what was most annoying: the bland food, the bland
clientele" or the "slow service."

Crustacean   23 | 17 | 19 | $49 |
1475 Polk St. (California St.), 415-776-2722; www.anfamily.com
Surveyors say "skip the Wharf and eat your crabs with
garlic sauce", "drunken or tamarind"–style at this recently
spiffed-up Nob Hill "gourmet" Vietnamese, and you'd better
be ready to "use your hands" because the "must-have"
namesake shellfish and "slurpy" noodles are "finger-lickin'
good"; staffers aim "to please" "without being annoying or
subservient" but critics snap that only in season is dinner
"worth the price of admission", given the "pretentious dress
code" (collared shirts only).

Deep Sushi ☒   24 | 20 | 15 | $34 |
1740 Church St. (bet. 29th & 30th Sts.), 415-970-3337;
www.deepsushi-sf.com
"Funky turntables, radical nigiri, crazy rolls" – this "super
hipster hangout in outer Noe" ain't no Japanese restaurant,
"it's a sushi revolution" with a "techno beat"; chefs "dressed
as if they're going to work on my car" instead "craft"
"amazing", "uncommon combinations" ("excellent veggie

options"); the place is as "cramped" and "overpriced" as a Tokyo apartment, though, and given the "punk" 'tude, lack of outdoor signage and "butt-numbing" seats, some suspect "no one cares if the customers are even there."

Delancey Street　　　16 | 15 | 20 | $25

600 The Embarcadero (Brannan St.), 415-512-5179
The magnanimous munch "with an air of philanthropy" at this South Beach nonprofit where their dining dollars buy "an amazing view" of the Bay while "helping people help themselves"; the Eclectic "comfort food" is "hit-or-miss", however, and though the staffers are "courteous and sincere", they're essentially "in training"; still, you can "do a good deed" by "eating here at least once" – and for heaven's sake "tip well."

DELFINA　　　26 | 19 | 23 | $43

3621 18th St. (bet. Dolores & Guerrero Sts.), 415-552-4055; www.delfinasf.com
Not "extravagant" or "pretentious", just "damn good", this Mission trattoria "always" "hits the mark" thanks to Craig Stoll's "delfina-tely delicious" "five-star" "seasonal Tuscan" fare "at three-star prices", "served by rocker chicks with a deep knowledge of food and wine"; ok, it's "as cramped as a phone booth" and "booked eons in advance", but now that they've set aside a counter for walk-ins "you're a fool if you don't go."

Desiree Café ⊠　　　▽ 21 | 15 | 16 | $16

San Francisco Film Ctr., 39 Mesa St. (Lincoln Blvd.), 415-561-2336; www.desireecafe.com
Foodies who "wish more big-time chefs came back down to earth instead of shooting for the most expensive star" have anointed Annie Gingrass (ex Hawthorne Lane) "queen of the Presidio" for her "tiny but wonderful" "gem" serving daytime eats only ("superb box lunches"); the Cal cuisine's concocted on the spot "so be prepared to wait"; N.B. now serving brunch on Fridays; closed weekends.

Destino　　　20 | 19 | 18 | $32

1815 Market St. (bet. Guerrero & Valencia Sts.), 415-552-4451; www.destinosf.com
"Interesting Nuevo Latino small plates" and "killer" pisco sours make this Castro destino-tion a contender "in what's become a competitive" culinary niche; its "Peruvian food with pizzazz" is "worth putting up with" the "jam-packed" and "outrageously loud" "South American–style" dining room and "off-and-on" service, although "tiny portions, the usual curse of the taperia", prompted a dip in Food ratings.

Dottie's True Blue Cafe　　　25 | 12 | 18 | $16

522 Jones St. (bet. Geary & O'Farrell Sts.), 415-885-2767
"Give me Dottie's baked goods or give me death" declare devotees of this "funky" New American "throwback" that's

"still, and maybe always, the best breakfast" joint around; its "colorful" Tenderloin setting doesn't "keep away the customers" who "wait half a day" for the "football-sized omelets" and "fat stacks of pancakes" "cranked out a mile a minute" that'll "fill you up" till dinner.

Dragon Well   21   16   19 $23
2142 Chestnut St. (bet. Pierce & Steiner Sts.), 415-474-6888; www.dragonwell.com
"Affordable" "Chinese food without all the heartburn" – but with "enough flavor so you don't miss the grease" – has habitués hailing every year as "the year of the dragon"; although the menu is "short", what's offered outshines the "typical 500 choices", and a "friendly" staff "attentively" handles the room, a "yuppified Marina hangout"; the "screaming-kids factor", however, yields a "stack of double-parkers picking up dinner" to go.

E&O Trading Company   19   21   17 $34
314 Sutter St. (bet. Grant Ave. & Stockton St.), 415-693-0303; www.eotrading.com
"Loud" and "busy" "at happy hour and dinnertime", this "recently redone" ex-microbrewery Downtown (with an offshoot in San Jose and one that opened post-*Survey* in Larkspur) rollicks with "tiki-influenced" Southeast Asian small plates amid an "extravagant" "tribal village" interior; still, some say variable service and "cheesy but fun" "umbrella" cocktails make it seem little more than a Far Eastern "proto-TGI Friday's"

E'Angelo ∌   20   10   17 $24
2234 Chestnut St. (bet. Pierce & Scott Sts.), 415-567-6164
For "old-school" Italian "without the hassle of North Beach", this "kitschy" Marina spot is "right on, from the red-and-white tablecloths" to the "flavorful, hearty" "family food" to the waiters "barking orders across the room"; a drop in Service score reflects the staff's "unpredictable" nature, but a recent ownership change may have calmed things down.

Ebisu   24   13   18 $33
1283 Ninth Ave. (Irving St.), 415-566-1770; www.ebisusushi.com
"Forget those hip places with trendy names" – to eat at this "colorful, lively" hole-in-the-wall Japanese "well-dressed yuppies" with a yen for the raw deal endure waits in "the cold, foggy Inner Sunset" in "lines that test the patience of a Buddhist monk"; once inside, old hands opt for the sushi bar and buy the "entertaining" chefs "sake shots" "to get awesome rolls not on the menu" plus "sashimi so fresh you want to slap it."

El Balazo   18   14   16 $10
1654 Haight St. (Clayton St.), 415-864-2140
The fare's "fast, good and cheap" at this Mexican on Haight Street that's as colorful as a tie-dyed T-shirt; its "'60s-

themed" menu of "burritos as big as your head" may be a
bit "too gringo" for some, but "garnish lovers" grin at the
"free extras" that help you "turn your common" *comida*
"into a masterpiece."

Elite Cafe   17 | 17 | 17 | $36 |
2049 Fillmore St. (bet. California & Pine Sts.), 415-346-8668
With its "festive" raw bar and hold-on-to-your-Hurricane
cocktails, this Upper Fillmore Cajun is still ragin'; if you
"stick to the Creole classics" (and eschew "overspiced"
and "blackened everything"), regulars report this art deco
vet "isn't bad" for dinner or brunch; amorists advise "settling
into one of the intimate booths" and "letting the oysters
do the trick."

Eliza's   22 | 16 | 16 | $22 |
2877 California St. (bet. Broderick & Divisadero Sts.), 415-621-4819
1457 18th St. (bet. Connecticut & Missouri Sts.), 415-648-9999
"Purists will frown on" the "nouvelle" noshes at these
"surrealistic" Pac Heights and Potrero Hill sisters, but fans
insist the "Cal-Chinese" tastes and esoteric ingredients
("try the ostrich") "will make you pull your head out of the
sand and wonder why you ate so many meals in Chinatown";
"don't expect to linger", however – "you are in, fed and out
in a flash" thanks to "poker-faced" staffers who are both
"brisk" and "brusque."

Ella's   22 | 14 | 19 | $21 |
500 Presidio Ave. (California St.), 415-441-5669;
www.ellassanfrancisco.com
Presidio Heights' "unpretentious", "family-friendly" fave
is HQ for Traditional American "breakfasts of champions",
which is why "locals and tourists" endure one "ella-va line"
to eat here; once in, they're soothed by a "welcoming" staff
proffering morning and midday food just "like grandma
makes, but bigger"; the frugal fret "for the price the eggs
should be made of gold", but at least "you'll have leftovers."

El Metate ⊄   ▽ 24 | 10 | 17 | $9 |
2406 Bryant St. (22nd St.), 415-641-7209
Partisans proclaim this "newish" taqueria (founded in
2002) the source of "indisputably the best burrito" in the
Mission plus "fish tacos worth a special trip"; as a result,
though it's "off the beaten path", the "cramped space" –
little more than a serape-wrapped counter and a handful
of tables – is "usually full", prompting patrons to "take the
food to go" or sit at one of the "outdoor tables."

El Raigon ☒   22 | 19 | 19 | $44 |
510 Union St. (Grant Ave.), 415-291-0927;
www.elraigon.com
"Finally, something besides pasta in North Beach" crow
carnivores about SF's first Argentinean steakhouse, where
"gauchos getcha" grilled chops you "could cut with a fork"

plus a "rich" array of "great South American wines"; as at other beeferies, everything's à la carte so "the tab rises rapidly", but that doesn't faze the "polo players" and "young gentry" who crowd the "deafening" brick-and-wood room adorned with antique ranching photos.

Emmy's Spaghetti Shack ⊄　　19 15 16 $21
18 Virginia Ave. (Mission St.), 415-206-2086
"Shack up" at this "ramshackle" Italian at the base of Bernal, where even "super-late" you can get "a mean plate of spaghetti" (as well as "more ambitious stuff") along with a "40 of Bud" chilled in "a champagne ice bucket"; however, unless you arrive "early to jockey" for one of the few tables – well before the real jockeys crank up the "spinnin' vibe beats" on weekends – you'll have to pasta time in "the adjacent Mexican bar."

Emporio Rulli　　21 22 15 $19
2300 Chestnut St. (Scott St.), 415-923-6464
Stockton Street Pavilion, 920 Post St. (bet. Powell & Stockton Sts.), 415-433-1122
www.rulli.com
While savoring the "divine desserts and elegant coffees" it's literally "la dolce vita" swoon sugar-happy habitués of this "wonderfully authentic" duo Downtown and in the Marina where fans "go for the chocolates" but "stay for everything else" ("great panini", "fresh soups"); luckily the "beautiful Roman decor" indoors and "terrific outdoor settings" encourage a "leisurely" visit because the "slow, disorganized service" ensures it; N.B. there's a location North of SF.

Enrico's Sidewalk Cafe　　16 19 16 $33
504 Broadway St. (Kearny St.), 415-982-6223;
www.enricossidewalkcafe.com
Beat nostalgics may howl "where did the real Enrico's go?" but this "North Beach classic" with patio is still the place "to hang out at for a while", with "entertainment" in the forms of live jazz and the neighborhood's "endless parade of humanity"; don't plan on an "intimate dinner", though, because the music is "incredibly loud" and the "overpriced" Cal-Med eats are "nothing to shout about."

Eos Restaurant & Wine Bar　　24 19 21 $41
901 Cole St. (Carl St.), 415-566-3063; www.eossf.com
"The bubble" has burst but this oenophiles' "mecca" in Cole Valley continues to sparkle, rising to the tapa the barrel after the kitchen's "switch to small plates"; the fanciful, "fantastic" Cal-Asian fusion is "perfectly matched" with vinos by "knowledgeable" staffers, which helps justify prices that are "a bit splurge-y" for a "loud", local spot; impromptu types report the "cozy" wine bar's your "best bet for spontaneous visits."

Eric's   22 | 14 | 16 | $20
1500 Church St. (27th St.), 415-282-0919
Noe Valleyites note there's "no need to fight the Chinatown crowds" when you can pop over to this "cheery" converted Victorian to get "tasty", "healthy" Chinese "basics you love" "at a reasonable price"; "service is spee-dee" due to the "move-'em-in-move-'em-out" mentality, but "screaming children and bustling, tight quarters" don't inspire lingering anyway – consider "carryout" instead.

Esperpento   18 | 14 | 15 | $25
3295 22nd St. (Valencia St.), 415-282-8867
At this "authentic", "loud", "colorful" Spanish, one of the Mission's many tapas bars, you can "go with a group of friends for numerous small plates and pitchers of sangria" without breaking the bank; however, you'll have to endure "exceedingly slow" and "horrible air circulation" ("you leave reeking" after an evening in this "garlic sweatbox").

Espetus Churrascaria   21 | 15 | 21 | $43
1686 Market St. (Gough St.), 415-552-8792; www.espetus.com
Beef eaters blissfully binge at this Brazilian churrascaria, a "noisy" Hayes Valley chop shop where a "never-ending" supply of "meats on swords" is delivered by attentive "wandering gauchos" until you flash the "convenient" stop sign; there's also an "amazing" all-you-can-eat salad bar for vegheads plus "strong caipirinhas", so "try to starve yourself before going" "to get your money's worth" since "meaty prices rack up like the ribs."

FARALLON   24 | 27 | 23 | $58
450 Post St. (bet. Mason & Powell Sts.), 415-956-6969; www.farallonrestaurant.com
A meal at this "magnificent", "whimsical" Downtown "aquarium" (complete with "amusing jellyfish chandeliers") is "like dining with Jacques Cousteau" "under the sea"; "elegant" fin fare of the first water (including "the greatest" raw shellfish platter) "flows" to your table courtesy of servers who are "on top of everything" – but pennywise patrons point out that all this "culinary pampering" can be a "cash-draining" experience.

1550 Hyde Café & Wine Bar   23 | 17 | 22 | $40
1550 Hyde St. (Pacific Ave.), 415-775-1550; www.1550hyde.com
"Proof that a wine bar can have great food too", this Russian Hill "hydeaway" delivers organic Cal-Med fare to "rival that of any of the snooty Downtown restaurants, at a lower price"; aptly, the 180-label cellar is "fantastic" ("not your usual mass-produced" stuff), and guidance from the "knowledgeable staff" is "amazingly helpful"; "the only drawbacks" to whine about are the "small size" (42 seats), "drab", "minimalist" decor and occasional "din."

FIFTH FLOOR
26 | 25 | 25 | $81

Hotel Palomar, 12 Fourth St. (Market St.), 415-348-1555;
www.hotelpalomar.com
"After many chef changes", this "swanky" "citadel of fine
cuisine" at SoMa's hip Hotel Palomar now boasts Melissa
Perello (ex Charles Nob Hill) as top toque; her "fabulous",
"inventive" New French fare is "impeccably" served by a
"top-notch" staff and paired with "perhaps the best wine
list" around (though with "too many" bottles "in the three-
and four-digit range") – all of which adds up to "astounding"
tabs (tip: "arrive in a Brink's truck").

Firecracker ⊠
21 | 18 | 18 | $27

1007½ Valencia St. (21st St.), 415-642-3470
This "fashionable" hot spot gets Missionites "fired up" with
its "light, flavorful" "Cal-Chinese" cookery, "eccentric, fun"
boho decor and "inviting atmosphere"; a "great cheap date"
declare devotees, but people who pan the "Americanized"
food and "at-ti-tude" see "no sparks."

Firefly
24 | 20 | 22 | $37

4288 24th St. (Douglass St.), 415-821-7652;
www.fireflyrestaurant.com
Despite the "well-deserved" "buzz", Brad Levy manages to
keep his "cozy" Noe Valley Eclectic "undiscovered" and
"unpretentious"; a "hip staff" "with no attitude" proffers
the "socially conscious", "multiethnic" "comfort food
extraordinaire"("those potstickers should be patented")
and "fairly priced" boutique bottlings; the combo (plus
a midweek prix fixe) makes this "neighborhood favorite"
"worth a special trip."

FLEUR DE LYS ⊠
27 | 27 | 26 | $87

777 Sutter St. (bet. Jones & Taylor Sts.), 415-673-7779;
www.fleurdelyssf.com
Step right up to the greatest show on Nob Hill (now also
appearing in Las Vegas) and be seated under a "romantic
circuslike tent" for culinary feats of derring-do – Hubert
Keller's "spectacular" prix fixe French dinner is an "epic
performance" ("foie gras, truffles and caviar coming out of
your ears", but "even vegetarians" can easily partake of
the "magic"); it's all staged by a "pampering" staff and
"marvelous sommelier", making an evening here a "civilized
splurge" that rewards "the effort of wearing a coat and tie."

Florio
21 | 19 | 19 | $40

1915 Fillmore St. (bet. Bush & Pine Sts.), 415-775-4300;
www.floriosf.com
"Ooh-la-la, very French!" coo the "upscale Pacific Heights
set" who liken this "charming" bistro to their favorite
Parisian boîtes "without the heavy cigarette smoke or even
heavier attitude"; the "homey" "Italian-leaning" menu
"never gets old" to some, though "bored" regulars wish

it were "a bit more extensive" ("how many steak frites restaurants do we need?").

Fog City Diner　　　19　18　18　$33
1300 Battery St. (The Embarcadero), 415-982-2000; www.fogcitydiner.com
"Don't let the word 'diner' fool you" – this New American on the Embarcadero with a "retro", "clubby atmosphere" puts an "elegant twist" on its "comfort food" to the satisfaction of tourists, locals and celebs alike; still, contrarians call the food "pricey" and service just "so-so": "resting on its laurels would be an understatement – this baby's out cold."

Foreign Cinema　　　21　24　19　$41
2534 Mission St. (bet. 21st & 22nd Sts.), 415-648-7600; www.foreigncinema.com
For best performance "in an edgy neighborhood", cinephiles give "two thumbs way up" to this Mission double bill where "alfresco diners" on the "heated patio" can take in a foreign or indie flick along with "creative" Cal-Med food ("the movies are great, but the food is better"); "on cool nights" it's better "inside" the "industrial-chic" space ("sit near the fireplace"); the only reel blooper in this *mise en scene* is the "spotty service."

Fournou's Ovens　　　21　21　21　$54
Renaissance Stanford Ct., 905 California St. (Powell St.), 415-989-1910; www.renaissancehotel.com
"Still good after 30 years" conclude connoisseurs who claim the "consistent" Cal-Med cuisine and "extensive" 500-label wine list are worth ascending Nob Hill to the Renaissance Stanford Court; if you "sit by the ovens" you can "watch as your meal is prepared" or look on from a window table as "cable cars climb California Street"; trendier types term the menu "unimaginative" and the experience "an expensive snooze."

Frascati　　　26　21　23　$41
1901 Hyde St. (Green St.), 415-928-1406; www.frascatisf.com
"It's not glitzy, it's just perfect" rave regulars about this "lively" Russian Hill "treasure" with a "fabulously romantic" balcony; its "knowledgeable and friendly staff" delivers "seasonal" Cal-Med dishes "elevated to an oh-my-God level of deliciousness" from a "small kitchen" that keeps the whole place "toasty warm"; since it takes "as much time to park as to eat" here, surveyors suggest you hop on the cable car that runs just outside the door.

Fresca　　　23　16　17　$31
2114 Fillmore St. (California St.), 415-447-2668
24 W. Portal Ave. (Ulloa St.), 415-759-8087
3946 24th St. (bet. Noe & Sanchez Sts.), 415-695-0549 ⊠
"Veni, vidi, seviche" declaim devotees of the "spicy seafood specialties" and marinated meats served at these modest

Peruvians in West Portal and Upper Fillmore (plus an unrated branch in Noe); the joints are "jumping, like the piped-in music" and "flames" from the open kitchen, but they're also "louder than a Who concert" and plagued by "sketchy service" and "eternal waits" "even with reservations."

Fringale ⊠ | 25 | 18 | 22 | $44 |

570 Fourth St. (bet. Brannan & Bryant Sts.), 415-543-0573;
www.fringalerestaurant.com
"Sophisticated" French-Basque specialties "sparkle" at this "loud" SoMa "staple", which regulars report "remains outstanding" with the arrival of new chef Thierry Clement (ex Frisson); most maintain it's "marvelous" but some say servers can be "aloof" or "curt" – as your neighbors may be also if you "knock elbows" with them at the "too-crowded" tables ("at least sardines are lying down"); N.B. a post-*Survey* ownership change may outdate scores.

Frisson | 19 | 25 | 18 | $56 |

244 Jackson St. (bet. Battery & Front Sts.), 415-956-3004;
www.frissonsf.com
A "groovy place to chill and swill", this "*Austin Powers*"–meets–"'60s airline lounge" has "local DJs spinning most nights" and "noisy" "twentysomething poseurs" cavorting under a "spiral of ceiling lights" in SF's "coolest room"; servers "should try harder" because the kitchen already is, having replaced its once-"avant-garde" fare with a more approachable New American menu; still, disoriented diners can't decide "do I dance, do I eat?"

Frjtz Fries | 18 | 14 | 13 | $14 |

579 Hayes St. (Laguna St.), 415-864-7654; www.frjtzfries.com
"Carb cravers" "give it up for the crispy, crunchy" frites "with a multitude of dipping sauces" and "great" "Belgian brews" at this "bohemian" teahouse in Hayes Valley, which also serves "crêpes galore", "tasty sandwiches" and "healthy" salads; unfortunately, the crew is "offhand" at best – and "don't expect any service" at all if you sit on the "cute patio" to "snarf" your "addictive treats."

Galette | 19 | 14 | 15 | $21 |

2043 Fillmore St. (bet. California & Pine Sts.), 415-928-1300
"Crêpe your way through an entire meal" for only a "few euros" at this Breton bistro in Pac Heights; sampling the "amazing" galettes and "scrumptious" moules frites is probably "best for a Sunday brunch" or dinner "where time is not of the essence", since the staffers may be "too busy talking with one another" to "pay attention to diners' needs."

GARDEN COURT | 19 | 28 | 20 | $47 |

Palace Hotel, 2 New Montgomery St. (Market St.), 415-546-5010;
www.gardencourt-restaurant.com
"What a spread" croon courtiers who come to the Palace Hotel's "opulent" Downtown dining room (the city's highest-

rated for Decor) to savor "grandiose" breakfast and brunch buffets that "go on for hours", high tea and other special "holiday" meals; sitting under the "unbelievable" stained-glass ceiling is "like having lunch in Queen Victoria's living room", so even if service is sometimes "impersonal" or "slow" and the American fare "more appropriate for a Holiday Inn Express", "it hardly matters"; N.B. a post-*Survey* chef change may outdate the Food score.

Garibaldis   22 | 21 | 21 | $41 |
347 Presidio Ave. (bet. Clay & Sacramento Sts.), 415-563-8841
As "comfortable as an old pair of jeans" – albeit a designer brand – this "convivial" yet "classy" Presidio Heights stalwart (with a larger, trendier Rockridge outpost) is "a solid choice"; staffed by "polished" personnel, the flower-filled room draws "upper-crust society people" for "serious cocktails" or "relaxing dinners" of "destination-quality" Cal-Med cuisine despite "can't-hear-your-tablemates" volume and "double-take prices"; N.B. chef changes at both locations may outdate the above Food score.

GARY DANKO   29 | 27 | 28 | $91 |
800 N. Point St. (Hyde St.), 415-749-2060; www.garydanko.com
A "foodie who hasn't" worshipped at this "temple of gastronomy" – ranked No. 1 for Food, Service and Popularity in this *Survey* – is "like an art lover who hasn't been to the Louvre"; "Gary Swanko" is a "master" of "perfection and finesse" whose "multihour", "design-it-yourself" New American meals end with a visit from the "extraordinary" artisanal cheese cart, all served without a "scintilla of pomposity" by "telepathic" waiters; though a few critics deconstruct the modern, almost minimalistic digs near the Wharf, most maintain "everything is superlative" – which is why reservations remain as elusive as the Mona Lisa's smile.

Gaylord India   19 | 17 | 19 | $33 |
*1 Embarcadero Ctr. (bet. Battery & Sacramento Sts.),
415-397-7775; www.gaylords1.com*
Once considered "*the* Indians in Frisco", these "white-tablecloth" curry couriers are "no longer the benchmark" but "still do a nice job" with the standards; the more "sophisticated" (if "aging") interiors, prix fixe buffet meals and service that's "higher-class" than that of "local Pakistani joints" also appeal to the Embarcadero "lunchtime crowd" and Menlo Park techies; N.B. as of fall 2005, the recently closed Ghirardelli Square location was slated to resurface at 201 Bridgeway in Sausalito.

Geranium   ▽ 19 | 20 | 18 | $25 |
*615 Cortland Ave. (Anderson St.), 415-647-0118;
www.geraniumrestaurant.com*
Flora fanciers fete this "sunny" "retro-chic" vegetarian cafe flowering in Bernal Heights (a "former butcher shop",

no less) for its "appealing" international comfort foods
(including vegan specials) that "convince" even carnivores
they "can live without meat for at least one meal"; that
meal may last awhile, given the "leisurely service", a sign
this newly sprouted spot is "still working out some kinks."

Giordano Bros. ⊘   – | – | – | I
303 Columbus Ave. (Broadway St.), 415-397-2767;
www.giordanobros.com
This hole-in-the-wall sandwich stop in North Beach has
promptly become a cheap-eats fave for its version of cheese
steaks: $6.75 'all-in-one sandwiches' packing coleslaw
and fries alongside the grilled meat and cheese, all served
in fresh, crusty French bread from the bakery next door.

Giorgio's Pizzeria   20 | 11 | 17 | $17
151 Clement St. (3rd Ave.), 415-668-1266; www.giorgiospizza.com
At this Inner Richmond "old-school pizzeria" the "checkered
tablecloths, Chianti bottles" and "plastic grapes hanging
from the ceiling" "haven't changed" since surveyors "first
went there" as children; nowadays their own "rugrats
invade" to "watch dough being thrown" on Wednesday's
"make-your-own-pizza nights", while adults again savor
the "delicious, thin-crust" pies (specimens that "could
survive in NYC").

Gira Polli   20 | 13 | 16 | $22
659 Union St. (bet. Columbus Ave. & Powell St.), 415-434-4472
The "prized rotisserie chickens" publicly "roast on a spit"
at this plain-Jane Southern Italian in North Beach, where
the "savory" "roto-grilled" birds and lamb come "with all
the fixings" at "half the price"; the "staff is always friendly"
to those who eat in, but most prefer "takeout" since the
room's "too darn small" (20 seats) and "bland" (the interiors
of the recently spiffed-up and expanded Mill Valley branch
get mixed reviews).

Globe ☾   20 | 17 | 18 | $39
290 Pacific Ave. (bet. Battery & Front Sts.), 415-391-4132
"Dark, "insidery" and open till 1 AM, this "chefs' after-work
hangout" Downtown is "what late-night dining should be",
and office workers report its "satisfying" "market-driven"
Cal-Ital fare and "sunny" sidewalk seating suit them fine
during "normal business hours" as well; but "inconsistent"
service has some saying this spot has "seen better days"
and hoping it'll come around now that the owners are back
in town with their just-opened Zuppa.

Goat Hill Pizza   20 | 10 | 16 | $16
300 Connecticut St. (18th St.), 415-641-1440
715 Harrison St. (3rd St.), 415-974-1303
www.goathillpizza.com
Proselytizers of this humble Potrero Hill pie parlor praise the
"amazing" sourdough crust "piled high" with "interesting"

toppings ("no goat", though) and dished out by servers who "remember the regulars", and they're devoted to the "Monday night all-you-can-eat" buffet; skeptics shrug "good pizza, but not enough" so for them to "join the Goat Hill cult"; N.B. the newer SoMa branch offers primarily takeout and delivery.

Godzila Sushi   19 | 9 | 15 | $26
1800 Divisadero St. (Bush St.), 415-931-1773
Lizard kings like this "pared-down" Pac Heights sushi bar for its "ultrafresh" fare served in "sizable" yet "inexpensive" portions ("when I get the check, I laugh") so they're happy to overlook "cafeteria-style seating" and "wacky" decor; however, critics stomp their feet about "ordinary" eats; N.B. ownership and chef changes may outdate scores.

Goood Frikin' Chicken   ▽ 20 | 6 | 16 | $13
10 29th St. (Mission St.), 415-970-2428
"Living up to its name" (make that "*great* frikin' chicken"), this new Mission cheep-eats spot is a veritable "Middle Eastern Boston Market" where the well-seasoned rotisserie cluckers come with three sides, all "for the price of a movie" (vegetarians crow it's also got the "best frikin' hummus"); most currently get it to go but as of this summer, plans were underway to add a 75-seat table-service space next door (which may outdate the above Decor score).

Grand Cafe   20 | 25 | 20 | $44
Hotel Monaco, 501 Geary St. (Taylor St.), 415-292-0101;
www.grandcafe-sf.com
"Foodies and architects" feel this Downtowner's "majestic" art nouveau interior is "almost equaled" by its "stylish", "jazzy" Cal-French bistro fare; add in a "perfect pre-theater location" (adjoining the Hotel Monaco), "lively" ambiance, "great wine list" and servers who "make you feel welcome" and the grand total is a "wonderful date restaurant" – now "if only the noise level lent itself to conversation."

Grandeho's Kamekyo   22 | 15 | 21 | $33
943 Cole St. (bet. Carl St. & Parnassus Ave.), 415-759-8428
2721 Hyde St. (bet. Beach & North Point Sts.), 415-673-6828
The grand, "innovative" rolls (plus "artfully presented" sushi and sashimi) can make you "love these places" report regulars of these Japanese sibs in Cole Valley and Fisherman's Wharf; sure, the interiors are "unassuming" and it's "a tad overpriced" to be an everyday haunt, but the "warmest wait staff" around ("come once a week and they'll know you by name") makes this "the *Cheers* of sushi bars."

Great Eastern ●   21 | 11 | 14 | $25
649 Jackson St. (bet. Grant Ave. & Kearny St.), 415-986-2500
At this "quintessential Chinatown" seafooder you can "pick your dinner from one of the many fish tanks" in the back or opt for other "reliable and solid" Sino specialties such as

"great dim sum" (selected from a menu instead of carts); fans feel the fare outweighs the stereotypical surroundings, but curmudgeons mutter it's a merely "mediocre" "tourist trap"; N.B. serves till 1 AM nightly.

Greens

23 | 22 | 21 | $38

Fort Mason Ctr., Bldg. A (Buchanan St.), 415-771-6222; www.greensrestaurant.com

After 26 years there's not as much "novelty" at this "veggie nirvana", but thanks to "imaginative" meat-free "haute cuisine" plus a slew of organic and sustainable wines, "even carnivores" happily "veg out" at this "ample, lofty" Marina institution; for Saturday's prix fixe dinners the "remarkably healthy-looking staff" "pull out the stops", and "views of the Golden Gate Bridge at sunset" just make "everything taste better"; trenchermen harrumph "portions are for hummingbirds" but still cost you a lot of green.

Habana

20 | 22 | 19 | $37

2080 Van Ness Ave. (Pacific Ave.), 415-567-7606; www.habana1948.com

"Now I see why Castro won't leave" comment comrades upon entering this eatery where the "slow and relaxed" "old-Cuba" "fantasy ambiance" makes "you forget Van Ness is just outside the door"; "groups trying to engender festivity" and a "comfortable buzz" "hang at the great bar" sipping "excellent mojitos" – but though the *comida* is "tasty" and "enjoyable" proletarians protest it "seems overpriced"; N.B. a post-*Survey* remodel may outdate the above Decor score.

Hamano Sushi

20 | 12 | 16 | $31

1332 Castro St. (24th St.), 415-826-0825; www.hamanosushi.com

Although "Hamano-san sold" this long-running Noe Valley Japanese several years back, sashimi "enthusiasts" still stop by "at least once a week" for "mouthfuls rather than morsels of raw fish"; they report there's "fun" to be had "sitting at the bar" but it's "utterly lost" if you sit in the "dull, cold" dining room, where the decor and servers aren't "out to make waves."

Harbor Village

22 | 18 | 16 | $32

4 Embarcadero Ctr. (bet. Clay & Sacramento Sts.), 415-781-8833; www.harborvillage.net

"Authentic daily dim sum and Cantonese food rivaling the best in Hong Kong" draw diners who are willing to pay a bit more than at "Chinatown dives" for this Sino's "beautiful" if "barnlike" setting on the Embarcadero ("great views from some tables"), lack of tourists and "complimentary validated parking on weekends"; "if you are looking for attentive service", however, "forget it" ("go hungry and eat fast").

Hard Rock Cafe
12 | 18 | 15 | $25

Pier 39, Bldg. Q1 (Beach St.), 415-956-2013; www.hardrock.com
"If you can take the loudness", this "formula" "rock 'n' roll
stroll down memory lane" – with the usual "mediocre"
American food – is a "dependable" option on the Wharf
when you're with a "hard-core rocker" or noisy children
("nobody will notice"); still, locals scold "if you come to SF
on vacation and eat here, you just aren't trying."

Harris'
24 | 21 | 23 | $53

*2100 Van Ness Ave. (Pacific Ave.), 415-673-1888;
www.harrisrestaurant.com*
"Hunks of meat in a window" attract a mature clientele to
this "retro" Russian Hill "must for serious carnivores", a
"locals' favorite" reminiscent of "'60s" "steak-and-martini
joints"; "everything is big, gracious and stately", from the
"fat", "dry-aged" chops to the leather booths and "old-
fashioned" service from "local characters" – not to mention
the beefy prices; N.B. live jazz Thursday–Saturday.

Hawthorne Lane
24 | 24 | 23 | $56

*22 Hawthorne St. (bet. Folsom & Howard Sts.), 415-777-9779;
www.hawthornelane.com*
"Now that the dot-com years are behind us", this "trendy"
"SoMa favorite" has matured into a plush, "quiet", "upscale
dining room" where "servers who go the extra step" present
"exquisite" Cal-Asian cookery and a "great but high-priced
list" of 500 wines; some surmise "it just misses that critical
edge" (e.g. "decor on the dull side"), but most maintain it's an
"outstanding", "sophisticated" spot "for a special dinner."

Hayes Street Grill
22 | 17 | 21 | $41

*320 Hayes St. (bet. Franklin & Gough Sts.), 415-863-5545;
www.hayesstreetgrill.com*
"In a town known for its seafood", this Hayes Valley fish
house continues to reel in regulars with "environmentally
sensitive" daily catches, "presented in straight-up fashion"
with "a choice of sauces"; though aesthetes ask "what is
up" with the "sterile interior", the "opera and symphony
crowd" considers the place a "standby" since the staff is
"excellent at getting you in and out in time for a show."

Helmand, The
24 | 16 | 21 | $31

*430 Broadway St. (bet. Kearny & Montgomery Sts.),
415-362-0641; www.helmandsf.com*
"Who knew they ate so well in Afghanistan?" marvel
"converts" who gobble up "fragrant, well-spiced" Kabul-
inspired cuisine at this sleeper co-owned by President
"Hamid Karzai's brother"; an "oasis" "among skin shops"
in the "crummy" part of North Beach, it offers "service
with a smile" in a "homey", "authentic atmosphere" that
makes you feel like "you're a world away", with dirt-cheap
tabs to further the fantasy.

Henry's Hunan ⊠

| 21 | 8 | 15 | $19 |

1016 Bryant St. (bet. 8th & 9th Sts.), 415-861-5808
110 Natoma St. (2nd St.), 415-546-4999
674 Sacramento St. (bet. Kearny & Montgomery Sts.),
415-788-2234

Hunan

924 Sansome St. (Broadway St.), 415-956-7727

"Henry taught the world to eat Hunan" almost 30 years ago at his original location, and his "addictive and distinctive" fiery fare still provides an affordable "hot fix" for "lunch crowds" throughout the city; "just flag" down a waiter and "after five to 10 minutes" your "gigantic portion" will appear ("have plenty of drinks and napkins handy"); the "no-frills" interiors may be "tragic" to some, but to others they're "perfect in this context" ("no pretense").

Herbivore

| 15 | 15 | 15 | $17 |

531 Divisadero St. (bet. Fell & Hayes Sts.), 415-885-7133
983 Valencia St. (21st St.), 415-826-5657
www.herbivore-restaurant.com

Green beings head to these Eclectic vegetarians in the Mission and the Western Addition for a "healthy meal" without the "holier-than-thou attitude" or the "wallet-breaking" prices; "vegans will be in heaven" but some "ovo-lactos and meat eaters" complain the "filling" fare is "bland as heck", while "spacy service" has wags wondering if staffers "smoked some herb of their own before work."

Hog Island Oyster Co. & Bar

| 25 | 17 | 19 | $29 |

The Embarcadero, 1 Ferry Bldg., #11A (Market St.), 415-391-7117;
www.hogislandoysters.com

To get oysters "any fresher", you'd have to "be the shucker" brag bivalve buffs who go hog wild "slurping down" "pristine" shellfish ("raw, fried, you name it") paired with "stellar wines" at this "casual setup" in the Ferry Building; loyalists love "watching the boats come and go", especially from the "outside communal picnic tables" (indoors it's a mite "cramped"), and remind those who "balk" at the "hefty price tag", at least "you don't have to drive up to Point Reyes."

Home

| 18 | 15 | 17 | $25 |

2100 Market St. (Church St.), 415-503-0333
2032 Union St. (bet. Buchanan & Webster Sts.), 415-931-5006
www.home-sf.com

Home is where the "hearty" American "comfort food" is, holler the hordes who dig in at this "energetic" (read: "loud") "Castro mainstay", now under new management; it's a "favorite for brunch, dinner" or "inexpensive cocktails" by the "fireplace on the patio" despite "so-so service" but detractors dis this "Marie Callender's on steroids" and declare "I'd rather stay home"; N.B. the Union Street location, which opened post-*Survey*, is unrated.

Hotei
18 | 16 | 17 | $18

1290 Ninth Ave. (Irving St.), 415-753-6045; www.hoteisf.com
Steaming bowls of Japanese soups crammed with "oodles of noodles", "tons of toppings and tasty sauces" are the draw at this Inner Sunset version of a Tokyo ramen bar; as the "less expensive" sib to Ebisu across the street, it also offers the "same great sushi without the long wait" – yet purists pout the "Americanized" chow and "surly service" deserve 40 lashes with . . . well, you know.

HOUSE
26 | 16 | 21 | $37

1230 Grant Ave. (bet. Columbus Ave. & Vallejo St.), 415-986-8612; www.thehse.com
Specialties of the house include "top-quality" "sushi-style" starters, the "legendary sea bass, grilled to perfection", and "awesome desserts" plus a "small yet smart wine list" at this "innovative, affordable" Asian fusion, a "tiny" "gem" hidden among North Beach's "touristy" eateries; though you can "forget about having a conversation" in the "loud", "cramped quarters", "friendly and knowledgeable staffers" nevertheless make you feel at home.

House of Nanking
21 | 5 | 11 | $18

919 Kearny St. (bet. Columbus Ave. & Jackson St.), 415-421-1429
"Chinatown's version of the Soup Nazi" draws "long lines" of locals and tourists for whom the "sit down–shut up"– "eat fast"–"get out" shtick is "part of the fun" and results in "delicious" dinners for mere pennies; "the owner promises to take care of you and then serves you what everyone else is getting (because he's taking care of them too)" – that explains how they "speed it to your table" and why the disenchanted dub this dump "House of Same Sauce."

House of Prime Rib
24 | 18 | 21 | $44

1906 Van Ness Ave. (Washington St.), 415-885-4605
At this Russian Hill "landmark" the "clubby", "kitschy" dining room might evoke "the days when the Rat Pack ruled Vegas" but 21st-century carnivores still contentedly consume its "gargantuan" "slabs" of "primo" prime rib (a "very moo-ving experience") and "satisfying" sides ("salads iced and spun to perfection"); the famished fret that "they always run late on your reservation" but once you're seated, servers are "willing to do anything and everything to make you happy"; P.S. the "martinis are a must."

Hunan Home's Restaurant
21 | 11 | 17 | $21

622 Jackson St. (bet. Grant Ave. & Kearny St.), 415-982-2844
"The concierge at the Ritz is right" – this "cheap", "no-frills" Chinatown joint is "the real deal", "packed with people who have been tipped off" as well as neighborhood "residents"; skip the "invented American" standards in favor of the "Hunan-style" eats, which the "obliging" staff is happy to make spicy as you like ("tell them you like it hot

and it'll cook you from the inside out"); N.B. there's a Los Altos branch with nicer decor South of SF.

Hyde Street Bistro   21 | 18 | 20 | $37 |
1521 Hyde St. (bet. Jackson & Pacific Sts.), 415-292-4415
Though cable cars make it unnecessary, "I'd walk up Russian Hill again" to visit this bistro, assert *amis* who adore the "simple French food done to perfection", the "intimate" interior and "funny, personable staff"; the "budget-friendly" prix fixe menu keeps this place "beloved by its neighbors", but motorists moan that unless "the parking gods are with you", "don't bring your car."

IL FORNAIO   18 | 20 | 18 | $35 |
Levi's Plaza, 1265 Battery St. (bet. Greenwich & Union Sts.), 415-986-0100; www.ilfornaio.com
"If there have to be chains", many wish they could all be like this "dependable," "upbeat" Italian on the Embarcadero and its Bay Area brothers, where the "smell of the fresh-baked breads" is "enough to make you quit Atkins"; contrary critics carp about "humdrum" pastas and so-so service, querying "whaddya expect from corporate cuisine?"

Iluna Basque   18 | 19 | 16 | $32 |
701 Union St. (Powell St.), 415-402-0011;
www.ilunabasque.com
"Hip" twentysomethings trundle into this "Euro-chic" North Beach "tapas lounge" (replete with communal table and "flat-screen TV images" of "the Old Country") where the "media-darling" chef-owner charms customers by "visiting each table", but his "flavorful" Basque "bites" can be "inconsistent", as is the service; still, supporters savor these "salty" munchies "served alongside a Tempranillo."

Impala   – | – | – | M |
501 Broadway (Kearny St.), 415-982-5299; www.impalasf.com
In a tourist-trafficked North Beach space that's undergone more changes than a Cher concert comes this new hopeful, which presents upscale but moderately priced Mexican fare in a spacious dining room decked out with rough-hewn tables and candlelit chandeliers; the *comida* is crafted by chef Kerry Simon, who knows a thing or two about cooking for tourists, since he also runs his own restaurant at Las Vegas' Hard Rock Hotel; N.B. there's a DJ and dancing in the downstairs lounge.

Incanto   24 | 23 | 22 | $41 |
1550 Church St. (Duncan St.), 415-641-4500; www.incanto.biz
"Mario Batali, eat your liver out" cheer ciao hounds enchanted by this "inventive" "neighborhood" Northern Italian that's also a "sophisticated" "destination" (an "exception in No-Eats Valley") thanks to its "earthy" offal meats and house-cured treats (from salumi to the *acqua con gaz* aerated on the premises); meanwhile, in the

colonnaded dining room that "could be in a palazzo" or at the wine bar, "knowledgeable sommeliers" guide you through "stellar" vintages from The Boot ("blind flights are a kick too").

Indian Oven   23 | 16 | 18 | $27 |
233 Fillmore St. (bet. Haight & Waller Sts.), 415-626-1628; www.indianovensf.com

"In the intense battle over Indian food in SF", this Lower Haight dal house may not be the "champion" but it's "still a contender", proffering "sublime", "taste-bud-tantalizing" fare that "doesn't come back to haunt you" in a more "civilized" "white-tablecloth" atmosphere than the "self-service Tandoor-loin" dives; "tight" quarters, "long waits" and "parking woes" don't deter devotees who'll "drive miles just for a taste."

Indigo   20 | 18 | 20 | $41 |
687 McAllister St. (Gough St.), 415-673-9353; www.indigorestaurant.com

The combination of "creative" New American fare (including an "excellent" prix fixe), a "rock-star wine list" and "reliably prompt" service "takes the blues out of the pre-theater rush" at this Civic Center "find"; once concert-goers have "shuffled over to the symphony", the "relaxing" decor ("blue, of course") "sets an exceptional mood" for enjoying the after-8 "$49 Ultimate Wine Dinner", a three-course meal with "unlimited" pours from a preselected roster.

Isa ☒   25 | 19 | 19 | $42 |
3324 Steiner St. (bet. Chestnut & Lombard Sts.), 415-567-9588; www.isarestaurant.com

"Fantastic," "flavorful" French small plates "pack a big wallop" at this Marina mainstay where the "wine list is killer" and the vibe is "so hip it hurts – mostly in the wallet"; the covered, heated patio with "twinkling lights" (a "special" "date place") is preferred by most to the recently expanded "Euro-industrial" interior, and though service can be "genuine and generous", "overselling", "overeager" staffers who "clear dishes with food still on them" may ruin the romance.

Izzy's Steaks & Chops   20 | 16 | 18 | $37 |
3345 Steiner St. (bet. Chestnut & Lombard Sts.), 415-563-0487; www.izzyssteaksandchops.com

Is he (or she) a beef eater? – then bring your favorite carnivore to this "vintage" cow palace for "amazing" chops with two "quintessential comfort-food" sides included, a "great value compared to high-end steakhouses"; the "clubby" "old-fashioned" spot is a bit out of place in the youthful Marina (there are also branches North and South of SF), but with "brisk, competent service" it's "worth a visit" "when the parents come to town."

Jack Falstaff   24 | 24 | 21 | $51 |
598 Second St. (Brannan St.), 415-836-9239; www.plumpjack.com
"PlumpJack's newest" entrant, this SoMa addition
located just a fly ball away from SBC Park has made a
"great start"; "fabulously priced wine is a given" but James
Ormsby's "marvelous" organic Californian 'slow food'
hits a home run as well, so "all the big shots" (including
"Mayor Gavin") are already making a "scene" in the "dark",
"sleek", "sexy" dining room or on the large heated patio,
despite service that's still slightly "off balance."

Jackson Fillmore   20 | 12 | 16 | $33 |
2506 Fillmore St. (Jackson St.), 415-346-5288
So "homey" the vino's "served in water glasses", this Upper
Fillmore trattoria is "still pumping out" "delicious" and
"very garlicky" Italian dinners after "20-plus years"; "it's
cheap enough" and "the free bruschetta whets the appetite
after a long wait outside", so regulars just "ignore the surly
staff" and "hole-in-the-wall" atmosphere – in fact, they
insist "the lack of decor gives it more charm" and "keeps
out the ultra-trendy" types.

Jai Yun ⊅   ▽ 24 | 8 | 16 | $47 |
923 Pacific Ave. (Mason St.), 415-981-7438; jaiyun.menuscan.com
"There's no menu", no ambiance ("unless Formica and
fluorescent lights are considered decor") and little English
at this "small" Chinatown sensation, but "adventurous
foodies" know it's all worth it for "the city's best Shanghai-
style" eats; the "rules" are: "make a reservation, bring your
own wine or beer", pick a banquet priced "to suit your
budget" ("$45 per person seems to be the sweet spot") and
then "sit back" to enjoy "two hours" of "spectacular" fare.

JARDINIÈRE   26 | 26 | 24 | $63 |
300 Grove St. (Franklin St.), 415-861-5555; www.jardiniere.com
No garden-variety eatery this: Traci Des Jardins' "Jazz
Age" "supper club" in Hayes Valley remains a "rhapsodic"
spot for the "culture crowd", though some suggest "skip
the theater" and "sit upstairs" "by the band" to "watch the
show below" at the "glamorous" bar; the "brilliant" Cal-
French menu with veggies "straight from the *jardin*" "wows"
diners, while a "superb" staff can help "divine what you're
actually longing for" – now if only you had "the proverbial
rich uncle" to fund it.

Jay's Cheesesteak   18 | 7 | 13 | $9 |
553 Divisadero St. (bet. Fell & Hayes Sts.), 415-771-5104
3285 21st St. (bet. Mission & Valencia Sts.), 415-285-5200 ⊅
"Yo, someone pinch me, am I in Philly or SF?" bluster
boosters of these "one-trick" wonders in the Western
Addition and Mission where the "lust-worthy" cheese steak
"sammiches" served by "gruff" staffers amid bare-bones
environs "conjure up images of *Rocky*"; the question's a

valid one, since there's "even a veggie version" venerated
by seitan worshipers.

Jeanty at Jack's
23 | 22 | 21 | $48 |

*615 Sacramento St. (bet. Kearny & Montgomery Sts.),
415-693-0941; www.jeantyatjacks.com*
"Jeanty has transformed Jack's – a city "institution" –
into an "upmarket" (and "vertical") Downtown boîte that
"captures lots of SF history" yet "oozes French bistro"
ambiance thanks to a slate of "classy and classic" Gallic
standards, bow-tied servers and three floors' worth of
"18th-arrondissement" decor; "it's not inexpensive", but
cheaper than "a trip to Paris" and – owing to its "cable
car–accessible" location – easier to reach than its higher-
rated "wine-country counterpart."

Joe's Cable Car
▽ 22 | 14 | 16 | $15 |

*4320 Mission St. (Silver Ave.), 415-334-6699;
www.joescablecar.com*
If you visit this "eccentric" cable car–cum-diner in the
Excelsior (a "San Francisco landmark" since 1965) and find
its "awesome burgers, fries and milkshakes" delivered
by "friendly Joe" himself "don't cheer you up, the neon
signs and the sounds of Louis Armstrong blasting will";
pattymeisters "appreciate" the "butcher grinding his own
chuck" but beef this place is "ridiculously expensive": "you
could get a good steak for this price."

Juban
20 | 17 | 18 | $29 |

*Japan Ctr., 1581 Webster St. (bet. Geary Blvd. & Post St.),
415-776-5822; www.jubanrestaurant.com*
See review in South of San Francisco Directory.

Julius' Castle
14 | 24 | 17 | $55 |

*1541 Montgomery St. (Union St.), 415-392-2222;
www.juliuscastle.com*
"On a clear day, you can see practically to heaven" at
this Telegraph Hill "hideaway" boasting "spectacular
views" of the city and the Bay from nearly "every table";
the "fantasy" setting suits tourists, lovers and "special-
occasion" celebrants, but even so this "calcified" landmark
(founded 1922) has "lost some of its luster", as reflected
in plunging ratings for both the "ho-hum", "overpriced"
Italian–New French fare and the "stale" service.

KABUTO ⊠
27 | 13 | 18 | $36 |

*5121 Geary Blvd. (15th Ave.), 415-752-5652;
www.kabutosushi.com*
"Insane" lines outside this "unassuming" Japanese nook
in the Outer Richmond are proof of its "run-don't-walk"
"popularity" and "mind-blowing" food ("transcendental"
maki and nigiri plus 30 "excellent sakes"); veterans advise
"be patient" when ordering ("spend some time reading
through the menu") – or just tell the sushi chef to "bring it

on" and get ready for some "sophisticated" "surprises";
N.B. a post-*Survey* ownership change may outdate scores.

Kan Zaman   17 20 16 $22
1793 Haight St. (Shrader St.), 415-751-9656
"Shimmying, shaking" belly dancers, "cool harem-style
seating" on pillows and "house spiced wine" "make dinner
secondary" at Haight-Ashbury's Middle Eastern "standby";
"attractive urbanites" come here not only for the "flavorful"
food ("great vegetarian options") but also "to smoke a
hookah after their hummus", and a rising Service score
suggests servers have an increasingly kan-do attitude.

Kate's Kitchen ⇥   20 13 16 $14
471 Haight St. (bet. Fillmore & Webster Sts.), 415-626-3984
"Bring your hollow leg or five extra stomachs" to this "more-
than-you-can-eat" storefront cranking out "big breakfast
plates" full of "Southern goodness" (still "the best hangover
cure" despite a slipping Food score); the "sketchy" Lower
Haight location and clientele are "not much to look at" but
the staff is "friendly" and the "pictorial U.S. map on the wall"
is fun for "playing I Spy."

Katia's Russian Tea Room   ▽ 20 16 22 $29
600 Fifth Ave. (Balboa St.), 415-668-9292; www.katias.com
Few are "rushin' to go here" but this "small", sunny spot in
the Inner Richmond is "one of SF's few places" serving
"authentic" food and "strong beers" from "the FSU (Former
Soviet Union)"; the "quirky", "gracious" owner whips up
"delectable piroshkis" and makes "even borscht a thing
to savor", while on weekends a "charming accordionist"
will "play requests."

Khan Toke Thai House   21 23 20 $25
5937 Geary Blvd. (bet. 23rd & 24th Aves.), 415-668-6654
Khan-freres compare this Outer Richmond longtimer to
"Thailand without the elephants and the heat", citing its
"sumptuous" "*King and I*–esque" interior, "gentle staff"
and "traditional" sunken seating as well as "authentic",
"delicious" food; be sure to "limber" up before your visit
so that "while standing in the crowded hallway" you can
"take off your shoes" and check to "make sure your socks
don't have holes."

Kingfish   19 20 16 $35
128 King St. (bet. 2nd & 3rd Sts.), 415-348-0648; www.kingfish.net
See review in South of San Francisco Directory.

King of Thai ⇥   19 7 14 $12
346 Clement St. (bet. 4th & 5th Aves.), 415-831-9953 ☽
639 Clement St. (bet. 7th & 8th Aves.), 415-752-5198 ☽
3199 Clement St. (33rd Ave.), 415-831-1301
420 Geary St. (bet. Mason & Taylor Sts.), 415-346-3121 ☽
(continued)

(continued)
King of Thai
184 O'Farrell St. (Powell St.), 415-677-9991 ☽
1507 Sloat Blvd. (Everglade Dr.), 415-566-9921
1541 Taraval St. (26th Ave.), 415-682-9958 ☽
Though these Thai cubbyholes are "not exactly pretty" (read: "divey"), frugal folks laud this local chain as "king of cheap eats" (ranging "from spicy broths to greasy fire-hot fried noodles" to "salty, earthy" roast duck); service is "efficient" and "fast-fast-fast" and since most branches are open until the wee hours, they're "great" "for a late snack."

Koh Samui & The Monkey   22 | 19 | 19 | $24
415 Brannan St. (bet. 3rd & 4th Sts.), 415-369-0007;
www.kohsamuiandthemonkey.com
"Top-of-the-line Thai" tout tasters who savor this SoMa Siamese's "nicely done staples" plus "slightly offbeat" specialties, "efficiently" served by a "helpful" staff; furthermore, thanks in part to the adjacent shop selling ethnic tableware, the "stylish" antiques-filled space qualifies as a "definite upgrade" from the average eatery, pleasing its crowd of "see-and-be-seen" "go-getters."

KOKKARI ESTIATORIO ⌧   25 | 25 | 22 | $49
200 Jackson St. (Front St.), 415-981-0983; www.kokkari.com
Known for "superlative" "dining experiences worthy of the gods of Olympus", this "thriving" Downtown "taverna" features a "fabulous fireplace" (where rotisserie meats and poultry are sometimes "spit-cooked") and "solicitous" servers who establish a "homey" "feel-good atmosphere"; yes, tabs are "somewhat expensive" but patrons who can't praise this "flavor-packed" cuisine enough ("addictive spreads", "succulent lamb" "done to perfection") declare it's "worth every drachma."

Koo   ∇ 24 | 20 | 22 | $30
408 Irving St. (bet. 5th & 6th Aves.), 415-731-7077;
www.sushikoo.com
Koo-linarians are "koo-koo" over this "upscale" Inner Sunset newcomer showcasing a mix of Asian-fusion shared plates and Japanese bites (including "unparalleled fish" so fresh it's as if someone "walked down to the Pacific and caught it that evening") served "without attitude"; the chef-owner is a veteran of "Tokyo Go Go and Ace Wasabi's", so expect "inventive" starters and "high-quality sushi."

Kuleto's   20 | 18 | 19 | $39
Villa Florence Hotel, 221 Powell St. (bet. Geary & O'Farrell Sts.),
415-397-7720
"Nothing ends a Union Square shopping trip" like some "hearty" Northern Italian eats at this "vibrant" "standby" in Downtown's Villa Florence Hotel; in the "so-very-SF" bar "tourists galore" hearken to the nearby "clang-clang-

clang of the cable cars", and though crowds cause service to "flag at times", they're also "testimony" this place is "still doing something right"; P.S. Kuleto's Trattoria in Burlingame is "convenient" if you're driving "to or from SFO."

Kyo-Ya ⌷   24 | 20 | 21 | $59
Palace Hotel, 2 New Montgomery St. (Market St.), 415-546-5090; www.kyo-ya-restaurant.com
"Exquisite, ultra-traditional sushi" seduces "connoisseurs and Japanese-speakers" who've discovered "the best of Tokyo" "in the middle of Downtown" SF; the "sleek", "serene" room in the Palace Hotel and "stratospheric prices" make this "place to impress" ideal for those with expense accounts; however, some surveyors say service is "superb", others opine it's "below par for this price range."

La Cumbre Taqueria ⊄   21 | 8 | 13 | $10
515 Valencia St. (bet. 16th & 17th Sts.), 415-863-8205
Ideal "for those on a budget", this Mission taqueria has been providing faithful folks with their "weekly burrito fix for years"; its "damn good" *comida* and "friendly," "fast" counter service make it a model for "imitators across the country", especially now that its "cold and ugly" decor has undergone a post-*Survey* revamp; P.S. for Peninsulans, the San Mateo outpost is a Mexican food "haven."

LA FOLIE ⌷   27 | 23 | 25 | $80
2316 Polk St. (bet. Green & Union Sts.), 415-776-5577; www.lafolie.com
Folie artist Roland Passot's "incomparable" fine-dining folly in Russian Hill is a true "spoil-someone kind of place"; his "sublime" French prix fixe menus "pay homage to all things rich", "sinful" and "surreal" ("every time they put down a plate, I wanted to take out my camera") and are "served expertly" by an "exceptional" crew; add in the "elegance" of the "recently redone front room" and the result is a "world-class restaurant."

La Méditerranée   20 | 14 | 17 | $20
2210 Fillmore St. (Sacramento St.), 415-921-2956
288 Noe St. (Market St.), 415-431-7210
www.cafelamed.com
"The food never changes", but why "fix it if it isn't broken" ask avid aficionados of the "delicious" eats served at "bargain" prices at these "informal", "quaint" "Middle Eastern oases" in the Castro, Upper Fillmore and East Bay (the patio at Berkeley's branch is "romantic"); moral: "walk in, pig out, leave extremely happy."

La Scene Café & Bar   ∇ 19 | 17 | 23 | $37
Warwick Regis, 490 Geary St. (Taylor St.), 415-292-6430; www.warwicksf.com
If you're making the scene at a Downtown theater, this long-running act at the Warwick Regis is a "comfortable" pre-

curtain (or "anytime") choice; the "delightfully quiet", "no-hassle atmosphere" attracts a "grown-up crowd" that likes the "accommodating staff" and "not great but good" Cal-Med meals; when you run the numbers – "three courses in 1 1/4 hours" for $30 – "it's even better."

Last Supper Club, The   –   –   –   M
1199 Valencia St. (23rd St.), 415-695-1199;
www.lastsupperclubsf.com
Having served its last supper under its original owners, this "dark, lively Mission haunt" – where the "whimsical" decor incorporates stained-glass windows and a bubbling fountain – is now owned by Ruggero Gadaldi (Pesce, Antica Trattoria); he hopes to retain regulars with Southern Italian antipasti, pasta and mains served family-style; meanwhile, along with their signature cocktails, "hot bartenders" pour vino from The Boot to boot; N.B. also serving alfresco brunch on weekends.

La Suite   22   20   20 $51
100 Brannan St. (The Embarcadero), 415-593-9000;
www.lasuitesf.com
"Paris by the Pacific" is the lowdown on this suite spot in the Embarcadero, a sibling of Chez Papa; it's a "true brasserie" where the "hot scene" "buzzes with energy", the Gallic eats are "excellent" ("big platters of *fruits de mer*", "outstanding cheese cart"), the wine list is "impressive" and the "adorable" staffers exhibit "real accents"; however, when the "cavernous" room is full, critics christen it "La Shout."

La Taqueria ⌀   24   8   13 $11
2889 Mission St. (25th St.), 415-285-7117
"Rice, schmice" – this Mission Mexican "doesn't rely on cheap carbs to fatten" its "legendary burritos", and as a result, other taquerias "can't match" these "perfectly flavored" "all-meat wonders" that come wrapped in "noticeably fresher, softer tortillas"; the *comida*'s "not the cheapest" around, but "hipster types" who happily "get in line" at this counter-service dive attest it's "reason No. 1 not to move out of SF"; P.S. the smaller San Jose branch is a "cleaned-up version."

Le Central Bistro ⧉   19   16   19 $38
453 Bush St. (bet. Grant Ave. & Kearny St.),
415-391-2233
"Local politicos", "eminent citizens" and a roster of regulars visit this "dependable" Downtowner for "good but not great" bistro cuisine that "hasn't gone nouvelle"; though devotees declare it "hasn't lost its verve" and deem the "old-time waiters" "fun", foes feel "stuffed-shirt" service and a "tired setting" ("asleep on its laurels") mean it "lacks the je ne sais quoi" of the competition around the corner.

Le Charm French Bistro   21 │ 16 │ 20 │ $34

315 Fifth St. (bet. Folsom & Shipley Sts.), 415-546-6128;
www.lecharm.com
At this "unpretentious" "bistro *magnifique*", "go for the
prix fixe" – such a "steal" many don't bother to "order
anything from the main menu" – and get three courses of
"homey", "delicious" French fare for $28; note that the
"romantic" "covered patio garden is the spot to reserve"
as that's "where you'll find the charm" lacking in the
"austere" dining room or the sketchy SoMa environs.

Le Colonial   21 │ 24 │ 19 │ $44

20 Cosmo Pl. (bet. Post & Taylor Sts.), 415-931-3600;
www.lecolonialsf.com
"Your quest" for this "sexy" Downtown French-Vietnamese
"hideaway" "will be well rewarded" – it's a portal "back to
a time of elegance" in "Indochina" ("the only reason to
celebrate colonialism"); it can be "great" for a "pre-theater"
dinner of "varied", "tasty" cuisine served by "pleasant" if
"not always alert" staffers, but the cash-conscious caution
you're "paying for ambiance" and opt instead for "lounge
snacks and cocktails" upstairs.

Le Petit Robert   20 │ 17 │ 17 │ $35

2300 Polk St. (Green St.), 415-922-8100; www.lepetitrobert.com
"The spirit of French food lives" in this "cute and competent"
Russian Hill cafe's "splendid mélange of traditional bistro
items" ("great onion soup"); despite some "attitude" from
the staff, neighbors enjoy "relaxing", "finishing a novel or
just holding hands" here, while valet parking has chauffeurs
shouting "*c'est la bonne vie!*"

Le Soleil   20 │ 11 │ 16 │ $21

133 Clement St. (bet. 2nd & 3rd Aves.), 415-668-4848
"While it ain't the Slanted Door", this "nice little" Inner
Richmond neighborhood "standby" shines nevertheless;
its "fine" Vietnamese fare ("great five-spice chicken")
"gives a good bang for the buck", and despite "spartan"
surroundings, sunny surveyors say it radiates with "sweet
service" and a "semi-upscale" vibe absent from "most
restaurants along Clement Street."

Levende ⊅   ▽ 20 │ 21 │ 19 │ $35

1710 Mission St. (Duboce Ave.), 415-864-5585;
www.levendesf.com
This "clublike" Mission nightspot's combo of "comfortable,
cushy tables and chairs", "expertly prepared" Eclectic small
plates, "a well-stocked bar" and nightly DJs comprises "a
one-stop shop" for evening entertainment; those lev cold
complain it's "not worth the price" or the "hipper-than-
thou" service, but supporters of Sunday's Boogie Brunch
ask "where else can you enjoy mellow morning music"
and a "make-your-own Bloody Mary bar"?

Le Zinc   18 | 20 | 17 | $33
4063 24th St. (bet. Castro & Noe Sts.), 415-647-9400;
www.lezinc.com
"The French Paradox comes to Noe Valley" in these "quaint"
quarters proffering *vin rouge* and "heavy" Gallic favorites;
whether inside the "Parisian" environs *avec* zinc-topped
bar or on the "delightful" *chien*-friendly garden patio, *amis*
"enjoy" the ambiance, if not the "high prices", and "never
feel rushed" – perhaps because the staff (much "improved"
"after a snooty start") is still stereotypically "slow."

Liberty Cafe & Bakery   22 | 17 | 20 | $30
410 Cortland Ave. (Bennington St.), 415-695-8777
Libertarians dub this "Bernal boîte" the "Platonic ideal" of a
"neighborhood restaurant" because it offers "all-American"
"stick-to-your-ribs (and -hips)" "haute home cooking"
("order anything with a crust") in "child-tolerant" environs;
claustrophobes call it "*too* cozy", however, and "slow
service" may have you "waiting forever", but "thanks to
the wine bar/bakery in the back, you won't mind."

Lime ◑   19 | 24 | 17 | $31
2247 Market St. (bet. Noe & Sanchez Sts.), 415-621-5256;
www.lime-sf.com
With its Eclectic small plates, "killer cocktails" and DJs
five nights a week, this Castro hot spot is "half restaurant
and all social scene", serving "creative" "global" goodies
in which "flavor and variety" trump "quantity"; surveyors
either love the "mod", "*Jetsons*-do-Japan" decor or wish
it would "go back to LA", while sourpusses urge "skip" the
"overpriced" eats (and the "scattered" servers) and stick
with "liquid nourishment."

Limón   24 | 19 | 20 | $34
524 Valencia St. (16th St.), 415-252-0918; www.limon-sf.com
"One of the few restaurants that's just as good" after a move,
this "yuppie" Peruvian-Asian in the Mission is still "seviche
heaven" thanks to its "intensely flavored" signature dish,
yet amigos also adore its other "delicious" "combinations
of fresh foods and South American spices"; the "stripped-
down" digs are also "roomier and quieter" than before
(spurring a spike in the Decor score), while servers are both
"knowledgeable" and "flirtatious."

Little Nepal   21 | 19 | 22 | $23
925 Cortland Ave. (Folsom St.), 415-643-3881
To get "the flavor of the Himalayas without the altitude
headache", diners scale Bernal Heights to this "Zen little
spot" dishing out Nepalese noshes with a deference that
makes some feel they're "in a temple" (staffers actually
"bowed when we entered"); it's clearly "the best, and
possibly only" of its ilk, and "a real find" too, as "crowds
forming" outside attest.

Los Flamingos   _ _ _ M
151 Noe St. (Henry St.), 415-252-7450
Sporting pink walls and the requisite flamingo flourishes, this newcomer on a residential block of the Castro near Duboce Park enlists chefs of two heritages, Mexican and Cuban, to oversee a menu evenly split between taqueria preparations and plantains, rice and beans; Sunday brunch includes chilaquiles and huevos rancheros.

L'Osteria del Forno ⊄   23 15 18 $27
519 Columbus Ave. (bet. Green & Union Sts.), 415-982-1124; www.losteriadelforno.com
"Something authentic" in North Beach's "touristland", this "vest-pocket" Northern Italian (26 seats) has a "small but perfect menu" (offering "only what can be made in an oven", as the name suggests) at "bargain" prices; service is sometimes "friendly", sometimes "a bit brusque", but "despite the crowds outside, once you're in they let you have a leisurely meal."

Lovejoy's Tea Room   20 23 22 $20
1351 Church St. (Clipper St.), 415-648-5895; www.lovejoystearoom.com
"All is love and joy" "over sandwiches, scones and sips" trill tea-totalers who cite this "high-estrogen" Noe Valley English tearoom as proof that "you don't have to go to a stuffy hotel" to enjoy a jolly afternoon cuppa (or the supplementary pub grub); instead, surveyors smilingly savor the "endless" batches of "top-notch whole-leaf" brews served here by a "motherly staff" amid a "mishmash of teapots, cozies and silverware."

Luella   ▽ 21 18 21 $41
1896 Hyde St. (Green St.), 415-674-4343; www.luellasf.com
In late 2004 Ben De Vries (ex Andalu) and his wife opened this "ultramodern" neighborhood haunt in Russian Hill; although he made his mark serving small plates, the Med-inspired menu here is divided between appetizers and entrees (his signature Coca-Cola-braised pork shoulder is "so soft it's spreadable"); the 10-seat bar serves an eclectic mix of wines, and the "dim", "well-appointed" dining room is ably handled by a "friendly staff."

Luna Park   20 17 18 $30
694 Valencia St. (18th St.), 415-553-8584; www.lunaparksf.com
"Tasty", "simple dishes done very well" are the hallmark of the Park, and if this Mission French–New American is "rarely great", at least it "doesn't take itself too seriously" ("love the make-your-own s'mores"); ordinarily "loud, hip" and "hopping", the "casual", "lively" locale can be "a bit of a zoo" on weekends – must be those "must-have" mojitos – so if it's "intimate conversation" you're after, "try getting a private table in the back."

Lüx ⊠   19 17 16 $42
2263 Chestnut St. (bet. Pierce & Scott Sts.),
415-567-2998

Luke and Kitty Sung (Isa) now have one more berth in the Marina: this Asian-Med with a "richly colored" interior, "inventive" *petits plats,* a "reasonably priced wine list" and a "jovial staff"; fans feel it "rivals its sister in every respect except" decor, but "underwhelmed" phos find this newbie – as "young and loud" as the crowd that frequents it – "inconsistent" "given its pedigree."

MacArthur Park   16 18 17 $36
607 Front St. (bet. Jackson St. & Pacific Ave.), 415-398-5700;
www.spectrumfoods.com

Dispatches from the front are mixed on this American veteran Downtown; old soldiers still salute its "fancied-up" BBQ (ribs are "the best pick"), its "large, open" interiors and staffers who are "there to please" but the new order reports the "tired" menu, "boring decor" and "spotty service" could use a "makeover"; N.B. the Palo Alto branch offers a prix fixe weekend brunch.

Maki   25 16 19 $33
Japan Ctr., 1825 Post St., 2nd fl. (bet. Fillmore & Webster Sts.),
415-921-5215

There "ain't no California rolls" at this "intimate" "hidden treasure" in Japantown – instead, it serves "delectable" and "rarely seen" "home-cooked" dishes (experts exhort "order from the specials" for a truly "divine experience"); service is suitably "attentive" but even cheerleaders complain about the "early" closing time and "tight tables"; N.B. more than 20 sakes on offer.

Mama's on Washington Square ⋒   25 14 17 $18
1701 Stockton St. (Filbert St.), 415-362-6421

Founded in 1967, this "sunny little parlor" on North Beach's Washington Square Park is a "brunch institution" and "everyone and their mama knows it"; the bakery's American breakfasts plated up by "friendly personnel" are "worth every penny and every minute" you spend in the "line that wraps around the building" on weekends, and though they stop lunch service at 3 PM, "there's so much food" you won't need dinner.

Mandalay   ∇ 24 14 20 $18
4348 California St. (6th Ave.), 415-386-3895

Neophyte noshers take the road to Mandalay for a cheap yet "exceptional" "intro to Burmese food" in the Inner Richmond; the "gracious", traditionally garbed staff is "helpful" in guiding novices through the "dead-on" "spicy" specialties ("amazing tea-leaf salad"), and though the ratings don't reflect it, regulars report the "decor has gotten better" – now there are "flowers at each table."

Mandarin, The   21 | 22 | 19 | $39 |
Ghirardelli Sq., 900 North Point St. (bet. Larkin & Polk Sts.),
415-673-8812; www.themandarin.com
SF's "original" "haute Chinese" (since 1968) boasts a
"spacious" templelike interior and "stunning views of
the Bay" that will make out-of-towners "exclaim" with
excitement, not to mention an "extensive" "high-end" menu
complemented by "attentive service", a "great wine list"
and convenient parking; ok, it's no longer "leading-edge"
and "by Chinatown standards" it's "expensive", but it's still a
welcome outpost of "quality" in touristy Ghirardelli Square.

Mangarosa   ▽ 20 | 19 | 18 | $37 |
1548 Stockton St. (bet. Green & Union Sts.), 415-956-3211;
www.mangarosasf.com
Rio meets risotto at this new coral-colored combo of
"Brazilian-style steakhouse" and Italian pastaria, a "nice
change in North Beach"; hopscotching between continents,
the menu incorporates everything from gnocchi to steak
'rechaud' on iron platters, fetched by "personable but
ditzy" staffers; meanwhile, weekend crowds pack the
bar to start a "night on the town" with "red mojitos" and
"bumping" "disco beats."

Manora's Thai Cuisine   24 | 16 | 19 | $22 |
1600 Folsom St. (12th St.), 415-861-6224
"After all these years" (since 1987), the SoMa crowd still
salutes this seasoned Siamese out at "the end of clubland";
chowing down on the "bright, fresh", "memorable" Bangkok
"standards" is "not quite as good as being in Thailand, but
close" ("get the beef larb as hot as you can stand it –
the endorphins will be your reward"); meanwhile, the
"genteel" service and "dark", "quiet" decor are fine "for
conversation" on "a first or second date."

Mario's Bohemian Cigar Store Cafe   18 | 15 | 17 | $17 |
566 Columbus Ave. (Union St.), 415-362-0536;
www.mariosbohemiancigarstore.com
"A cigar store without cigars", this "well-worn" sandwich
shop by Washington Square Park still serves up a "slice of
bohemia à la North Beach"; ok, "there is not much choice
here", but loyalists love downing the "cheap" "wonderful
Italian focaccia sandwiches" "made to order in the pizza
oven" and the "homemade Campari" at sidewalk tables
("great for people-watching").

MarketBar   16 | 17 | 15 | $33 |
The Embarcadero, 1 Ferry Bldg., #36 (Market St.), 415-434-1100;
www.marketbar.com
With its smashing "view of the Embarcadero" this "casual"
brasserie is a "comfortable" spot for refueling "after the
farmer's market", and given the "location, location, location"
its Mediterranean fare is "better than it needs to be";

"alfresco dining is preferable" (despite "erratic" service outside) because there's "barely enough room to swing a cat" in the "noisy" interior.

Marnee Thai   23 | 15 | 17 | $22

2225 Irving St. (bet. 23rd & 24th Aves.), 415-665-9500
1243 Ninth Ave. (bet. Irving St. & Lincoln Way), 415-731-9999
These Sunset Siamese twins are known for their "spicy, amazing" and "inexpensive" Thai specialties; the Irving Street original is said to have "better ambiance" ("fresh orchids") and a vibe that's "chaotic, in a good way": a "noisy" room with "tables jammed together" where the owner "tells you what to order"; the "second location", on Ninth Avenue, is "more modern and spacious" but alas has "no Mae to come and tell fortunes."

MASA'S ☒   28 | 25 | 27 | $92

Hotel Vintage Ct., 648 Bush St. (bet. Powell & Stockton Sts.), 415-989-7154
When and if you dine at this "extraordinary" New French in Downtown's Hotel Vintage Court, "throw caution to the wind" – "splurge" on French Laundry alum Gregory Short's "breathtaking" nine-course tasting menu, which "lasts three hours and turns into about 12 courses after the amuses bouches and over-the-top dessert cart"; the minimalist room is "formal by San Francisco standards" (a jacket is required) but "they treat you like a star" "regardless of who you are" so "save your Benjamins" – "it's a must-do at least once, preferably more."

Massawa   ▽ 20 | 8 | 18 | $19

1538 Haight St. (bet. Ashbury & Clayton Sts.), 415-621-4129
"Like most Eritrean places", this Haight Street stalwart is "nothing to look at" – but with its "out-of-this-world flavors" and "super-nice staff" this one "kicks the competition out of the water"; take a "group of close friends" for budget "fun" (kids under five eat free) over "sublime" stews that "you eat with your hands"; there's even "African beer to accompany your meal."

Matterhorn Swiss Restaurant   19 | 16 | 18 | $36

2323 Van Ness Ave. (bet. Green & Vallejo Sts.), 415-885-6116
"You can practically hear the cows mooing while grazing on the Matterhorn" at this ersatz Alpine lodge on Van Ness, proffering a dozen kinds of "excellent", "gooey" and "filling fondue" ideal for "chilly SF nights"; servers are "helpful" if not always "enthusiastic", but the cash-conscious give this Swiss a miss, calling it "overpriced" "considering you're cooking your own food."

Maverick   – | – | – | M

3316 17th St. (Mission St.), 415-863-3061; www.sfmaverick.com
As the funky U.S. map on its wall suggests, this Mission newcomer presents a refreshingly different repertoire of

regional American dishes; the handsome cocoa-brown
shoebox dining room, with an adjoining wine bar, is barely
recognizable (it used to be Limón), and thanks to newly
installed windows that open up to the street, neither is
the sound level.

Max's 16 | 13 | 16 | $23 |
*Bank of America Bldg., 555 California St., concourse level
(bet. Kearny & Montgomery Sts.), 415-788-6297* ☒
1 California St. (Market St.), 415-781-6297 ☒
398 Geary St. (Mason St.), 415-646-8600
*Opera Plaza, 601 Van Ness Ave. (Golden Gate Ave.),
415-771-7301*
www.maxsworld.com
"Carnegie Deli it ain't" but this Bay Area chain pumping out
"*Super Size Me*" portions" of "Jewish soul food" will "cure
corned-beef" cravings; in fact, "everything at this place is
huge", from the "encyclopedic menu" to the "tempting"
desserts to the "voices" of the "singing waiters" at the
Opera branches – to the considerable number of critics
who claim this "high-end Denny's" "act" is "uninspired"
"to the max."

Maya 22 | 21 | 19 | $39 |
*303 Second St. (bet. Folsom & Harrison Sts.), 415-543-2928;
www.mayasf.com*
"This ain't no burrito parlor" – this SoMa "haute" hacienda
specializes in "*Like Water for Chocolate*"–style "high-end
Mexican" ("fascinating food" in "fabulous sauces") that
amigos assert is "worth the extra" pesos; the "candlelit
room" is "sophisticated" too, even if service ranges from
"so-so to slow-slow"; P.S. Maya Next Door is a "cheaper"
"way to get your guacamole on the run" at lunchtime.

Mayflower 22 | 10 | 14 | $24 |
6255 Geary Blvd. (27th Ave.), 415-387-8338
"One of the better venues" for dim sum and Hong Kong–
style Chinese specialties ("exotic live fish, lobster and
shrimp"), this Outer Richmond operation has a "high AQ
(Asian Quotient)", so "be prepared" for a truly "authentic"
experience – the atmosphere's "blah" and folks whose
forebears came over on that other Mayflower surmise "no
one seems to speak English here."

Maykadeh ▽ 22 | 16 | 18 | $31 |
*470 Green St. (bet. Grant Ave. & Kearny St.), 415-362-8286;
www.maykadehrestaurant.com*
Regulars recommend this North Beach Persian because
the "wonderfully fragrant" cuisine and "sleek" yet "sedate"
surroundings "take you away to another place", plus the
meals are an "unbelievable value, especially for this part
of town"; some who come to supper are "greeted as old
friends" but others say they're subject to "surly" service.

McCormick & Kuleto's   19 22 18 $39
900 North Point St. (Larkin St.), 415-929-1730; www.msmg.com
"Ravishing" Bay vistas "provide the wow" at this "classic
seafooder" known for its "vast selection" of "reliably
good" "raw, fried and grilled" fish served "courteously";
the Wharf location means it's "touristy to say the least" but
quality's high enough to satisfy locals when they "bring
family members visiting SF"; contradictory critics carp "killer
view, dead menu" and suggest that service flounders.

Mecca   22 24 21 $43
*2029 Market St. (bet. Dolores & 14th Sts.), 415-621-7000;
www.sfmecca.com*
Like its namesake, this Upper Market locale "still draws a
crowd"; here it's for the "party" scene fostered by DJs' "loud
house beats" and a "round bar" for "people-watching",
though denizens declare that "you won't be disappointed"
"if you stay" for the New American fare with "Southern
flair"; in fact, say some, this "swank" spot seems to "have
it all", including "top-shelf libations", an "eclectic and
classy clientele" and "flirty service."

Medjool   ∇ 21 25 18 $31
*2522 Mission St. (bet. 21st & 22nd Sts.), 415-550-9055;
www.medjoolsf.com*
A "welcome newcomer" to the Mission, this "hipster
hangout" establishes a "cool vibe" with its "ambitious
layout" ("a cafe, restaurant and club all in one huge
space"), "sky-high ceilings" – literally, thanks to "rooftop
alfresco dining" – and colorful "loftlike decor", plus Med-
inflected small plates, but the "sexy atmosphere" is marred
by "a staff that could use some seasoning."

Mela Tandoori Kitchen   _ _ _ I
(fka Shalimar Gardens)
*417 O'Farrell St. (Taylor St.), 415-447-4041;
www.melatandoori.com*
This recently renamed and redesigned subcontinental in
the so-called Tandoorloin is a gussied-up offshoot of the
Shalimar set; a subterranean space with Moghul Palace
touches (e.g. low-slung tables made of incised tin and
carved wood) and live DJs on Friday and Saturday nights, it's
"the most cost-effective" place for "high-end" Indian-
Pakistani eats when "you want ambiance with your meal."

Mel's Drive-In ●   13 14 14 $16
*3355 Geary Blvd. (bet. Beaumont & Parker Aves.), 415-387-2244
2165 Lombard St. (Steiner St.), 415-921-2867
801 Mission St. (4th St.), 415-227-4477
1050 Van Ness Ave. (Geary St.), 415-292-6357
www.melsdrive-in.com*
"They get the '50s atmosphere right" at this diner chain
decked out with "*American Graffiti* memorabilia", and its

"reasonably priced" "classic American" grub makes it a "safe choice" when you're toting tots or filling up "after a night on the town"; even so, mel-contents maintain "hit-or-miss service" and "bland" food mean you can "skip it."

Memphis Minnie's BBQ Joint   21 11 15 $16
576 Haight St. (bet. Fillmore & Steiner Sts.), 415-864-7675; www.memphisminnies.com
'Cue connoisseurs happily "follow the mouthwatering smell" to this "cutesy", "almost self-serve" rib shack in the Lower Haight for "jaw-droppingly smoky and delicious" brisket and pork; however, opinion is split over the sides ("the best this side of the Mason-Dixon" vs. "so-so"), and the Dixie-bred declare "real BBQ doesn't cost this much."

Mescolanza   22 16 21 $30
2221 Clement St. (bet. 23rd & 24th Aves.), 415-668-2221; www.mescolanza.net
"One of the city's best-kept secrets", this "comfortable", "cozy" "gem" delights diners who have "stumbled onto" this Outer Richmonder and "loved every morsel"; the "homey" Northern Italian dinners may not be "fancy" but they're "toothsome", and the "attention to detail across the board" extends to the "wonderful staff."

MICHAEL MINA   27 24 26 $107
Westin St. Francis, 335 Powell St. (bet. Geary & Post Sts.), 415-397-9222; www.michaelmina.net
"Gary Danko, watch your back" grin fanatical foodies who favor this new "monument to conspicuous consumption" in Downtown's Westin St. Francis; its "choreographed" staffers "energetically" present "extravagant" New American "multipart tastings" ("amazing trios") matched with "Rajat Parr's outstanding wine pairings"; however, aesthetes find it "hard to believe they spent millions" on this "beautifully appointed airplane hangar" plagued by "constant noise from the hotel lobby"; P.S. Mina's Aqua "classics" (e.g. lobster pot pie) "have moved here."

Mifune   18 11 14 $16
Kintetsu Bldg., 1737 Post St. (bet. Buchanan & Webster Sts.), 415-922-0337
It's "noodle heaven at this bargain-priced old-timer in J-town", a no-frills setup with "fast service" that's "good for children who want to slurp" as well as anyone craving a warm one-pot meal "on a cold or rainy day" – so despite "a strip-mall feel" it remains a "convenient lunch stop" and a "favorite for families."

Mijita   20 13 12 $15
The Embarcadero, 1 Ferry Bldg., #44 (Market St.), 415-399-0814; www.mijitasf.com
Traci Des Jardins (Jardinière) "can tell you the provenance of the chicken or the corn in the tortillas" at her "highbrow"

Ferry Building "taco bar", but most maintain "her massive talent is wasted" on "upscale Mexican fast food"; even so, this counter-service Embarcadero eatery buzzes at lunch as staffers crank out a "limited" array of "mouthwatering" *comida*; peso pinchers say it's costly "compared to other taquerias", but then again "these aren't your usual tacos."

Millennium 24 | 20 | 22 | $43

Savoy Hotel, 580 Geary St. (Jones St.), 415-345-3900;
www.millenniumrestaurant.com

Vegan vittles "made glorious and gourmet" and paired with "organic wines" make this handsome Downtowner at the Savoy Hotel a "delightful" pre-theater option for vegheads and "open-minded carnivores"; even those a "little afraid going in" become "believers" after enjoying "large portions" and "kind treatment" in the "airy" setting decorated with recycled materials, even if prices are a mite high "for nothing but veggies."

Miss Millie's 22 | 17 | 17 | $25

4123 24th St. (bet. Castro & Diamond Sts.), 415-285-5598

"*The* hot spot for brunch" for "Noe Valley yuppies" who "inundate it every weekend", this "funky" American proffers "filling, delicious" (and, yes, "expensive") "comfort-food" breakfasts in portions so "immense" "you'll gain three pounds per meal"; the chef-owner's "unusual" but "palate-pleasing" "mixtures of familiar flavors" can also make for a "great romantic dinner if you get a back booth" – the one caveat is that the kitchen and staff can be "glacially" slow.

Mochica ▽ 21 | 18 | 18 | $30

937 Harrison St. (5th St.), 415-278-0480; www.mochicasf.com

San Francisco's latest upscale Peruvian, this inviting SoMa entrant overcomes an "awkward location" just off the freeway with a colorful, contemporary interior and chef-owner Carlos Altamirano's arsenal of spice-laced apps and entrees; highlights include five "really good" varieties of seviche and the national dish, *lomo saltado* (a stir-fry of steak strips, onions, tomatoes and potatoes).

Moki's Sushi & Pacific Grill 23 | 16 | 18 | $27

830 Cortland Ave. (Gates St.), 415-970-9336; www.mokisushi.com

"Set to look like a Polynesian hut", this "laid-back" "Hawaii-themed" sushi joint in Bernal Heights rolls out "creative" maki that "aren't exactly what you would find in Japan", as well as "jumping-off-the-plate fresh" grilled fish "with a Pacific flair" and "outstanding salads with unusual combinations"; at the same time, though, "long waits" and "glacial service" leave many cold.

MoMo's 17 | 18 | 16 | $35

760 Second St. (King St.), 415-227-8660; www.eatatmomos.com

This South Beach American across from SBC Park has a "split personality"; when the Giants are at home fans find

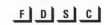
it a "great warm-up for the game" with "surprisingly good" eats, while "in the off season" it's far mo' "mellow"; opponents balk at the bar's "crazy" "meat-market" scene and call the food "only so-so" and service "spotty": "no grand slams here."

Monte Cristo Cafe   ─ | ─ | ─ | M |
4 Embarcadero Ctr., promenade level (Drumm St.), 415-362-0646; www.montecristocafesf.com
This sprawling restaurant and nightclub located on the promenade level of Embarcadero 4 features a long, curved open kitchen that prepares a *très* French bistro menu; lunches appeal to Downtown business types, but in a bid to loosen up the stiff surroundings, dinner is served till 10 PM and a DJ performs afterward till 2 AM.

Moose's   22 | 21 | 21 | $44 |
1652 Stockton St. (bet. Filbert & Union Sts.), 415-989-7800; www.mooses.com
Ed and Mary Etta Moose "know what it takes" to succeed in the restaurant business: combine "elegant" New American cuisine "at fair prices" with a "polished" staff, "ambiance galore" and a "rotating" slate of jazz acts – and don't forget valet parking, a "lifesaver in North Beach"; the result is a SF "institution" offering "lovely park views" along with attractive "two-legged scenery."

Morton's, The Steakhouse   23 | 20 | 22 | $59 |
400 Post St. (bet. Mason & Powell Sts.), 415-986-5830; www.mortons.com
The "mammoth" steaks are "cooked to perfection every time" at this Downtown outpost of the "clubby", "classy" Chicago-based chophouse chain; in addition, the "extensive wine list" "impresses" and the "servers are knowledgeable without being snooty", but grumblers beef about big bills, saying "go on an expense account" or simply "steer clear."

Mo's   20 | 10 | 14 | $16 |
1322 Grant Ave. (bet. Green & Vallejo Sts.), 415-788-3779
Yerba Buena Gardens, 772 Folsom St. (bet. 3rd & 4th Sts.), 415-957-3779
www.mosgrill.com
There's nothing wimpy about the "hefty", "sloppy", "juicy" patties at these "fun, fast and fab" diners in North Beach and SoMa; in fact, the proprietors "grind their own beef and cut their own fries" so the value is "unbelievable", though there's no "ambiance" ("splendid views" of Yerba Buena Gardens notwithstanding) or "gracious service."

MYTH ☒   24 | 25 | 23 | $52 |
470 Pacific Ave. (bet. Montgomery & Sansome Sts.), 415-677-8986; www.mythsf.com
"So hard to get into you'd think" it didn't really exist, this "stunning" Jackson Square newcomer has been "hyped

to mythic proportions" and largely lives up to the legend, thanks to Gary Danko alum Sean O'Brien's "inventive", "subtle" New American cuisine, a "sultry" scene "worthy of *Sex and the City*", "professional, pleasant" staffers and an "owner who makes everyone feel like a VIP"; what's more, dinner here won't "break the bank", owing in part to "superb wines" priced "almost at cost."

Naan 'n Curry ◐   19 6 9 $12
642 Irving St. (7th Ave.), 415-664-7225
533 Jackson St. (Columbus Ave.), 415-693-0499
398 Eddy St. (Levenworth), 415-775-1349
www.naanncurry.com
"Thank Shiva" for this chainlet of "no-frills" BYO "favorites" (including a branch in Berkeley) that slings "sizzling, spicy, scrumptious" and so-cheap subcontinental specialties (naan "as big as your head") ; "blasting Indo-pop" music and a "serve-yourself" setup can combine to create "sensory overload" even though "decor is lacking."

Nectar Wine Lounge   17 24 21 $31
3330 Steiner St. (bet. Chestnut & Lombard Sts.), 415-345-1377;
www.nectarwinelounge.com
The "thirtysomething Marina crowd" isn't the only "sexy" thing at this "sophisticated" lounge – so are the "fantastic descriptions" on the "ever-changing" international *carte du vin* (they "read like a J. Peterman catalog") that inspire aspiring oenophiles to "explore" with the help of "educated staffers" and "personable owners"; though "overpriced", the Cal-fusion "finger food" does "complement the array of 40-plus wines by the glass."

Nick's Crispy Tacos ≠   21 10 14 $11
2101 Polk St. (Broadway), 415-409-8226
Carnitas-craving Russian Hill residents swear the "best fish tacos in town (go figure)" are served by CIA grad Nick at a "cheesy" "red-velvet" dance club where they "wouldn't be caught dead at night"; during the day, however, when it's decked out with "piñatas and picnic tablecloths", the "counter-service" space is a "hilarious" setting for a "quick" Mexican bite and a *cerveza* without moseying over to the Mission; P.S. "when Rouge opens, Nick's closes."

Nob Hill Café   20 14 19 $29
1152 Taylor St. (bet. Clay & Sacramento Sts.), 415-776-6500;
www.nobhillcafe.com
Nob Hill "locals" hobnob at this "surprisingly inexpensive" "hangout" for its "simple" Northern Italian cuisine "done right" (including a "brunch so good it'll make you forget your hangover") and "laid-back atmosphere"; the "plain", "small" interiors are "very quaint" but surlier sorts snarl they don't enjoy "getting squished"; P.S. it's also a "great place to spot the SF Twins", Marian and Vivian Brown.

North Beach Pizza
18 | 9 | 14 | $16

1310 Grant Ave. (Vallejo St.), 415-433-2444
1499 Grant Ave. (Union St.), 415-433-2444 ◗
4787 Mission St. (bet. Persia & Russia Aves.), 415-586-1400 ◗
Pier 39 (bet. Grant & Stockton Sts., off The Embarcadero),
415-433-0400
800 Stanyan St. (Haight St.), 415-751-2300 ◗
3054 Taraval St. (41st Ave.), 415-242-9100 ◗
www.northbeachpizza.com
Surveyors who salivate over the "thick crust", "generous"
toppings and "gooey cheese" on the slices at this local
chain say the original branch is a "must-stop" in North
Beach (and open-late locations are a godsend "after a
night at the bars"); others opine "now that they're all over
the place" "quality has dropped" ("bland, bland, bland");
N.B. locations also East and South of SF.

North Beach Restaurant ◗
22 | 17 | 21 | $41

1512 Stockton St. (bet. Green & Union Sts.), 415-392-1700;
www.northbeachrestaurant.com
With "old-school" Tuscan entrees (from "before Cal-Italian
was invented"), a 700-label wine list and "classic" interiors,
this "wonderfully traditional" North Beach stalwart is "still
at the top of its game" "after a million years" (well, more
like 35); longtimers "listen to the recommendations" of the
"experienced" staffers, who "will not steer you wrong."

One Market ☒
21 | 20 | 19 | $49

1 Market St. (Steuart St.), 415-777-5577; www.onemarket.com
"Tourists meet bankers" at Bradley Ogden's "sprawling"
Embarcadero space with "great views of the Bay"; its
"ambitious" New American eats are "very tasty" "80
percent of the time" and with this "all-U.S. wine list" "you
don't miss Europe" – but "don't go for a quiet romantic
meal" since this place is "priced, decorated" and staffed
"to impress expense-account diners" and "noisy" enough
that "you could broker a merger here and not be overheard."

Oola Restaurant & Bar ◗
20 | 22 | 18 | $41

860 Folsom St. (bet. 4th & 5th Sts.), 415-995-2061;
www.oola-sf.com
Evoking the "dot-com days", this SoMa newcomer has early
adopters aflutter about its "swanky", "loftlike space" where
"hipsters galore" swill "signature cocktails"; the "delicious"
French-American bistro fare is "reasonably priced" (though
some say "oola-la" only when "Ola is in the kitchen") and
though "aloof" service irks a few, "night-owls" hoot "finally
you can dine like a prince after midnight."

Original Joe's
17 | 13 | 17 | $26

144 Taylor St. (bet. Eddy & Turk Sts.), 415-775-4877
At this Italian-American "institution" in the Tenderloin,
"the only thing older than the staff" ("unfailingly efficient"

"men in tuxedos") is the "ancient" "Rat Pack decor"; nevertheless "nostalgists" "appreciate the funkiness" and the "tradition", not to mention "comforting" food that tastes "the same all the time", though trendier types tsk tsk this Joe's just "average"; N.B. the similarly "old-school" San Jose namesake is not officially affiliated with the Original.

Osha Thai Noodles ●   21 15 17 $17
696 Geary St. (Leavenworth St.), 415-673-2368
819 Valencia St. (19th St.), 415-826-7738
If you're craving "flavorful", "fresh" and "really, really fast" Thai tidbits – perhaps "after an evening of happy-hour-and-beyond drinks" – "you won't find anything better or cheaper" than this "grungy" Tenderloin vet (serving till at least 1 AM) or its "über-hip offshoot" in the Mission (till midnight); the latter, with "funky mixed drinks" and "pseudo-tropical" decor, has "taken the menu (and prices) up a few notches."

OZUMO   24 25 19 $48
161 Steuart St. (bet. Howard & Mission Sts.), 415-882-1333;
www.ozumo.com
"Trendy" types seeking a "taste of Tokyo under the Bay Bridge" flock to this "bubble survivor" in the Embarcadero where in an elemental, "positively Zen" dining room "master sushi chefs" dazzle diners with "gorgeous" maki and "robata grill" creations, and in the lounge "DJs keep hipsters happy" – or maybe credit goes to the "specialty cocktails" and dozens of sakes; still, nothing kills a buzz faster than "slow service" and a tab that'll have "money o-zooming out of your wallet."

Pacific   22 20 21 $51
Pan Pacific Hotel, 500 Post St. (Mason St.), 415-929-2087;
www.panpac.com
Cognoscenti claim this "sleeper" in Union Square's Pan Pacific Hotel is "worthy of great praise", thanks to its "creatively prepared" California-style Pacific Rim cookery and staffers who "take care of you"; it's "never crowded" so "you can actually have a good conversation", though some sniff the setting is "too close to the lobby to feel like a first-rate restaurant."

Pacific Café   21 15 21 $30
7000 Geary Blvd. (34th Ave.), 415-387-7091
"Way off the tourist trail" in the Outer Richmond, this "classic SF" seafooder has been reeling 'em in for 30-plus years for "fresh fish" "without pretension" but with salad, soup and sourdough gratis (a "tremendous bargain"); nostalgists smile at the "snazzy '70s interior", which is "obviously not a hindrance" – this place is "packed every night" and few mind the "oppressive waits" thanks to "friendly staffers" pouring "free wine" for folks in line.

Pacific Catch
21 11 17 $15

*2027 Chestnut St. (bet. Fillmore & Steiner Sts.), 415-440-1950;
www.pacificcatch.com*
"A step up from a sandwich place", this tiny Marina seafood
joint hooks pescatarians with its Pacific Rim–style "fast-
food fish" that's "healthy", "perfectly grilled", "served
quick" and "priced right"; regulars recommend the wasabi
bowls ("a creative mix of flavors") and the "unbelievable"
sweet-potato fries and politely suggest getting your meal
to go, since the "tight quarters" will be "overwhelmed"
once "this place gets discovered"; N.B. a new Corte Madera
location is forthcoming.

Pakwan
23 6 10 $13

501 O'Farrell St. (Jones St.), 415-776-0160
3182 16th St. (bet. Guerrero & Valencia Sts.), 415-255-2440 ▽
The "delectable curries" at these Tenderloin and Mission
BYOB subcontinentals drive diners to admiring alliteration
about the "aromatic, authentic and affordable" "Pakistani
pleasure palaces"; though many dislike "surly" staffers,
"grimy tables" and having to "bus your own table", rhyme-
happy "lamb lovers" advise "ignore the decor" and "savor
the flavors"; N.B. there's also a location in Hayward.

Palio D'Asti ✍
20 18 20 $41

*640 Sacramento St. (bet. Kearny & Montgomery Sts.),
415-395-9800; www.paliodasti.com*
Adorned with a mural of the eponymous race, this Italian
stallion is a Financial District workhorse, drawing "power-
lunching" crowds during the week and providing service
that "accommodates business needs"; meanwhile, given
its "extensive" Cal-Ital wine list and special Piemontese
menus, some wonder why people "overlook" this "upscale"
"charmer"; P.S. "great free pizzas during happy hour."

Pancho Villa Taqueria ◗
23 9 15 $11

3071 16th St. (bet. Mission & Valencia Sts.), 415-864-8840
"Time to crown" Pancho "the king and get it over with"
proclaim partisans of this "classic Mexican joint" in the
Mission who villamently vaunt its cafeteria-style "assemble-
your-own" meals served "day or night"; for a "gut-busting
taco" or "succulent burrito" ("I swear there was an entire
pig in mine once") they "brave the fluorescent lighting"
and "prison-ward" decor, thankful for "strolling minstrels
and the omnipresent security guy"; N.B. San Mateo's branch
is geared more toward gringos.

Pane e Vino
21 17 19 $33

*1715 Union St. (Gough St.), 415-346-2111;
www.paneevinotrattoria.com*
A loaf of bread, a jug of wine and "good vibes" are the stock
in trade of this "lively" "come-as-you-are" Northern Italian,
considered a "standout" in Cow Hollow; crowds gather

at this "traditional" trattoria for "well-executed pastas, seafood" and "Neapolitan-style pizza" matched with 80 vinos and served with "friendliness", though a few fret that since relocating it's resting "on previous laurels."

Park Chalet   13 22 13 $27
1000 Great Hwy. (bet. Fulton St. & Lincoln Way), 415-386-8439;
www.beachchalet.com
Like the nearby Beach Chalet, this "glassed-in greenhouse" in the Outer Sunset above Golden Gate Park caters mostly to out-of-towners who'll tolerate the "overpriced" New American eats and "problem service" for the sake of the view; "locals displace tourists" on "warm days" when the retractable walls are open or on "nights when bands play."

Park Grill   19 19 22 $45
Park Hyatt Hotel, 333 Battery St. (Clay St.), 415-296-2933;
www.hyatt.com
"Polished service" and a "quiet" room make this "gem" at Downtown's Park Hyatt "well suited" for "power breakfasts" and "business lunches"; fans favor the "fresh, attractive" New American grill fare yet "sparse attendance" for dinner suggests this place "isn't on anybody's favorites list."

Parma   23 16 21 $27
3314 Steiner St. (bet. Chestnut & Lombard Sts.), 415-567-0500
"It's in the hub of the Marina" yet after a quarter of a century this "low-key Italian" remains "unknown to many" – and that's "their loss" surmise savvy surveyors; "wonderful owners" "straight from the old country" "know how to make you feel at home", dishing out affordable, "authentic" *cucina* like "mama used to make" in an "unpretentious", "noisy" space evoking a Roman alley.

Pasta Pomodoro   15 13 16 $18
816 Irving St. (9th Ave.), 415-566-0900
2304 Market St. (16th St.), 415-558-8123
1865 Post St. (Fillmore St.), 415-674-1826
4000 24th St. (Noe St.), 415-920-9904
655 Union St. (Columbus Ave.), 415-399-0300
1875 Union St. (Laguna St.), 415-771-7900
www.pastapomodoro.com
"Conveniently" located around the Bay Area, this "basic" Italian chain satisfies pastafarians who point out "prices are low, portions generous", service "functional" and food "reliable", making it "always a good choice for the kids"; meanwhile purists pout the "manhandled" "ingredients should be treated with a little respect."

Pauline's Pizza ☒   23 13 18 $21
260 Valencia St. (bet. Duboce Ave. & 14th St.), 415-552-2050
"Even pizza snobs who don't like fancy-schmancy pies" succumb to this Mission munchery's hot, "haute" creations, which feature "exotic" toppings ("edible flowers") on

"crispy thin crusts"; the "casual" spot is "pleasant to dine in" too, thanks to "white linens", a "down-home attitude" and "imaginative salads" – although you'll need those crayons to "keep you occupied" during the "painful waits."

paul k   20 18 19 $39
199 Gough St. (Oak St.), 415-552-7132; www.paulkrestaurant.com
"Hip", "modern furnishings meet" "intensely flavored" Med meze "executed with Californian class" (and "excellent wine pairings") at this "avant-garde" Hayes Valley boîte; "some complain" about the "famous waiter's" "dramatic" "performance" of the dessert menu – inescapable in the "elbow-to-elbow", "noisy" interior – but fans respond "lighten up . . . it's one of SF's amusing dining secrets."

Pazzia ⊠   24 14 21 $28
337 Third St. (bet. Folsom & Harrison Sts.), 415-512-1693
When did "North Beach move south of Market" ask *amici* crazy about this "authentic", "affordable" Tuscan trattoria; the "office-building" exterior belies the warmth inside, generated by "charming owner Massimo" and his "fresh-off-the-boat" staffers as well as the wood-burning oven from which come the "delectable" dishes ("awesome pizza"); the "noisy" "dining room is a bit cramped" but the "cheery" vibe compensates.

Pesce   24 18 20 $34
2227 Polk St. (bet. Green & Vallejo Sts.), 415-928-8025
"If you love seafood, sharing and surprises, you'll be hooked on this "stylish" yet "informal" Russian Hill spot "from the Antica folks"; it showcases "fish-themed" Venetian nibbles with "clear, intense flavors" that are "so good you want to order double"; the "friendly staff" and "great prices for the area" "more than make up for the need to juggle the place settings" in the "tight" room.

Pho Hoa-Hiep II   ∇ 20 7 12 $11
1833 Irving St. (bet. 19th & 20th Aves.), 415-664-0469
See review in East of San Francisco Directory.

Picaro   18 15 16 $25
3120 16th St. (bet. Guerrero & Valencia Sts.), 415-431-4089
Unlike trendier Mission taperias, this "bargain" Spaniard has "no glitz" and "no waits"; "large groups" gulp "garlicky" snacks, "pound sangria" and make noise that could "deafen even those used to Def Leppard concerts" (you might "have to wave your arms to get the staff's attention").

Piperade ⊠   25 22 22 $45
1015 Battery St. (Green St.), 415-391-2555; www.piperade.com
"Every taste offers not only spice but soul" at this "haute Basque" "heaven", where you can count on "phenomenal" food ("foie gras with baby squid – delicious!"), "interesting wines" "not available elsewhere" and "delightful" chef-

owner Gerald Hirigoyen "shaking hands and smiling his way through" the "welcoming", "rustic" room; the "center table can be fun for large groups" and the "well-trained" staff "gives you the straight skinny", but what really makes this "rare" Downtown "gem" precious is its "available parking."

Pizzeria Delfina   – | – | – | I

3611 18th St. (Guerrero St.), 415-437-6800; www.delfinasf.com
Craig Stoll's Neapolitan- and New York–inspired pizzeria, located in a snug Mission space adjacent to his acclaimed Delfina, serves an affordable short list of thin-crust pies supplemented by seasonal antipasti, a daily entree from the oven and an all-Italian wine list; while the setting is industrial (white tiles, stainless-steel kitchen), there's doting service at the tables, counter and half-dozen sidewalk seats.

Pizzetta 211 ⊟   25 | 14 | 13 | $21

211 23rd Ave. (California St.), 415-379-9880
"In the outskirts of the Outer Richmond", this "microscopic pizza joint" with "Euro flair" turns out "crackling-crust pizzettas" and "artisanal salads", all "unique combos" of "superb ingredients"; although food and wine selections are "as few as the tables" in the "tiny" room ("a little larger than my bathroom") and the "snotty" staff puts out big "attitude", regulars realize "great pizza" has its price and keep "lining up for it" before the kitchen "runs out."

PJ's Oyster Bed   18 | 15 | 16 | $30

737 Irving St. (9th Ave.), 415-566-7775; www.pjsoysterbed.com
With "generous portions and friendly service", it's no wonder that the Inner Sunset's only venue for Creole seafood still attracts a "loud, high-energy" crowd for "fun, fun, fun"; still, some jambalaya junkies dismiss decor that's "a bit dingy" and a menu that's "kinda tired", suggesting the party's over and "maybe PJ's should be put to bed."

Platanos   19 | 18 | 18 | $29

598 Guerrero St. (18th St.), 415-252-9281; www.platanos-sf.com
Patrons "go bananas" for the "good-value" midweek prix fixe dinners served with "great sangria" at this "breezy", tropical-themed Nuevo Latino in the Mission; amigos appreciate the "refreshingly different" Central American flavors and "substantial" servings, and though some sniff the à la carte fare is "overpriced", it all goes down a bit easier thanks to a staff that "tries hard."

Plouf ☒   22 | 16 | 18 | $36

40 Belden Pl. (bet. Bush & Pine Sts.), 415-986-6491;
www.ploufsf.com
"The feeling is so French, you'll want to light a cigarette" at this Downtown seafooder on "cozy and adorable Belden Place", where on a "warm evening" or a "sunny workday" eating alfresco is "worth it for the atmosphere alone"; despite a "hectic feel" and "brusqueness" from "efficient"

but "harried" servers, downing "delicious mussels" "with bread to soak up the broth" is a "wonderful experience."

PlumpJack Cafe   24 | 21 | 23 | $49 |
3127 Fillmore St. (bet. Filbert & Greenwich Sts.), 415-563-4755; www.plumpjack.com
Even "without Gavin at the helm", the "professionals in the kitchen and on the floor" of the PlumpJack Group's Cow Hollow "flagship" "make it look easy" say the "budding wine connoisseurs and *Sideways* fans" who bend elbows – and literally rub elbows – with its "rich or famous regulars"; they savor the "inspired" Cal-Med cookery at this "aptly named place" that delivers a "dose of urban sophistication without requiring a tie"; P.S. the Squaw Valley branch is a "must-visit" for "the discerning ski crowd."

Pomelo   21 | 14 | 19 | $21 |
1793 Church St. (30th St.), 415-285-2257
92 Judah St. (6th Ave.), 415-731-6175
www.pomelosf.com
"Based on rice or noodles", the "tasty", "creative" and "healthy" "global comfort food" at these "quaint" Eclectic siblings is "a steal" for "students" seeking an "affordable" "on-the-go dinner"; both spaces have "crowded seating" and "hit-or-miss" service, but there's one big difference: Noe Valley offers weekend brunch, but the Inner Sunset original serves lunch only during the week.

Ponzu   20 | 21 | 19 | $37 |
Serrano Hotel, 401 Taylor St. (bet. Geary & O'Farrell Sts.), 415-775-7979; www.ponzurestaurant.com
This "energetic and creative" eatery in Downtown's Serrano Hotel is "convenient" "before the theater" for "well-presented" Pan-Asian small plates; some say the space's "cool", sleek decor "makes the unhip feel like they've joined the happening crowd", but others opine the "dark" room is too "gloomy" and the bites a bit "bland."

Pork Store Café   20 | 10 | 16 | $14 |
1451 Haight St. (bet. Ashbury St. & Masonic Ave.), 415-864-6981
3122 16th St. (bet. Guerrero & Valencia Sts.), 415-626-5523
Plenty of little piggies go to market at this no-frills Traditional American twosome where the famous, "filling" breakfasts send habitués to "hog heaven"; food and service can be "good one day, lousy the next", but always appreciated is the "free coffee" that's served to those waiting outside on Haight Street for a table; N.B. the Mission location serves dinner Wednesday–Saturday.

POSTRIO   24 | 24 | 23 | $58 |
Prescott Hotel, 545 Post St. (bet. Mason & Taylor Sts.), 415-776-7825; www.postrio.com
"Impress" out-of-town guests with "splashy" "big-city dining" at "Puck's poster child" for New American cuisine –

or at least with "perfect" pizza "while waiting at the bar"; most maintain the Rosenthal brothers do a "tremendous job" in the kitchen, assisted by "efficient, courteous" servers in "handsome" yet "lively" surroundings at Downtown's Prescott Hotel; still, a few perceive "declining quality" in the "loud" room "filled with tourists" and sniff "Wolfgang Yuck."

Powell's Place   – – – I
1521 Eddy St. (Fillmore St.), 415-409-1388
More than a year after surrendering his original Hayes Valley digs, gospel singer Emmit Powell returns to his role as the king of soul – soul food, that is; his new spot in the Fillmore Jazz District may feature fancier New Orleans–style touches like ceiling fans and palm trees, but Powell's still providing the same affordable dishes, including what many consider the best fried chicken in town.

Public, The ☒   20 20 18 $36
1489 Folsom St. (11th St.), 415-552-3065; www.thepublicsf.com
There's "great people-watching" at this "exposed-brick loft" in SoMa, a "dim", "posh-industrial" venue for "dates and groups" that serves "gussied-up" Cal-Med "comfort food that more than comforts"; the pennywise proclaim the "price performance is hard to beat", even if the public servants are "not the friendliest"; N.B. a post-*Survey* change of ownership and chef may outdate the above Food score.

Puerto Alegre   19 12 17 $16
546 Valencia St. (bet. 16th & 17th Sts.), 415-255-8201
With its Service score rebounding after a dip last year, this family-run Mission cantina has surveyors summing up its situation as "you get what you pay for, but at least they're friendly"; in truth, this "festive" place is "known for its margaritas" (aka "fun served by the pitcher"), while the "secondary" food turns out to be "tasty" "basic Mexican": "all the quality of a taco cart in a sit-down restaurant."

Q   19 16 17 $22
225 Clement St. (bet. 3rd & 4th Aves.), 415-752-2298
The decor may be "questionable" and the cuisine is no quintessence of culinary art – but questers still queue up at this "lively", "unpretentious", "bohemian" Inner Richmond BBQ, where the kitchen "piles on" its "hearty" American "home cooking" ("soul food for white people"); overall, folks either love or hate this place, equating it to a "drag queen in a '70s disco: cheap, loud and funky."

QUINCE   27 23 25 $61
1701 Octavia St. (bet. Bush & Pine Sts.), 415-775-8500; www.quincerestaurant.com
Though admittedly "expensive", Pacific Heights' "precious little boîte" is "wonderful in all respects"; its "muted decor" enables "lucky" diners to "focus" on the "meticulously prepared", "delicately flavored", "über-fresh" French–

Italian fare and "outstanding wines"; bring a "dictionary to decipher the menu" – or enlist the "extraordinarily well-trained" servers – but do "leave Atkins behind for the night" because the "ethereal" "handmade pastas are clearly where the chef's heart is."

Ramblas
20 | 18 | 18 | $27

557 Valencia St. (bet. 16th & 17th Sts.), 415-565-0207;
www.ramblastapas.com
Regulars who ramble over to this "trendy" yet "comfortable" Mission Spaniard recommend its "tempting" tapas if you haven't already snacked on small plates "at one of the 15 other places" nearby; there's "no wait" here to partake of pitchers of "potent sangria" that are "half price before 7 PM", making it ideal for "beginning a girls' [or guys'] night out" despite rumbles about "spotty service."

R & G Lounge
23 | 13 | 16 | $26

631 Kearny St. (bet. Clay & Sacramento Sts.), 415-982-7877;
www.rnglounge.com
Lounge lizards who love this "efficient" Chinatown center of "authentic down-home Cantonese" declare its "wonderful" seafood "could be served to royalty" ("the signature salt-and-pepper crab deserves a place in the hall of fame"); cognoscenti confide "upstairs there's better service and nicer atmosphere" but "the same food" is "much cheaper" "if you eat in the basement."

Red's Java House
16 | 10 | 15 | $10

Pier 30 (Bryant St., off the Embarcadero), 415-777-5626
Riddled with "character", this "bare-bones" Traditional American near the Bay Bridge on the Embarcadero is "one of the only blue-collar places left on the waterfront" ("a double cheeseburger, a Bud" and "an oceanfront view" for around $6); its "friendly" servers have fed "everyone from construction workers to suits" to longshoremen for more than 50 years.

Restaurant LuLu
21 | 19 | 18 | $40

816 Folsom St. (bet. 4th & 5th Sts.), 415-495-5775;
www.restaurantlulu.com
With some 600 wines and "smoky, modern, hearty" French Provençal food to its credit, this "large and open" SoMa showcase is a lulu, all right; though the menu changes daily, and service is "up-and-down", regulars feel they can rely on this longtimer as a "dependable, fall-back option" "after a movie at the Metreon", despite the "deafening" din.

Rigolo
18 | 12 | 12 | $19

3465 California St. (Laurel St.), 415-876-7777;
www.rigolocafe.com
Pascal Rigo combined two parts "casual cafe" with one part boulangerie and cooked up this "appealing" New French in Laurel Village that's popular "with the mom-and-

stroller crowd" for its "wonderful pizzas" and pastries; considering counter service is "still getting the kinks out" and indoor seating is "uncomfortable", opt for takeout.

Ristorante Bacco   23 | 18 | 21 | $34 |
737 Diamond St. (bet. Elizabeth & 24th Sts.), 415-282-4969; www.baccosf.com
"Hidden" in Noe Valley, this "homey", "soothing" trattoria "delivers on its promise" of "delectable" *cucina* with "heavenly pastas" and "*molto bene* risotto" prepared from scratch plus "interesting" Italian wines; "friendly waiters" who have real "accents (or are good at faking it)" make folks feel "comfortable" and "satisfied" – and "they always have a table for you."

Ristorante Ideale   ∇ 21 | 16 | 21 | $33 |
1309 Grant Ave. (Vallejo St.), 415-391-4129
"You only need a Vespa" to make the "authentic" Italian picture complete, assert *amici* of this "pasta pick" in North Beach; its "intensely flavored" fare "isn't fancy, just really good", and the "staff couldn't be nicer" (hence its higher Service score this year); but the "cozy" room is "noisy" and a few regulars remark the kitchen can be "inconsistent."

Ristorante Milano   25 | 16 | 23 | $35 |
1448 Pacific Ave. (bet. Hyde & Larkin Sts.), 415-673-2961; www.milanosf.com
Russian Hill residents "would like to keep this little hideout a secret", but word has gotten out about the "splendid" Northern Italian specialties "cooked to perfection" and "high-caliber" service that "makes you feel like a special guest" ("home should be as good as this"); some swoon over "romantic ambiance" as well, so although critics consider the confines "cramped" and dislike delays in being seated "even if you have a reservation", most insist it's "worth its wait in gold."

Ristorante Umbria ⊠   19 | 16 | 18 | $30 |
198 Second St. (Howard St.), 415-546-6985
"I'll be back" vow visitors to this "cute" SoMa trattoria, a "tried-and-true" choice for "surprisingly good" Northern Italian eats; chef/co-owner Giulio Tempesta is "always there with a smile and a grand welcome", and its business-district location is convenient for a midday meal, though "they really need to take lunch reservations."

RITZ-CARLTON DINING ROOM ⊠   27 | 27 | 28 | $87 |
Ritz-Carlton Hotel, 600 Stockton St. (bet. California & Pine Sts.), 415-773-6198; www.ritzcarlton.com
The arrival of Ron (aka "I-Ron" Chef) Siegel, who has incorporated his "love for Japanese seafood" into the "enchanting" New French menu, "has added the final ingredient" to this "heaven on Nob Hill"; an "impeccable" staff that "grants your every desire, even reading glasses",

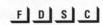
and an "elegant" "old-world" ambiance ("so quiet you can hear your ice melt") appeal to an older crowd, but "the candy cart makes a kid out of anyone"; given that it's "the Rolls-Royce of SF dining", expect similar sticker shock.

RITZ-CARLTON TERRACE   23 | 24 | 25 | $53

Ritz-Carlton Hotel, 600 Stockton St. (bet. California & Pine Sts.), 415-773-6198; www.ritzcarlton.com

"Super-attentive" service that's "not at all stuffy" is the hallmark of this "quiet" "oasis" on Nob Hill, a humbler alternative to the Ritz's Dining Room, so "bring friends and relatives" and sit out in the "beautiful courtyard" for the "high-class" (aka "steep") brunch with "classy live jazz"; though less "memorable", the Med dinners (served Sunday and Monday) are still "tasty and imaginative."

rnm ⊠   23 | 24 | 20 | $40

598 Haight St. (Steiner St.), 415-551-7900; www.rnmrestaurant.com

This "happening hipster hangout" "hidden in the Lower Haight" is a "stylish", "sleek and sexy" spot "in a punk neighborhood"; all agree Justine Miner's "creative" New American small plates "shine" (the "fabulous" prix fixe dinners provide "huge value"), but surveyors split on the service – some are satisfied with the "capable" staffers while others huff about their "hipper-than-thou 'tude."

RoHan Lounge ◐   ▽ 20 | 22 | 17 | $24

3809 Geary Blvd. (bet. 2nd & 3rd Aves.), 415-221-5095; www.rohanlounge.com

Although soju is "everywhere now", SF's first bar/restaurant devoted to the Eastern elixir remains a "one-of-a-kind" "social scene" in the Inner Richmond; the "stylish, retro" red room with DJs spinning "funky music" on weekends may be a "better place to drink than eat", but the "Pan-Asian small plates" (mostly "Korean with a slight twist") are "interesting" and "delicious" too.

Rosamunde Sausage Grill ⇕   24 | 8 | 17 | $9

545 Haight St. (bet. Fillmore & Steiner Sts.), 415-437-6851

"Everybody needs a little piggy" now and then, and there's "no better" version in town than those from this stainless-steel American "sausageria" in the Lower Haight – more than a dozen types of "mouthwatering" brats (including a vegan dog) that you can "wash down" with a "frosty" "pint" at the bar next door; regulars rely on the counter servers' "toppings suggestions" and appreciate that "they'll pound on the wall for you" when it's ready.

Rose Pistola   21 | 21 | 19 | $42

532 Columbus Ave. (bet. Green & Union Sts.), 415-399-0499

"Still cooking after all these years" according to admirers, North Beach's "date-perfect" Ligurian locale dishes up "enticing" Northern Italian fare that's "pricey, but worth it" given the venue's "gorgeous" (and "boisterous") interior; critics complain about "slow service" and conclude "the rose is wilting": it's "more about buzz and attitude than food."

Rose's Cafe   19 | 18 | 18 | $27
2298 Union St. (Steiner St.), 415-775-2200
Everything's coming up roses at this "idyllic" Pac Heights Northern Italian, especially on weekends when it's "packed" with "shining yuppies" eating "out-of-this-world brunches" ("breakfast pizza? what's not to love?") as they "sit at the sidewalk tables" "people-watching"; still, some say "slow" or "surly" service is a thorn in their side.

Rotee   ▽ 21 | 14 | 17 | $16
400 Haight St. (Webster St.), 415-552-8309; www.roteesf.com
Two can feast on "ridiculously good, ridiculously cheap" curries "for under $25" at this Indo-Pak in the Lower Haight's "new Indian food ghetto"; it's "counter service–only", but with its "bright colors" and "great" "DJ music" the modest room is "inviting" except to coughing critics who choke at the "smoke" ("please fix the ventilation").

Rotunda   20 | 23 | 19 | $36
Neiman Marcus, 150 Stockton St. (bet. Geary & O'Farrell Sts.), 415-362-4777
For light eaters who "find the sound of cash registers soothing", Neiman Marcus' "spacious", "spectacular" (and recently remodeled) New American cafe is ideal for afternoon tea or "a glass of champagne" and "$28 lobster club sandwich"; "service varies", unsurprisingly, but nobody much minds as long as they can "grab a table along the rotunda" overlooking Union Square.

ROY'S   22 | 22 | 21 | $46
575 Mission St. (bet. 1st & 2nd Sts.), 415-777-0277; www.roysrestaurant.com
"Oh boy, Roy's!" laud lei-men for whom the "island-fresh", "savory seafood" conjures up "a bit of Hawaii" in SoMa, especially with "welcoming" staffers who embody the ethos of the Aloha State; most find the "serene, lovely" room "unchainlike, despite the multiple locations" but a few roiled respondents "want more originality for their buck."

Rubicon ⧄   23 | 20 | 23 | $59
558 Sacramento St. (bet. Montgomery & Sansome Sts.), 415-434-4100; www.sfrubicon.com
"Wine authority" Larry Stone's "Bible-like", 1,600-label list prompts "suits" and celebs to pick their vino "first, then the food" at Drew Nieporent's Downtown "expense-accounter"; although the sommelier is some folks' "main reason to eat here", connoisseurs credit Stuart Brioza's "artful" fare with boosting this Cal–New French back into "SF's top tier" – even if its "industrial" interior evokes "NYC" instead; N.B. lunch served on Wednesdays only.

Rue Lepic
─ │ ─ │ ─ │ M

900 Pine St. (Mason St.), 415-474-6070; www.ruelepic.com
This intimate 35-seat Nob Hill bistro has been doling out
French standards since 1940 in an impossibly romantic
setting, replete with mirrored pillars and large windows
overlooking one of the steepest hills in the city; these days,
Japanese-born chef Michiko Boccara carries the Gallic
torch for her retired husband with her artfully presented
preparations of sweetbreads, escargot and duck à l'orange;
multicourse prix fixe dinners are also available.

Rue Saint Jacques
─ │ ─ │ ─ │ I

1098 Jackson St. (Taylor St.), 415-776-2002;
www.ruesaintjacques.com
On the slope of Nob Hill, this charming new bistro offers a
romantic perch to watch the cable cars pass while settling
into brown leather banquettes and California-kissed French
fare; despite the tony zip code and rich offerings (foie gras,
confit), the menu is affordable (topping out at $20 for a sole-
wrapped lobster tail), as is the international wine list, with
many choices served by the glass and half-bottle.

Ruth's Chris Steak House
23 │ 19 │ 21 │ $56

1601 Van Ness Ave. (California St.), 415-673-0557;
www.ruthschris.com
"Cows dream of becoming" one of the "buttery" steaks
"cooked to perfection" at Nob Hill's link of the national
chain; carnivores commune in the "classic" dining room
and commend the "professional staff" ("from the bus boys
to the manager") – their only beef is "high prices", so this is
best "for a special occasion or an expense-account meal."

Saigon Sandwiches ⌀
24 │ 3 │ 12 │ $6

560 Larkin St. (Turk St.), 415-474-5698
"Yes, that Food score and cost entry are correct" – this
"tiny" Tenderloiner provides this *Survey*'s Best Bang for
the Buck by "cranking out" "fabulous and incredibly cheap"
Vietnamese *banh mi* "at warp speed"; denizens "down to
their last $5" declare they "don't care that there's no service
or decor" because "if there's a better sandwich for $2 in
the Bay Area, I haven't found it"; N.B. closes at 5 PM.

Sam's Grill &
20 │ 16 │ 20 │ $37

Seafood Restaurant ⊠

374 Bush St. (bet. Kearny & Montgomery Sts.), 415-421-0594
"The freshest seafood cooked any way you want it" – as
long as you don't want any "foo-foo sauces" – has been
reeling diners in to this "clubby" Downtown "institution for
power lunches" since it opened in 1867; the "curtained
private booths are a wonderful anachronism", as are the
"crusty" "staffers in white jackets who attend to your
every need", but less nostalgic noshers fuss that this "fair
fare has no flair."

Sanraku Four Seasons   22 | 14 | 19 | $31
Sony Metreon Ctr., 101 Fourth St. (Mission St.), 415-369-6166
704 Sutter St. (Taylor St.), 415-771-0803
www.sanraku.com
There's "nothing fancy but the fish" at these Japanese
joints straddling Market Street that offer "authentic", "fresh"
sushi and sashimi, "fair prices and a come-as-you-are
attitude"; however, tourists and locals alike prefer the
"minimalist" Sutter Street location ("walking distance from
Union Square hotels") to the Metreon's "food-court" branch,
where "the lack of quick service" distracts diners who worry
about "missing that movie."

Sauce ◐   – | – | – | M
131 Gough St. (Oak St.), 415-252-1369; www.saucesf.com
Although "there hasn't been fanfare" (yet) about this "great
new neighborhood joint" in the Civic Center area, this
baby's got sauce thanks to a "fun" staff proffering "large
portions of gourmet" New American "comfort food" at
"such reasonable prices"; it's also "one of the few places
to eat late" (till midnight), making it a "subdued" "oasis"
for a bite and a belt post-symphony.

Savor   18 | 15 | 17 | $20
3913 24th St. (bet. Noe & Sanchez Sts.), 415-282-0344
When you crave "pancakes for dinner", "the appeal" of
this "convenient", "comfortably funky" Noe Valley staple
"crêpes right up on you"; the "serviceable" and "semi-
healthy" Med meals served in "big portions" seem most
"savory" when you sit on the "charming" patio.

Scala's Bistro ◐   22 | 21 | 20 | $42
Sir Francis Drake Hotel, 432 Powell St. (bet. Post & Sutter Sts.),
415-395-8555; www.scalasbistro.com
The Drake Hotel's "festive" dining room festooned with
"stunning fresh flowers" is "jammed at lunch and dinner"
due to "reliable" and "surprisingly" "inspired" Northern
Italian and French cuisine that's a "bargain for Downtown";
scalawags sigh it's "as noisy as a henhouse" but "warm,
on-the-spot service" and a kitchen that's open late attract
everyone from Union Square shoppers to theatergoers.

Scoma's   21 | 16 | 18 | $40
Pier 47, 1 Al Scoma Way (bet. Jefferson & Jones Sts.),
415-771-4383; www.scomas.com
"Yes, there are more tourists here than on the cable car", but
this Fisherman's Wharf "sentimental favorite" also lures
lots of locals with its "extremely fresh", "simply prepared"
seafood and "friendly", "honest" service; the "dated"
interior may not "look like much", but if you sit "near one
of the walls of windows" with a view of the "unmatched"
waterscape, "you won't notice" anyway; the outpost in
Sausalito is "every bit as good" with even "better" scenery.

Sears Fine Food
17 | 10 | 16 | $18

439 Powell St. (Sutter St.), 415-986-0700; www.searsfinefood.com
Founded in 1938 and reopened in 2004 after "subtle" renovations, this "classic" Downtown diner is an "almost legendary spot for breakfast", drawing tourists and locals alike, some of whom huff that the "cranky" "help needs help"; overall surveyors are split on whether "it's just as good as before" or "some of the old charm is gone."

SEASONS
24 | 26 | 26 | $61

Four Seasons Hotel, 757 Market St. (bet. 3rd & 4th Sts.), 415-633-3838; www.fourseasons.com
An "extremely elegant Downtown location" with "large picture windows" "overlooking Market Street" sets the scene for "excellent" (and "expensive") Cal-French cuisine accompanied by hundreds of fine wines; "all the details are attended to" by "gracious" staffers who may well be "mind readers", fostering a "quiet" atmosphere and as "smooth" an operation "as you'd expect" from a restaurant at a Four Seasons hotel.

Shabu-Sen
▽ 19 | 14 | 16 | $23

1726 Buchanan St. (bet. Post & Sutter Sts.), 415-440-0466
Diners who have a yen for Japanese food and don't mind "cooking it" themselves are warming up to this "authentic" new "hot pot" place "in J-Town" that specializes in only two items, shabu-shabu and sukiyaki; both dishes are prepared tableside by the customers themselves from "ample portions" of meats, veggies and noodles, while servers remain on hand to assist neophytes and refill glasses of sake or draft beer.

Shalimar ⊅
23 | 3 | 10 | $14

532 Jones St. (Geary St.), 415-928-0333
1409 Polk St. (Pine St.), 415-776-4642
www.shalimarsf.com
This chainlet's "crazy good" Pakistani-Indian fare is so "fiery hot and delicious" ("I couldn't feel my tongue afterwards") it renders "everything else irrelevant" – namely the "high-school cafeteria service" and "grubby" rooms – not to mention the delightfully "rock-bottom prices"; P.S. "diehards stick to" the "Tandoor-loin" location, while "Polk and Pine has become the yuppie" choice and Fremont's branch attracts eager East Bay crowds.

Shanghai 1930 🄯
20 | 22 | 19 | $40

133 Steuart St. (bet. Howard & Mission Sts.), 415-896-5600; www.shanghai1930.com
"I thought I was in a Charlie Chan film" say surveyors smitten by this swanky Sino near the Embarcadero; over-the-top "chic" crimson interiors provide the backdrop for live music, some 500 wines (reds a specialty, naturally) and "complicated" regional cuisine; however, "don't expect

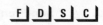
Chinatown prices" or speed ("service via the slow boat from China") or you're liable to "feel Shanghaied."

SILKS
24 | 26 | 25 | $59

Mandarin Oriental Hotel, 222 Sansome St. (bet. California & Pine Sts.), 415-986-2020; www.mandarinoriental.com
Best known as a Downtown power-dining destination, the Mandarin Oriental's Cal-Asian fusion "gem" is "delightful" for a "civilized" meal anytime, thanks to a "dreamy", "hushed environment" ("tasteful" antique silk hangings, "stunning wood floors") that "allows for long conversation" plus "impeccable" service from "waiters who'll address you by name"; the "exquisite" food is also "top-notch", but trendoids who tsk-tsk it's "too sedate" prefer more exciting options "for the same money."

SLANTED DOOR, THE
25 | 22 | 20 | $43

The Embarcadero, 1 Ferry Bldg., #3 (Market St.), 415-861-8032; www.slanteddoor.com
Charles Phan's Vietnamese powerhouse still knocks the "socks, shoes, pants, shirt and even underwear off" its many phans; since its relocation to a "sleek", "glass-and-steel" Ferry Building space with "sweeping Bay Bridge views" its crowd is more "touristy", but the "sassy" "spin" on Saigon street food and "eclectic wine list" "still rock" and servers are "helpful", if harried, in the "deafening" environs; the only "slant in the door" remains "reservation frustration" but the adjacent "small take-out" shop helps somewhat.

Slow Club
23 | 20 | 19 | $33

2501 Mariposa St. (Hampshire St.), 415-241-9390; www.slowclub.com
This "fine-dining dive bar" in the Mission enables locals to "stop by for espresso and pastries in the morning" and "drop in" "without a reservation" for "candlelit dining" at night; all appreciate the "reasonably priced" New American eats ("what home cooking would be if you married a Michelin-starred chef"), while scenesters also say the "edgy", "low-rent" vibe "is the allure"; sadly, some find the "surly" staff way too "slooooooow."

So
∇ 20 | 12 | 16 | $14

2240 Irving St. (bet. 23rd & 24th Sts.), 415-731-3143
Colorful and "popular", this family-owned Asian "noodle joint" catering to "trendier" types in the Outer Sunset is known for "SF's biggest bowls" of soup and for "spicy" soba, though regulars urge "try their dry-fried chicken wings" and "great potstickers"; the digs and service are just "so-so", but so what when you can fill up for less than $15?

Sociale ⊠
24 | 22 | 23 | $40

3665 Sacramento St. (bet. Locust & Spruce Sts.), 415-921-3200
At this casual, rustic Italian "tucked away (literally)" "down an alley" in Presidio Heights, the preferred perch is on the

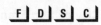
pooch-friendly patio where socialites chat "about debutante balls, summering in Europe" and "trust funds"; meanwhile, the "delectable" dishes and "welcoming staff" make even average-income *amici* "want to go back" – just "keep the number on your cell phone's speed dial" because reservations are a must.

South Park Cafe ⌧ 22 | 18 | 20 | $36

108 South Park St. (bet. 2nd & 3rd Sts.), 415-495-7275
This "understated, unpretentious" bistro "right on South Park" remains a "best-kept secret" even after two decades of serving up "*très* French" fare (e.g. homemade blood sausage); in-the-know *amis* assert this "friendly" nook is a "favorite" "before a ballgame" or dinner after "you've missed the train" and need to eat "in under an hour"; N.B. "the three-course prix fixe is an incredible deal."

STRAITS CAFE 21 | 20 | 17 | $34

3300 Geary Blvd. (Parker Ave.), 415-668-1783;
www.straitsrestaurants.com
Chris Yeo's "whimsically decorated" Singaporean – which specializes in "small plates" of "eyebrow-raising" "delights from all over East Asia" plus "imaginative cocktails" – is now a "burgeoning" Bay Area chain; the pennywise point out "sharing plates can either add up or be economical" but believe the staff's suggestions are "right on the money", particularly at SF's "intimate" Inner Richmond original, which offers "better service" than do the "ear-shattering", "see-and-be-seen" South Bay branches.

Street Restaurant ▽ 23 | 18 | 21 | $32

2141 Polk St. (bet. Broadway & Vallejo Sts.), 415-775-1055;
www.streetrestaurant.com
Word on the street is that this smallish, "hip" yet "comfy" "hangout" in Russian Hill offers "big portions" of New American "upscale diner fare" (including housemade sausages and breads), wines "to suit any palate" and friendly servers "familiar with them", resulting in the area's "best quality-to-price ratio"; some complain it's "too darn noisy", but din-tolerant diners declare "get here early or you'll be shut out by the regulars."

SUMI 22 | 19 | 23 | $41

(fka Ma Tante Sumi)
4243 18th St. (bet. Castro & Diamond Sts.), 415-626-7864;
www.suminthecastro.com
Delivering "tantalizing" Asian-inspired French fare, this "great little fusion restaurant in the Castro" is an "epicurean adventure" in a "mediocre" dining neighborhood; exec chef "Sumi is often there", and the "phenomenal" staff "makes sure every need is met" in the "tight" but mercifully "quiet" quarters (another "rarity") that have recently been "revitalized" with a "much-needed face-lift."

Suppenküche
21 | 16 | 18 | $27

601 Hayes St. (Laguna St.), 415-252-9289; www.suppenkuche.com
At this "warm, bustling" Hayes Valley *wursthaus* the "super"
kitchen turns out "top-notch"German "country cooking"
while the bar's "fantastic" Bavarian brews "transport" you
to Munich; "come with an open mind and a good topic for
conversation" since seating is at communal "picnic tables"
and the social interaction (like the "decibel levels") "rises
exponentially" as the suds-filled "boots get passed around."

Sushi Groove
24 | 20 | 18 | $37

1516 Folsom St. (bet. 11th & 12th Sts.), 415-503-1950 ⊠
1916 Hyde St. (bet. Green & Union Sts.), 415-440-1905
"Twenty- and thirtysomethings" get their groove back at
this sushi-specialist twosome turning out "outstanding"
"traditional and original rolls" in "over-the-top combos"
("heaven melted on rice"); whether at the "tiny" Russian
Hill original or its "tragically hip" SoMa sib (with nightly
DJs and "clubbers in various states of disarray"), the staff
"sometimes serves" food, "sometimes 'tude" – at "inflated
prices", even – but most feel the chefs "continue to deliver."

SUTRO'S AT THE CLIFF HOUSE ⊠
20 | 25 | 19 | $44

1090 Point Lobos Ave. (Sutro Heights Park), 415-386-3330;
www.cliffhouse.com
A "stunning improvement" over the "kitschy" "landmark"
formerly at this Outer Richmond location, this "airy" two-
story glass tower suspended on the Point Lobos cliffs has
"out-of-towners and locals alike" gasping at its "jaw-
dropping" "views of the ship traffic and the entrance to the
Golden Gate"; most maintain the Cal cuisine is "surprisingly"
"impressive for a tourist spot", so though nostalgics "miss"
the earlier incarnation's "old-fashioned charm" and service
is slightly "underwhelming", it's worth the "steep prices" –
at least during "daylight hours."

Swan Oyster Depot ⊠⊅
26 | 11 | 22 | $26

1517 Polk St. (bet. California & Sacramento Sts.), 415-673-1101
"Forget the Wharf" – instead, head to Nob Hill to this
"landmark" "multigenerational seafood wholesaler, open
for lunch service only"; ok, the "tiny" space with "teetering
stools" "almost as high" as its circa-1912 counter may look
like an "ugly" duckling, but it's beautiful to those "devouring"
the "perfect lunch" ("superb Louie" and "fantastic" raw
oysters) and "chatting" with the "friendly" "fishmonger"
brothers serving it up; "go early and often", as finatics
"line up" "on the sidewalk to get in."

Sydney's Restaurant
15 | 17 | 16 | $28

415 Presidio Ave. (California St.), 415-409-0400;
www.sydneysrestaurant.com
Presidio Heights *landsmen* laud this "lively", "swank"
Jewish Community Center yearling for its "cool bar", $12

early-bird and "garage parking in the same building" and acknowledge that new chef John Beardsley (ex Azie) has recently "spiced up the place" with a lighter Eclectic menu; even so, they feel it's still "struggling to find its groove" after abandoning its Jewish-style "comfort food", and say "laughable" service "needs to work out the kinks."

Tablespoon   23   21   21 $42

2209 Polk St. (Vallejo St.), 415-268-0140;
www.tablespoonsf.com

Russian Hill residents feel "lucky" to find a "trendy" spot that "still values great service and a warm welcome"; an "impressive" New American menu that's "limited in size but not imagination" offers both "homey food and foam-y food", plus there's a "great wine list, even by the glass"; though the "mod", "sexy" space can get "cramped" and "noisy", diners deal with it so they can "order half-portions" as "late-night snacks" without forking over a lot of cash.

Tadich Grill ⧄   21   18   19 $38

240 California St. (bet. Battery & Front Sts.), 415-391-1849

Financial District "power-lunchers", "local celebs and socialites" willingly "wear bibs" to slurp down "excellent cioppino" at this "chauvinist bastion" that's "been around since the Gold Rush"; the "glitz-free", "no-pretense" experience extends to "fresh, unadorned seafood" and "strong drinks" proffered by an "all-male staff" "as crusty as the fabulous sourdough bread" (though a few wish they'd toss the "salty" attitude "overboard").

Taiwan   17   7   13 $15

445 Clement St. (6th Ave.), 415-387-1789
See review in East of San Francisco Directory.

Takara   ▽   21   12   17 $27

22 Peace Plaza (bet. Laguna & Webster Sts.), 415-921-2000

"Delightfully untouristy" compared to most of its J-town ilk, this Japanese joint "has a good selection" of "authentic" combos and cooked dishes; the "shabu-shabu and sukiyaki hot pots" – "prepared for you tableside" in quantities big "enough for two" – are "recommended", making up for sushi that's just "ordinary" and "humdrum" traditional decor.

Tallula   20   21   17 $39

4230 18th St. (bet. Collingwood & Diamond Sts.), 415-437-6722;
www.tallulasf.com

"The setting alone" – a "bohemian", "phantasmagorical" "townhouse" – is "reason enough to search out" this "intriguing" Castrolite that deals in "French-Indian tapas" ("like something visualized while on LSD at a Ravi Shankar concert") and "creative uses of sake"; however, a falling Food score suggests that this place, once considered "so unique that we forgive the price" and the "spotty service", no longer is.

Tamal 🗷   ▽ 21 | 14 | 22 | $25

1599 Howard St. (12th St.), 415-864-2446; www.tamalsf.com
Tamales are what's hot at this mod, colorful "little wine-and-tapas bar", a "welcome addition" to the "culinary wasteland" of southern SoMa; cooking teacher and food historian Moaya Scheiman, the chef-owner, has put together a menu of "fantastic, creative Nouvelle Latino" small plates (including "interesting and tasty" versions of the eponymous starter), deftly delivered by staffers along with "personalized service."

Tao Cafe   ▽ 20 | 18 | 18 | $25

1000 Guerrero St. (22nd St.), 415-641-9955; www.taocafe.com
"Keep this one under your hat" whisper fans of this Franco-Vietnamese in the Mission where an "effervescent and fast" expat "lovingly prepares" and serves "authentic food of her childhood" ("bargain prix fixe dinners") in a cafe decorated to evoke the 1930s Indochinese colonial era; however, cognoscenti confess "service could be better."

Taqueria Can-Cun ●🗗   23 | 8 | 14 | $8

1003 Market St. (6th St.), 415-864-6773
2288 Mission St. (19th St.), 415-252-9560
3211 Mission St. (Valencia St.), 415-550-1414
"Bums and loft-dwelling yuppies alike swear by the burritos" from this "late-night" taqueria trio where "grilled tortillas" and "avocado chunks" "make all the difference"; herbivores "bow to the super-veggie" versions while carnivores wink "the *lengua* [tongue] or *cabeza* [brains] are worth trying if you're the adventurous type" – either way "watch out for the salsa" ("you'll smile, then you'll hurt"); the locations may be "sketchy", but "gaudy decor and the Mexican jukebox add a certain charm to the experience."

Tartare 🗷   25 | 24 | 24 | $67

550 Washington St. (bet. Montgomery & Sansome Sts.),
415-434-3100; www.tartarerestaurant.com
Rah-rah raw-food regulars revere George Morrone's Downtown boîte specializing in "thought-provoking" and "exquisite" fish and meat tartares along with "ultrarich", fully cooked French fare ("duck-fat fries to harden the arteries but gladden the heart") and "quirky wine pairings"; admirers also appreciate that "the chef makes his rounds to each table" in this "serene" "jewel-box" dining room that manages to be "both elegant and erotic"; N.B. in early fall 2005 plans were afoot to alter the menu (which may outdate the above Food score) and change the name to George.

TARTINE BAKERY   26 | 15 | 14 | $14

600 Guerrero St. (18th St.), 415-487-2600;
www.tartinebakery.com
"Judging by the lines outside on Sunday mornings", carb connoisseurs believe this Mission *boulangerie* is "orders

of magnitude better" than its city competitors; those who
finally get in willingly withstand waiting salivaters' "shooting
stares" in order to savor the "sacramental cakes", "fluffy
quiches" and "spectacular sandwiches"; but balkers blanch
at the "bad-tempered staff", "bone-crunching crowds" and
general "craziness"; N.B. as of August 2005 a wine bar
sibling was slated for 561 Valencia St.

Taylor's Automatic Refresher   21 | 13 | 15 | $15
The Embarcadero, 1 Ferry Bldg., #6 (Market St.), 866-328-3663;
www.taylorsrefresher.com
See review in North of San Francisco Directory.

Ten-Ichi   20 | 12 | 18 | $30
2235 Fillmore St. (bet. Clay & Sacramento Sts.), 415-346-3477;
www.tenichisf.com
If you're itching for Japanese, this "popular" Upper Fillmore
longtimer is "not flashy but steady" and "quiet"; the kitchen
dishes out "utterly dependable" sushi plus traditional
"Asian comfort food" (sukiyaki, yosenabe), but there's "not
much in terms of decor" and "service is slow", so some
bristle it's "not worth the excruciating wait."

Thai House   22 | 13 | 17 | $18
2200 Market St. (bet. 15th & Sanchez Sts.), 415-864-5006
Thai House Express
599 Castro St. (19th St.), 415-864-5000
901 Larkin St. (Geary St.), 415-441-2248 ◗
Though the original Castro location of this chainlet has
closed, its "spartan" "renovated-IHOP" offshoot situated
at "one of the most colorful intersections in town" remains
a great perch for "people-watching" as a "chipper" crew
ferries "coconutty and spicy" "Thai chow" hither and yon;
in addition, the late-night Express "satellites" (one in the
Tenderloin, one near 19th Street) are perfect "if you have
15 minutes" "before or after hitting the bars."

Thanh Long   23 | 16 | 18 | $42
4101 Judah St. (46th Ave.), 415-665-1146; www.anfamily.com
"Crustacean's big sister" in the Outer Sunset lays out
Vietnamese feasts "fit for King Neptune", namely the
signature "huge" roasted crabs and garlic noodles that
"would make Emeril blush"; diners at "table after table"
are "up to their elbows" sucking down the specialty as
"personable" servers traverse the "casual" space; all but
the crabbiest gladly shell out for valet parking even as they
snap the fare's too "costly."

Thep Phanom Thai Cuisine   25 | 16 | 18 | $25
400 Waller St. (Fillmore St.), 415-431-2526; www.thepphanom.com
At this "titillating" two-decade-old Thai the "food is phanom-
enal" affirm fanatics fond of its "creative, fresh, always
delicious" eats ("wonderfully fragrant curries" have a
"subtlety that's very hard to find" elsewhere); the "tiny,

intimate space" is undoubtedly "a bit cramped" but "kind"
servers manage to remain "even-tempered" as they
maneuver through "the nightly chaos"; P.S. those who
don't love the Lower Haight location suggest "take a taxi"
to avoid "problem parking" or walking through the area.

Three Seasons   23   20   19 $34
3317 Steiner St. (bet. Chestnut & Lombard Sts.), 415-567-9989;
www.threeseasonsrestaurant.com
The "artful" small plates with "wonderful flavors and
reasonable prices" at this Vietnamese venue "never
disappoint", and neither does its "good-looking Marina
crowd" "dressed to kill"; on the other hand, the "spartan"
setting and sometimes "undertrained" staff "still need a
bit of work"; P.S. branches in Palo Alto and Walnut Creek
ratchet up the collective Decor score with their "colonial"
air and "Zen" interior, respectively.

Ti Couz   23   16   16 $20
3108 16th St. (Valencia St.), 415-252-7373
Supporters of this "noisy", "crowded" Mission standby
swear its "authentic", "addictive", "affordable" buckwheat
galettes and sweet crêpes that "cannot be skipped" are
"the best this side of the Seine"; "expect a wait" at this
"happening" ti party, but "delicious cocktails, ciders and
beers" will help you pass the time; however, surveyors split
on service ("funky" and "friendly" vs. "pretentious").

Tita's hale 'aina   20   15   19 $20
3870 17th St. (bet. Noe & Sanchez Sts.), 415-626-2477;
www.titashaleaina.com
Bored serfs "craving the look, sound and taste of Hawaii"
head to this "little slice of aloha" in the Castro that hosts
"broke-da-mouth plate lunches", weekend brunches and
"*ono*" dinners (including full-boar luaus once a month); just
"make sure you wear expandable pants" and be prepared
to hang loose because the staff operates on island time.

Tokyo Go Go   22   22   18 $32
3174 16th St. (bet. Guerrero & Valencia Sts.), 415-864-2288;
www.tokyogogo.com
"The trendoids" (and yet another chef) "have moved on", but
go-go-getters still talk up this "yuppie" Mission Japanese
as the place to go for "pretty darn good" maki and nigiri
("innovative" rolls), a "great sake selection" and a "cool"
pop-art interior; gregarious gourmands go go straight to
the sushi bar where the "chefs are fun and welcoming",
since the "staff isn't so much."

Tommaso's   25   15   19 $26
1042 Kearny St. (bet. Broadway St. & Pacific Ave.),
415-398-9696; www.tommasosnorthbeach.com
North Beach has clearly "evolved over the years" (witness
the nearby "topless bars") but *amici* are glad to report this

Neapolitan "red-sauce palace" hasn't; "owned by the same family" since 1935, it still serves the "traditional" Italian "family-style" "favorites" ("lasagna just like nonna's" and "heavenly" wood-fired pizza) in a basement "reeking of history", and the personnel "know how to make everyone feel at home" "even with tourists, screaming babies and lines out the door."

Tommy Toy's Cuisine Chinoise   24   23   23 $55

655 Montgomery St. (bet. Clay & Washington Sts.), 415-397-4888; www.tommytoys.com

"Worth the splurge" for an hour or two of "opulence and fawning", this Downtown "favorite" serves "exquisite Chinese feasts for the eyes and palate" in a "classy but dark" room "dripping with formality"; seen-it-alls shrug the "menu and presentation haven't changed" for years but return nevertheless for the "excellent value" of the midday prix fixe; P.S. "do not let the waiters order for you" – "the bill can be incredibly high."

TONGA ROOM   12   25   15 $36

Fairmont Hotel, 950 Mason St. (bet. California & Sacremento Sts.), 415-772-5278; www.fairmont.com

"The old tiki torch days" are still aflame at the Fairmont Hotel's "high altar of kitsch" atop Nob Hill, where the Pan-Asian nibbles delight "mostly tourists drinking overpriced piña coladas, eating mediocre egg rolls and having a great time doing it"; most agree that "the drinks are where it's at" and that for an island-inspired happy hour the indoor "tropical rainstorms are worth the price of admission", but the consensus is "don't bother" staying for dinner.

Ton Kiang   25   13   17 $27

5821 Geary Blvd. (bet. 22nd & 23rd Aves.), 415-387-8273; www.tonkiang.net

Dim sum devotees descend on this Outer Richmond Chinese renowned for its "unsurpassed variety" of "fabulous", "intensely flavored" yet "accessible" fare; "service is brisk" (even "borderline frantic" on weekends, lending the scene "an *Alice in Wonderland* feel"), and while some surveyors suspect "you're paying for the tablecloths", the "yuppie crowd seems to think it's worth the money and the wait"; N.B. the staff also hawks a heckuva good Hakka menu.

TOWN HALL   24   21   21 $47

342 Howard St. (Fremont St.), 415-908-3900; www.townhallsf.com

"SF meets New Orleans" at this "hot, happening" SoMa sophomore, the talk of the town owing to the Rosenthal brothers' "bold" "homestyle" New American fare and their "flexible" staff's ability to make diners "feel pampered, smart and connected"; like the food, the "upscale", brick-walled room is "luxuriant but simple", but the "party vibe" that some call a "nice buzz" seems as "relaxing as a post-game locker room" to others; P.S. spur-of-the-moment types appreciate the "community table for walk-ins."

Town's End Restaurant & Bakery   20 | 14 | 18 | $24
South Beach Marina Apts., 2 Townsend St. (The Embarcadero), 415-512-0749

Even more than its "view of the Bay", the "absolutely heavenly baked goods" draw hungry habitués to this New American "combo bakery and restaurant" for breakfast and brunch – especially the mini-muffins and scones served before the meal by an "indifferent" staff; afterwards you can "take a walk on the Embarcadero" to burn the calories; P.S. Tuesday's prix fixe dinner is an "excellent deal."

Trader Vic's   16 | 21 | 17 | $43
555 Golden Gate Ave. (Van Ness Ave.), 415-775-6300; www.tradervics.com

See review in East of San Francisco Directory.

Trattoria Contadina   23 | 16 | 20 | $33
1800 Mason St. (Union St.), 415-982-5728

"One of the best casual Italians in the city" rave regulars recalling the "divine", "delicious" dishes at this North Beach "local favorite" that isn't "flooded with tourists" despite a location near the cable car; "personable and professional" staffers "go out of their way to make you comfortable" in "cozy" (or "cramped") quarters, while "reasonable" tabs bespeak "great value" – consequently veterans advise "don't forget to make reservations."

Truly Mediterranean   22 | 6 | 14 | $10
3109 16th St. (Valencia St.), 415-252-7482; www.trulymed.com

Well "worth the garlic breath", these schwarmas and falafels "wrapped with precision" in "perfectly grilled lavosh" are "as close to truly Mediterranean food as you will find in the U.S." maintain Middle Eastern mavens who value this "reliable" cafeteria-style "hole-in-the-wall" in the Mission (the original, and last remaining, link of a onetime chainlet); given the sparse seating and "grim surroundings", though, "take it to go."

Tsunami Sushi & Sake Bar ◑ ☒   21 | 21 | 19 | $32
1306 Fulton St. (Divisadero St.), 415-567-7664; www.tsunami-sf.com

"So many fish, so little time" grin wave runners who relish the "trendy but tasty" Japanese fare (plus "California-ized sushi") and the "vast, educational selection of sakes" at this "hip, modern" eatery in a "gritty", "slowly gentrifying" section of the Western Addition; dinner here is "a little expensive for the neighborhood", though, and surveyors say servers can either be "willing to help" or "unaware you are there."

Tu Lan 🗷⇗   21 2 9 $13
8 Sixth St. (Market St.), 415-626-0927
Allegedly "Julia Child's favorite Vietnamese", this SoMa
spot serves "dirt cheap", "delicious eats" that "come
quick and in large quantities"; though the unimpressed
stress the decor's "nonexistent" and that both the staff
and the neighborhood are "darned unfriendly", "hard-core
foodies" shrug that's just "tu bad."

2223 Restaurant   21 19 20 $38
2223 Market St. (bet. Noe & Sanchez Sts.), 415-431-0692
"Still setting the standard in the Castro", this "reliable"
Californian–New American serves up "adroitly executed"
"comfort food" that's "rich but unpretentious, much like
the clientele", a "well-heeled and same-sexed" crowd
that also appreciates the "flirty waiters" and "excellent
martinis"; the "bustling" (read: "noisy") contemporary
room with its "changing art shows" is "hip enough for your
friends" yet "elegant enough for your parents."

Universal Cafe   23 18 19 $34
*2814 19th St. (bet. Bryant & Florida Sts.), 415-821-4608;
www.universalcafe.net*
Regulars report the "high-class", "inspired" seasonal
New American eats at this eternally "hopping" Mission
"institution" are universally admired; some surveyors are
"absolutely addicted to weekend brunches" alfresco
while others prefer downing dinners inside the "slightly
industrial" room that manages to be both "homey" and
"stylish"; note that servers may "befriend you instantly"
then leave you "waiting a long time for food and drink."

U Street Lounge   – – – M
*1980 Union St. (Buchanan St.), 415-409-0150;
www.ustreetlounge.com*
Destined to become a Cow Hollow fixture, this ambitious
newcomer offers the trendster trifecta: eclectic Cal-Med
nibbles from chef Michael Schley (formerly of PlumpJack
and the French Laundry), a lounge where DJs spin down-
tempo beats and bartenders pour specialty cocktails, and
weekend brunch – all of which can be enjoyed quasi-
alfresco, thanks to a retractable, vaulted glass ceiling.

Venticello   23 22 20 $42
*1257 Taylor St. (Washington St.), 415-922-2545;
www.venticello.com*
Amici advise take a "date you want to impress" to this
"charming" "slice of Tuscany" atop Nob Hill where the
"fulfilling" Northern Italian dishes "never disappoint", the
"cozy and intimate" atmosphere "radiates warmth" and
staffers "go out of their way to make your meal special";
critics call it "cramped" and a bit "pricey for pasta" but
everybody appreciates easy access via cable car.

Vivande Porta Via　　　22 | 14 | 18 | $34
2125 Fillmore St. (bet. California & Sacramento Sts.),
415-346-4430; www.vivande.com
"Cleverly disguised as a deli", Carlo Middione's Pac Heights
prepared-foods purveyor is also a "fine trattoria" serving
"savory Italian cuisine" (much of it "handmade on the
premises") with a "helpful", "homey" attitude; the "casual"
space attracts locals "more concerned with the palate
than the decor" who are willing to tolerate the "spartan
room with ache-inducing chairs" or try out the recently
installed wine bar.

Walzwerk ⌀　　　20 | 16 | 19 | $25
381 S. Van Ness Ave. (bet. 14th & 15th Sts.), 415-551-7181;
www.walzwerk.com
Perhaps "defying common sense", this East German *haus*
in the Mission dishes out "authentic", "tasty (and heavy)"
Mittel-Europa "vittles" and "amazing beer" from behind
the erstwhile Iron Curtain amid "quirky", "kitschy" pre-
unification decor that "will have you waxing nostalgic about
class warfare" – but it "werks every time."

Washington Square Bar & Grill　　　18 | 19 | 19 | $38
1707 Powell St. (bet. Columbus & Union Sts.),
415-982-8123
You get a "wonderful warm feeling" at this "jovial" Italian-
influenced New American in North Beach, thanks to
"reliable" "classic dishes" ("great burgers" plus "more
creative offerings") presented by servers who manage to
be "attentive without overdoing it"; still, surveyors who ate
at an earlier incarnation debate whether it's "great to have
the old standby back" or "the Washbag is washed up."

Watercress　　　20 | 15 | 18 | $31
(fka Watergate)
1152 Valencia St. (bet. 22nd & 23rd Sts.), 415-648-6000
Though management and chef have changed, Missionites
maintain this Californian-French remains a "solid choice"
for "homey" prix fixe three-course dinners that deliver
"high quality for little money"; servers are sometimes said
to be "caring", sometimes "sassy", but there's across-the-
board agreement that the recent makeover definitely
diminished the decor ("bland", "antiseptic", "strangely
stuffy and old-ladyish").

Waterfront Restaurant & Cafe　　　17 | 21 | 18 | $43
Pier 7, The Embarcadero (Broadway St.), 415-391-2696;
www.waterfrontsf.com
Given its name, nautical decor, "serene" Embarcadero
location and "spectacular" Bay vistas, "naturally" this
four-decade-old "institution" specializes in "varied, fresh"
seafood, though it also offers a smattering of "tasty" land-
based Cal cuisine; old salts suggest you "ask to be seated

out on the patio", "drink some wine and savor the view" – "after a while you don't care" about the "shaky service" or "forgettable" fare.

Watergate 21 | 19 | 20 | $46

1177 California St. (bet. Jones & Taylor Sts.),
415-474-2000
Nobody's nixin' the "bargain" $35 prix fixe dinners at this French-Asian that's breaking in its "large" new location atop Nob Hill; indeed, with "incredible sauces" and a few "delightful indulgences" the "quality food" "does not disappoint", and neither does the "friendly staff"; still, some wish the menu "could be changed to keep it fresh" and opponents censure the "weird" room's "stuffy", "no-pulse" feel.

Winterland ☒ – | – | – | E

2101 Sutter St. (Steiner St.), 415-563-5025
Decades ago this Japantown space was a concert venue for the likes of the Dead and Janis Joplin, but since its recent conversion into a snazzy, thoroughly modern dining destination for local swells, the performer everyone's cheering for is chef Vernon Morales (formerly of New York City's Daniel), who orchestrates an "eclectic" El Bulli-esque seasonal New American menu; late-nighters can snack on hearty, "reasonably priced" bistro nibbles in the stylish lounge with its low-slung sofas and louvered, peek-a-boo partitions.

Woodward's Garden ☒ ▽ 25 | 17 | 21 | $44

1700 Mission St. (Duboce St.), 415-621-7122;
www.woodwardsgarden.com
An "excellent restaurant in a terrible neighborhood" ("hidden" beneath the freeway overpass construction), this "under-the-radar" Missionite staffed by "hardworking people" has been serving "tremendously creative" New American cookery since 1992; constituents call it a "quiet", "unpretentious" place for a "romantic splurge", though most maintain the "cozy" 45-seat dining room – which can get "crowded" and "uncomfortable" – could stand a "makeover"; N.B. despite the name, there's no garden.

XYZ 20 | 21 | 18 | $45

W Hotel, 181 Third St. (Howard St.), 415-817-7836;
www.xyz-sf.com
New American fare "with flair" and a 600-label cellar have made this "hot spot" at SoMa's W Hotel a "solid business-lunch place", but respondents report it's also "date"-worthy thanks to an upstairs lounge with weekend DJs and dancing; service is just "ok", however, and the decor is not for everyone (some find it "cool", others "cold") – if you "go for the scene" and the "sophisticated young crowd", be sure to "wear black and bring money."

Yabbies Coastal Kitchen   23 19 21 $38
2237 Polk St. (bet. Green & Vallejo Sts.), 415-474-4088;
www.yabbiesrestaurant.com
Seekers of "outstanding" seafood "get out of Downtown"
and head toward Russian Hill for a bite at this "bustling"
"neighborhood treasure" that's "perfect for a date"; the
"upscale nets 'n' floats decor", "low-key" yet "attentive"
service and award-winning wine list have diners repeatedly
returning to "eat with the fishes."

YANK SING   25 16 18 $32
Rincon Ctr., 101 Spear St. (bet. Howard & Mission Sts.),
415-957-9300
49 Stevenson St. (bet. 1st & 2nd Sts.), 415-541-4949
www.yanksing.com
For "sum handsum dim sum" "and then some" surveyors
sing the praises of this "high-end" Downtown duo where
"efficient" staffers serve from "roving" carts brimming with
"amazing", "addictive" (if "Americanized") Chinese "finger
food"; be sure to "pace yourself or you're going to roll out
of the restaurant" and your tab "will grow faster than China's
population"; P.S. both branches take reservations, while
the Rincon Annex "has parking" too.

YaYa   - - - I
2424 Van Ness Ave. (bet. Green & Union Sts.), 415-440-0455;
www.yayacuisine.com
Foodies craving Mesopotamian flavors can get their yayas
out at this 60-seater in Cow Hollow; most of chef-owner
Yahya Salih's dishes deploy Middle Eastern ingredients in
eye-opening combinations (e.g. ravioli stuffed with dates,
cardamom and cinnamon in a yogurt-walnut sauce), while
the interior is adorned with large murals of Babylonian
landscapes; a few Moroccan and Lebanese bottles dot the
wine list, but overall its contents are NorCal locals.

Yuet Lee ●⋈   20 5 11 $18
1300 Stockton St. (Broadway St.), 415-982-6020
"Swimming in a tank one minute, steaming on your plate"
the next, the "excellent" fish at this Chinatown Cantonese
"redefines fresh" ("exquisite salt-and-pepper squid") –
plus it's "cheap, cheap, cheap"; "fast service" and late
hours ("until 3 AM!") also make this veteran a "perfect"
stop "after clubbing", notwithstanding the "zero-decor",
off-puttingly "Day-Glo" digs.

Yumma's   ▽ 21 9 17 $11
721 Irving St. (bet. 8th & 9th Aves.), 415-682-0762
"Yumma is right" yell those who yearn for the "authentic
Middle Eastern" grub ("superb falafel") served at this Inner
Sunset "neon-and-Formica" "mom-and-pop place" where
the "service couldn't be nicer"; regulars recommend you
go "when you crave" an "inexpensive", "quick" lunch "by

yourself", as seating is limited to "the counter in the window" or on the "sweet backyard garden patio."

Zante Pizza & Indian Cuisine   18 5 10 $15

3489 Mission St. (Cortland St.), 415-821-3949; www.zantespizza.com
Earning an "A+ for cultural cross-pollination", this Bernal Heights Indian "puts zing in the ubiquitous pizza pie" by making it from "naan crusts and spicy toppings" ("don't be scared" – "cauliflower is delicious"); staffers aren't terribly "warm", though, and the "never-fancy" interiors have "gotten shabbier" so consider "ordering for delivery."

Zao Noodle Bar   14 12 13 $16

2406 California St. (Fillmore St.), 415-345-8088; www.zao.com
Zao hounds appreciate the "simple, tasty" noodles on offer at this "easy-on-the-pocketbook" Upper Fillmore Pan-Asian, a handy spot for "solo eaters" to grab a "lightning-fast" lunch ("just step up to the counter and start slurping"); however, critics call it "cold and corporate" and bash its "big bland bowls"; N.B. Palo Alto and Emeryville have branches as well.

Zarzuela ⊠   22 17 20 $33

2000 Hyde St. (Union St.), 415-346-0800
"Everyone seems to be having fun" at this "lively and crowded" "little piece of Spain in Russian Hill" where "some of the nicest waiters in the city" serve "excellent" sangria and "wonderfully authentic" tapas; as a result surveyors say it's a "sexy date spot" ("refreshingly hipster-free"), and although the "homey", rustic space "can be noisy" it's "charming" to take in the "lovely view of the Hyde Street cable car from the front room."

Zazie   21 17 18 $23

941 Cole St. (bet. Carl St. & Parnassus Ave.), 415-564-5332
"Unpretentious" and "reasonably priced", this "reliable" French bistro with a "kind staff" is "usually bursting at the seams on Sunday morning", when Cole Valleyites line up for its "lovely brunch"; regulars report that on sunny afternoons the "beautiful secret garden" "can't be beat", and at dinnertime the "cozy atmosphere" and "creative food pairings" are a "charming" combo.

ZUNI CAFÉ ●   24 20 20 $43

1658 Market St. (bet. Franklin & Gough Sts.), 415-552-2522
"One restaurant where you actually should get the chicken", Judy Rodgers' Hayes Valley Mediterranean is a "miracle of consistency" where "straightforward" ingredients are "prepared brilliantly without extravagance"; what's more, the "buzzing bar" in this "chic" yet "comfortable" "fishbowl" is HQ for SF "movers and shakers" ("the way everyone checks one another out, I thought it was a gay bar"), so

though critics complain service is "abrupt" and "smug", devotees doggedly defend this "venerable" venue.

Zuppa
564 Fourth St. (Bryant St.), 415-777-5900

Globe owners Joseph and Mary Manzare point their compass toward Southern Italy at their newest trattoria, where rustic wood-fired pizzas, pastas and salumi are served in a strikingly modern industrial space with high ceilings, concrete walls and exposed beams; the main downstairs area, which features a row of counter seats overlooking an open kitchen and a community table seating 18, is sure to rollick with a high-voltage SoMa vibe, while upstairs, semi-private nooks offer more subdued settings.

Zushi Puzzle ∇ 27 11 21 $35
1910 Lombard St. (Buchanan St.), 415-931-9319;
www.zushipuzzle.com

"Why is" this "low-key" Marina Japanese "never packed"? puzzle zushi lovers who conclude it's because this spot's still a "secret" – though "not for long", since the "original rolls" are "as inventive and exciting as their funky names", the "impeccably fresh" "sashimi is some of the city's best" and yet "prices aren't too high"; veterans vow that if you "sit at the minuscule bar" and "get to know Roger", the "owner/sushi chef", he'll "make you feel like a star."

East of San Francisco

Top Ratings East of SF

Excluding places with low voting, unless indicated by a ▽.

Top Food

28 Erna's Elderberry Hse.
27 Chez Panisse Café
   Rivoli
   Chez Panisse
26 Lalime's
   Pearl Oyster Bar
25 Bay Wolf
   Kirala
   Zachary's Pizza
   Cafe Esin

   Oliveto
   Dopo
   Citron
24 Wente Vineyards
   Bo's Barbecue
   À Côté
   Tratt. La Siciliana
   O Chamé
   PlumpJack Cafe
   Va de Vi

By Cuisine

American
23 Bendean
22 Lark Creek
   Rick & Ann's
   Bette's Oceanview
21 Blackberry Bistro

Californian
28 Erna's Elderberry Hse.
27 Chez Panisse Café
   Chez Panisse
24 Wente Vineyards
23 Zax Tavern

Chinese
24 Great China
21 Restaurant Peony
   Shen Hua
17 Taiwan
   Jade Villa

French
25 Citron
24 À Côté
   Soizic
23 Jojo
   La Rose Bistro▽

Indian
24 Vik's Chaat Corner
23 Ajanta
   Shalimar
   Pakwan
22 Breads of India

Italian
25 Oliveto
   Dopo
24 Tratt. La Siciliana
   Prima
21 Pizza Antica

Japanese
25 Kirala
24 O Chamé
   Uzen
22 Grasshopper
19 Yoshi's

Mediterranean
27 Chez Panisse Café
   Rivoli
   Chez Panisse
26 Lalime's
25 Bay Wolf

Mexican/Pan-Latin
23 Fonda Solana
   Doña Tomás
21 Cactus Taqueria
   Picante Cocina
   Tacubaya

Southeast Asian
24 Soi Four
23 Three Seasons
22 Battambang
   Le Cheval
21 Nan Yang

By Special Feature

Breakfast/Brunch
25 Oliveto
24 Wente Vineyards
23 Café Fanny
22 La Note
    Rick & Ann's

Late Night
23 Fonda Solana
22 Koryo BBQ
20 Everett & Jones BBQ
18 Caspers Hot Dogs
17 Taiwan

Newcomers (Rated/Unrated)
23 Zatar▽
    Bendean
21 Bing Crosby's
– Adagia
– Olivia

Outdoor Seating
25 Bay Wolf
24 Wente Vineyards
    À Côté
22 La Note
20 Café Rouge

People-Watching
27 Chez Panisse Café
24 À Côté
23 César
22 Grasshopper
21 downtown

Romance
28 Erna's Elderberry Hse.
27 Chez Panisse
26 Lalime's
25 Citron
24 Wente Vineyards

Small Plates
26 Pearl Oyster Bar
24 À Côté
    Va de Vi
    Soi Four
23 Fonda Solana

Winning Wine Lists
28 Erna's Elderberry Hse.
27 Chez Panisse Café
    Chez Panisse
23 César
21 downtown

By Location

Berkeley
27 Chez Panisse Café
    Rivoli
    Chez Panisse
26 Lalime's
25 Kirala

Oakland
26 Pearl Oyster Bar
25 Bay Wolf
    Zachary's Pizza
    Oliveto
    Dopo

Top Decor

28 Ahwahnee Din. Rm.	Chez Panisse Café
27 Erna's Elderberry Hse.	**22** Blackhawk Grille
26 Wente Vineyards	Oliveto
25 Bing Crosby's	Bay Wolf
24 Postino	Zax Tavern
Pearl Oyster Bar	Prima
23 Chez Panisse	**21** Garibaldis
Bridges	Va de Vi
O Chamé	PlumpJack Cafe
Rivoli	Venezia

Top Service

28 Erna's Elderberry Hse.	Zax Tavern
26 Chez Panisse	Bridges
25 Rivoli	Soizic
Chez Panisse Café	Mezze
24 Wente Vineyards	Oliveto
Bay Wolf	**21** Prima
Lalime's	Cafe Esin
23 PlumpJack Cafe	Lark Creek
22 Jojo	Pearl Oyster Bar
Citron	Postino

Top Bangs for the Buck

1. Caspers Hot Dogs	11. Juan's Place
2. Cactus Taqueria	12. Barney's
3. Picante Cocina	13. Zachary's Pizza
4. Vik's Chaat Corner	14. Pakwan
5. Tacubaya	15. Udupi Palace
6. Fenton's Creamery	16. FatApple's
7. Asqew Grill	17. Naan 'n Curry
8. Bette's Oceanview	18. Jimmy Bean's
9. Mama's Royal Cafe	19. Rick & Ann's
10. Café Fanny	20. Blue Nile

Other Good Values

Battambang	La Méditerranée
Bendean	Lo Coco's
Bo's Barbecue	Mezze
Breads of India	Nan Yang
Cafe Esin	Pearl Oyster Bar
César	Pizza Antica
Chow	Shalimar
Dopo	Soi Four
Great China	Tratt. La Siciliana
Koryo BBQ	Uzen

East of San Francisco

	F	D	S	C

À CÔTÉ | 24 | 21 | 20 | $36 |

5478 College Ave. (Taft St.), Oakland, 510-655-6469;
www.citron-acote.com

"Swishy cocktails", "primo vinos" (40 by the glass) and
"imaginative", "fabulously shareable" French-Med tapas
help make this Rockridge "neighborhood favorite" "one of
the best scenes in Oakland"; the "sophisticated", dim den
draws "elbow-bumping" crowds despite its drawbacks
(the "soulful small plates" can be "pricey", the room
"noisy" and parking "tough") because the "terrific frites",
"efficient", "friendly" service and "lovely" garden patio
"haven't lost any of their charm"; N.B. no reservations.

Adagia Restaurant | – | – | – | M |

Westminster House, 2700 Bancroft Way (College Ave.),
Berkeley, 510-647-2300

Chef Lawrence Jossel (ex Chez Nous) is big man on campus
now that he's heading up the kitchen at UC Berkeley's
historic Westminster House; although it serves three
meals a day to students, profs and the non-matriculated
public, the handsome dining room will never be mistaken
for a mess hall thanks to smart Californian cookery (grilled
romaine salad, steak bordelaise) and well-studied service.

AHWAHNEE DINING ROOM, THE | 19 | 28 | 20 | $48 |

Ahwahnee Hotel, 1 Ahwahnee Rd., Yosemite National Park,
209-372-1489; www.yosemitepark.com

"Don't even think about" coming to Yosemite without visiting
this "pioneering" hostelry insist "city slickers" who "wind
down after hiking" in the "breathtaking" dining room
overlooking "towering granite walls and waterfalls"; true,
the "imaginative but under-realized" Cal-American fare
delivered by youngsters "trying to find themselves" pales by
comparison to the "awe-inspiring surroundings", but it's
still "better than you could expect in the woods"; P.S. "lunch
may be best" – after all "the view's the thing."

Ajanta | 23 | 19 | 20 | $25 |

1888 Solano Ave. (bet. The Alameda & Colusa Ave.),
Berkeley, 510-526-4373; www.ajantarestaurant.com

"East Bayers know" that amid Berkeley's "glutted market"
of "McIndian food" this "classy sit-down" establishment
is the "real deal"; "you feel like a rajah" thanks to "savory,
succulent" and "constantly changing" "regional" menus
that showcase "fresh ingredients" "prepared with care",
"free-range meats" and even "terrific Indian wines"; a

recent renovation has deep-sixed the racy murals from the Ajanta caves, but respondents report the "modern decor remains fetching" and the service is as "attentive" as ever.

Albany Bistro   ▽ 18 | 15 | 19 | $31

1403 Solano Ave. (Carmel Ave.), Albany, 510-528-1237; www.albanybistro.com

Although this Albany address looks like your "run-of-the-mill hip bistro", the "eccentric" Eclectic East-West cuisine is anything but basic; surveyors are sharply divided, as those who "never leave this Bay Area burb" praise "good food" and "friendly service" while others "who get out more often" dis "overdescribed dishes" that "aren't quite on the mark."

Asqew Grill   19 | 12 | 14 | $13

Bay Street Mall, 5614 Bay St. (Shellmound St.), Emeryville, 510-595-7471; www.asqewgrill.com

See review in City of San Francisco Directory.

Balboa Cafe   18 | 18 | 18 | $31

1995 Squaw Valley Rd. (Squaw Peak Rd.), Olympic Valley, 530-583-5850; www.plumpjack.com

See review in City of San Francisco Directory.

Barney's Gourmet Hamburgers ⊅   19 | 12 | 14 | $14

1600 Shattuck Ave. (Cedar St.), Berkeley, 510-849-2827
1591 Solano Ave. (Ordway St.), Berkeley, 510-526-8185
5819 College Ave. (Chabot Rd.), Oakland, 510-601-0444
4162 Piedmont Ave. (Linda Ave.), Oakland, 510-655-7180
www.barneyshamburgers.com

See review in City of San Francisco Directory.

Battambang ⊠   22 | 12 | 18 | $21

850 Broadway (9th St.), Oakland, 510-839-8815

The "amazing flavors", "complex, multilayered sauces" and "unexpected surprises (pineapples in my special rice!)" at this "nondescript" Oakland Chinatown "perennial" have habitués wondering "why Cambodian is not already the next Thai"; in the meantime, the "gracious" staff is "patient with novices", and the "diverse" and "unusual" menu keeps this "favorite" "pleasantly distinct among the East Bay's many Asian budget restaurants."

BAY WOLF   25 | 22 | 24 | $46

3853 Piedmont Ave. (Rio Vista Ave.), Oakland, 510-655-6004; www.baywolf.com

Set in an "old Victorian home with a warm atmosphere" and heated veranda, this Oakland Cal-Med "pioneer" overseen by a "solicitous, gracious" staff just "gets better with age, like a fine California Cabernet" (e.g. those in its "impressive wine inventory"); meanwhile, the chefs can make the house-specialty duck "do everything but sit up and beg" – all of which makes this "class act" a "neighborhood restaurant and genuine destination all in one"; N.B. beer and wine only.

Bendean   23 | 16 | 19 | $35 |
1647 Solano Ave. (Ventura St.), Berkeley, 510-526-3700
For "idealized versions of international comfort foods"
delivered "without pretension", no one can bend it like the
"brilliant" Berkeley chef behind this "noisy but festive"
New American newcomer; some gripe the "harsh industrial"
interiors "seem out of place on cozy Solano Avenue" and the
"cheerful" staff is "still working the kinks out", but early
adopters aver it's a "welcome addition to the neighborhood";
P.S. don't miss the "incredible" $13 prix fixe offered 5–6 PM.

Bette's Oceanview Diner   22 | 16 | 18 | $17 |
1807 Fourth St. (Hearst St.), Berkeley, 510-644-3230
"You can't see the ocean, or even the Bay" from here, but
you bette you "can sure smell" "breakfast perfected" at
this "bustling" "faux-'50s" eatery, the "Berkeley brunch
standard" thanks to "creative, tasty" American "diner food
without the grease"; curmudgeons "could choke on the
nostalgia" and expire from the "obligatory wait" but the
faithful "kill time" shopping or get takeout from the "deli/
bakery/cafe next door"; N.B. breakfast and lunch only.

BING CROSBY'S   21 | 25 | 19 | $45 |
1342 Broadway Plaza (Main St.), Walnut Creek, 925-939-2464;
www.bingcrosbysrestaurant.com
Bing-abilia abounds at this "lavish, large" Crosby-themed
establishment that's "loaded with noise and nostalgia"; from
its "country-club-attire requirement" and "jazzy" piano
bar to its "serviceable" throwback American menu and
specialty martinis, it "feels like an old-time NYC restaurant";
ok, "it's expensive and phony" and "service has a long way
to go" but it's nevertheless become the "new hangout" for
a Walnut Creek crowd aged "21 to 81."

Bistro Liaison   21 | 20 | 20 | $34 |
1849 Shattuck Ave. (Hearst Ave.), Berkeley, 510-849-2155;
www.liaisonbistro.com
"Well-prepared classics" and authentic *vin pays* "at *plat
du jour* prices" "bring Paris within your reach" at this
"attractive" French bistro in Berkeley where you can eat
alfresco "under an umbrella" and choose dessert from a
list "rubber-stamped" on the paper tablecloth; thanks to a
"cheerful" staff that's "sensitive to timing needs" diners
deem this place "ideal for a romantic rendezvous" at midday
or a "pre-theater dinner" but deplore how "noisy" and
"cramped" the room gets "when full."

Blackberry Bistro   21 | 15 | 15 | $19 |
4240 Park Blvd. (Wellington St.), Oakland, 510-336-1088;
www.blackberrybistro.com
This colorful, "sunny" sidewalk cafe in Oakland serves some
of the "best breakfasts in the East Bay" plus "wonderfully
fresh" and "interesting" American brunches and lunches;

"problem is, everyone knows" about it so unless you "get there before the yuppies with their BlackBerries" "the wait can be long", and once you sit down servers' timing can be "terrible – you'll get your drinks as you take your last bite."

Blackhawk Grille   20   22   20 $43

The Shops at Blackhawk, 3540 Blackhawk Plaza Circle (Camino Tassajara), Danville, 925-736-4295; www.blackhawkgrille.com

"Whether you shop or not" at the surrounding plaza, this "upscale" Danville destination is "worth a stop" say surveyors who savor its "seasonal, fresh" and "delicious" Cal cuisine on the waterside patio "under the stars"; regulars report the "secluded" location, "plush fabrics" and 400-label cellar lend the place a "romantic" vibe, but cynics criticize "outdated" decor and "pricey", "pedestrian" fare, and crack "don't forget to dress up or you'll find yourself parking cars."

Blue Nile   18   16   16 $19

2525 Telegraph Ave. (Dwight Way), Berkeley, 510-540-6777

A onetime "standard-bearer for Horn-of-Africa restaurants" in Berkeley, this "quiet, calm" and "earthy" Ethiopian remains a "favorite of UC students" who mead and greet over "homemade honey wine" and "flavorful", "thick" stews; a few are blue over the "low-rent" bamboo-and-beads interior and prices that "keep creeping up", but others insist this is "still the best ambiance" you can get "on a budget."

Bo's Barbecue ⊠∌   24   11   17 $19

3422 Mt. Diablo Blvd. (Brown Ave.), Lafayette, 925-283-7133

'Cue lovers (from "Lafayette soccer moms and dads" to fanatics "from parts East making the trek") queue up at this smoke shack for "fantastic ribs" and "expertly cooked" Texas-style brisket akin to "what they must serve in heaven"; it comes with a "nice mesclun salad", an "amazing wine selection" and "a hug" from the "ultimate gentleman host/chef"; P.S. "thanks to the recent expansion, you might even be able to find a place to sit."

Breads of India &   22   10   14 $19
Gourmet Curries ∌

1358 N. Main St. (Cypress St.), Walnut Creek, 925-256-7684
2448 Sacramento St. (Dwight Way), Berkeley, 510-848-7684

The long line "tells the story" about this BYO Berkeley curry courier (and its unrated Walnut Creek sibling), home of naan-pareil namesake breads and "delectable" organic entrees, all of which "change nightly"; turnoffs include "sassy-bordering-on-rude" service and "cramped" surroundings ("feels like you're sitting in a janitor's closet"), but hey, you can "eat like a king at paupers' prices"; P.S. "be friendly – the chances of sharing a table with strangers are high."

Bridges Restaurant   23 | 23 | 22 | $48

44 Church St. (Hartz Ave.), Danville, 925-820-7200;
www.bridgesrestaurant-bar.com

Perhaps "most notable for being featured in *Mrs. Doubtfire*"
this "elegant" Danville destination is also known for its
scenic "deck with the golf course and rolling hills in
the background" – but a remake by the new owner and
returning-alum chef (as of late 2004) aim to make the "lively"
Cal-Asian fusion fare the star of this show; now if only
management could render the servers less "snippy" and
the bill "less of a strain on your wallet."

Bucci's ⌦   20 | 18 | 19 | $29

6121 Hollis St. (bet. 59th & 61st Sts.), Emeryville, 510-547-4725;
www.buccis.com

"Mama Bucci is a gem" and so is her "little oasis" in "dot-
com Emeryville"; "convenient to shopping" and offices, the
"roomy", "arty" space and its "pleasant patio" draw nine-
to-fivers for "fantastic" breakfast pastries and espresso or
"creative" Cal-Med lunches and dinners ("delicious thin-
crust pizzas") while also presenting food for thought via
"pithy sayings" written on the wall-mounted chalkboards.

Cactus Taqueria   21 | 12 | 14 | $11

1881 Solano Ave. (The Alameda), Berkeley,
510-528-1881
5642 College Ave. (Keith Ave.), Oakland, 510-658-6180

Although these crowded, contemporary, "chaotic" Mexican
"muncherias" in Berkeley and Oakland "function like fast-
food joints" ("friendly cashiers keep the lines moving"),
the "updated" *comida* is "far better" thanks to hormone-
free meat and chicken and "high-quality" ingredients in
everything ("awesome crispy tacos", "top-notch" burritos);
hence it's a "highly recommended" and "inexpensive
haven" for "struggling students", "middle-class families"
and BART-bound commuters.

Cafe Cacao   20 | 18 | 16 | $25

Scharffen Berger Chocolate Maker Factory, 914 Heinz Ave.
(7th St.), Berkeley, 510-843-6000; www.cafecacao.biz

This cocoa bean–themed Berkeley cafe is a predictably
"popular place to take the kids" after "touring the Scharffen
Berger factory", but even "adults embarrass themselves"
when they get a whiff of the "ambrosial" scent from the
"inventive" American–New French savories ("fun chocolate
pasta") and, of course, "sublime desserts"; critics aren't so
sweet on the "disorganized" service or "industrial" digs.

Cafe Esin ⌦   25 | 17 | 21 | $39

2416 San Ramon Valley Blvd. (Crow Canyon Rd.), San Ramon,
925-314-0974; www.cafeesin.com

A "hidden treasure" in a "sea of chain restaurants", this
"pearl of the San Ramon Valley" shines thanks to "flavorful"

"new takes" on Med–New American "standards" and "world-class desserts" brought to table by an "attentive" and "unpretentious" staff; "the ambiance, what there is, could use some improvement" but it's a "small price to pay" for the "this-is-my-one-night-out-away-from-the-kids-and-I'm-going-to-make-the-most-of-it" crowd craving "fine dining" without having to "head into the city."

Café Fanny   23 | 12 | 15 | $16

1603 San Pablo Ave. (Cedar St.), Berkeley, 510-524-5447
"Its reputation is so large" but the "space is tiny" at this "quirky yet quintessential" Berkeleyite named after owner Alice Waters' daughter, where "sociable" (if sometimes "distracted") counter servers proffer petite portions of "f-ing fantastic", "aromatic coffee" and "exquisite" French sandwiches ("organic, of course"); "you'd think people wouldn't fight" so "Berserkley" to "eat in a parking lot" – let alone pay "sucker" prices – "but you'd be wrong"; N.B. no dinner.

Café Rouge   20 | 18 | 18 | $35

Market Plaza, 1782 Fourth St. (bet. Hearst Ave. & Virginia St.), Berkeley, 510-525-1440; www.caferouge.net
"One part butcher plus one part restaurant plus one part bar equals happy Atkins-ites" calculate carnivores while considering this "high-ceilinged", "companionable" "temple to red meat in Berkeley" ("it must be on the endangered species list"); also known for its charcuterie and "flavorful" French-Med menu, it's "one of the few" dinner options "in the heart of Fourth Street" – which compensates for "hoity-toity" service, "minuscule" servings and prices that have some seeing *rouge*.

Caffé Verbena   17 | 18 | 18 | $32
(fka Verbena)

Walter Shorenstein Bldg., 1111 Broadway (bet. 11th & 12th Sts.), Oakland, 510-465-9300; www.caffeverbena.com
With its "pricey", "adroitly prepared" Cal-Italian offerings and "elegant surroundings", this "upscale" "bottom-dweller in a high-rise tower" in Downtown Oakland is a real "treat" for the neighborhood; it's "been through more changes than Cher" yet remains a "power-lunch paradise" for the "office set" and a "sophisticated setting" for "happy hour"; still, "uneven" food and service leave it "struggling to find its niche" in the evenings.

Casa Orinda   17 | 17 | 17 | $31

20 Bryant Way (Moraga Way), Orinda, 925-254-2981
Although respondents reckon its "authentic 1950s Western" decor "hasn't changed since your grandparents were pulling up in their '36 Packard", this "retro" "home on the range" in Orinda may well serve "the best fried chicken in the world"; otherwise, they caution, the "consistent"

"Middle American" fare is merely middling, while service moves "slower than the honey on those biscuits."

Caspers Hot Dogs ⊄ | 18 | 7 | 16 | $7 |

545 San Pablo Ave. (bet. Brighton Ave. & Garfield St.), Albany, 510-527-6611
5440 Telegraph Ave. (55th St.), Albany, 510-652-1668
6998 Village Pkwy. (Dublin Blvd.), Dublin, 925-828-2224
951 C St. (bet. Main St. & Mission Blvd.), Hayward, 510-537-7300
21670 Foothill Blvd. (bet. Cotter Way & Kimball Ave.), Hayward, 510-581-9064 ●
6 Vivian Dr. (Contra Costa Blvd.), Pleasant Hill, 925-687-6030
2530 Macdonald Ave. (Civic Center St.), Richmond, 510-235-6492
1280A Newell Hill Pl. (San Miguel Dr.), Walnut Creek, 925-930-9154

"Fans of the cheese dog since grade school" avow that "if you haven't tried" the "legendary" franks at this "living-museum" East Bay chain "you should be investigated by HUAC for being un-American"; it's "nothing fancy" – the "kitschy decor" and "sassy waitresses' uniforms" "haven't changed since it opened" circa 1934 – so "don't expect anything" beyond a "snappy casing and lots of condiments" at "retro" prices ("comes complete with a spork").

César | 23 | 21 | 19 | $30 |

1515 Shattuck Ave. (bet. Cedar & Vine Sts.), Berkeley, 510-883-0222; www.barcesar.com

"Leading the East Bay tapas revolution" since 1998, this "hip (not hippie)", "happening" Berkeley bar and restaurant – crammed with tiny tables and a "convivial" communal table – "overflows" well into the night with who's-who crowds snacking on "thoughtfully constructed", "vivid" Iberian small plates and "drinking well-paired wines" (600 labels) or examples of "exotic" "mixology"; on the downside, there are always "long lines on the weekends" and you're apt to "run up a bill faster than on a Tokyo cab ride."

Cha Am Thai | 20 | 14 | 17 | $19 |

1543 Shattuck Ave. (Cedar St.), Berkeley, 510-848-9664
See review in City of San Francisco Directory.

CHEZ PANISSE ⊠ | 27 | 23 | 26 | $75 |

1517 Shattuck Ave. (bet. Cedar & Vine Sts.), Berkeley, 510-548-5525; www.chezpanisse.com

Alice Waters' "celebrated" "cathedral to organic", "just-off-the-tree" "pristine" Californian ingredients still draws devout "pilgrims" who peer into the open kitchen as if "watching the bishop give communion"; the "Draconian this-is-what-you'll-have" preset Med menu "leaves little to choice but much to savor" in the "gorgeous" Berkeley bungalow, so while heretics grumble "nothing much has changed" true believers counter "nothing much changes in the Sistine Chapel either."

CHEZ PANISSE CAFÉ ⊠   27 | 23 | 25 | $45 |

1517 Shattuck Ave. (bet. Cedar & Vine Sts.), Berkeley,
510-548-5049; www.chezpanisse.com

"Alice Waters for the rest of us", this "relaxed" "Arts and
Crafts" "attic hidden above Chez Panisse" presents "locally
grown", "simple" Cal-Med creations (with a dose of "moral
superiority") "as scrumptious" as the mother ship's – "only
cheaper" and offered à la carte – presented by a "knowing"
yet "authentically friendly" staff; long-in-the-tooth longhairs
muse it's "a lot like downstairs before the place became
a mecca", and what's more this is one "major treat" that
"even a graduate student can afford every now and then."

CHOW/PARK CHOW   19 | 15 | 17 | $21 |

La Fiesta Sq., 53 Lafayette Circle (Mt. Diablo Blvd.),
Lafayette, 925-962-2469

See review in City of San Francisco Directory.

Citron   25 | 21 | 22 | $46 |

5484 College Ave. (bet. Lawton & Taft Aves.), Oakland,
510-653-5484; www.citronrestaurant.biz

Known for its seasonally changing Cal–New French cuisine
"without the arrogant sneer" or the "SF premium", this petite
Rockridge "crown jewel of East Bay dining" is considered
a "matchbox Chez Panisse"; "don't come if you're in a hurry"
because it's the kind of "place to discuss the excellent
wine list at length" with the "knowledgeable staff" as you
"linger" over each "toothsome" course, preferably on
the "terrific" back patio where there's more elbow room;
N.B. lunch Tuesday–Saturday.

Doña Tomás ⊠   23 | 19 | 18 | $29 |

5004 Telegraph Ave. (bet. 49th & 51st Sts.), Oakland,
510-450-0522

"Strong" "suck-'em-down" margaritas are the *specialité
de la maison*" at this "spirited" cantina in Oakland that "also
gets points" for "elevating Mexican food to an artistic level"
using "top-notch local ingredients" ("I cry by my third bite
of the carnitas plate"); unfortunately, the "service suffers"
and "acoustics stink" when you get "smothered by the
yuppies" in the "crowded", rustic dining room and patio,
and the food's "not cheap" – "but it's worth it" to take a
"two-hour culinary vacation."

Dopo ⊠   25 | 15 | 20 | $28 |

4293 Piedmont Ave. (Echo St.), Oakland, 510-652-3676

"No longer" Oakland's "best-kept secret", this "cheerful",
"shoebox"-sized "neighborhood trattoria" lures "hordes"
with its "short but sweet menu" of "affordable", "dare I say
'dope'" "thin-crust pizzas" and "outstanding homemade
pastas"; "watching the chefs work" can be "part of the
charm", but some lament this instant "classic" has "lost
some of its magic" (and Service and Decor scores) now

that "you need the patience of Job to wait for a table" ("time to start taking reservations").

downtown   21 | 20 | 20 | $40 |
2102 Shattuck Ave. (Addison St.), Berkeley, 510-649-3810;
www.downtownrestaurant.com
"If you're going Downtown" – be it "for the Berkeley Rep", "Cal sports, musical entertainment or an intimate dinner" – "go to downtown" where "delicious" Cal-Med cuisine ("fish dishes reign supreme") joints "Uptown atmosphere" and "great" live jazz that "adds a high note"; although time-pressed ticket-holders often wonder "waiter, where art thou?" in the "big" "noisy" room, the refreshingly "adult" vibe generally "makes up for any bumps in the road."

Duck Club, The   20 | 20 | 20 | $43 |
Lafayette Park Hotel & Spa, 3287 Mt. Diablo Blvd.
(Pleasant Hill Rd.), Lafayette, 925-283-3700;
www.lafayetteparkhotel.com
This "upscale" "suburban" hotel outpost in Lafayette is part of a chain of "dignified", "classic" settings where you can "carry on a conversation" over "reliable" "but not inventive" New American eats; as a result, they're just "ducky" for a "reliable" "business lunch" or "elegant" dinner "if you're staying" on the premises; meanwhile, more adventurous diners squawk the vibe is just "a little too stuffed-shirt"; N.B. there are locations North and South of SF too.

Eccolo   19 | 20 | 18 | $44 |
1820 Fourth St. (bet. Hearst Ave. & Virginia St.), Berkeley,
510-644-0444; www.eccolo.com
Opened in 2004, this "modern" Berkeley "trattoria" from "pedigreed" chef Chris Lee (ex Chez Panisse) showcases a daily-changing "rustic" "seasonal" Northern Italian menu and "well-chosen" Boot-centric vintages "like you would get in top *enoteche*"; the *cucina* is "authentic" and "fresh" but otherwise the "limited menu" of "not exactly heartwarming" offerings ("lamb's tongue, nettles") plus lingering "service kinks" leave some surveyors skeptical.

ERNA'S ELDERBERRY HOUSE   28 | 27 | 28 | $80 |
48688 Victoria Ln. (Hwy. 41), Oakhurst, 559-683-6800;
www.elderberryhouse.com
Although this Oakhurst "jewel" is "nestled in the hills" "a few miles from Yosemite", you'll be "magically transported to Europe" when you step inside its "elegant", "palace"-like interior, where you're "treated like royalty" right down to the "handwritten menus" that record every "exquisite" course of your costly prix fixe Californian–New French meal; perhaps the only way to "make your dinner even better" is to "stay overnight at the château" "after consuming all the well-selected wines."

Everett & Jones Barbeque   20 | 10 | 12 | $18

296 A St. (Myrtle St.), Hayward, 510-581-3222 ●♅
126 Broadway (2nd St.), Oakland, 510-663-2350
2676 Fruitvale Ave. (bet. Davis & 27th Sts.), Oakland, 510-533-0900
3415 Telegraph Ave. (34th St.), Oakland, 510-601-9377 ♅

Carnivores with a jones for 'cue confirm these "legendary"
East Bay smokeries serve up "lip-smackin', finger-lickin'
good" ribs and sauces ("hot, hotter and call-the-fire-
department") that are "authentic down to the Wonder
Bread" and "paper plates"; however, "except for the Jack
London space" (with "fantastic" weekend jazz and R&B),
the locations are basically "seedy" "take-out windows"
with "cheeky" service.

FatApple's   17 | 13 | 16 | $16

1346 Martin Luther King Jr. Way (bet. Berryman & Rose Sts.),
Berkeley, 510-526-2260
7525 Fairmount Ave. (bet. Colusa & Ramona Aves.), El Cerrito,
510-528-3433

"Repeat customers" run to these "habit-forming" sibs in
Berkeley and El Cerrito to "fatten their apples" on "down-
home breakfasts" and other "basic" diner food; "friendly"
servers and a "casual", "kid-friendly" vibe make it "popular"
with families, even if detractors dis them as "lackluster
Americana masquerading as yuppie comfort chic."

Fenton's Creamery   19 | 15 | 13 | $14

4226 Piedmont Ave. (Entrada Ave.), Oakland, 510-658-7000;
www.fentonscreamery.com

"Come with an empty stomach or a close friend" to this retro
"ice-cream shoppe" in Oakland (a "Piedmont landmark"
since 1894) where "we all scream" for sundaes "so big
they might make you cry"; surveyors suspect it "survives
on its small-town reputation", slagging "sloppy" service
and suggesting "skip" the "generic" meals – or at least
"eat dessert first."

Fonda Solana ●   23 | 21 | 19 | $33

1501 Solano Ave. (Curtis St.), Albany, 510-559-9006;
www.fondasolana.com

A "fun" "late-night choice", this "well-run", "convivial"
Albany Pan-Latin attracts "funky East Bay types" seeking
"innovative", "palate-tickling" tapas and "super drinks"
("its rep for great mojitos keeps someone working the lime
juicer like mad"); its "high ceilings and brick walls" result
in a "hip SF" aesthetic and "quasi-industrial feel – but also
a lot of din for dinner", while wallet-watchers warn "don't
go feeling too hungry" because "those little plates add up."

Garibaldis   22 | 21 | 21 | $41

5356 College Ave. (Manila Ave.), Oakland, 510-595-4000;
www.garibaldis-eastbay.com
See review in City of San Francisco Directory.

Grasshopper   22   19   19 $31

6317 College Ave. (Claremont Ave.), Oakland, 510-595-3559;
www.grasshoppersake.com

"Knock out-of-towners' socks off" with a trip to this modern,
"Zen-like" Oaklander for a culinary "adventure" via the
"creative", "eclectic" – or even "a bit weird" – Pan-Asian
small plates; though the flavors are "a treat", portions are
"drastically tiny" so "if you want to eat your fill, expect to
drop a lot of yen" – then again, after "a glass or two of
cool, unfiltered sake", "who cares?"; N.B. habitués are
hopping mad this place stopped serving lunch.

Great China   24   10   13 $18

2115 Kittredge St. (Shattuck Ave.), Berkeley, 510-843-7996

Notwithstanding "aging" decor and the "iffy" service, this
Berkeley Sino scene gets "ridiculously crowded" with
connoisseurs who crow over "the best Peking duck" plus
other "authentic", "intensely flavored" Chinese chow, all
offered at "amazing" prices; consequently, unless you're
"early", "prepare to stare at the aquarium for a while."

Gregoire   –   –   –   I

2109 Cedar St. (Shattuck Ave.), Berkeley, 510-883-1893;
www.gregoirerestaurant.com

For "amazing French" fare at bargain prices, Berkeleyites
think inside the box and head to this "tiny, mostly take-out
place" for "wondrous lunches and dinners" whipped up
"in a microscopic kitchen with Gallic attitude"; it's a veritable
"yuppie drive-thru" where you "order from the window",
but "you don't miss the service (much) once you have the
food" ("the potato puffs are better than sex") to eat *chez
vous* or at "picnic tables" on the front sidewalk.

IL FORNAIO   18   20   18 $35

1430 Mt. Diablo Blvd. (bet. Broadway & Main St.),
Walnut Creek, 925-296-0100; www.ilfornaio.com

See review in City of San Francisco Directory.

Jade Villa   17   11   13 $18

800 Broadway (bet. 8th & 9th Sts.), Oakland, 510-839-1688

Though "not always sure" what they're eating, dumpling
divers declare "it pays to be adventurous" at this Oakland
Chinese that rolls out a daily "variety of dim sum" at midday;
the "big room with little atmosphere" can "handle large
parties" but the faint of heart fret "don't look too closely at
the walls" – instead, keep an eye out for servers, who are
"sometimes rude, but mostly just absent."

Jimmy Bean's   21   11   13 $16

1290 Sixth St. (Gilman St.), Berkeley, 510-528-3435;
www.jimmybeans.com

East of Eden (aka SF) lies this "very casual" (as in counter-
service), "funky" Berkeley diner where the "only thing that

beats the coffee" are the "outstanding", "innovative" Cal-inflected breakfasts and lunches; it's a "chill place" but "be prepared to be aggressive for tables – everyone else is" – or, failing that, bear in mind that the hours have been extended, so you can "always get in" for dinner.

Jojo ⊠　　23 | 18 | 22 | $44

3859 Piedmont Ave. (bet. 40th St. & Macarthur Blvd.), Oakland, 510-985-3003; www.jojorestaurant.com
"Absolute masters of simplicity", the chef-owners at this Oakland "sleeper" offer up "inspired variations on Provençal" bistro "classics" "without pretension" but with some "very good wines" and "fabulous, not to be missed" desserts; the "personable" service and the "intimate" 35-seat space make many "feel like a personal guest" in someone's home, as does the fact that "there's no bar or waiting area"; even so, go, go – "it's worth" the "wait outside" and the "high prices."

Jordan's　　▽ 21 | 23 | 19 | $50

Claremont Resort & Spa, 41 Tunnel Rd. (Claremont Ave.), Berkeley, 510-549-8510; www.claremontresort.com
"Out-of-town guests" will love the "beautiful setting" of this vintage-style Berkeley resort dining room ("Zelda and Scott Fitzgerald might have dined there") with "awesome" panoramic views of the Bay and a "rightfully famous Sunday brunch"; even the weekdays' rather "predictable" Cal–Pacific Rim "hotel food", however, "outpaces the service by a wide margin", making the experience "too expensive" "for what you get"; N.B. no dinner served on Tuesdays.

Juan's Place　　17 | 13 | 19 | $15

941 Carleton St. (9th St.), Berkeley, 510-845-6904
After "more than 30 years", this "raucous", "nostalgia-filled" Berkeley "dive" still shows "college students", "neighborhood old-timers", "Emeryville professionals" and "the odd softball team" a "very good time"; "huge portions" of "cheap", "greasy" "pre-cilantro Mexican" *comida* accompany the party-fueling "wine margaritas" and Baja beers, all served up by a crew that's "friendly in a brisk sort of way."

Kirala　　25 | 17 | 18 | $33

2100 Ward St. (Shattuck Ave.), Berkeley, 510-549-3486; www.kiralaberkeley.com
"Everybody knows" this "modern", "crowded" "Berkeley favorite" serves "generous portions" of "absolutely the freshest, most exquisitely prepared sushi" plus "amazing" robata items; "when the food is so good" fin-atics feel they "can't complain about the price" or about "distracted service" – though the wistful worn out by "painfully long waits" ("there are no off-peak hours") wonder "do they take reservations yet?" (the answer is no).

Koryo Wooden Charcoal BBQ ☑ | 22 | 8 | 13 | $22 |

4390 Telegraph Ave. (Shattuck Ave.), Oakland, 510-652-6007
Grills gone wild is the come-on at this cult "do-it-yourself
Korean BBQ", considered the "cornerstone of Telegraph
Avenue's Kimchi Row"; "if you can get past the fluorescent
lights", "folding chairs" and "gruff service", you'll "eat like
a king" thanks to "great bibimbop", kalbi and an array of
"pickled snacks" perfect for "late-night cravings" (till 2 AM
on weekends); just "bring your appetite" and a "change of
clothes" because you'll end up "full and smelly."

LALIME'S | 26 | 20 | 24 | $43 |

*1329 Gilman St. (bet. Neilson St. & Peralta Ave.), Berkeley,
510-527-9838; www.lalimes.com*
Who needs that "other Berkeley restaurant" when you
can come to this "venerable" venue; an ever-changing
roster of "innovative" Cal-Med cuisine and regional wines
keeps the experience "fresh" even as the "welcoming"
staff and "serene, pretty" two-story setting evoke "dining
at your wealthy aunt's home" (albeit surrounded by "tweedy
professors"); given the "realistic prices" and "relaxing" vibe,
locals would prefer to "keep this gem hidden."

La Méditerranée | 20 | 14 | 17 | $20 |

*2936 College Ave. (Ashby Ave.), Berkeley, 510-540-7773;
www.cafelamed.com*
See review in City of San Francisco Directory.

La Note | 22 | 21 | 18 | $23 |

*2377 Shattuck Ave. (bet. Channing Way & Durant Ave.),
Berkeley, 510-843-1535; www.lanoterestaurant.com*
Café Clem ☒
*2703 Seventh St. (bet. Carleton & Pardee Sts.), Berkeley,
510-204-9602; www.cafeclem.com*
Gallic gourmands embrace this "French kiss in the heart of
Berkeley" where "*délicieux* breakfasts", "welcoming" bistro
decor (including a "gorgeous patio") and "not-always-
timely service" seemingly "send Shattuck Avenue diners
to rue de Provence"; "*mais oui*", waits can be "hours long"
and seating "tight" for weekend brunch, but frustrated
Francophiles can also get their fix via "limited" "candlelit"
dinners Thursday–Saturday, some *avec* a "charming
accordion player"; N.B. new sibling Cafe Clem is unrated.

Lark Creek | 22 | 20 | 21 | $38 |

*1360 Locust St. (bet. Civic Dr. & Mt. Diablo Blvd.),
Walnut Creek, 925-256-1234; www.larkcreek.com*
Like his Larkspur longtimer, Bradley Ogden's stripped-
down Walnut Creek "standby" specializes in his signature
"straight-shooting Americana (meatloaf, pot roast, etc.)"
and all-U.S. wine list in "classy", "comfortable" indoor/
outdoor digs; some scoff at shelling out big bucks for "basic
food", but there's also "creative regional fare" on offer if

you're willing to "wade through the menu"; and though the friendly staff delivers "service with a smile", it's up to you to provide the "bullhorn for conversation."

La Rose Bistro   ∇ 23 | 19 | 23 | $32

2037 Shattuck Sq. (Addison St.), Berkeley, 510-644-1913
An "unexpected find on a street not known for high-end restaurants", this "romantic", "family-run" Berkeley bistro "needs to be discovered" so "fans" can continue to enjoy chef-owner Vanessa Dang's "ambitious", "amazing variety" of "exquisitely arranged", Asian-accented Cal-French creations; service may not always be "suave" or swift (a real demerit when you're dining "in the theater district"), but the "friendly enthusiasm makes you root for the whole crew."

Le Cheval   22 | 15 | 16 | $22
1007 Clay St. (10th St.), Oakland, 510-763-8495; www.lecheval.com
Le Petit Cheval 🖾 ⇗
2600 Bancroft Way (Bowditch St.), Berkeley, 510-704-8018
"City Hall's power crowd meets neighborhoodies" at this "Oakland melting pot", a family-owned "fave" for "French-Vietnamese fusion"; the stable "menu never disappoints" ("try the lemongrass chicken") and the equine-themed room is "open and spacious", though some who look this gift horse in the mouth bridle at the "loud", "barnlike atmosphere" and the galloping "speed" of the "food delivery"; N.B. the Berkeley branch is unrated.

LEFT BANK   18 | 20 | 17 | $37
60 Crescent Dr. (Monument Blvd.), Pleasant Hill, 925-288-1222; www.leftbank.com
See review in North of San Francisco Directory.

Lo Coco's Restaurant & Pizzeria   21 | 13 | 18 | $22
1400 Shattuck Ave. (Rose St.), Berkeley, 510-843-3745
4270 Piedmont Ave. (Echo Ave.), Oakland, 510-652-6222 ⇗
www.lococospizzeria.com
The "best meatball award" goes to these "funky" *fratelli* of Sicilian pizzeria in Oakland and Berkeley where "a mix of blue-collar" types and "millionaires" line up (or "preset their phones") for the "wonderful" Sicilian pizzas and other "gutsy", "nothing-fancy" "family-style" Southern Italian "served by genuine local characters"; ok, they're "cramped" and "crowded", but when you need your "spaghetti fix" "you can't go wrong here."

Louka   _ | _ | _ | E
267 Hartz Ave. (Diablo Rd.), Danville, 925-743-9180; www.loukarestaurant.com
This elegant, earth-toned Danville destination has replaced the acclaimed French restaurant La Salamandre; the same "friendly owners" and their new chef "have turned to an Eclectic small-plates" menu (not surprisingly, the Gallic goodies are singled out for being "outstanding"); the *petits-*

plats concept carries through to dessert (an array of micro-sweets) and even the wine list, offering 3- or 6-oz. pours; not surprisingly, some louka askance at the "high prices" of these "super-small portions."

Mama's Royal Cafe ∌   20 | 13 | 15 | $15

4012 Broadway (40th St.), Oakland, 510-547-7600
"Hangover-healing", "down-home" American breakfasts ("fat has never left the vocabulary") inspire local bohos to dub this "quirky" "greasy spoon" "Oakland's only legit brunch destination"; "paper-napkin art" and vintage "aprons decorating the walls" provide diversion as you try to flag down the "colorful characters who provide the service", but be warned that given the "relaxed atmosphere" and "reputation", lines can be "indecent."

Marica   ▽ 23 | 18 | 20 | $36

5301 College Ave. (Bryant Ave.), Oakland, 510-985-8388
The line on this "underappreciated" Rockridger is that afishionados "can catch a good seafood dinner" here for a "reasonable price"; habitués are hooked on the "excellent twice-cooked lobster" ("enough reason to come here") and other "delectable" fish dishes exhibiting "a touch of Hong Kong", and appreciate that this "smallish space" with "exposed-brick walls" has "few pretensions" – you may even get a "nice personal visit from the owner."

Max's ▨   16 | 13 | 16 | $23

Oakland City Ctr., 500 12th St. (bet. Broadway & Clay St.), Oakland, 510-451-6297; www.maxsworld.com
See review in City of San Francisco Directory.

Mezze   23 | 21 | 22 | $38

3407 Lakeshore Ave. (bet. Hwy. 580 & Mandana Blvd.), Oakland, 510-663-2500; www.mezze.com
The chef "pushes the creative envelope" at this "sleeper" serving "fabulous Cal-Med fusion cuisine"; though it's a bit "pricey for the neighborhood" – near Oakland's Lake Merritt – the "appealing casual/chic interior", proprietors who "treat patrons like family" and a "full bar with inventive cocktails" have many diners deeming it a "destination."

Naan 'n Curry ∌   19 | 6 | 9 | $12

2366 Telegraph Ave. (bet. Channing Way & Durant Ave.), Berkeley, 510-841-6226; www.naanncurry.com
See review in City of San Francisco Directory.

Nan Yang Rockridge   21 | 14 | 20 | $22

6048 College Ave. (Claremont Ave.), Oakland, 510-655-3298
"Out-of-the-ordinary" and "reasonably priced" Burmese is "the novelty and the hook" at this Oakland "hangout" where "sincere" servers help "adventurous" eaters select from among the "authentic", "delicious" specialties (e.g. "über-unctuous garlic noodles with mango" and "green tea salad

I could eat every day for the rest of my life"); though the modest decor includes genuine native artifacts, a pack of patrons points out "who cares what's on the wall when the food is so good?"

Nizza La Bella   20 | 19 | 21 | $32 |
825-827 San Pablo Ave. (bet. Solano & Washington Aves.), Albany, 510-526-2552
Despite an "oddball location", this "lively" Albany bistro has developed a "bona fide cult following" for its "gutsy" and "dependable" French-Italian "comfort food" plus "flawless classic cocktails" mixed by bartenders who "really know what they're doing"; a "warm interior, intoxicating scents" and "attentive" servers also help make this "a happy place", even if an unhappy few find staffers "not very welcoming."

North Beach Pizza ●   18 | 9 | 14 | $16 |
1598 University Ave. (California St.), Berkeley, 510-849-9800; www.northbeachpizza.com
See review in City of San Francisco Directory.

O Chamé ⊠   24 | 23 | 21 | $31 |
1830 Fourth St. (Hearst Ave.), Berkeley, 510-841-8783
"No worry in the world cannot be soothed" by a "bowl of steaming udon" at this "heaven-Zent" "oasis" on Berkeley's Fourth Street; the "tasty, fresh", "down-home" (if high-priced) Japanese "comfort food", "always in lockstep with the seasons", is served in portions that "leave you feeling refreshed and balanced" (read: "small"); set in a "peaceful", almost "monastic" room populated by "helpful" servers, the experience "brings Serenity Now" to those who don't mind "a little pretension" with their noodles.

OLIVETO CAFE & RESTAURANT   25 | 22 | 22 | $48 |
5655 College Ave. (Shafter Ave.), Oakland, 510-547-5356; www.oliveto.com
Supporters salute "brilliant", "passionate" chef/co-owner Paul Bertolli, deeming his rustic Rockridge Italian "great in general" and downright "trekworthy" when there's a "special" "epicurean event" on; though the "unpretentious", "ingredient-driven" dishes (rotisserie meats, "breathtaking homemade pastas") are "outstanding" and the service "professional", the bill may "cause you to stop breathing"; by contrast, the casual Cafe downstairs provides a less "precious", less pricey yet still "delightful respite."

Olivia ⊠   – | – | – | M |
1453 Dwight Way (Sacramento St.), Berkeley, 510-548-2322; www.oliviaeats.com
Nathan Peterson, who spent the greater part of two decades at Bay Wolf, is striking out on his own, offering a compact, frequently changing Med-Eclectic menu at this little Berkeley joint; the colorful, medieval-looking storefront would look at home in any of the countries represented by

the globe-trotting fare (enchiladas, duck confit, tians), and an egalitarian pricing structure charges one flat fee for each course (entrees are restrained at $19); an all-French wine list rounds out the offerings.

Pakwan ≠   23 | 6 | 10 | $13
26617 Mission Blvd. (Sorenson Rd.), Hayward, 510-538-2401
See review in City of San Francisco Directory.

Pasta Pomodoro   15 | 13 | 16 | $18
5614 Shellmound St. (Powell St.), Emeryville, 510-923-1173
5500 College Ave. (Lawton Ave.), Oakland, 510-923-0900
www.pastapomodoro.com
See review in City of San Francisco Directory.

PEARL OYSTER BAR &   26 | 24 | 21 | $39
RESTAURANT 🖾
5634 College Ave. (bet. Keith Ave. & Ocean View Dr.),
Oakland, 510-654-5426; www.pearloncollege.com
"Upping the hipness quotient for" Oakland's College Avenue, this freshly spawned seafooder has floated "straight to the top" due to its "beautifully presented", Asian-inflected "tapas from the sea"; meanwhile, a "super-cool", "sleek" shell – replete with "down-tempo beats" and lighting that changes colors – "makes you forget you're 100 yards from the Berkeley line"; a "terrific staff" "offers guidance" on the "innovative wine list" but highball-hankering habitués harrumph "all they need to offer now are cocktails."

Pho 84   – | – | – | I
354 17th St. (Franklin St.), Oakland, 510-832-1338
"Despite what the name implies" Oakland's "longtime favorite" value Vietnamese venue has a lot more than its "Californian"-style pho (read: "not as greasy as mom's") going for it, "as evidenced by the huge crowds"; "everything is extremely fresh" and "tasty" ("flavorful chicken and seafood") and though the decor is "nothing fancy", it's "pleasant" enough, as is the "friendly staff."

Phoenix Next Door 🖾≠   ▽ 25 | 13 | 15 | $19
1788 Shattuck Ave. (Delaware St.), Berkeley, 510-883-0783
"Their pasta is the stuff dreams are made of" say surveyors "shocked at how good" "homemade" noodles can be when "adorned with the innovative sauces" cooked up at this "tiny", "absolutely no-frills" Italian in Berkeley; the "lax", "disorganized" service, however, is the stuff of nightmares; P.S. the cash-only joint's "only open for a couple of hours daily for lunch", though you can "visit the adjoining" shop/bakery and buy all the fixings to take home.

Pho Hoa-Hiep II   ▽ 20 | 7 | 12 | $11
1402 E. 12th St. (14th Ave.), Oakland, 510-533-0549
There's "nothing better on a cold, rainy day" than the "inexpensive", "huge and tasty pho bowls" dished out "in

less than 10 minutes" at this "family-run" Vietnamese hole-in-the-wall in Oakland (and its branches in Daly City and San Francisco's Outer Sunset); the kitchen also offers a variety of "consistently good" noodles and rice plates "to cater to all types", though the decor is less approachable ("kind of dingy").

Piatti   17   18   18 $34
100 Sycamore Valley Rd. W. (San Ramon Valley Blvd.), Danville, 925-838-2082; www.piatti.com
"The crowds attest to the quality and prices" at this Danville link of a regional chain that "gets the job done" with "safe", "familiar" Italian fare "prepared American-style" from "fresh, seasonal ingredients"; each location has its own personality and amenities, but overall, "you get what you expect" – "comfortable" surroundings and "kid-friendly" service – and "it is easy to do worse"; N.B. there are locations North and South of SF too.

Picante Cocina Mexicana   21   14   15 $14
1328 Sixth St. (bet. Camelia & Gilman Sts.), Berkeley, 510-525-3121
"Thousands of Berkeley families can't be wrong"; after more than two decades, this "politically correct" taqueria "from the folks behind Chez Panisse" still draws a "cult following" for its "outstanding" menu of "organic" Mexican munchies (e.g. "unbelievable carnitas"); the "chaotic" counter-service cantina is especially "child-friendly" because the "so-cheap *comida*" is "prepared in a blink of an eye" but "despite its name, nothing is remotely spicy."

Pizza Antica   21   17   17 $23
3600 Mt. Diablo Blvd. (Dewing Ave.), Lafayette, 925-299-0500; www.pizzaantica.com
See review in South of San Francisco Directory.

Pizzaiolo 🖂   –   –   –   I
5008 Telegraph Ave. (51st St.), Berkeley, 510-652-4888
Charlie Hallowell, onetime Chez Panisse cook–turned–pizza maker, is enticing Oaklanders with the promise of a perfect pie at this upscale, dinner-only pizzeria with a tiled wood-fired oven, handsome dining room and cozy back patio; a daily-changing menu showcases a half-dozen crackle-crusted creations topped with organic goodies, with a handful of pastas, *contorni* and the like rounding out the reasonably priced offerings; N.B. no reservations.

Pizza Rustica   19   10   15 $19
5422 College Ave. (bet. Kales & Manila Aves.), Oakland, 510-654-1601
6106 La Salle Ave. (Moraga Ave.), Oakland, 510-339-7878
www.caferustica.com
"They do two things" – "chichi, New Age crispy-crust pizzas" ("the Potesto is the besto") and rotisserie chickens –

"and they do them well" at this "unique" retro-style Oakland pie purveyor and its "take-out" offshoot in Montclair; "service is slower than it needs to be", though, so consider "ordering to go" or taking advantage of the "reasonably quick delivery" service; P.S. the College Avenue location's tiki-themed Conga Lounge is "fun with friends."

Plearn Thai Cuisine   20 13 17 $20
2050 University Ave. (bet. Milvia St. & Shattuck Ave.), Berkeley, 510-841-2148
Ok, they're not quite "as authentic as in Bangkok" but the "standard dishes" still "sparkle on the tongue" at this veteran Thai, boast its budget-minded Berkeley boosters; less sanguine sorts state it's "more crowded than good", with decor that's "showing its age" and staffers who aren't always "attentive"; nevertheless all agree it's a "solid lunchtime choice" that gives "great value."

PlumpJack Cafe   24 21 23 $49
PlumpJack Squaw Valley Inn, 1920 Squaw Valley Rd. (Hwy. 89), Olympic Valley, 530-583-1576; www.plumpjack.com
See review in City of San Francisco Directory.

Postino   21 24 21 $43
3565 Mt. Diablo Blvd. (Oak Hill Rd.), Lafayette, 925-299-8700; www.postinorestaurant.com
For a "special occasion – or at any time", this "wonderful", "atmospheric" 1905 post office building in Lafayette draws diners who dig its "well-priced", "toothsome" Italian cookery and choice of 200 local and international wines, presented by a "knowledgeable" crew; in all, it's a "definite repeat kind of place" that remains "a good choice on this side of the Caldicot Tunnel."

Prima   24 22 21 $42
1522 N. Main St. (bet. Bonanza St. & Lincoln Ave.), Walnut Creek, 925-935-7780; www.primaristorante.com
An "institution" with "staying power", this "upscale" Walnut Creeker has been serving up "amazingly consistent" Italian cuisine that may not "stretch the imagination but pleases the palate" for almost three decades; known for its primo vino (1,600 labels), wine-cellar dining rooms, "jazz three nights a week" and staffers who "care for you as if you were a guest in their fine home", it's "grown into a destination for area oenophiles"; still, peckish people protest "portion sizes are ridiculously small for the price."

Restaurant Peony   21 14 13 $24
Pacific Renaissance Plaza, 388 Ninth St. (bet. Franklin & Webster Sts.), Oakland, 510-286-8866
"If you can stand the wait" to "get a table" ("an eternity") and then endure as "the carts make their way to you", you can "feast" on a "wide array" of "unusual", "aromatic" dim sum at this "immense", "raucous, Hong Kong–style"

"teahouse" in Oakland's Pacific Renaissance Plaza; the "white tablecloths" and "family-style" banquet dinners make it "more upscale" than nearby competitors, but "it would help" if "the noise level would dim some" and the staff's English-speaking skills rise some.

Rick & Ann's   22   15   17 $19
2922 Domingo Ave. (bet. Ashby & Claremont Aves.), Berkeley, 510-649-8538; www.rickandanns.com
"The dream brunch destination" declare devotees of this Berkeleyite, citing its "amazing" American eats, "lovely outdoor seating" and "homey ambiance" (a communal table in the middle "encourages you to get to know your neighbor"); however, "consistent" servers sometimes seem "overtaxed" by the huge crowds, and "looooong waits" can be something of a nightmare ("plan to get through the whole Sunday paper" while in line "on weekends").

RIVOLI   27   23   25 $43
1539 Solano Ave. (bet. Neilson St. & Peralta Ave.), Berkeley, 510-526-2542; www.rivolirestaurant.com
At this Berkeley "oasis", revelers rejoice in Wendy Brucker's "wonderfully innovative" Cal-Med "comfort food", which can be paired with bottles from an "enviable wine list" with the assistance of "personable", "perfectly professional" staffers; meanwhile, there's a "raccoon floor show" taking place in the "lighted back garden", so though a minority grouses "the tables are too damn crowded" nature lovers declare the "delightful" experience "rivals those at the East Bay's big-name restaurants."

Saul's Restaurant & Delicatessen   18   15   16 $18
1475 Shattuck Ave. (bet. Rose & Vine Sts.), Berkeley, 510-848-3354; www.saulsdeli.com
When you "have a hankering" for a "corned-beef sandwich on fresh rye" or a "bagel with a schmear", schlep over to Berkeley's "simulacrum" of "the New York deli experience" where a "popular take-out counter" obviates "long waits for a table" or for "distracted waiters"; although "high prices are authentic", "NYC it ain't" ("you call that pastrami?").

Scott's Seafood   -   -   -   E
2 Broadway (Water St.), Oakland, 510-444-5969
1333 N. California Blvd. (Mt. Diablo Blvd.), Walnut Creek, 925-934-1300
www.scottsseafood.com
For over 25 years, this "reliable" Bay Area chain (with links East and South of SF) has been plying businessmen and families with "consistent, dependable", straightforward American seafood – plus dry-aged beef "for the non-fish eaters in your party" – respectable wines and sophisticated settings; Sunday jazz brunches are offered at every branch except San Jose, and some offer views as well – notably

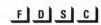
those of the waterfront from Oakland's Jack London Square and of the cityscape from San Jose's sixth-floor outpost.

Sea Salt
– | – | – | M

2512 San Pablo Ave. (Dwight Way), Berkeley, 510-883-1720; www.seasaltrestaurant.com

From the folks behind Lalime's comes this affordable Berkeley seafooder that feels like a cross between a New England fish shack and a California garden party; the all-day menu of sustainably caught fin fare ranges from lobster rolls to Italian *crudos,* and can be enjoyed in a variety of settings, including a sunny dining room, backyard patio and raw bar.

Shalimar ⊘
23 | 3 | 10 | $14

3325 Walnut Ave. (Paseo Padre Pkwy.), Fremont, 510-494-1919; www.shalimarsf.com

See review in City of San Francisco Directory.

Shen Hua
21 | 18 | 17 | $22

2914 College Ave. (bet. Ashby Ave. & Russell St.), Berkeley, 510-883-1777

For a "refreshing departure" from "everything-tastes-the-same syndrome" reviewers recommend Berkeley's "family-friendly" Mandarin mainstay that serves "high-quality" "Chinese haute cuisine"; the interior is "bright", "clean and airy" to boot, so even the "speediest, rudest service" and "terrible noise ("like dining in a train station") "don't seem to sway the faithful crowds."

Soi Four
24 | 20 | 19 | $30

5421 College Ave. (bet. Kales & Manila Sts.), Oakland, 510-655-0889; www.soifour.com

At Oakland's "hipster Thai" "hot spot" the kitchen four-mulates "beautiful" small plates of "light", "delectable" delicacies with "flavors rarely found outside of Asia", and the bar pours "inventive cocktails"; "polite" servers can be "indifferent" at times, however, and though spenders say the fare's "less pricey" than the "upscale" scene would suggest, wallet-watchers wonder "does street food cost this much in Bangkok?"

Soizic
24 | 19 | 22 | $36

300 Broadway (3rd St.), Oakland, 510-251-8100; www.soizicbistro.com

A "nondescript" exterior and an "odd location" "on the Oakland waterfront" ("you'd miss it if you weren't looking for it") have kept this "offbeat" entry "under the radar all these years" – but those in-the-know confide that its "innovative", "diverse" Cal-French menu is full of "clean, fresh flavors"; add in an "always-charming staff" and an "understated" interior and the result is a "find" that's a "great alternative" in "touristy Jack London Square"; P.S. "parking is easy."

Tacubaya   21 | 15 | 14 | $15
1788 Fourth St. (bet. Hearst Ave. & Virginia St.), Berkeley, 510-525-5160
This "very crowded", "citrus-colored", counter-service taqueria on Berkeley's "trendy Fourth Street" – a daytime "counterpart to the beloved Doña Tomás" – may be "pricey", but the kitchen uses Niman Ranch meats and "impeccable" local, organic ingredients to "perfectly prepare" regional Mexican "items not found everywhere else" (including "many vegetarian and vegan options"); veterans advise "don't let curt cashiers" or "long lines" "scare you away."

Taiwan ●   17 | 7 | 13 | $15
2071 University Ave. (Shattuck Ave.), Berkeley, 510-845-1456
A "local hot spot" near UC Berkeley, this no-frills nook dishes out "excellent, authentic" noodles aplenty plus "traditional" Taiwanese fare and a "vast menu" of "the usual suspects" from the mainland as well; though Taipei personalities find the front "window to view dumpling-making" "entertaining", most maintain if you "take out, the decor improves"; N.B. the SF offshoot offers dim sum all day long.

Three Seasons   23 | 20 | 19 | $34
1525 N. Main St. (Bonanza St.), Walnut Creek, 925-934-4831; www.threeseasonsrestaurant.com
See review in City of San Francisco Directory.

Townhouse Bar & Grill ☒   21 | 19 | 20 | $31
5862 Doyle St. (bet. 59th & Powell Sts.), Emeryville, 510-652-6151; www.townhousebarandgrill.com
The rough exterior of this "barnlike" Emeryville venue "belies a warm interior" where a "hospitable" staff serves up "reliable", "hearty" and rather "sophisticated" Cal cuisine; it's "always packed with suits", perhaps because it's equally suited to "after-work drinks at the bar or a fancy celebration dinner."

Trader Vic's   16 | 21 | 17 | $43
9 Anchor Dr. (Powell St.), Emeryville, 510-653-3400; www.tradervics.com
The "wacky tiki-tacky decor" and "signature drinks" "satisfy nostalgists" who take "a trip back in time" at this Emeryville emporium, with its "marvelous" Bay views and Polynesian eats; given the high prices, though, "come for the scene, not for the food or the service"; P.S. the "excellent" Palo Alto outpost is preferred over the new Downtown SF branch.

Trattoria La Siciliana   24 | 16 | 16 | $28
2993 College Ave. (Ashby Ave.), Berkeley, 510-704-1474
Thanks to a "huge selection" of "brilliant and satisfying entrees" (including "excellent" pastas redolent of "garlic and more garlic") plus "heavenly" Sicilian wines, this Berkeley Southern Italian attracts "throngs of hungry

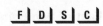
diners" who'll "wait on the street" just to enter the "noisy"
"shoebox of a space"; fans find the "exuberant staffers"
"hilarious", though critics complain they're "inflexible."

Udupi Palace ⌿   19 | 8 | 14 | $14
*1901-1903 University Ave. (Martin Luther King Jr. Way),
Berkeley, 510-843-6600
Springtown Plaza, 941 Bluebell Dr. (Springtown Blvd.),
Livermore, 925-960-1942
www.udupipalace.net*
It's easy being green at these "authentic" Berkeley and
Livermore vegetarian Indians, thanks to "gigantic" combo
plates, "mammoth *dosas*" and other "cheap, delicious
eats"; still, sticklers sniff at "bare-bones" interiors, "abrupt
service" and fare that "isn't as good as it used to be" (as
reflected in a falling Food score); P.S. South Bay sorts
"prefer the Sunnyvale location."

Uzen ⌷   24 | 17 | 18 | $30
*5415 College Ave. (bet. Hudson St. & Kales Ave.), Oakland,
510-654-7753*
Savvy Rockridgers "avoid the dreaded waits" at several
"surrounding" sushi spots by selecting this "well-kept
secret" where "the chef may ignore you, but he speaks
volumes" with his "fantastic", "creative" nigiri and sashimi
along with "conventional" rolls and "other Japanese
standards"; meanwhile, "service is a little slow" and the
"small", "spartan" digs aren't exactly oozin' ambiance,
prompting some to suggest "freshening up the decor."

Va de Vi   24 | 21 | 20 | $39
*1511 Mt. Diablo Blvd. (Main St.), Walnut Creek, 925-979-0100;
www.va-de-vi-bistro.com*
"Adventurous" Eclectic cuisine ("every flavor a good one"),
"fabulous wine flights" and "big-city ambiance in the 'burbs"
of Walnut Creek make this handsome small-plates specialist
a "grazer's paradise"; "efficient" servers bounce between
the "beautiful patio" and the "noisy, exciting" and "packed"
interior, where tables may be "tiny" but bills get big fast.

Venezia   20 | 21 | 19 | $27
1799 University Ave. (Grant St.), Berkeley, 510-849-4681
This "longtime" Berkeley "standby" "works on every level",
from the "tasty", "authentic" pasta (an "excellent value")
to the "always welcoming" servers to the "creative"
(some say "campy") setting that mimics a Venetian piazza
"complete with a clothesline", "a real fountain and trompe
l'oeil buildings painted on the walls."

Venus   22 | 17 | 20 | $23
*2327 Shattuck Ave. (Durant Ave.), Berkeley, 510-540-5950;
www.venusrestaurant.net*
Lovers of this Berkeley venue swoon over its "imaginative",
"light" Californian cookery (especially the "superb",

"satisfying breakfasts") that "emphasizes seasonal local produce and organic meats" "without being righteous about it"; though hard-hearted sorts grumble the "noisy" dining room is "not particularly pleasant compared to the food", affectionate aficionados admire its "terrific, youthful vibe" and assert the "warm and friendly" servers are "always attentive."

Vic Stewart's   21 | 21 | 21 | $45

850 S. Broadway (bet. Mt. Diablo Blvd. & Newell Ave.), Walnut Creek, 925-943-5666
"A shrine to the prime beef barons", this "clubby" Walnut Creek chophouse is a "cool train-car themed" eatery in an erstwhile depot (with "private booths" in an attached 1909 Pullman car) where a "caring but not intrusive staff" ensures your "slabs of meat" are "cooked exactly as you want them"; the pennywise warn this excursion can be a "wallet-buster" – try to engineer it so that "your parents take you to dinner."

Vik's Chaat Corner   24 | 4 | 10 | $11

726 Allston Way (bet. 4th & 5th Sts.), Berkeley, 510-644-4412; www.vikdistributors.com
Ok, so the "bare-bones" "industrial decor" at this "teeming" "self-service" Berkeley venue evokes "that school-cafeteria feeling", but ardent admirers advise a visit "to see what all the chaater is about" – namely "generous portions" of "zesty" "mouthwatering Indian snacks" that are "fresh, filling, fast" and "shockingly cheap"; N.B. closes at 6 PM.

WENTE VINEYARDS   24 | 26 | 24 | $47

5050 Arroyo Rd. (Wetmore Rd.), Livermore, 925-456-2450; www.wentevineyards.com
At this "first-class" Livermore Cal-Med set among "rolling hills" and grapevines, "you feel like an actor in a Merchant/Ivory film" sitting on the "elegant terrace in summer" or by the "warm fire in winter" to dine on "creative" "gourmet" cuisine (the "house-cured pork chop is a must") and imbibe selections from a 450-label wine cellar; servers "make each dish sound like a well-written poem", so regulars' only regret is that the chef hasn't "broadened the menu."

Yoshi's at Jack London Square   19 | 20 | 17 | $34

Jack London Sq., 510 Embarcadero W. (Washington St.), Oakland, 510-238-9200; www.yoshis.com
"World-class jazz" played twice nightly elevates the "wide selection of Japanese fare" suitable for "longtime sushi lovers and newbies" at this "comfortable yet stylish" Oakland club; "eating here ensures" "preferential seating" for the show and "accommodating" servers will get you there on time, though sushi snobs sniff that the "overpriced", "ho-hum" fish serves as an "inauspicious opener for the amazing" aural acts.

ZACHARY'S CHICAGO PIZZA 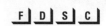 25 | 12 | 15 | $17 |
1853 Solano Ave. (The Alameda), Berkeley, 510-525-5950
5801 College Ave. (Oak Grove Ave.), Oakland, 510-655-6385
www.zacharys.com
"These people have deep-dish down" declare devotees
of the "primal-pleasure" "pizza without peer" at these
"casual" Berkeley and Oakland siblings, "homes away from
home for Chicagoans"; "energetic and friendly" servers
proffer pies as quickly as they can, but can't prevent waits
that are "notoriously long" in the "campy, crowded and
cacophonic" rooms; "call ahead for takeout" "unless you
have the patience of Job."

Zao Noodle Bar 14 | 12 | 13 | $16 |
5614 Bay St. (Shellmound St.), Emeryville, 510-595-2888;
www.zao.com
See review in City of San Francisco Directory.

Zatar 🖼🏷 ▽ 23 | 22 | 23 | $31 |
1981 Shattuck Ave. (University Ave.), Berkeley, 510-841-1981;
www.zatarrestaurant.com
"An oasis in the East Bay's Middle Eastern–food Sahara",
this "tiny" yet "beautiful" and "upscale" Berkeley riad
proffers "astonishing", "subtle", "complex" Med cuisine
that goes way "beyond kebabs and falafel"; the "terrific"
chef-owner uses "only organic" meats and produce (much
of it from his own half-acre backyard garden), so though
wallet-watchers warn "it's pricey for its grade", they admit
they'd "rather spend money on homegrown ingredients than
white tablecloths"; N.B. closed Sunday–Tuesday.

Zax Tavern 23 | 22 | 22 | $39 |
2826 Telegraph Ave. (bet. Oregon & Stuart Sts.), Berkeley,
510-848-9299; www.zaxtavern.com
"It all works" at Berkeley's "frequently overlooked and
underrated" Cal-Med bistro, where a "small but interesting
menu" – which runs the gamut from an "affordable burger"
to more "exquisite" entrees – enables "both foodies and
meat-and-potatoes guys to enjoy the meal"; "sophisticated,
understated" interiors and "friendly, attentive service" also
help make this a "wise choice" for "celebrating a special
occasion" or just "comfortable eating and visiting."

North of San Francisco

Top Ratings North of SF

Excluding places with low voting, unless indicated by a ∇.

Top Food

28 French Laundry	Lark Creek Inn
Sushi Ran	Willi's Wine Bar
Farmhouse Inn	John Ash & Co.
27 Cafe La Haye	**25** Foothill Cafe
Terra	Marché aux Fleurs
Hana Japanese	Cafe Beaujolais
La Toque	Willi's Seafood
Fork	Auberge du Soleil
26 Cole's Chop House	Pilar
Bistro Jeanty	zazu

By Cuisine

American
- **28** French Laundry
- **27** Terra
- **26** Lark Creek Inn
- **25** Martini House
- **24** Celadon

Asian
- **28** Sushi Ran
- **27** Hana Japanese
- **22** Royal Thai
- **21** Gary Chu's
- **20** Robata Grill

Californian
- **28** Farmhouse Inn
- **27** Cafe La Haye
- Fork
- **26** John Ash & Co.
- **25** Cafe Beaujolais

Eclectic
- **26** Willi's Wine Bar
- **24** Celadon
- **23** Willow Wood Mkt.
- Wappo Bar
- Ravenous Cafe

French
- **27** La Toque
- **26** Bistro Jeanty
- **25** Marché aux Fleurs
- Bouchon
- Syrah

Italian
- **25** zazu
- **24** Bistro Don Giovanni
- Tra Vigne
- Santi
- Cucina Rest./Wine Bar

Mediterranean
- **25** Auberge du Soleil
- **24** Insalata's
- **23** Willow Wood Mkt.
- Manzanita
- **20** Hurley's

Seafood/Steakhouses
- **26** Cole's Chop House
- **25** Willi's Seafood
- **23** Fish
- **21** Père Jeanty
- Scoma's

By Special Feature

Breakfast/Brunch
26 Lark Creek Inn
   John Ash & Co.
25 Auberge du Soleil
24 Santi
   Insalata's

Newcomers/Rated
27 Cyrus▽
26 Rest. Budo▽
24 Cook St. Helena▽
21 Maria Manso's▽
   Fuentes Tapas▽

Newcomers/Unrated
   Boca
   Bungalow 44
   Flavor
   Picco
   Press

Outdoor Seating
26 Lark Creek Inn
   John Ash & Co.
25 Auberge du Soleil
   Martini House
20 Pinot Blanc

People-Watching
25 Martini House
   Bouchon
24 Bistro Don Giovanni
   Tra Vigne
   Mustards Grill

Romance
28 Farmhouse Inn
27 Cyrus▽
25 Cafe Beaujolais
24 Madrona Manor
23 El Paseo

Small Plates
27 Fork
26 Willi's Wine Bar
25 Willi's Seafood
23 Cindy's Backstreet
   Stomp

Tasting Menus
28 French Laundry
27 Hana Japanese
   La Toque
25 Auberge du Soleil
24 Domaine Chandon

Wine Bars
28 Sushi Ran
26 Willi's Wine Bar
25 Martini House
23 fig cafe & winebar▽
21 Wine Garden Food▽

Winning Wine Lists
28 French Laundry
27 Terra
   La Toque
25 Auberge du Soleil
   Martini House

By Location

Marin County
28 Sushi Ran
27 Fork
26 Lark Creek Inn
25 Marché aux Fleurs
24 Insalata's

Mendocino County
25 Cafe Beaujolais
24 Albion River Inn
   Rest. at Stevenswood
22 Little River Inn
   MacCullum House

Napa County
28 French Laundry
27 La Toque
26 Cole's Chop House
   Bistro Jeanty
25 Foothill Cafe

Sonoma County
27 Hana Japanese
26 Willi's Wine Bar
   John Ash & Co.
25 Willi's Seafood
   zazu

Top Decor

28	Auberge du Soleil		Terra
26	Domaine Chandon		Dry Creek Kitchen
	French Laundry		La Toque
25	John Ash & Co.		Meadowood Grill
	Madrona Manor		Wine Spectator
	Martini House	23	Poggio
	Lark Creek Inn		Caprice
	Farmhouse Inn		Albion River Inn
	El Paseo		Napa Valley Train
24	Tra Vigne		Bouchon

Top Service

27	French Laundry		John Ash & Co.
	Farmhouse Inn	23	Albion River Inn
26	La Toque		El Paseo
25	Marché aux Fleurs		Cole's Chop House
	Terra		Madrona Manor
	Lark Creek Inn		Syrah
	Auberge du Soleil		Fork
24	Cafe Beaujolais		zazu
	Cafe La Haye		Celadon
	Domaine Chandon		Bistro Jeanty

Top Bangs for the Buck

1. Downtown Bakery	11. Gira Polli
2. Joe's Taco Lounge	12. Royal Thai
3. Jimtown Store	13. Lotus of India
4. Barney's	14. Willow Wood Mkt.
5. Taylor's Automatic	15. Pizzeria Tra Vigne
6. Emporio Rulli	16. General Café
7. Alexis Baking Co.	17. Max's
8. Dipsea Cafe	18. Pearl
9. Amici E. Coast Pizza	19. Gary Chu's
10. Las Camelias	20. Wappo Bar

Other Good Values

Bistro Jeanty	Insalata's
Bistro Ralph	Market
Cafe La Haye	Mustards Grill
Celadon	Ravenous Cafe
Christophe	Santi
Cindy's Backstreet	Syrah
fig cafe & winebar	Willi's Seafood
Fish	Willi's Wine Bar
Foothill Cafe	zazu
girl & the fig	Zuzu

North of San Francisco

F	D	S	C

Albion River Inn
24 | 23 | 23 | $47

3790 North Hwy. 1 (Albion Little River Rd.), Albion, 707-937-1919;
www.albionriverinn.com

"What a view" rave regulars of this "romantic getaway" "nestled among the bluffs" of Mendocino where floor-to-ceiling windows offer vistas of the "Albion River flowing into the ocean" while an inviting "fireplace and piano player" help create a "cozy, classy" feel indoors; what makes the place "worth every mile of the drive", though, are the "outstanding" Californian cookery and "tremendous" single malts (160 labels) and wines (650), served by a "warm and efficient" staff that "remembers you year to year."

Alexander Valley Grille
▽ 21 | 26 | 20 | $42

(fka Chateau Souverain Café at the Winery)
400 Souverain Rd. (Hwy. 101, Independence Ln. exit),
Geyserville, 707-433-3141; www.chateausouverain.com

"A delightful place to while away a Saturday" "waxing eloquent over a great Russian River Pinot Noir", Chateau Souverain's Geyserville estate entices enthusiasts with its "sweeping view of the Alexander Valley" ("exactly what you hope for in the wine country") and "delicious" Cal-French fare; oenophiles enjoy "a bottle (or two)" on the patio "in the summer sun" or in the "beautiful dining room during inclement weather", but vent about "variable service" and the proprietary vinos ("diversity is a good thing!").

Alexis Baking Company
20 | 11 | 13 | $15

(aka ABC)
1517 Third St. (School St.), Napa, 707-258-1827;
www.alexisbakingcompany.com

The "aromas floating out onto the street" from the "killer pastries" and "delicious coffee drinks" at this "funky", "cramped" bakery in Napa "will win you over before you even get to your seat"; the "mecca for delectables" "gets an A" for its "awesome breakfasts" and "limited" New American lunches, but loses points for "long waits" and prices too high to reflect "the quality of service" from the "17-year-olds" working the counter.

All Season's Cafe & Wine Shop
23 | 16 | 20 | $38

1400 Lincoln Ave. (Washington St.), Calistoga, 707-942-9111

"You really know you're in" vineyard country at this "quaint" Downtown Calistogan where the "nice people" let you pick your potions "at retail in their shop and drink them with dinner" (in 3- or 5-oz. pours or by the bottle, plus corkage) as "perfect pairings" with the "excellent seasonal" Cal eats; aesthetes assert the bistro suffers from "a diner-meets–wine shop decor", but there's a reason this "old-timer" has "survived" all these seasons; N.B. customized tasting menus are available.

Amici's East Coast Pizzeria   20 | 12 | 16 | $18
1242 Fourth St. (C St.), San Rafael, 415-455-9777; www.amicis.com
See review in City of San Francisco Directory.

Angèle   22 | 21 | 20 | $42
540 Main St. (3rd St.), Napa, 707-252-8115; www.angele.us
"About as French as Downtown Napa gets", this "warm and pretty" country-style Gallic offers "exactly the comfort food you crave" exult satisfied souls who feel exalted by "wonderful views" from the "relaxing" riverside patio and the "lively bar" packed with "lots of locals" – but bedeviled detractors "don't feel comforted" by the "expense" or the often "forgetful service"; N.B. a post-*Survey* chef change may outdate the above Food score.

Applewood Inn & Restaurant   23 | 20 | 22 | $43
13555 Hwy. 116 (River Rd.), Guerneville, 707-869-9093;
www.applewoodinn.com
"Tucked away in the redwoods" near the Russian River, this apple farm–turned–"luxe" Guerneville "hideaway" is a "perfect wine-country" destination for "romantic trysts" "by the fireplace" and foodie forays; the "novel" and "delicious" Cal cuisine "reflects the area" as does an equally "good, locally focused" *carte du vin,* all proffered by a "friendly" staff that delivers "tip-top service"; the place's "wonderful atmosphere" may even make you "forget about the fog-shrouded drive" home and "splurge" on an overnight stay.

AUBERGE DU SOLEIL   25 | 28 | 25 | $71
Auberge du Soleil, 180 Rutherford Hill Rd. (Silverado Trail),
Rutherford, 707-967-3111; www.aubergedusoleil.com
"Nestled up above the Silverado Trail", this Rutherford French-Med is "romance central"; score a "table by the windows" for "soul-cleansing", "breathtaking views of the Napa Valley", peruse a 1,500-label list that's so fat it "needs an index" and bask in the pleasure of "flawless, seamless service", but realize that "if you have to ask how much" the "superb" tasting menu costs, "you can't afford it"; N.B. the arrival of chef Robert Curry (ex CIA's Wine Spectator) postdates the Food score.

Barndiva   ▽ 17 | 23 | 15 | $40
231 Center St. (Matheson St.), Healdsburg, 707-431-0100;
www.barndiva.com
Making its debut in 2004, this "up-and-coming" "new barn"-cum–"hip hangout" in Healdsburg gets an ovation for its spacious, "dramatic" interior (50-ft. mahogany bar, glass-walled wine cellar) and "gorgeous, magical" back patio

overlooking lush gardens; the "fun" menu of "playful" Eclectic small plates – composed of local ingredients in 'light', 'spicy' or 'comfort' preparations – generally hits the right notes, but prices are "high" and service falls flat; "with time, it should find its balance."

Barney's Gourmet Hamburgers   19 12 14 $14
1020 Court St. (4th St.), San Rafael, 415-454-4594; www.barneyshamburgers.com
See review in City of San Francisco Directory.

BISTRO DON GIOVANNI   24 22 22 $42
4110 Howard Ln. (bet. Oak Knoll & Salvador Aves.), Napa, 707-224-3300; www.bistrodongiovanni.com
What with "superb", "satisfying" *cucina,* a "welcoming" staff, "beautiful" interiors and a "gorgeous terrace", this "Italian trattoria in wine country" makes *amici* feel they're "visiting a favorite cousin's villa in Tuscany", which is why this "darling of Napa Valley" "bustles every night" with "local winemakers" and "society" sorts "hanging out in jeans"; though some slam long waits ("never go without a reservation") they concede "once inside, you know why."

BISTRO JEANTY   26 21 23 $46
6510 Washington St. (Mulberry St.), Yountville, 707-944-0103; www.bistrojeanty.com
Philippe Jeanty's "rustic, homey" Yountville outpost feels like a "casual and friendly" "French country inn" right down to the "vintage posters" on the walls, "accommodating" service and "heavenly", "hearty" Gallic classics; the fare may be "as rich as a Lotto winner" but you don't have to be, and though it's still "tough as ever to get a reservation" walk-ins can sit at the large communal table or at the bar "rubbing elbows with Napa wine notables."

Bistro Ralph ⊠   23 17 22 $41
109 Plaza St. (Healdsburg Ave.), Healdsburg, 707-433-1380
Chef-owner Ralph Tingle's "still whipping up" "fresh, snappy" Cal–New American fare and "visiting tables" at his "comfortable", "fun bistro" on the square in Healdsburg; a "chic staff" ("the coolest cats in town") pours "killer martinis" and displays its "great wine knowledge" when matching entrees with the "well-priced Sonoma-only list", so though some suggest the "small" menu "could stand to change more often", most maintain "'if it ain't broke, don't fix it' applies here."

Bistro V   – – – M
2295 Gravenstein Hwy. (Hwy. 116), Sebastopol, 707-823-1262; www.bistro-v.com
Silicon Valley transplant Rick Vargas has turned an old French stalwart in Downtown Sebastopol into this charming 50-seat bistro; the moderately priced French-Italian menu

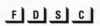
encompasses veggie, meat and seafood dishes, as well as a handful of Peruvian specialties in honor of Rick's heritage.

Boca —| —| —| M|

340 Ignacio Blvd. (Rte. 101), Novato, 415-883-0901

Tartare chef George Morrone prepares the cuisine of his mother's heritage at his second restaurant, an Argentinian steakhouse in Novato with rustic decor resembling a cattle ranch estancia; the focal point of the moderately priced menu is steak (both corn- and grass-fed) cooked in a wood-burning oven, but there are also empanadas, housemade sausages and a smattering of fish dishes.

Boonville Hotel ∇ 21| 19| 20| $37|

Boonville Hotel, 14050 Hwy. 128 (Lambert Ln.), Boonville, 707-895-2210; www.boonvillehotel.com

"Yes, it's in the boonies", so most folks who've discovered this Boonville "haven of comfort" are "probably staying the night" or "on the way to the coast", yet what they find are "unexpectedly well-crafted, fresh" Cal–New American eats and a "good" "local wine list"; whether you "stop in for a 'horn' (Boontling for drink)" or a meal in the "quaint" Shaker-style dining room or on the sizable garden patio, this is a "superior" option out where the "pickin's are slim."

Bouchon ◐⊄ 25| 23| 22| $49|

6534 Washington St. (Yount St.), Yountville, 707-944-8037; www.frenchlaundry.com

"Calling it the poor man's French Laundry does not do justice" to Thomas Keller's "vibrant", "convivial" "Yountville version of La Coupole"; *oui*, "it can get noisy and the tables are tight" but the "sublime", "super-fresh veggies, perfect meat" and "pro service" ("the waiter was a culinary encyclopedia") "would put any Paris bistro to shame"; "flexible hours" are a "godsend" for "winery-hoppers" and night-owls who can "impress or decompress" at the "classic zinc-plated bar" over "oysters and bubbles."

Brannan's Grill 22| 22| 20| $38|

1374 Lincoln Ave. (Washington St.), Calistoga, 707-942-2233; www.brannansgrill.com

"You won't rave about nuance" when dining at this "reliable" steakhouse in Calistoga but "you'll enjoy the straightforward simplicity" of the "better-than-average" American fare and "sleek", "masculine" mahogany-accented room with a bar dating back to 1870; best of all, the staff "never rushes you" and can help you navigate an "excellent" 275-label wine list that "appeals to tourists and locals alike."

Brix 22| 22| 21| $44|

7377 St. Helena Hwy./Hwy. 29 (Washington St.), Yountville, 707-944-2749; www.brix.com

Overlooking "beautiful vineyards" and "gardens in which the chefs hand-pick their vegetables", the "lovely terrace" of this Californian in Yountville is idyllic for "dinner on a summer evening" or a "great Sunday brunch", but if you want to ensure your server doesn't get "sidetracked as the crowds amass" you can "eat at the bar with the locals" instead; the "wines are incredible" too – now if only the "reliably very good" but only "marginally inspired" cuisine were equally "amazing."

Buckeye Roadhouse 23 23 21 $40

15 Shoreline Hwy./Hwy. 1 (west of Hwy. 101), Mill Valley, 415-331-2600; www.buckeyeroadhouse.com
Opened in 1937, this Mill Valley "old-world lodge" – complete with "roaring fireplace, lofty ceilings" and "forest denizens' heads adorning the walls" – has morphed into a "roadhouse of the rich and famous"; it's a "perennial fave" because the "BBQ pit smoking outside" turns out "intensely flavored", "stick-to-the-ribs American" cookery with "Marin flair" and because the bar's "retro cocktails" attract a slew of "lively" "fortysomething singles."

Bungalow 44 – – – M

44 E. Blithedale Ave. (Sunnyside Ave.), Mill Valley, 415-381-2500; www.Bungalow44.com
This Mill Valley newcomer housed in an Arts and Crafts–style bungalow is the latest upscale American grill from the folks behind the Buckeye Roadhouse; offering good value for all its pretensions, it caters to a local Marin crowd with affordable yet gussied-up comfort foods, rare wines and clever cocktails, which can be enjoyed either in the warm and inviting dining room or on the adjacent patio.

Cafe Beaujolais 25 21 24 $47

961 Ukiah St. (School St.), Mendocino, 707-937-5614; www.cafebeaujolais.com
A notorious, "glorious (albeit expensive) gem on the North Coast", this fave still "justifies its local fame" even to SF fans, who are "ready to drive those three hours just to dine" here; housed inside a "charming Victorian" with "tranquil gardens" is a true "lair of sophistication" showcasing "great" "modern" Cal-French "country-style food" with a wine list to match; "impeccable" work by the staff has boosted Service ratings as well.

Cafe Citti ∇ 20 12 16 $24

9049 Sonoma Hwy./Hwy. 12 (Shaw Ave.), Kenwood, 707-833-2690
For the ultimate "side-of-the-road" Northern Italian noshing, winery-hoppers "pull over" to this "inexpensive" highway haunt in Kenwood full of "locals and garlic"; "carbo-load on the freshest pastas" or chow down on "juicy rotisserie chicken" but expect "DIY" service where you "order at the counter and then find a table to park yourself" in the "diner"-like digs or "on the patio."

CAFE LA HAYE 🗷   27 | 20 | 24 | $45

140 E. Napa St. (bet. 1st & 2nd Sts.), Sonoma, 707-935-5994;
www.cafelahaye.com
Gourmets have a haye-day at John McReynolds' and Saul
Gropman's "pocket bistro" ("not much bigger than a couple
of phone booths") just "off the square" in Sonoma; the "arty"
venue is typically filled with "more locals than tourists" but
it's "worth its own trip from the city"; the "microkitchen"
"consistently" and "miraculously" produces "superb",
"sophisticated" Cal–New American dishes, the boutique
bottles are "fairly priced" and the "professional" crew is
"as much in love with the food as you are."

Caprice, The   20 | 23 | 22 | $50

2000 Paradise Dr. (Mar West St.), Tiburon, 415-435-3400
The "knockout view" of the Bay and the city "is the thing"
at this "old-money" waterside Tiburon institution ("racing
sailboats seem about to use your salt shaker as a turning
mark"), where the "stunning" setting plus "soft candlelight"
and crackling fires "puts you in the mood" for a tête-à-tête
or a splurge with "your parents"; surveyors say the "tasty"
yet "not imaginative" Cal-Continental "standards" and
"worn" decor seem "stuck in the '70s", but a post-*Survey*
change of chef might inject a bit of caprice.

Carneros   21 | 20 | 21 | $45

The Lodge at Sonoma, 1325 Broadway (Leveroni Rd.),
Sonoma, 707-931-2042; www.thelodgeatsonoma.com
"*Carneros* means sheep but there is nothing sheepish"
about the faithful flock who "make the effort to get" to this
"sleeper" in The Lodge at Sonoma; the "creative" and
"consistently good" Cal cuisine features "flavors fresh from
the garden" and the "wood-burning ovens" "at good prices"
(same goes for its regional wine list), and service is solid
and "friendly"; still, ratings suggest it hasn't "recovered
yet" from the "loss of its previous chef."

Celadon   24 | 22 | 23 | $42

The Historic Napa Mill, 500 Main St. (5th St.), Napa,
707-254-9690; www.celadonnapa.com
"Everyone should try" this Napa Mills veteran, "the first
child of Greg Cole" (Cole's Chop House); fans "keep coming
back" for his "novel preparations" of "memorable" "Asian-
inspired American and European comfort food" that's
"always accompanied by personal service from Greg"
himself; additional assets include the cellar's "strong half-
bottle selection" and an "atmospheric" patio "complete
with fireplace"; N.B. full bar now available.

Chapter and Moon   ▽ 18 | 14 | 18 | $24

32150 N. Harbor Dr. (Shoreline Hwy.), Fort Bragg, 707-962-1643
Sure, "driving through a trailer park seems an odd way" to
get to a "great eatery", but those few that make this lunar

landing moon about this humble "waterfront" spot in Fort Bragg; you can "watch the activity" in Noyo Harbor while savoring "moderately priced" "gourmet homestyle" American chow that's "so well presented one hates to take the first bite."

Charcuterie   20 | 15 | 19 | $31

335 Healdsburg Ave. (Plaza St.), Healdsburg, 707-431-7213
"This is Healdsburg, not Strasbourg", yet this "charming" nook dishes up "reliable", "expertly made" and affordable French bistro fare; "stuffed" and satisfied SF surveyors "would drive the 90 miles again just for that pork sandwich" even if some regulars rue the routinized menu ("hasn't changed in seven years"); meanwhile, given the place's name and the pork dishes on the menu, sensitive souls find the interior's "pink pig theme" "a bit distracting."

Christophe   22 | 19 | 22 | $34

1919 Bridgeway (Spring St.), Sausalito, 415-332-9244
For a hit of "France without the jet lag" or currency woes, you can't beat this "lovely", "unpretentious" and "verrreee Fransch" bistro, a "gem hidden in plain view on the outskirts of Sausalito" for nearly three decades; the menu "may not be the most innovative", but the Gallic "classics" proffered "with élan" by the "warmly welcoming (if nannylike in their attention)" staffers in the petite "shabby"-chic dining room are "a screaming bargain", particularly the "early-bird and prix fixe menus."

Cindy's Backstreet Kitchen   23 | 20 | 21 | $39

1327 Railroad Ave. (bet. Adams & Hunt Sts.), St. Helena, 707-963-1200; www.cindysbackstreetkitchen.com
"After days of nothing but fancy restaurants" this "small-townish", "laid-back" St. Helena haunt where "even visitors feel like locals" is "just what's needed"; "if you like Mustard Grill" (owner Cindy Pawlcyn's original wine-country venue) "you'll love" her "refreshingly gourmet take" on Cal–New American "home cooking" ("divine duck burgers"), served here in a "cheery" 1829 house with a "lovely patio" and a "convivial" vibe (you may even "strike up a conversation with the couple at the next table").

COLE'S CHOP HOUSE   26 | 22 | 23 | $55

1122 Main St. (bet. 1st & Pearl Sts.), Napa, 707-224-6328
Set in an 1866 historic building, Greg Cole's Napa meatery "satisfies that red-meat craving" with "dry-aged", "juicy porterhouses" and "wonderful sides"; the clientele admits the "array of beef" "will clog the heart and separate you from the Benjamins" but it's "just what you need for that Screaming Eagle" or another full-bodied fave from the "fabulous" 220-label list; locals, though, prefer quaffing "great martinis" and "chatting" with the "accommodating staff" at the "happening" bar.

Cook St. Helena ⌧   ▽ 24 15 20 $35
1310 Main St. (Hunt Ave.), St. Helena, 707-963-7088
Hometown cook Jude Wilmoth's "comfortable" "new place
on the block" is a "worthy replacement" to "venerable
locals' favorite" Green Valley Cafe, in part because "the
philosophy remains unchanged": a "wonderful blend" of
"well-prepared but not over-the-top fancy" Northern Italian
fare and a "good wine list" at "reasonable prices"; although
the "crowded storefront" with a "semi-open kitchen" can
get "noisy", it's where "Napa Valley natives" go when they
"don't want to cook" but also don't want "high-end dining."

Cork   - - - I
317 Johnson St. (Bridgeway), Sausalito, 415-332-2975
This handsome mom-and-pop wine bar with a back patio is
the brainchild of SF restaurant vets who longed for a casual,
cozy spot in Sausalito to gather for a drink; although there's
a limited selection of Italian fare (inexpensive panini,
crostini and salads fashioned from local, organic purveyors),
oenophiles will pop their corks over the vast, international
selection of boutique vintners; N.B. bottles-to-go are sold
at slightly less than market price.

Cucina Paradiso   ▽ 25 16 22 $34
*Golden Eagle Shopping Ctr., 56 E. Washington St.
(Petaluma Blvd.), Petaluma, 707-782-1130;
www.cucinaparadisopetaluma.com*
With "fabulous housemade pastas" and "great, relaxed"
Southern Italian cookery "at its finest", this "plain-Jane
restaurant" hidden in a Downtown Petaluma strip mall
"outshines" its fancier neighbors; it's a real "sleeper" but
"locals know" the wine bar is "surprisingly extensive", the
dolci are "to die for" and the "charmingly" accented staffers
"let you take your time" over your meal, whether you're
dining inside or on the riverside patio.

Cucina Restaurant & Wine Bar   24 17 20 $36
*510 San Anselmo Ave. (Tunstead Ave.), San Anselmo,
415-454-2942*
"Jack Krietzman and his staff did it again" cheer *amici*
of this San Anselmo trattoria; the chef/co-owner "makes
everyone feel welcome" in this "simple dining room" that's
"as narrow and crowded as a Venetian bus" so locals are
willing to endure a "long wait" for the "hearty", "satisfying"
Tuscan *cucina* and an "extensive, if pricey wine list" that
"could actually pass muster in Italy" ("a rarity in Marin").

Cyrus   ▽ 27 27 28 $84
*Les Mars Hotel, 29 North St. (Healdsburg Ave.), Healdsburg,
707-433-3311; www.cyrusrestaurant.com*
If you think Sonoma County dining means casual, this pricey
prix fixe–only Contemporary French in Healdsburg's new
Les Mars Hotel will come as a salutary surprise; owners

Nick Peyton and chef Douglas Keane (veterans of Gary Danko and Jardinière, respectively) are aiming for flat-out luxury, from the Burgundian-style room's vaulted ceiling to a caviar and champagne cart; N.B. namesake Cyrus Alexander pioneered the nearby Alexander Valley wine region, though the extensive cellar covers the globe.

Della Santina's   21 17 19 $35
133 E. Napa St. (1st St. E.), Sonoma, 707-935-0576;
www.dellasantinas.com
For its "shades of Italy" in sunny Sonoma, Santinistas shout "bravo" to this Tuscan trattoria, "a favorite of local winemakers" that offers "top-notch", "earthy" *cucina* "like your grandmother made" plus vintages from The Boot; the "great back garden" is most "welcoming", as is an owner who "treats you like family, or should I say *la famiglia*"; however, the disgruntled grumble "if or when *il padrone* leaves the premises, so does the service."

Deuce   ▽ 21 19 21 $37
691 Broadway (Andrieux St.), Sonoma, 707-933-3823;
www.dine-at-deuce.com
The "delightful" garden patio at this "wonderful converted" 1880 farmhouse may well be the "best outdoor dining" setting in Sonoma, state smitten surveyors; the place also proffers "solid" if "not outstanding" New American cuisine, county-centric wines and a "visiting-the-family" vibe from the "caring" owners, but few take a shine to its "flat and dull" art deco interior.

Dipsea Cafe, The   19 15 17 $19
200 Shoreline Hwy./Hwy. 1 (Tennessee Valley Rd.), Mill Valley,
415-381-0298
2200 Fourth St. (W. Crescent Dr.), San Rafael, 415-459-0700
www.dipseacafe.com
"Located near hiking paths and biking trails", these "sunny" San Rafael and Mill Valley cafes are predictably packed with "overactive" "athletic types and their families" carbo-loading on the "oversized portions" of "healthy" American-style breakfast/lunch grub; clockwatchers caution that even if "you can find a parking spot for your Range Rover", "long waits" and "haphazard service" may pose problems "if you aim to get over to Stinson before the crowds."

DOMAINE CHANDON   24 26 24 $61
1 California Dr. (Hwy. 29), Yountville, 707-944-2892;
www.chandon.com
How do voters love this Yountville "wine and dine"-ry? – "let me count the bubbles": from the "knowledge-elevating" free tour and "great list" including its "own sparkling brews" to the "heavenly" Californian cuisine "luxuriously presented" by the "formal", "well-trained" service to the "gorgeous, bucolic" view from the patio tables, it's "as good

a restaurant as Chandon is a champagne"; though prices
are "high", "you definitely get what you pay for" – "after 20-
plus years", it's still the area's "quintessential" "special-
occasion place" (some surveyors even say "skip that French
dry cleaning place and come here").

Downtown Bakery & Creamery ⊄   24   11   18 $12
308A Center St. (Matheson St.), Healdsburg, 707-431-2719;
www.downtownbakery.net
Locals concede this "quaint-as-hell bakery straight out of
Norman Rockwell" is "not really a restaurant", but "when
people ask about wineries to visit", they "instead suggest
these perfect" pastries, ice creams and sandwiches "for
the ultimate tasting"; despite little more than a bench for
seating (not counting "the park across the street"), a rising
Service score suggests it's the "best place to get your carb
fix in Downtown Healdsburg" – "the smell alone is filling."

Dry Creek Kitchen   23   24   20 $58
Hotel Healdsburg, 317 Healdsburg Ave. (Matheson St.),
Healdsburg, 707-431-0330; www.hotelhealdsburg.com
Although Charlie Palmer's "hip" Aureole "transplant" in the
Hotel Healdsburg "oozes" "NYC" "sophistication", this
"innovative" New American "captures the culinary wonders
of Sonoma – fresh produce, local livestock and fishing, and
of course" the regional vino (BYO from the home county and
corkage is waived); now "if only this place could iron out
service issues" and recalibrate the "Manhattan prices" for
"minimal portions" it'd be "equal to Palmer's reputation."

Duck Club, The   20   20   20 $43
Bodega Bay Lodge & Spa, 103 Coast Hwy. 1 (Doran Park Rd.),
Bodega, 707-875-3525; www.bodegabaylodge.com
See review in East of San Francisco Directory.

El Dorado Kitchen   –   –   –   M
El Dorado Hotel, 405 First St. W. (W. Spain St.), Sonoma,
707-996-3030; www.eldoradosonoma.com
A pair of former French Laundry chefs oversees this hip
new kitchen on the Sonoma Square that's the successor to
a long-running Piatti outpost; the moderately priced Med-
inspired bistro menu features gutsy pastas, meats and pizzas
that can be enjoyed in a variety of settings, including a
communal table, two cocktail lounges and a poolside
courtyard shaded by a fig tree.

El Paseo   23   25   23 $51
17 Throckmorton Ave. (bet. Blithedale & Sunnyside Aves.),
Mill Valley, 415-388-0741
Spanish name notwithstanding, this "unbelievably romantic"
restaurant "tucked into a breezeway in the heart of Mill
Valley" is likened to an "elegant country inn in France";
satisfied surveyors say this cluster of "intimate" "candlelit"
rooms qualifies as the quintessential "special-occasion"

spot because of its luxe "traditional" Gallic-Continental repertoire, "award-winning" 1,400-label wine list and "elegant" service, though some "under 60" suggest the place feels a bit "outdated" ("bring your grandparents").

Emporio Rulli | 21 | 22 | 15 | $19 |
464 Magnolia Ave. (bet. Cane & Ward Sts.), Larkspur, 415-924-7478; www.rulli.com
See review in City of San Francisco Directory.

FARMHOUSE INN & RESTAURANT, THE | 28 | 25 | 27 | $58 |
Farmhouse Inn, 7871 River Rd. (Wohler Rd.), Forestville, 707-887-3300; www.farmhouseinn.com
It's easy to keep 'em down on the farm at this Forestville "favorite" "in the Russian River area" that's "exactly what one would hope for in wine country"; set in a "tranquil", "country-chic" inn, it showcases "sublime" Cal cuisine and "top-notch" local wines, proffered by a "knowledgeable", "pampering" staff that practically holds a "personal seminar over the cheese course" served tableside from rolling carts; N.B. open Thursday–Sunday only.

fig cafe & winebar | ▽ | 23 | 19 | 20 | $36 |
(fka the girl & the gaucho)
13690 Arnold Dr. (Warm Springs Rd.), Glen Ellen, 707-938-2130; www.thefigcafe.com
"If you can't make it to the real thing Downtown", Sondra Bernstein's Glen Ellen offshoot will satisfy your cravings for "seriously good" French comfort food at comforting prices in an atmosphere that's "just like home – but better"; a few amigos still "miss the Gaucho" (which it replaced in 2003) but most locals don't give a fig now that it serves brunch and offers a win-win wine solution – stocking a great selection of Rhônes (all available by the glass) and providing complimentary corkage as well.

Fish ⊄ | 23 | 14 | 13 | $28 |
350 Harbor Dr. (foot of Clipper Yacht Harbor), Sausalito, 415-331-3474; www.331fish.com
"What a great catch" is the line on this "bare-bones", "dockside" Sausalito seafood "warehouse" run by an "ex-Masa's chef"; it's "pricey, considering you order at the counter" but the real lure here is the "creative", sustainable fin fare "brought from the boat into the kitchen"; "just don't expect Masa's interior" as this is more "like attending a picnic": "eating on benches", "drinking wine from old jelly jars and looking at the houseboats."

Flavor ⊠ | – | – | – | I |
96 Old Courthouse Sq. (Santa Rosa Ave.), Santa Rosa, 707-573-9600; www.flavorbistro.com
With its "cosmopolitan" vibe and "great service", this "incredibly popular" "uptown-style" newcomer in Santa

Rosa "feels like it could be in NYC" but the Eclectic cuisine – "a mix of fancy and simple", Mediterranean, European and Pacific Rim influences that even includes a kids' menu – is a love letter to California wine country; it "features locally, sustainably grown" ingredients, accompanied by an all-Sonoma wine list and beers from nearby Moonlight Brewing Company on tap, which hopsheads hypothesize "is reason to go all by itself."

Foothill Cafe 🗷 25 | 15 | 22 | $37 |
J&P Shopping Ctr., 2766 Old Sonoma Rd. (Foothill Blvd.), Napa, 707-252-6178
Napa regulars rhapsodize about the "fantastic food" ("get the ribs") at this "secret gem" set "blissfully far" from the usual tourist route; the "phenomenal" American barbecue-style grub and a staff that "knows how to serve" more than make up for "one of the world's ugliest shopping-center locations"; "bargain" prices make it easy to foot the bill; N.B. now closed on Sundays.

FORK 🗷 27 | 19 | 23 | $47 |
198 Sir Francis Drake Blvd. (Tunstead Ave.), San Anselmo, 415-453-9898; www.marinfork.com
"Lick-your-fork scrumptious" small plates "pack big flavors" at San Anselmo's "favorite dress-up restaurant", where the "refreshing", "imaginative" Californian–New French cuisine is "on par with the best in the Bay Area"; though the setting "is on the spare side" ("like a Quaker schoolhouse"), the "truly wonderful tasting menus" and "warm, attentive" host make this "foodie hangout" "worth a trip"; N.B. founder Scott Howard has departed, but little will change since the toque has passed to longtime staffer Bob Simontacchi.

Frantoio 21 | 21 | 19 | $38 |
152 Shoreline Hwy./Hwy. 1 (west of Hwy. 101), Mill Valley, 415-289-5777; www.frantoio.com
Though it's "incongruously" "nestled next to a motel", this "surprisingly elegant" Mill Valley Northern Italian "sleeper" is "a delight, whether for a quick pizza or a full meal" (e.g. "satisfying pastas"), thanks in part to servers who make diners "feel as welcome as they would be at home (maybe more)"; tip: sit near the restaurant's "giant stone olive press", an "amazing piece of machinery" that "turns while diners eat."

FRENCH LAUNDRY, THE 28 | 26 | 27 | $154 |
6640 Washington St. (Creek St.), Yountville, 707-944-2380; www.frenchlaundry.com
Thomas Keller's "countryside" Yountville cottage is home to "outstanding" "dinner theater in the best sense of the phrase"; "the service is a ballet, and the food a symphony" of "exquisite" tasting meals (some vegetarian) in which "magnificent" French–New American cuisine is paired

with "stunning" wines by "sommeliers who read minds"; yes, the reservations system is a "hassle" and the meal will cost you "an arm and a leg", but after "the best five hours ever spent" "you will agree that you didn't need that extra arm or leg anyway."

Fuentes Tapas and Wine Bar   ▽ 21 | 12 | 15 | $29
(fka Wappo Taco)
1458 Lincoln Ave. (Washington St.), Calistoga, 707-942-8165
While diners can still snag one of Calistoga's finest folded meals at this former home of Wappo Taco, the owner (who also runs the more upscale Wappo Bistro) has replaced the budget Mexican menu with a full-blown, gussied-up small plates one featuring hot and cold tapas; he stocks an array of Spanish and Chilean wines to complement the *cerveza* offerings, too.

Fumé Bistro & Bar   ▽ 20 | 17 | 19 | $34
4050 Byway St. E. (Wine Country Ave.), Napa, 707-257-1999;
www.fumebistro.com
With all the culinary competition in Napa, it's "easy to forget how good this place is until the scents from the kitchen greet you at the front door"; what's more, "the price is right" for the "dependable" and "creative" New American food, and the "pleasant ambiance" and "no-attitude" staff make it a "favorite of locals"; even if the indoor decor "isn't much to admire", there's a "nice outdoor sitting area."

Gary Chu's   21 | 18 | 19 | $31
611 Fifth St. (bet. D & Mendocino Sts.), Santa Rosa,
707-526-5840; www.garychus.com
This "local boy made good" makes good use of "fresh ingredients" in the "classic and nouveau" Sino fare at his "upscale" Santa Rosa spot; given the "efficient" service, "elegant" room and "the owner's personality" (which alone is "worth the tab") – not to mention the fact that there's "little competition" in the area – Chu believers choose this "superior" site to sate their "Chinese-flavor cravings."

General Café   19 | 14 | 16 | $24
Napa General Store, 540 Main St. (5th St.), Napa, 707-259-0762;
www.napageneralstore.com
An erstwhile mill in Downtown Napa, this is now "the area's best country market" for your "ritzy picnic" needs; at noon in its "crowded" cafe section diners dig in to "sandwiches, salads and pizzas" and "gaze at the river" from the sizable terrace, and insiders predict that "as soon as it's general knowledge" that chef Nam Phan (ex Slanted Door) now offers an evening menu of "upscale" Pan-Asian small plates Wednesday–Saturday, "we won't be able to get in" at all.

Gira Polli   20 | 13 | 16 | $22
590 E. Blithedale Ave. (Camino Alto), Mill Valley, 415-383-6040
See review in City of San Francisco Directory.

girl & the fig, the   23 | 21 | 21 | $40 |
Sonoma Hotel, 110 W. Spain St. (1st St.), Sonoma, 707-938-3634;
www.thegirlandthefig.com
The "daring combinations" at this "always imaginative"
French bistro at the Sonoma Hotel "may make you say
'hmmm' when you read them" on the menu but the chefs –
who are "really in tune with local produce, wines and
cheeses" and "let the ingredients sing" – "definitely know
what they are doing"; "attentive yet discreet" servers
attend the "warm and cozy" interior, surpassed only by the
"beautiful" back patio as a "perfect romantic getaway."

Gordon's   ▽ 22 | 16 | 16 | $23 |
6770 Washington St. (Madison St.), Yountville, 707-944-8246
A "daily stop" for locals, this "strictly breakfast and lunch"
counter-service cafe in Yountville harbors a "small-town
atmosphere", thanks to "made-from-scratch" American
eats and "terrific" owner "Sally G. working the crowd";
though the down-home spot "isn't big on ambiance" the
"fight for the tables can be competitive", as can the line for
"their fabulous, sells-out-quickly sour-cream coffee cake";
N.B. no longer serving Friday dinners.

Guaymas   17 | 19 | 15 | $33 |
5 Main St. (Tiburon Blvd.), Tiburon, 415-435-6300;
www.spectrumrestaurantgroup.com
The "breathtaking" view from the deck at this Tiburon
Mexican "can't be beat", so supporters say "with the Bay
and the city as natural wallpaper", "adventurous" "coastal
cuisine" and "great – and I mean great – margaritas", "how
can one go wrong?"; yet a contingent of critics carps "they
just can't get it right", complaining about "disappointing"
food and "dismissive" servers.

HANA JAPANESE RESTAURANT   27 | 17 | 21 | $41 |
Doubletree Plaza, 101 Golf Course Dr. (Roberts Lake Rd.),
Rohnert Park, 707-586-0270; www.hanajapanese.com
"Omakase, oh my god" sigh salivating surveyors who sagely
let chef-owner Ken Tominaga "do his thing" for them at his
"tiny" Rohnert Park place next to the Doubletree Plaza,
"easily" one of the "best Japanese restaurants north of
SF"; proffered by "unobtrusive" staffers, the "impeccable
sashimi and sushi" and "Asian-European dishes" are
downright "swoon-worthy", so while more pretentious
spots "may have better decor" (this one "reeks of plastic
strip-mall") the Sonoma County chefs who "flock" here
"on their days off" couldn't care less.

Harmony Club   ▽ 20 | 24 | 21 | $46 |
Ledson Hotel, 480 First St. E. (Napa St.), Sonoma, 707-996-9779;
www.ledsonhotel.com
With "elegant" old-world decor and sidewalk seating "right
on the square", this "pricey but fun" tasting room–cum–

supper club in Sonoma's Ledson Hotel showcases "deftly prepared" Eclectic small plates that harmonize with the "fabulous local wines" (some say *too* local – "it would be great if they carried wines other than" their own); late at night there's live music (piano during the week, jazz and blues on weekend nights) to boot.

Hurley's Restaurant & Bar | 20 | 19 | 21 | $42 |
6518 Washington St. (Yount St.), Yountville, 707-944-2345; www.hurleysrestaurant.com
Though less famous than some of its Yountville competition, this "no-attitude" Cal-Med serves "creative" "seasonal fare" ("great wild game") to "complement local wines" – and "you don't have to reserve months in advance"; the "lovely patio" and "nice fireplace" make it a "favorite of locals" in every season, and a "wonderful and considerate" staff has sent this year's Service score soaring.

Il Davide | 21 | 18 | 19 | $34 |
901 A St. (bet. 3rd & 4th Sts.), San Rafael, 415-454-8080
When in San Rafael, do as the locals do and head to this Tuscan trattoria that draws the likes of "reclusive Hollywood stars" who reside nearby; the "reasonably priced" and "satisfying" Italian chow, paired with some "interesting wines", goes down easily in the mural-enhanced, "noisy" interior or on the patio, and if service can sometimes be "slow", at least "they aren't rushing you out of there."

IL FORNAIO | 18 | 20 | 18 | $35 |
Corte Madera, 223 Corte Madera Town Ctr. (Madera Blvd.), Corte Madera, 415-927-4400; www.ilfornaio.com
See review in City of San Francisco Directory.

Insalata's | 24 | 22 | 20 | $40 |
120 Sir Francis Drake Blvd. (Barber Ave.), San Anselmo, 415-457-7700; www.insalatas.com
"Brilliant" chef Heidi Krahling "packs 'em in" to this "outpost of tastiness" in San Anselmo for her "flavorful", "fresh and inventive" Mediterranean "cuisine inspired by the season"; proponents proclaim the staffers "proficient" and the casual room "spacious" and "vibrant" ("love the oversized still-life paintings"), but critics complain about "noise" and "hit-or-miss" service, often opting for "take-out items" instead.

Izzy's Steaks & Chops | 20 | 16 | 18 | $37 |
55 Tamal Vista Blvd. (Madera Blvd.), Corte Madera, 415-924-3366; www.izzyssteaksandchops.com
See review in City of San Francisco Directory.

Jimtown Store | 20 | 18 | 17 | $16 |
6706 Hwy. 128 (1 mi. east of Russian River), Healdsburg, 707-433-1212; www.jimtown.com
Out in "the boonies" of Healdsburg, "this quirky little" combo of "retro" "roadside" "general store", deli and take-out shop

is the "perfect pit stop" for putting together an "upscale wine country picnic"; you half expect to see "Auntie Em making" the "overpriced" "goodies", and it takes "20 minutes for a sandwich" – but while you wait you can "browse the shelves" filled with "old-fashioned candies, toys" and "kitschy" "knickknacks."

Joe's Taco Lounge & Salsaria 20 | 18 | 17 | $16 |

382 Miller Ave. (Montford Ave.), Mill Valley, 415-383-8164
It "doesn't get more fun than this funky", kitschy Mill Valley "shrine to hot sauce" ("Pee-Wee's Mexican Playhouse") featuring "eclectic" artifacts, "friendly service" and the "best fish tacos this side of border control"; it's "the perfect spot after hiking on the mountain or driving back from the beach" and the "one of the few casual places to eat in pricey Marin" so expect "perpetual crowds"; P.S. "no hard-liquor license means burritos *sin* margaritas."

JOHN ASH & CO. 26 | 25 | 24 | $54 |

Vintners Inn, 4330 Barnes Rd. (River Rd.), Santa Rosa, 707-527-7687; www.johnashrestaurant.com
After a quarter of a century, this "landmark" at the Vintners Inn remains a "perennial contender for tops in the Santa Rosa area"; from inside the "lovely" "Spanish hacienda" or "outside among the vines" you can "watch a future vintage Chardonnay growing as you dine" on "inventive and inspiring" Cal cuisine (paired with "fantastic" local vintages), presented by an "accommodating", "gracious" staff; in short, it's "what people expect" in a wine-country restaurant "but seldom find."

Julia's Kitchen 23 | 18 | 22 | $49 |

COPIA, 500 First St. (bet. Silverado Trail & Soscol Ave.), Napa, 707-265-5700; www.copia.org
Fans feel Mrs. Child "would be proud" to see how her Napa Cal-French namesake has "morphed" from a "very solid place to eat after a tour of COPIA" into a "delightful culinary" "destination" in its own right; while the modern decor is now "warmer and less sterile" most "sightseers" still "sit on the patio" to "fully enjoy" the garden-grown food, always "wonderfully fresh" but sometimes rendered "overly fancy"; P.S. locals can stop by on "Thursday nights for a $29 prix fixe and free corkage."

K&L Bistro ⊠ ▽ 26 | 18 | 23 | $40 |

119 S. Main St. (Bodega Hwy./Hwy. 12), Sebastopol, 707-823-6614
"Alas, I only ate there once" lament those who can't get enough of this "Parisian-style" bistro that "foodies whisper about" and who vow they'll "return to taste again" after trying the "excellent steak frites" and other "superb" "authentic" French fare; though the "intimate interior" is "tiny" (you're "squeezed in tight"), "gracious" servers help make this "the place for fine dining in Sebastopol."

Kenwood   24 | 20 | 22 | $45

9900 Sonoma Hwy./Hwy. 12 (Warm Springs Rd.), Kenwood, 707-833-6326; www.kenwoodrestaurant.com

Although this "upscale roadhouse" in Kenwood "does not look like much" from the highway, cognoscenti confide it's actually one of the "wine country's best-kept secrets"; an alfresco interlude drinking "great" local wines, savoring "really satisfying" French–New American food and taking in the "amazing" pastoral views from the patio is exactly what you'd "expect Sonoma to be"; true, the bar can be "noisy" and "crowded", but "good service" and "interesting art" are compensations; N.B. closed Monday–Tuesday.

Kitchen at 868 Grant   ▽ 23 | 18 | 22 | $36

868 Grant Ave. (Sherman Ave.), Novato, 415-892-6100

As homey and cozy as its name, this rustic 45-seat storefront on Novato's newly spiffed-up main boulevard spotlights the classic American cookery of Christopher Douglas (once a star of Foreign Cinema); his compact, inexpensive menu is full of familiar favorites like crab cakes and skirt steak and is paired with an equally well-edited and affordable wine list.

La Ginestra   18 | 12 | 19 | $27

127 Throckmorton Ave. (Miller Ave.), Mill Valley, 415-388-0224

"Straight out of the '60s", this "old-school", "family-run" Mill Valley "landmark" serves "homey" Southern Italian fare, sometimes too "promptly"; regulars stick to the "excellent pizzas" and homemade ravioli (the rest is "no big whoop"), and caution that the "no-reservations" policy makes for a "noisy" night as "too many families with kids" wait for a booth.

LARK CREEK INN, THE   26 | 25 | 25 | $51

234 Magnolia Ave. (Madrone Ave.), Larkspur, 415-924-7766; www.larkcreek.com

"Set in an 1889 Victorian" "nestled among beautiful gardens and redwoods", Bradley Ogden's Larkspur legend "feels far away from the city" – but relax, it's "only 20 minutes" to this "secluded" spot, HQ for his signature "homey" yet "artful", "direct-from-the-market" American fare ("sublime Sunday brunches") and list of U.S. wines; with "pampering" staffers creating a "genteel", "clubby and genial" vibe, Marin mavens maintain "it would be hard to do better than this."

LaSalette   ▽ 25 | 20 | 23 | $40

Sonoma Plaza, 452 First St. E. (bet. Napa & Spain Sts.), Sonoma, 707-938-1927; www.lasalette-restaurant.com

"Finally something in wine country that's not French or Italian" rejoice revelers about this Sonoma Plaza showplace where Manuel Azevedo's "artful", "satisfying" Portuguese fare and an "extensive" selection of Iberian wines and ports are proffered by a staff of "knowledgeable waiters"; its "new, larger location" is "terrific", featuring an open kitchen, wood-burning oven and tile murals, so "save the airfare" to Lisbon and drive here instead – "it is worth the trip from anywhere."

Las Camelias
20 | 16 | 18 | $23

912 Lincoln Ave. (bet. 3rd & 4th Sts.), San Rafael, 415-453-5850; www.lascameliasrestaurant.com

"Not your average taqueria", San Rafael's "Mexican gem" concocts an array of "tasty" specialties (e.g. "mole to maim for"); "nice servers" and two "rustic" but "charmingly decorated" dining rooms featuring work by local artists help make this a "*muy bueno*" experience for families.

LA TOQUE
27 | 24 | 26 | $103

Rancho Caymus Inn, 1140 Rutherford Rd. (east of Hwy. 29), Rutherford, 707-963-9770; www.latoque.com

"Plan on spending three-plus hours" enjoying the prix fixe French dinners ("high art") and "remarkably humane service" at Ken Frank's "spacious" Rutherford "version of a farmhouse in Burgundy" – and plan to splurge and "go all the way with wine" pairings "matched better than most couples"; the experience may "cost as much as Napa Valley real estate", but since there's "none of the snobbiness" or "drama of getting a reservation" found at nearby rivals, at least you won't feel like you've been "taken to the cleaners."

Ledford House
▽ 23 | 23 | 23 | $43

3000 N. Hwy. 1 (Spring Grove Rd.), Albion, 707-937-0282; www.ledfordhouse.com

Mendocino "locals as well as visitors" "return over and over" to this "redone home"–cum–"coastal restaurant" in Albion for its "must-eat" Californian-Mediterranean cuisine, "fabulous wine list", "nice" nightly jazz and, most important, the "spectacular" "Pacific panorama" afforded by every table; "during the cold wintertime and on foggy nights" comfort-lovers also commend the fireplace; yes, it's "pricey", but the owners "treat you like family" and "oh, those sunsets."

LEFT BANK
18 | 20 | 17 | $37

Blue Rock Inn, 507 Magnolia Ave. (Ward St.), Larkspur, 415-927-3331; www.leftbank.com

At this Larkspur branch of Roland Passot's chain of suburban brasseries, Francophiles find the Gallic "bistro ambiance" ("high ceilings", vintage "food posters") *très jolie* and the menus rather "ambitious"; the fare itself is "decent" but "not exceptional" and "service is maddeningly inconsistent"; apropos the group in general, surveyors shrug "the more they grow, the less good they get"; N.B. there are locations South and East of SF as well.

Little River Inn   22 | 20 | 22 | $40
Little River Inn, 7901 N. Hwy. 1 (Little River Airport Rd.),
Little River, 707-937-5942; www.littleriverinn.com
When stopping at this coastal Mendocino "golf course
veteran", "at least have a drink" in Ole's Whale Watch Bar
with its "magnificent" ocean vista; the "beautiful dining
room with fresh flowers" and "wonderful" service is very
"inviting", but the Little River band supping or brunching
there on its "delightful" Cal fare don't get the same view.

Lotus Cuisine of India   22 | 17 | 20 | $27
704 Fourth St. (bet. Lincoln & Tamalpais Aves.), San Rafael,
415-456-5808; www.lotusrestaurant.com
"Delicious" Indian food in San Rafael, "who knew?" marvel
masala mavens at this "surprising find" that's "packed most
evenings"; if you "go on a warm night when they roll the roof
open" for a starlight dinner and the staff "treats you like a
very special guest", Lotus eaters aver you won't be sari;
though it's a bit "expensive", like everything else in the zip
code, "you can't beat the $8 all-you-can-eat lunch buffet."

Lucy's   ∇ 18 | 17 | 19 | $31
6948 Sebastopol Ave. (bet. Main St. & Petaluma Ave.),
Sebastopol, 707-829-9713; www.lucysrestaurant.com
This "fun locals' restaurant" with a primo "Downtown
location" is *the* place to go in Sebastopol"; by day, fans
flock "for the hearth-baked pizzas" ("the rest" of the Cal-
Med offerings are "decent but not special"), and by night,
cocktailers congregate for the "bartenders' innovative
concoctions"; "the decor and the staff are funkier than the
food", but the vibe's so "comfortable" and "unpretentious"
no one seems to care.

MacCallum House   ∇ 22 | 21 | 20 | $43
MacCallum House Inn, 45020 Albion St. (bet. Kasten &
Lansing Sts.), Mendocino, 707-937-5763;
www.maccallumhouse.com
A "charming" Mendocino inn in a "restored Victorian" is
home to this "warm, inviting" and "dependable" dining
room with "traditional decor" and a "gorgeous" porch
"overlooking the gardens"; "exciting" chef Alan Kantor is
a "local treasure" whose Californian menu "focuses on
organic and local farms", so it's a pity "his big tastes"
sometimes "get squashed in the crunch" of "too many
tables in too small a space" or overshadowed by the "flip-
a-coin great vs. grunt" service.

MADRONA MANOR   24 | 25 | 23 | $56
Madrona Manor, 1001 Westside Rd. (W. Dry Creek Rd.),
Healdsburg, 707-433-4231; www.madronamanor.com
"Just outside" of Healdsburg lies this "romantic getaway",
an 1881 Victorian B&B with grounds "so beautiful you don't
want to sit down" at your indoor table (fortunately there's

"patio dining in the warm months") – but once you do, the "simple but amazing" New American food (much of it "fresh from their garden") is "good enough to refocus you" on your plate; thanks to high-priced tasting menus, 400 "outstanding wines" and "very cordial service", respondents recommend it for those slightly "formal" "special occasions."

Manka's Inverness Lodge   ∇ 24 | 26 | 19 | $72 |
30 Callendar Way (Argyle St.), Inverness, 415-669-1034; www.mankas.com

If you like to see "your favorite woodland creatures" stuffed and mounted on the walls and appreciate "the cooking of same" "you'll feel at home" at this "out-of-the-way" West Marin "Arts and Crafts hunting lodge"; a "wonderful dog" keeps watch by the "real wood fireplace" where the chefs prepare their "amazing", regionally produced Californian fare; the "dreamlike" prix fixe dinners can last "four hours", however (everyone "cheered when we were served the last dessert of the evening"), and the "self-importance of the staff is a real turn-off."

Manzanita   23 | 19 | 22 | $41 |
336 Healdsburg Ave. (North St.), Healdsburg, 707-433-8111

This "low-key spot" in Downtown Healdsburg "doesn't get much press, but it should" swear "locals" who maintain the "warm" "professional service" is among the best in town; you can "eat in the wine cellar", "at the bar" (where there's "always a chance to spot a famous winemaker") or in the "comfortable", rustic main room that's filled with "lovely smells from the wood-burning fireplace" where much of the "diverse and inventive" Mediterranean fare ("from fish" to "delicious pizza") is prepared.

Marché aux Fleurs ⊠   25 | 22 | 25 | $42 |
23 Ross Common (off Lagunitas Rd.), Ross, 415-925-9200; www.marcheauxfleursrestaurant.com

Boosters bestow bouquets on this "absolute winner" in Ross, which flourishes due to "superb" New French fare "emphasizing organic and seasonal ingredients" and a "fascinating collection" of boutique bottles "from around the globe"; the owners, a "husband-and-wife team" ("chef and wine expert", respectively), "treat you like houseguests" and proffer a "quiet" "patio under a tree" that's "marvelous" for "Marin summer-evening dinners."

Maria Manso's World Cuisine ⊠   ∇ 21 | 16 | 22 | $41 |
1613 Fourth St. (F St.), San Rafael, 415-453-7877; www.mariamanso.com

The few who've found this "small", "simple" but "really great" "new addition to San Rafael" think the world of its "innovative" chef (ex Asia de Cuba), raving "what a treat" "to see someone taking chances with food"; her "delicious" Eclectic repertoire incorporates a handful of Cuban and

Asian dishes that lend this "friendly" spot a resemblance to her previous domain – fortunately, "you don't have to be hip to get in."

Market
22 | 20 | 21 | $36 |

1347 Main St. (bet. Adam & Spring Sts.), St. Helena, 707-963-3799; www.marketsthelena.com

"Real food served real well" "without the wine-country snobbery" makes this "lively" yet "low-key" St. Helena American a "much-needed regular restaurant for locals" and binged-out tourists; as the "friendliest staff settles you into your booth" it's like sitting in "your grandma's" kitchen being "stuffed full of your favorite foods" – though here they've been "classed up" (by the pair behind Healdsburg's tonier Cyrus) and paired with an "excellent" selection of "modestly priced" wines.

MARTINI HOUSE
25 | 25 | 23 | $54 |

1245 Spring St. (bet. Main & Oak Sts.), St. Helena, 707-963-2233; www.martinihouse.com

For a "first-class Napa dining experience" in the heart of St. Helena, respondents recommend Todd Humphries' "sophisticated" New American creations ("a flight of mushrooms took me higher than the ones from the '60s") presented by a "knowledgeable" crew in Pat Kuleto's "Craftsman-style cottage"; choose a table indoors, alfresco in a "Garden of Eden" or, if you're sans reservations, down in the "festive" "cellar bar" where you can "browse" the "engaging wine list" or "share a martini."

Max's
16 | 13 | 16 | $23 |

60 Madera Blvd. (Hwy. 101), Corte Madera, 415-924-6297; www.maxsworld.com

See review in City of San Francisco Directory.

Meadowood Grill
21 | 24 | 22 | $56 |

Meadowood Resort, 900 Meadowood Ln. (Howell Mountain Rd., off Silverado Trail), St. Helena, 707-963-3646; www.meadowood.com

"Croissants and croquet – does it get any better" than this "very resort-y" St. Helena "'in' spot for the old money"; the "unforgettable setting" overlooking "rolling green grass" alone "makes you want to join the game", although the "unrushed atmosphere", "attentive service", "very deep wine list" and "pricey" Cal cuisine are "great too"; some snap it's a "pale imitation of what was the Restaurant at Meadowood" and wonder when "that venue will reopen" (the answer as of fall 2005: within a few months).

Mendo Bistro
∇ 23 | 18 | 21 | $31 |

The Company Store, 301 N. Main St., 2nd fl. (Redwood Ave.), Fort Bragg, 707-964-4974; www.mendobistro.com

With its liberal use of "local produce", "fantastic" county-centric wine list and "nice view of Old Downtown Fort

Bragg", chef-owner Nicholas Petti's "relaxed", "big and
barny" bistro is well "worth the short drive up from Mendo";
offering "more than just the famed crab cakes", the "user-
friendly" New American menu allows "vegetarians and
carnivores alike" to "create their own entrees" (via a "nice
long list" of ingredients, cooking techniques and sauces),
while a staff of "hustling hotties" helps out.

Mi Casa   _ _ _ M
(fka First Crush)
*24 Sunnyside Ave. (Blithedale Ave.), Mill Valley,
415-381-7500*
The owners of the popular SF wine bar First Crush have
transformed their Mill Valley outpost into a homey Mexican
restaurant featuring original folk art and a mural with a
cactus motif; the menu spotlights Oaxaca and the Yucatán
Peninsula (think elaborate moles and mussels steamed in
agave wine) and employs organic produce and free-range
meats whenever possible.

Mirepoix Ⓢ   ▽ 27 | 18 | 26 | $46
*275 Windsor River Rd. (Bell Rd.), Windsor, 707-838-0162;
www.restaurantmirepoix.com*
"Keep an eye on this" little-known Windsor "diamond in the
rough" that presents "top-level", "thoughtful" and daily-
changing New American cookery with a "nice selection of
local wines" all "for about half the price of the same in SF";
given the "cozy surroundings" (including a 25-seat patio
and five-seat bar) and the "personable" owners, "you feel
like you're eating at a friend's house"; P.S. if you BYO
Sonoma bottle that's "not on the list", corkage is free.

Model Bakery   ▽ 21 | 12 | 14 | $13
*1357 Main St. (bet. Adams & Spring Sts.), St. Helena,
707-963-8192; www.themodelbakery.com*
"Just the smell" of the "great old-world bakery" at work
starts "the taste buds working" swoon St. Helena locals
who "get their morning fix" at this vintage venue; it's "not
open for dinner" and "best for takeout since table seating is
minimal", but "their ace breads", "excellent pastries" and
savory (if increasingly "pricey") brick-oven pizzas and
panini make it a "favorite spot to lay down a base for a day
of wine-tasting."

Monti's Rotisserie & Bar   ▽ 20 | 20 | 18 | $39
*Montgomery Village Shopping Ctr., 714 Village Ct. (Farmers Ln.),
Santa Rosa, 707-568-4404; www.montisroti.net*
One of the "hottest places in Santa Rosa" despite its
"shopping-center locale", this rustic, tile-and-wrought-
iron eatery conjures up "simple, uncomplicated" and
"consistently well-prepared" Med munchies, but skeptics
suggest skipping the "full Monti" and opting for the "hip"
bar with 42 wines by the glass ("either a 6-oz. or 9-oz. pour")

and "wonderful martinis"; surveyors are split on service, meanwhile, as some call staffers "professional" and "helpful" and others carp they "could use a little training."

Moosse Cafe ▽ 23 20 21 $34

Blue Heron Inn, 390 Kasten St. (Albion St.), Mendocino, 707-937-4323; www.theblueheron.com

"Hooray for the new ownership" hail habitués of the Blue Heron Inn's "cheerful" and "consistently good" Californian cafe, who have raised its Food, Decor and Service scores following a chef and management change in May 2004; just a block from the Pacific, this "jewel among the tourist shops" has an "airy", "tasteful ambiance" that particularly "lends itself to lunch", and though speedier sorts say the staff moves "in slow motion", locals simply suggest "get a tea, open your book and relax – it's Mendocino."

Mustards Grill 24 19 21 $43

7399 St. Helena Hwy./Hwy. 29 (bet. Oakville Grade Rd. & Washington St.), Napa, 707-944-2424; www.mustardsgrill.com

Don't wait for the "annual Mustard Festival" to visit "Cindy Pawlcyn's venerable" "upscale" "truck stop" in Napa; after 20-plus years, this "Dorian Gray" remains "the alpha and omega" of wine-country dining thanks to "phenomenal" New American "comfort food" (a "relative bargain"), a "terrific" cellar (natch) and the staff's "collective can-do" attitude and "desire to please"; it all "makes up for the ear pain" inflicted in the "packed" dining room and at the bar, a "haunt" for "Valley vintners" and the reservationless.

Napa Valley Grille 22 20 20 $41

Washington Sq., 6795 Washington St. (Madison St.), Yountville, 707-944-8686; www.napavalleygrille.com

This "pleasant-looking" Yountville chain link has visitors vacillating; confreres consider the "wholesome", "reliable" Cal cuisine served by a "nice" staff "an excellent value" and contentedly "sit outside" for "a wonderful lunch"; however, naysayers note "nothing innovative" here and nail the scene as "a little too plastic."

Napa Valley Wine Train 17 23 20 $66

1275 McKinstry St. (bet. 1st St. & Soscol Ave.), Napa, 707-253-2111; www.winetrain.com

Ok, it's "touristy", but well-trained Napa-sters term a trip on these "vintage railroad cars" to take in the "changing view" of "vineyards gliding by" and "enjoy the sunset" a "memorable", "lovely" and (literally) "moving" experience ("what it may have been like to be a 1940s high roller"); steamed critics complain the "uninspired", "overpriced" Cal meals (some with paired wines) are "not as good as the ride", however, and snarky surveyors scorn it as "the great train robbery."

955 Ukiah   ▽ 22 | 20 | 22 | $42
955 Ukiah St. (School St.), Mendocino, 707-937-1955;
www.955restaurant.com
Despite the "magical lighting" over the winding walkway
to this wainscoted "artist's studio turned restaurant" in
Mendocino Village, the enlightened emphasize that the
"real stars" here are the "well-priced" bottles on a "fine
regional wine list" and the "marvelous" New American–
New French food; a "cheerful" staff that "treats guests like
family" lends shine to this "relaxed and reliable" retreat.

Olema Inn   ▽ 22 | 22 | 21 | $41
Olema Inn, 10000 Sir Francis Drake Blvd. (Hwy. 1), Olema,
415-663-9559; www.theolemainn.com
Exuding an "honest, plain-Jane atmosphere" and plenty of
"heart", this "charming" 1876 inn in Olema offers "Tomales
Bay oysters by the boatload" along with "richly flavored"
Cal-Med cookery, all served "simply and efficiently"; active
out-of-towners aver it's an "enchanting place" to "rest
weary hikers' or kayakers' bones", while West Marinites
make sure to drop by on Mondays ("Locals' Night") for small
plates and live music; N.B. weekend lunches in summer only.

Osake ☒   ▽ 22 | 18 | 20 | $36
2446 Patio Ct. (Farmer's Ln.), Santa Rosa, 707-542-8282;
www.garychus.com
"The best sushi in Santa Rosa" comes from, surprise,
"local Chinese restaurateur Gary Chu" at his "spacious",
contemporary Japanese – indeed, the "gregarious" owner
himself may well be the one "making your maki" out of
"impeccably fresh" seafood; "for those who can't eat raw
fish" he also offers "high-caliber" hot dishes, plus 15 sakes
and a "limited" selection of Sonoma wines; it's all "great
as long as you're not in a hurry – service can be slow."

Pangaea   ▽ 22 | 17 | 20 | $41
39165 S. Hwy. 1 (east side of the Hwy.), Gualala, 707-884-9669;
www.pangaeacafe.com
Though it recently relocated to a "cute", "easier-to-get-
to" converted home in the "small seaside town" of Gualala,
this "lusty" Cal-French cafe still serves up "big, satisfying
flavors reflecting the North Coast" ("succulent homemade
charcuterie"), well complemented by the "chef's personally
selected wines" (including many biodynamics); thanks to
"very good service" the vibe is "relaxed", and summertime
lunchers swoon "sitting on the front porch is magnificent";
P.S. closed Monday–Tuesday.

Pearl ☒   22 | 18 | 21 | $33
1339 Pearl St. (bet. Franklin & Polk Sts.), Napa, 707-224-9161;
www.therestaurantpearl.com
"Nothing and no one is fussy" at this "unpretentious" Napa
mom-and-pop shop – it's just "local ingredients, local

wines and local residents" enjoying "simple, subtle" "yet creative" Californian eats ("good oysters", natch) in a "casual", colorful "enclave" run by "owners who really care about their guests"; given the "affordable" prices and "excellent value", no wonder it's "not so secret anymore."

Père Jeanty   21   21   20 $46
6725 Washington St. (Madison St.), Yountville, 707-945-1000; www.perejeanty.com
"Steaks, chops and more, with a French flair" are what's for dinner at Philippe Jeanty's more "affordable" Gallic "roadhouse" with the "charm and food of Provence" yet just "a quick walk from the hotels in Yountville"; carnivores cry *vive la* "marvelous""new meat menu" and appreciate the "easygoing", "chummy service" and "breezy patio" "on a nice afternoon or evening"; however, some with "high expectations" beef this boîte is "lackluster" and prefer the "parent" down the street.

Piatti   17   18   18 $34
625 Redwood Hwy. (Hwy. 101), Mill Valley, 415-380-2525; www.piatti.com
See review in East of San Francisco Directory.

Piazza D'Angelo   18   18   18 $33
22 Miller Ave. (bet. Sunnyside & Throckmorton Aves.), Mill Valley, 415-388-2000; www.piazzadangelo.com
For a quarter of a century this "popular" Mill Valley Italian has been locals' "habitual" "haven for cocktails or dinner", while plenty of others come primarily for the mixture of "beautiful people", "Botoxed broads", "balding men who drive Ferraris" and "graying yuppies" that populates this "friendly", "noisy" "singles scene"; consequently few squawk about the "not especially creative but reliable" fare or "spotty service."

Picco   -   -   -   M
320 Magnolia Ave. (King St.), Larkspur, 415-924-0300
Bix's Bruce Hill brings the small-plate phenomenon to Downtown Larkspur with a moderately priced, locally and seasonally driven Eclectic menu that allows diners to create shared multiple-course meals; regulars will recognize the interior of recycled redwood and exposed brick from the space's previous incarnation as Roxanne's, but the 15-ft.-long bar is now more prominent (it's run by wine director Michael Ouellette, also of Restaurant Budo).

Pilar ⊠   25   19   23 $47
807 Main St. (3rd St.), Napa, 707-252-4474; www.pilarnapa.com
TV chef Pilar Sanchez and husband Didier Lenders' "darling" "up-and-coming" bistro is the "real new star" in the "increasingly interesting Napa city dining scene"; the "dynamic duo at the stove" produce an "extraordinary"

seasonal menu that's "limited" in scope but broad in inspiration (a "wonderful blend of Spain, California" and France), as is a "nice" us-and-them wine list (half Golden State, half international); although the space is "small" and "crowded", "the friendliness of the servers" fosters a "comforting" atmosphere.

Pinot Blanc   20   22   20 $49
641 Main St. (Grayson Ave.), St. Helena, 707-963-6191;
www.patinagroup.com
Whether you're "dining alfresco" on the "lovely", "tranquil patio" or "by the fireplace" in the "comfortable", slightly "formal" dining room under the care of a "pleasant" crew, the "luxurious setting" of this St. Helena member of the Patina Group (aka "Pinot North") "promises the perfect wine-country dining experience" "at considerably less cost than the big boys"; unfortunately, though, the French-inspired Cal cuisine suffers from "inconsistencies", making it "low man on the Splichal totem pole."

Pizza Azzurro ⊠   ▽ 21   11   17 $20
1400 Second St. (Franklin St.), Napa, 707-255-5552
The "thin crust and absolutely wonderful toppings" are "damn good" pronounce pie-eyed partisans of this "laid-back and no-nonsense" "gourmet pizzeria" that's a "nice break from the pretentious restaurants in Napa"; the corner spot is "not exactly warm in atmosphere" but inexpensive local wines and "high-quality, quick food" (e.g. "simple, fresh salads") help "compensate."

Pizzeria Picco & Wine Shop   ⌐ ⌐ ⌐   I
316 Magnolia Ave. (King St.), Larkspur, 415-945-8900
A casual counterpart to newcomer Picco next door, this Larkspur pizzeria and wine bar from chef-owner Bruce Hill (also of Bix) tosses authentic Neapolitan pies and piadini (pizza crusts topped with salad) in a Lilliputian setting dominated by a massive wood-burning oven; while the crust (rolled so thin it cooks in a mere 90 seconds) is pure southern Italy, local Marin ingredients are showcased in everything from the toppings to the homemade organic soft-serve ice cream.

Pizzeria Tra Vigne   19   16   17 $25
(fka Vitte)
Inn at Southbridge, 1016 Main St. (Pope St.), St. Helena,
707-967-9999
"Fancy restaurants are nice, but sometimes you want" a "quick bite" at an "inexpensive place" admit locals and fatigued foodies who head to this St. Helena haunt for a "limited" selection of Tra Vigne–style "casual" grub ("delicious pizza", "amazing piadini", wines by the glass at "great prices"); meanwhile the setting, at the Inn at Southbridge, is also "very kid-friendly" – "you can eat,

they can play pool and everyone is happy"; N.B. BYO with no corkage fee.

Poggio Ristorante
21 | 23 | 19 | $41 |

777 Bridgeway (Bay St.), Sausalito, 415-332-7771;
www.poggiotrattoria.com

"The best thing" to befall the "tourist-infested" Sausalito waterfront of late may be this sprawling re-creation of an "Italian seaside" "sidewalk cafe" and bar, report reviewers; the "soulful", "rustic" food and "lovely" vino served in a "gorgeously lit", "dark-wood" space with "views of the SF skyline" have even "locals venturing out onto Bridgeway" – only the "ragged but always friendly service" is a bit doggio.

Press
– | – | – | VE |

587 St. Helena Hwy. (White Ln.), St. Helena, 707-967-0550;
www.pressthelena.com

Despite its homey farmhouse-style decor and seemingly straightforward American menu, this luxe St. Helena newcomer is definitely the place to impress in Napa Valley; the dream team behind the venue is vintner Leslie Rudd, who oversees the exclusive Napa Valley wine list, and former White House chef Keith Luce, who prepares a seasonal ingredient–driven repertoire of pricey prime roasts and grill items from the custom-built rotisserie, many of which are finished and carved tableside.

Ravenous Cafe
23 | 18 | 19 | $37 |

420 Center St. (North St.), Healdsburg, 707-431-1302

"You will not leave ravenous" rave respondents who regularly repair to this "cute" Cal-Eclectic "family spot" (across the street from Healdsburg's Raven Film Center); the "plentiful", "innovative bistro food" ("best burger") is made with Sonoma County vegetables "so fresh they might offend you", and stargazers say "sipping wine" "on the patio on a summer night" is swell; despite "amateurish" service and a slightly off-putting "pumpkin-colored" interior, locals "often say 'orange you glad it's here?'" N.B. a nearby sibling, Ravenette, reopened recently but is unrated.

Rendezvous Inn & Restaurant
▽ 26 | 20 | 22 | $45 |

647 N. Main St. (Bush St.), Fort Bragg, 707-964-8142;
www.rendezvousinn.com

An appropriately "romantic setting for a rendezvous", this "elegant old home" with its "cozy" Craftsman-style decor and "friendly" staff is the "best bet for a dining experience in Fort Bragg", offering "imaginative", seasonally driven New French dinners of the "first rank" (the locally focused "wine list is tops" too); supporters say "personable chef-owner" Kim Badenhop (who "trained under Georges Blanc") is an "excellent technician who deserves a better-appointed venue" ("if this were in Mendocino it would be packing them in").

Restaurant at Stevenswood, The ▽ 24 | 23 | 25 | $53
Stevenswood Lodge, 8211 Shoreline Hwy./Hwy. 1
(1.5 minutes south of Mendocino), Little River,
707-937-2810; www.stevenswood.com
"Surrounded by a tranquil garden", this "jewel in the forest"
in Little River gleams brightly thanks to chef Mark Dym's
"excellent", "innovative" Mediterranean cuisine; additional
facets include a "lovely", art-filled dining room with "an
inviting fireplace" and only "a handful of tables" that
enables the "great staff" to "make you feel like the most
important folks in Mendocino"; N.B. closed Wednesdays.

Restaurant Budo ☒   ▽ 26 | 27 | 22 | $70
1650 Soscol Ave. (bet. 1st St. & Lincoln Ave.), Napa,
707-224-2330; www.restaurantbudo.com
Word on the grapevine is this Napa neophyte is the valley's
"new star"; chef/co-owner James McDevitt (formerly of
Scottsdale's Restaurant Hapa) has crafted the "closest thing
to a NYC restaurant north of the Bay", pairing "innovative"
Asian-accented New American fare with wines from a
"marvelous" "50-page" list; pessimists pronouce the cluster
of "sleek but warm" rooms "too fancy" for the area, but
early adopters optimistically opine they "can't wait to go
back" next summer to dine on the "great patio."

Ristorante Fabrizio ☒   ▽ 21 | 14 | 22 | $33
455 Magnolia Ave. (Cane St.), Larkspur, 415-924-3332
"Who can resist" chef-owner and "great host" Fabrizio
Martinelli, who "meets and greets almost everyone" at his
"family-run" Larkspur Italian where nonna is "usually at
the corner table surveying the scene"; "uncomplicated"
yet "never disappointing", the Northern Italian dishes are
a "good value" and the "simple", "very charming" room is
a "nice place" for a "romantic dinner" (though they tend to
"cater to a more mature crowd").

Robata Grill & Sushi   20 | 16 | 18 | $33
591 Redwood Hwy./Hwy. 101 (Seminary Dr. exit), Mill Valley,
415-381-8400; www.robatagrill.com
This Mill Valley maki manse offers robata-grilled items too,
"a pleasant combo for sushi lovers and landlubbers" alike;
the "quiet", "relaxed" "traditional" dining room and "prompt
if impersonal" service make it a "down-to-earth" scene –
even if a few snark that by comparison to competitors this
"basic" spot is like "the Denny's of Japan."

Royal Thai   22 | 16 | 19 | $26
610 Third St. (Irwin St.), San Rafael, 415-485-1074;
www.royalthaisanrafael.com
"Of the gazillions of Thai restaurants in San Rafael", this
"always hopping", "well-established" Marin mainstay is
a "reliable" "favorite"; partisans proclaim its "authentic"
Siamese eats the "best this side of Bangkok" and deem

dinner at this "funky" yet "comfortable" Victorian a royal *oui* thanks to "smiling staffers who make you feel welcome."

Rustico   – | – | – | I

39 Caledonia St. (bet. Johnston & Pine Sts.), Sausalito, 415-332-4500; www.windowsofitaly.com

Overlooking a tree-lined stretch of Downtown Sausalito, this cozy storefront trattoria features butter-yellow walls, dark-wood wainscoting and a fireplace, while its affordable menu of rustic Southern Italian cuisine showcases homemade pastas like meat tortellini and pappardelle with wild boar ragout, as well as hand-thrown pizzas.

Rutherford Grill   22 | 18 | 20 | $34

1180 Rutherford Rd. (Hwy. 29), Rutherford, 707-963-1792; www.houstons.com

"Ok, so it's really just Houston's" but "when you need a change from wine-country haute cuisine" this "casual", Rutherford all-American (owned by the aforementioned corporation) fits the bill; admirers assert the "bartenders know their stuff" and the "well-trained employees" serve up "solid", "consistent" (if "a bit boring") "comfort food", so although detractors dis the "chain feel and flavor", it's "always crowded" nevertheless.

Sabor of Spain ⌧   – | – | – | I

1301 Fourth St. (C St.), San Rafael, 415-457-8466; www.saborofspain.com

This San Rafael specialty store, which imports food, wine and tchotchkes from the Iberian Peninsula, has added a modern, casual vinoteca that prepares 'Alta Cocina' (or 'high end') traditional tapas and entrees fashioned from locally grown Marin and Sonoma county ingredients; 25 Spanish wines are available by the taste, with another 75 by the bottle, all of which are sold in the adjacent shop.

Santé   ∇ 23 | 22 | 22 | $58

Fairmont Sonoma Mission Inn & Spa, 100 Boyes Blvd. (Sonoma Hwy.), Sonoma, 707-939-2415; www.fairmont.com

"Even the low-cal choices are enticing" now that "new chef" Bruno Tison is cooking up "very fine" (if "pricey") Cal cuisine at this Sonoma Mission Inn veteran; it's now a "worthy alternative" for those "too tired to venture out after a day at the spa" so though "robes aren't allowed in the dining room (about the only place you have to put on real clothes)", denizens don't mind getting dressed to "wine and dine in the serene" Craftsman-style environs.

Santi   24 | 20 | 22 | $44

21047 Geyserville Ave. (Hwy. 128), Geyserville, 707-857-1790; www.tavernasanti.com

It's "not your usual spaghetti dinner" – instead you get some of the "wine country's most authentic Tuscan" specialties

("spicy and inventive pastas", signature osso buco) at this
rustic, "real-deal" trattoria, where "you'll find, in winter, a
cozy fire crackling" and in summer, a "romantic terrace",
plus a staff happy to introduce you to some "excellent
local wines"; all in all, say santi-sfied surveyors, it's "the
biggest reason to visit" "the one-street town of Geyserville"
("there's not much else here").

Scoma's   21   16   18 $40
*588 Bridgeway (Princess St.), Sausalito, 415-332-9551;
www.scomassausalito.com*
See review in City of San Francisco Directory.

Sea Ranch Lodge Restaurant   ▽ 19   22   20 $46
*Sea Ranch Lodge, 60 Sea Walk Dr. (Hwy. 1), Sea Ranch,
707-785-2371; www.searanchlodge.com*
Friends find it "hard to argue" with the "spectacular views"
of the Sonoma coast ("watch the whales cavort") or the
"classic and enduring '60s architecture" at this Sea Ranch
restaurant; while the Cal-style seafood is "good" "for a
lodge in the middle of nowhere", locals who make the
"Highway 1 trek" opt to "sit in the solarium" for a drink and
a bite – same "romantic setting" and vistas, "only cheaper."

Seaweed Café   ▽ 27   19   26 $39
*1580 Eastshore Rd. (Hwy. 1), Bodega Bay, 707-875-2700;
www.seaweedcafe.com*
Though the place has "no view" of Bodega Bay, a small
squadron of swooning surveyors swear this "tiny" bistro
"in a nothing strip mall" is a "real catch" on the "teeming-
with-tourist-traps" Sonoma coastline; chef/co-owner
Jackie Martine whips up "creative", "Japanese-influenced"
Californian seafood-oriented dinners (with organic
ingredients and wines from the soil "west of Highway 101")
and weekend brunches while staffers pay "very personal
attention" to patrons in the "delightful", newly enlarged
dining room; N.B. closed Sunday–Tuesday.

Sharon's By the Sea   ▽ 21   15   19 $28
*Noyo Harbor, 32096 N. Harbor Dr. (Hwy. 1), Fort Bragg,
707-962-0680*
*Hill House Inn, 10701 Palette Dr. (Lansing St.), Mendocino,
707-937-3200*
www.sharonsbythesea.com
Fin-fare fans who favor this "tiny", "funky" Fort Bragg "fish
trap" on a pier "in the depths of Noyo Harbor" figure you'll
be hooked after "one taste" of the "simple", "very fresh"
Italian-accented seafood; it's "lovely" "to watch the boats
and seals go by" from the outdoor deck, and though the
room can be "cramped" and "drafty", it's "convenient if
you want to avoid the bustle and expense of Mendocino",
where Sharon's got a "rose-colored", country-style outpost
at the Hill House Inn.

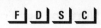
Sonoma Meritage & Oyster Bar ▽ 22 | 19 | 20 | $37

165 West Napa St. (bet. 1st & 2nd Sts.), Sonoma, 707-938-9430; www.sonomameritage.com

Boosters of this bivalve bar and eatery boast of its French–Northern Italian fare ("excellent fresh fish") at prices so "reasonable" you won't have to shell out a lot of clams; its modern, "lively new digs" (with a "beautiful outdoor area" and "better parking") just off the plaza in Sonoma attract "a crowd" that's "seemingly there to party", including the "chef who mingles with the tables" and bartenders who pour local meritage wines and "specialty martinis"; N.B. closed Tuesdays.

Stomp ▽ 23 | 19 | 21 | $47

Mount View Hotel, 1457 Lincoln Ave. (bet. Fair Way & Washington St.), Calistoga, 707-942-8272; www.stomprestaurant.com

A "great new choice" – with possibly the "worst restaurant name ever" – this "upscale" freshman at Calistoga's Mount View Hotel features Californian small and large plates along with some 40 wines available in 2-oz. and 5-oz. pours; the "owners are trying hard" with their "trendy, stacked" cuisine, but some folks dig their heels in, insisting it's "too pretentious for the location" ("very, very expensive") and instead stepping over to the adjacent cafe, Little Feet, which stomps on weekends thanks to live music.

St. Orres ▽ 23 | 26 | 23 | $54

36601 Shoreline Hwy./Hwy. 1 (2 mi. north of Gualala), Gualala, 707-884-3303; www.saintorres.com

"A Mendocino classic" since 1979, this "wacky" Gualala B&B's "spectacular" "hand-built dining room with a ceiling soaring into a Russian-style" "onion-domed roof" is "unlike any other" as are Rosemary Campiformio's "adventurous" Cal prix fixe dinners ("dramatic presentations" of "wild game and mushroom" dishes) with "eight to 10 daily specials" that the "exquisitely trained" staffers recite by heart; longtimers suggest the menu could use a "little refreshing", but nevertheless liken the "elegant" experience to "slipping into a warm bath."

SUSHI RAN 28 | 21 | 22 | $46

107 Caledonia St. (bet. Pine & Turney Sts.), Sausalito, 415-332-3620; www.sushiran.com

Voted the Bay Area's premier Japanese restaurant, this Sausalito "treasure" (the "Nobu of Marin") has it all: "solicitous service", "calming decor", an "incredible sake selection" and, of course, "exquisite", "sublime" sushi and sashimi ("like you're eating music"); rhapsodic regulars also recommend the "out-of-the-(bento)-box" cooked plates ("highly imaginative without being absurd"); "yes, you may have to wait, but with the wine bar next door that's not a hardship."

Syrah   25 | 19 | 23 | $44
205 Fifth St. (Davis St.), Santa Rosa, 707-568-4002;
www.syrahbistro.com
In a part of the world where "too many restaurants take
the name of a varietal", this "ambitious" Cal-French bistro
in Santa Rosa's Railroad Square area is "among the best";
"make sure to loosen your belt" for chef-owner Josh Silvers'
"out-of-this-world" tasting menu and predictably "dynamite
Rhône wines", all "knowledgeably" served in a "rustic",
copper-accented room; scenery snobs scorn the "mediocre
location" near "the 101 overpass", but satisfied surveyors
serenely shrug "que Syrah, Syrah."

Taylor's Automatic Refresher   21 | 13 | 15 | $15
933 Main St. (bet. Charter Oak Ave. & Pope St.), St. Helena,
707-963-3486; www.taylorsrefresher.com
"Where else can you get a bottle of wine with your burger"
but this St. Helena "retro" "roadside diner" where "there's
something for everyone" on the American menu ("awesome
ahi sandwiches", "indulgent milkshakes") plus a couple
dozen local bottlings; despite counter service (you "could
starve to death" in the long line) and seating that's outdoors
only, wallet watchers warn "you'll pay sit-down prices";
N.B. a branch in SF's Ferry Building has tables inside and out.

TERRA   27 | 24 | 25 | $61
1345 Railroad Ave. (bet. Adams & Hunt Sts.), St. Helena,
707-963-8931; www.terrarestaurant.com
Even San Franciscans claim it's "worth the pilgrimage" to
this "fabulous restored 19th-century stone building" "off the
main drag in St. Helena" for Hiro Sone's "deeply satisfying",
"spectacularly original" New American fare (incorporating
Italian, French and Japanese flavors), wife Lissa Doumani's
desserts that "dance on your palate", the "extensive wine
list" and the attentions of an "exceptional" staff; of course,
"if you're already in town, it's a slam dunk."

TRA VIGNE   24 | 24 | 22 | $50
1050 Charter Oak Ave. (Hwy. 29), St. Helena, 707-963-4444;
www.travignerestaurant.com
Italophiles idolize this "charming farmhouse" just off
Highway 29 ("Tuscany in St. Helena") whether they're dining
under the "soaring ceilings" indoors or in the "*bellissimo*"
courtyard; at its best the "rustic, earthy" *cucina* is "brilliant"
("you could drink their olive oil like water") and staffers
display "awesome knowledge" of the ever-changing wine
list, so it remains "difficult to get a reservation" – although
a vocal faction frets "inconsistency is marring the beauty."

Underwood Bar & Bistro   ∇ 22 | 24 | 20 | $38
9113 Graton Rd. (Edison St.), Graton, 707-823-7023
"Step past the velvet curtain and you're zapped out of the
one-block town of Graton" and into an "effervescent" "NYC"

nightspot; the "awesome" oysters and "sophisticated" Southern Med meals are "surprisingly good" but "West County residents" "tend to favor" the spot for its "late-night tapas-style menu and well-stocked, friendly bar" (though not for its "slow service"); "when the joint is jumpin'" and "conversation is a near impossibility", "good outside seating" provides an acoustic alternative.

Uva Trattoria & Bar   ∇ 20 | 16 | 19 | $31 |
1040 Clinton St. (Main St.), Napa, 707-255-6646;
www.uvatrattoria.com
Despite its proximity to the opera house in Downtown Napa, this "comfortable", colorful Southern Italian trattoria isn't particularly the province of culture vultures; instead it's primarily patronized by families who dine early on "darn good", "moderately priced" pizza and pasta (much of it "available in half portions") and then, later in the evening, by a "trendy younger crowd" enjoying "live music", a limited late-night menu and "personable service."

Victorian Gardens   ∇ 22 | 24 | 24 | $73 |
The Inn at Victorian Gardens, 14409 S. Hwy. 1
(8 mi. north of Pt. Arena), Manchester, 707-882-3606;
www.innatvictoriangardens.com
"Unique fails to describe" this culinary oasis, set in a small, "delightful" Manchester B&B that's surrounded by a 92-acre farm and run by the "wonderful" Zamboni family; "Luciano cooks from his very Roman heart", whipping up nightly prix fixes with appropriate pairings for "16 or fewer" guests (practically a "family gathering") in his two dining rooms; generous wine pours and leisurely five-course dinners have admirers advising "book one of the rooms so you don't have to drive afterwards."

Wappo Bar Bistro   23 | 20 | 19 | $34 |
1226 Washington St. (Lincoln Ave.), Calistoga, 707-942-4712;
www.wappobar.com
"Adventurous, unexpected flavor combinations" ("truly amazing duck carnitas") paired with any of 190 international boutique wines help make this "unpretentious" Calistoga Eclectic with "real soul" "popular with locals"; some prefer the "casually elegant" redwood interior but most maintain "sitting under the grape arbor" on the "romantic patio" is a "must", even on occasions when the service is "off."

Water Street Bistro ⇗   ∇ 23 | 16 | 18 | $20 |
100 Petaluma Blvd. N. (Western Ave.), Petaluma, 707-763-9563
"Who cares if you have to go up to the counter and order" at this "unpretentious" little French bistro when the result is an "apparently limitless" variety of "appealing", "organic" breakfasts and lunches for your delectation on a patio with a view of the Petaluma River; fortunately, when the place stays open for dinner – on summer Fridays and Saturdays

plus once a month for eight-course themed repasts – there's "welcoming" table service as well; N.B. cash only.

Willi's Seafood & Raw Bar   25 22 21 $40
403 Healdsburg Ave. (North St.), Healdsburg, 707-433-9191; www.willisseafood.net
Adorned with bright cool colors, wrought-iron ceiling fans and a 20-ft. slate wall fountain, this "noisy and lively" Healdsburg seafooder provides "great energy" along with "fun, fantastic fish" tapas ("that lobster roll – wow!") and a "wide variety" of Sonoma wines offered by the glass or half-bottle; service is "polite" and "unobtrusive" but "uneven", and cost-conscious consumers carp those small plates can cost a small fortune: "if you're hungry, be prepared to spend a lot."

Willi's Wine Bar   26 18 21 $43
Orchard Inn, 4404 Old Redwood Hwy. (River Rd.), Santa Rosa, 707-526-3096; www.williswinebar.net
Owners Mark and Terri Stark give you the Willi's at Santa Rosa's "relaxing" 1886 Orchard Inn, where they offer "excellent", "always-changing" Eclectic "small plates with big flavors" ("think global" with a dash of "local color") along with 40 vinos by the glass; rhapsodizing regulars report that "mixing and matching" tapas, cheese samplers and wine flights will "satisfy every kind of flavor craving" – but caution "prices add up shockingly quickly."

Willow Wood Market Cafe   23 14 17 $26
9020 Graton Rd. (Brush St.), Graton, 707-522-8372
In-the-know tourists in the "rustic village" of Graton wouldn't miss this "funky" "hangout" where "simple", "standout" Eclectic, Med-inspired "bargain" meals and "terrific local wines" "aspire to heights beyond these confines"; the down-home space was recently upgraded (though "not prettied up") with expanded counter seating and new hardwood floors, and though a few weep about servers "too laid-back to remember what you asked for", most willingly overlook that for the sake of the "delightful" experience.

Wine Garden Food and Wine Bar   ▽ 21 19 21 $40
6476 Washington St. (Oak Circle), Yountville, 707-945-1002; www.napawinegarden.com
Run by the "friendliest staff" in Yountville, this retro-style newcomer proffers an "extensive menu" of "delectable" Regional American small plates and "expansive list of wines by the glass" (including a dozen themed flights), all of which come from grapes grown by the owners' family; still, unsatisfied trenchermen whine "prices need to come down and portion size needs to go up" – if you keep ordering till you're full the "bill ends up a shocker"; N.B. live piano music on Saturday nights.

Wine Spectator Greystone | 23 | 24 | 23 | $46 |
Culinary Institute of America, 2555 Main St. (Deer Park Rd.), St. Helena, 707-967-1010; www.ciachef.edu
"A spectacular medieval stone edifice" is home to this "Harvard of cuisine" in St. Helena, a "must-visit" for enthusiastic epicures who can sit near the "unique, wide-open" exhibition kitchen to "watch the cooks at work" whipping up "divine" Californian cuisine ("even having an iced tea here is an event") or "get a seat on the terrace" with a "commanding view of the valley"; not everyone is impressed, though, as some report "spotty" service and sigh that "the beauty of the landmark isn't yet matched by the food."

Yankee Pier | 18 | 15 | 17 | $30 |
286 Magnolia Ave. (bet. King St. & William Ave.), Larkspur, 415-924-7676; www.yankeepier.com
Cape crusaders claim Bradley Ogden's New England–style "sea shanty" in Larkspur is without peer "for homesick East Coasters" whose "kids play in the sandbox on the patio" while they have a "quick slurp at the raw bar" or "scarf" "real lobster rolls and Ipswich fried clams"; but cranky Yankees cry "arr, matey", this "hit-or-miss" grub isn't worth "shelling out buried treasure" for; N.B. offshoots have surfaced in San Jose and SFO.

Zaré | – | – | – | M |
5091 Solano Ave. (Oak Knoll Ave.), Napa, 707-257-3318; www.zarenapa.com
Now that he's closed his longtime eponymous Downtown restaurant, chef-owner Hoss Zaré is exercising his talents in Napa with this casual, moderately priced venue featuring his signature Cal-Med dishes, as well as new creations fashioned from produce grown on-site; a spacious patio and live entertainment on Friday and Saturday evenings give diners a chance to stretch out; N.B. Zaré plans to transform the property eventually into a culinary complex featuring, among other things, a more upscale eatery, wine bar, B&B and bakery.

zazu | 25 | 18 | 23 | $42 |
3535 Guerneville Rd. (Willowside Rd.), Santa Rosa, 707-523-4814; www.zazurestaurant.com
Though its location on the outskirts of Santa Rosa "defines out-of-the-way", this "rustic", "funky roadhouse" with a "warm ambiance" turns out to be a "revelation", say surveyors; assisted by a "gracious" staff, the "passionate, creative, whimsical chef-owners" concoct "sumptuous", "innovative" New American–Northern Italian cuisine; on Wednesdays, Thursdays and Sundays, local zealots zazoom on over for the popular 'pizza and Pinot' nights, featuring a trio of pies "mixed and matched" with three wines from the "fabulous", mostly regional list.

Zin   21 | 18 | 20 | $38
344 Center St. (North St.), Healdsburg, 707-473-0946;
www.zinrestaurant.com
"Upscale" yet "homey" New American eats ("like mom
would make if only she went to cooking school") accompany
a positively zinful list of largely local bottlings at this
Healdsburg open-kitchen "winner"; the "high-energy" "but
still sophisticated" venue is a "cool setting" "for a glass of
wine or two", not to mention the "blue-plate daily specials"
("a tasty bargain"), despite occasionally "shaky" service
from a usually "friendly" crew.

Zinsvalley ☒   ▽ 20 | 18 | 19 | $33
Browns Valley Shopping Ctr., 3253 Browns Valley Rd.
(bet. Austin & Larkin Sts.), Napa, 707-224-0695;
www.zinsvalley.com
"The average tourist won't find" this "friendly" bistro ("one
of the best secrets in the valley") gloat Napa locals who
particularly enjoy its "hearty" New American cuisine
when dining on the "huge patio out back" ("awesome on
summer nights" with its creek view and freshening fountain);
meanwhile, wine lovers think they have "zinned and gone
to heaven" when they discover the list of "great Zinfandels
at good prices" and the free-corkage policy.

Zuzu   24 | 19 | 22 | $36
829 Main St. (bet. 2nd & 3rd Sts.), Napa, 707-224-8555;
www.zuzunapa.com
Napa's tapas nook is a "funky", rustic "little spot" that's
"great if you have food-commitment-phobia": you can "nosh
your way" through a variety of "superb", "shareable"
Spanish and Latin American snacks, which makes "a great
change" from the area's customary cuisines; like others
of its ilk, it's "high-energy" (read: "loud") and "not very
relaxing", but the "cozy" room and the "pleasant" servers
still have "charm to spare."

South of San Francisco

Top Ratings South of SF

Excluding places with low voting, unless indicated by a ▽.

Top Food

28 Manresa
27 Sierra Mar
   Marché
   Le Papillon
   Marinus
26 Cafe Gibraltar
   Fresh Cream
   Evvia
25 Bouchée
   Chez TJ

   Tamarine
   Café Marcella
   Amber India
   John Bentley's
   La Forêt
   Passionfish
   Pacific's Edge
24 O'mei
   Viognier
   Emile's

By Cuisine

American
25 John Bentley's
   Pacific's Edge
24 Village Pub
   231 Ellsworth
   Parcel 104

Asian
25 Tamarine
23 Three Seasons
21 Straits Cafe
20 Pho Hoa-Hiep II▽
19 E&O Trading Co.

Californian
27 Sierra Mar
25 Bouchée
24 Viognier
   Navio
23 Flea St. Café

Chinese
24 O'mei
   Koi Palace
22 Fook Yuen Seafood
21 Hunan Home's
   Hong Kong Flower

Continental
23 Chantilly
   Anton & Michel
21 Taste Cafe▽
   Maddalena's
20 Shadowbrook

French
28 Manresa
27 Marché
   Le Papillon
   Marinus
25 Chez TJ

Italian
23 Casanova
22 Osteria
21 Pizza Antica
20 Rist. Capellini
   Kuleto's

Japanese
27 Kaygetsu▽
24 Flying Fish Grill
22 Fuki Sushi
20 Blowfish Sushi
   Juban

Mediterranean
26 Cafe Gibraltar
   Evvia
23 Stokes
   71 Saint Peter
22 Cetrella Bistro

Seafood
25 Passionfish
24 Flying Fish Grill
23 Pisces
19 Barbara's Fishtrap
18 Yankee Pier

Top Food

By Special Feature

Breakfast/Brunch
25 La Forêt
24 Koi Palace
    Navio
    Gayle's Bakery
23 Flea St. Café

Outdoor Seating
27 Sierra Mar
    Marinus
23 Casanova
    Roy's Pebble Beach
22 Spago Palo Alto

People-Watching
26 Evvia
25 Tamarine
24 Village Pub
22 Spago Palo Alto
20 Zibibbo

Romance
27 Sierra Mar
    Marché
    Le Papillon
    Marinus
25 La Forêt

Singles Scenes
22 Seven
20 Zibibbo
19 Pearl Alley Bistro▽
    E&O Trading Co.
    Kingfish

Small Plates
25 Tamarine
23 Stokes
    Three Seasons
21 Straits Cafe
20 Zibibbo

Tasting Menus
28 Manresa
27 Marché
    Le Papillon
    Marinus
25 Pacific's Edge

Winning Wine Lists
27 Sierra Mar
    Marinus
26 L'Auberge Carmel▽
25 Bouchée
    Pacific's Edge

By Location

Carmel/Monterey
27 Marinus
25 Bouchée
    Pacific's Edge
24 Flying Fish Grill
23 Casanova

Half Moon Bay/Coast
26 Cafe Gibraltar
24 Navio
22 Cetrella Bistro
    Pasta Moon
21 Mezza Luna

Palo Alto/Menlo Park
27 Marché
26 Evvia
25 Tamarine
23 Bistro Elan
    Flea St. Café

Peninsula
24 Viognier
    Koi Palace
    Ecco
    231 Ellsworth
23 Pisces

Santa Cruz/Capitola
25 Oswald's▽
24 O'mei
    Gayle's Bakery
21 Gabriella Café▽
20 Shadowbrook

Silicon Valley
28 Manresa
27 Le Papillon
25 Chez TJ
    Café Marcella
    La Forêt

Top Decor

29 Sierra Mar
28 Pacific's Edge
27 Navio
26 Marinus
   Shadowbrook
25 Roy's Pebble Beach
   Marché
   La Forêt
24 Chez TJ
   Tamarine

Nepenthe
Manresa
23 Cetrella Bistro
   Village Pub
   Anton & Michel
   Le Papillon
   Evvia
   Chantilly
   Casanova
22 Fresh Cream

Top Service

27 Marinus
26 Sierra Mar
   Le Papillon
25 Manresa
   Chez TJ
   La Forêt
   Marché
24 Navio
   Pacific's Edge
   Plumed Horse

23 John Bentley's
   Maddalena's
   Village Pub
   Chantilly
   Anton & Michel
   231 Ellsworth
   Passionfish
   Emile's
   Fresh Cream
   Cafe Gibraltar

Top Bangs for the Buck

1. Pancho Villa
2. Burger Joint
3. La Cumbre Taqueria
4. La Taqueria
5. Gayle's Bakery
6. Udupi Palace
7. Cool Café
8. Amici E. Coast Pizza
9. North Beach Pizza
10. Pasta Pomodoro

11. Zao Noodle
12. Dish Dash
13. Hunan Home's
14. Passage to India
15. Pizza Antica
16. jZcool
17. Barbara's Fishtrap
18. O'mei
19. Amber India
20. Chef Chu's

Other Good Values

Basque Cultural Ctr.
Cetrella Bistro
Duarte's Tavern
Flea St. Café
Flying Fish Grill
Hong Kong Flower
Izzy's Steak
Juban
Koi Palace
Mezza Luna

Montrio Bistro
Passionfish
Pasta Moon
71 Saint Peter
St. Michael's
Stokes
Straits Cafe
Tamarine
Tarpy's Roadhouse
Three Seasons

South of San Francisco

F	D	S	C

Adrian's Gourmet Kitchen 🖃

−	−	−	I

26135 Carmel Rancho Blvd. (Carmel Valley Rd.), Carmel, 831-624-1494; www.adriansgourmetkitchen.com

Yo Adrian – this casual Carmel Continental cafe and gourmet take-out shop has become the hottest breakfast and lunch spot on the Monterey Peninsula; the brainchild of chef-owner Brian Reed (formerly of Sent Sovi and the Ivy in London), it's dominated by a deli case brimming with a daily-changing selection of soups, salads, sandwiches and grilled meats, and customers can also have omelets made to order; among the clientele are day-trippers looking for a latte and pastry pick-me-up and locals getting dinner to go.

Alexander's Steakhouse

−	−	−	E

Vallco Shopping Ctr., 10330 N. Wolfe Rd. (Vallco Pkwy.), Cupertino, 408-446-2222

'East meets Beef' is the conceit behind this clubby Cupertino steakhouse where high-tech industry moguls are plied with pricey Asian-style preparations like Kobe beef sashimi, in addition to more traditional cuts; a five-ft.-long showcase grill, retail meat counter and exhibition cellar housing an extensive array of wine and sake round out the look of the modern, bi-level dining room.

Amber India

25	19	20	$30

Olive Tree Shopping Ctr., 2290 W. El Camino Real (Rengstorff Ave.), Mountain View, 650-968-7511
377 Santana Row (Olsen Dr.), San Jose, 408-248-5400
www.amber-india.com

For the "undisputed pinnacle" of "fancified" Indian eats that may well be "the best outside of London" – not to mention "the motherland itself" – homesick emigrés head to these Mumbai "magnets" in San Jose and Mountain View where even the spice-wary can savor "ecstasy"-inducing butter chicken and other "exceptional" entrees without "the fear of rumble belly"; both locations boast "good service", but the youth vote goes to the more "contemporary", "innovative" and "happening" Santana Row "sister."

Amici's East Coast Pizzeria

20	12	16	$18

790 Castro St. (Church St.), Mountain View, 650-961-6666
226 Redwood Shores Pkwy. (Twin Dolphin Dr.), Redwood Shores, 650-654-3333

(continued)

(continued)

Amici's East Coast Pizzeria
69 Third Ave. (San Mateo Dr.), San Mateo, 650-342-9392
www.amicis.com
See review in City of San Francisco Directory.

Anton & Michel Restaurant   23 | 23 | 23 | $54
Mission St. (bet. Ocean & 7th Aves.), Carmel, 831-624-2406;
www.carmelsbest.com
For "old-world resort-town dining at its best", you can't
beat this "quiet oasis in busy Carmel"; sitting "in front of
the fireplace" or by the "fountain in the courtyard calms
you" while the "well-trained staff" "treats you like royalty"
and prepares "excellent" Californian-Continental classics
("great tableside Caesar", flambéed desserts); although
the "formal" "European" room and "menu could use some
imagination", this vintage spot, cellaring 900 vintages, is
still "wonderful" – just "don't expect anything trendy."

A.P. Stump's   21 | 22 | 20 | $46
163 W. Santa Clara St. (bet. Almaden Blvd. & San Pedro St.),
San Jose, 408-292-9928; www.apstumps.com
Though its "chic" "modern interior" with its glassed-in
wine cellar remains "one of the best-appointed settings"
in the area, this "high-end" destination near San Jose's
H.P. Pavilion "abandoned" its Cal-Med menu at the end
of 2004 and was promptly "reincarnated" as a meatery
showcasing "excellent" but "less creative" chops and fish
dishes matched by a "nice" *carte du vin*; nevertheless, some
stump speakers sigh it's now "just another steakhouse"
that "feels like you got there after the party ended."

Arcadia   22 | 21 | 21 | $55
San Jose Marriott, 100 W. San Carlos St. (Market St.), San Jose,
408-278-4555
With its "playful and inventive" New American cuisine,
"elegant, contemporary" environs and a staff that mostly
"minds the details like Martha would", San Jose's "lower-
end Michael Mina" outpost at the Marriott is an "impressive
gourmet option" for those who "want Downtown SF class
in a South Bay location"; nevertheless, the pennywise
pronounce the celeb chef's "upscale comfort food" "overly
complex" and "too pricey" ("if I'm having lobster, I don't
want it in a corn dog").

A Tavola   21 | – | 19 | $36
1041 Middlefield Rd. (Jefferson St.), Redwood City, 650-995-9800
www.atavoladining.com
Both "family-friendly" and "wannabe hip", this recently
relocated "high-quality neighborhood restaurant" now
"livens up" Redwood City with "creative" Cal-Ital chow
that's "a cut above most" in the area (as is the tab); the
"dependable" dishes help make up for the shortcomings of

a staff that's "attentive" but "inexperienced"; N.B. the move took place post-*Survey*.

Barbara's Fishtrap ⌀   19 | 11 | 16 | $22
281 Capistrano Rd. (Hwy. 1), Princeton by the Sea, 650-728-7049

At this "laid-back" "chowderhead's paradise" overlooking Princeton Harbor, you can "watch the fishermen haul in their catch while you munch" on "basic, uncomplicated" fin fare ("deep-fried everything") and quaff an "impressive selection" of 70 beers; don't expect much of the "gruff service" ("weekends are a madhouse") or the "funky" decor (some dub the spot "Barbara's Greasetrap"), but "for what it is – a fish grotto on the water – this place rocks."

Basin, The   ▽ 21 | 17 | 20 | $37
14572 Big Basin Way (5th St.), Saratoga, 408-867-1906; www.thebasin.com

Exuding a "warm atmosphere in chilly Saratoga", this "noisy but amiable" neighborhood haunt is a handy HQ for "eavesdropping on the movers and shakers of Silicon Valley"; the "great" martini bar (shaking 20-plus variations) and oak-shaded outdoor patio are its "main attractions", but the "diverse" New American cookery with Spanish and Italian influences and an "emphasis on local products" is also "enjoyable" – if "a little on the expensive side" for such a "relaxed and casual" place.

Basque Cultural Center   20 | 12 | 18 | $28
599 Railroad Ave. (bet. Orange & Spruce Aves.), South San Francisco, 650-583-8091; www.basqueculturalcenter.com

They admit "it ain't Parisian wining and dining" but boosters nevertheless bask in the "no-pretenses" "local charm" of this working cultural center in South SF, where "generous" four-course meals of "hearty", "reliable" Classic French and Spanish "standards" – not to mention the "cheapest martini for miles" – deliver "solid value for the price"; the vibe is strictly "old-world" (alas, "no jai alai") so it's "popular with the geriatric crowd."

Bella Vista ⌧   ▽ 20 | 21 | 22 | $49
13451 Skyline Blvd. (5 mi. south of Rte. 92), Woodside, 650-851-1229; www.bvrestaurant.com

"Like the name says, beautiful views" of "the redwoods", Silicon Valley and the South Bay are "the main attraction" at this "romantic spot" in Woodside; indoors, it's a "trip back" in time featuring tuxedoed waiters "who make the Caesar salad at your table" and decant primo vintages from the "excellent" 600-bottle wine list; however, the "classic" Italian and French specialties, executed "well albeit not especially creatively", received a not-so-"bella" dip in ratings.

Bistro Elan ☒   23 18 21 $45
448 California Ave. (El Camino Real), Palo Alto, 650-327-0284
For "a dash of panache in Palo Alto", you can't go wrong
at this "relaxed", "intimate" Californian–French bistro where
an "oh-so-enticing menu" spotlights the "highest-quality
raw ingredients" and a "professional" staff presents
"innovative" preparations "without pretension"; if some
sigh the portions and the "noisy" "minimalist" interior both
seem "comically small", you can remedy the latter by sitting
on the "gorgeous" back patio "when the weather is right."

Bistro Vida   18 19 19 $34
*641 Santa Cruz Ave. (El Camino Real), Menlo Park,
650-462-1686*
It's *la vida* low-key at this "casual", "authentic"-looking
cafe where the owner himself "greets and seats you" and
proffers a "homey", "down-to-earth" French bistro menu; as
a result "BMW-driving" Menlo Park "locals out shopping"
are glad to have this as a quieter alternative to nearby
"better-known hot spots", even if the food doesn't quite
"live up to the decor or the atmosphere."

Blowfish Sushi To Die For   20 21 16 $37
*335 Santana Row (off Stevens Creek Blvd.), San Jose,
408-345-3848; www.blowfishsushi.com*
See review in City of San Francisco Directory.

Bouchée   25 21 22 $62
*Mission St. (bet. Ocean & 7th Aves.), Carmel, 831-626-7880;
www.boucheecarmel.com*
"How could anyone visit Carmel" without dining at this
"sophisticated", "understated" Tuscan-hued "gem"? ask
aficionados; they adore its "incredibly creative", "intensely
flavored" – and "*trop cher*" – haute Cal menu ("the cheese
course is an epiphany"), "phenomenal wine selection" (sans
markup thanks to the "attached shop") and owner who
"embodies hospitality at its finest"; it may have "lost some
buzz" to its "new sister, L'Auberge Carmel", but it's still far
"more interesting" than the "mediocrity" found elsewhere.

Brigitte's French Mediterranean   – – – M
Gourmet & Healthy Cuisine ☒
*351 Saratoga Ave. (Pruneridge Ave.), Santa Clara,
408-246-2333; www.brigittescuisine.com*
It may be a mouthful, but "the name says it all" at this
"fantastic" "Parisian bistro" incongruously located in a
Santa Clara "strip mall" overlooking a golf course; the
"fresh", "wonderful", market-driven French-Mediterranean
munchies are "light on the fat" (and your wallet, thanks to
a slew of prix fixe options) but heavy on flavor, and menus
"change daily"; what's more, "you can always be sure of
meeting" co-owner Brigitte herself, who "stops by often to
check on your meal and service."

Buca di Beppo   13   16   16 $24

Pruneyard Shopping Ctr., 1875 S. Bascom Ave. (Campbell Ave.), Campbell, 408-377-7722
643 Emerson St. (bet. Forest & Hamilton Aves.), Palo Alto, 650-329-0665
Oakridge Mall, 925 Blossom Hill Rd., San Jose, 408-226-1444
www.bucadibeppo.com

"Loud", "bawdy and fun", these Silicon Valley outposts of the "Italian TGI Fridays" are "great for groups" since you can "feed a family of 12" on "supersized" family-style servings of "garlic-infused", "high-carb", "ersatz red-gravy" "shovel food" for the "change you found in your couch"; the help may be "peppy" or "grumpy" and waits can be "horribly long" but *cucina* connoisseurs couldn't care less, dismissing it as "Buca di Pepto"; N.B. SF's SoMa has one too.

Burger Joint ●   20   13   16 $11

San Francisco Int'l Airport, Int'l Terminal, Boarding Area A, South San Francisco, 650-583-5863
See review in City of San Francisco Directory.

CAFE GIBRALTAR   26   21   23 $39

425 Ave. Alhambra (Palma St.), El Granada, 650-560-9039;
www.cafegibraltar.com

A "coastal wonder" offering "big-city gourmet" eats and a "beautiful view of the ocean", this El Grenada Med is "quite out of the way" but "so worth" the trip; the "tantalizing", "savory", often-changing repasts are infused with "rich, complex flavors seldom found" outside this "seductive" room where booths are lined with "sit-down pillows"; moreover, "you will not find a nicer pair than the owners" – but some say the "surfer-dude" servers should be Moor polished "to match the cuisine and prices."

Café Marcella   25   19   22 $41

368 Village Ln. (bet. Hwy. 9 & Santa Cruz Ave.), Los Gatos, 408-354-8006; www.cafemarcella.com

This "understated" "little bistro in the heart of Downtown Los Gatos" is a "longtime" favorite, and under new chef Michael Schibler (formerly of Emile's) it continues to please with "creative", "delicious" French-Med fare, a "superb wine list" and "divine service"; although "not the place for a quiet dinner" (due to "noise just shy of a jet engine's"), it's "otherwise a wonderful", "charming" destination "when you're in the mood" for "some hustle and bustle" with your foie gras.

Casanova   23   23   22 $51

Fifth Ave. (bet. Mission & San Carlos Sts.), Carmel, 831-625-0501; www.casanovarestaurant.com

"After a day" of "retail therapy" in Carmel, shoppers and their Casanovas head to this "*très belle*", *très cher* "romantic hideaway" that appears to be a "quaint cottage on the outside" but actually contains a warren of themed rooms and patios for enjoying "delicious, rustic" country French and Northern Italian fare, "wonderful wines" and the "knowledgeable" career waiters who serve them; those who've fallen out of love with this vintage venue shrug it's "fulla" tourists, "fulla dogs and a little bit fulla" itself.

Cascal 19 | 22 | 17 | $33 |
400 Castro St. (California St.), Mountain View, 650-940-9500; www.cascalrestaurant.com
Silicon Valleyites "don't need to drive to SF for tapas" ever since this "upbeat" "hot spot" opened in Downtown Mountain View; instead they flock to this "festive" den for "eclectic, satisfying" Pan-Latin provisions (including "fun small plates" that are "indeed rather small"), plus "fresh-made mojitos" and "fabulous live music on Friday and Saturday nights"; a puckish few posit a "connection" between the "great sangria" and the seemingly "hungover waiters" often "overwhelmed by the crowds."

Central Park Bistro 19 | 20 | 18 | $37 |
181 E. Fourth Ave. (San Mateo Dr.), San Mateo, 650-558-8401; www.centralparkbistro.com
Despite its bucolic-sounding name, this "cute bistro" is the "hippest place in San Mateo", luring in the local "movie-theater crowd" with a "great bar, live jazz on weekends" and New American "small-plates fusion fare" that's definitely a "step up" in price and quality from the usual suburban suspects; critics, though, complain the food "doesn't quite 'get there'" and neither do the servers ("I thought I might never get my drink").

Cetrella Bistro & Café 22 | 23 | 20 | $44 |
845 Main St. (Monte Vista Ln.), Half Moon Bay, 650-726-4090; www.cetrella.com
Why "rush back" to SF when you can get "city sophistication by the coast" at this Half Moon Bay venue; "whether you eat in the bar" or in the sprawling "rustic-chic" dining room with a "big central fireplace to keep you warm", a crew of "attentive" servers presents a "finger-licking good" "mix of Northern Mediterranean flavors" throughout the meal (especially its renowned brunch), while "some of the best live jazz" acts swing by on Thursday–Saturday evenings.

Chantilly ⊠ 23 | 23 | 23 | $56 |
3001 El Camino Real (Selby Ln.), Redwood City, 650-321-4080; www.chantillyrestaurant.com
At this "old-money", "old-world" Redwood City veteran "expect opulent luxury from the moment you walk in the door" until the presentation of "roses for the ladies upon departure"; although both the decor ("brocade walls, dark woods") and the "delicious" Continental cuisine may feel "heavy" and "a little stuffy upon first impression", this

"refined" retreat "fills a niche" as "one of the rare formal places on the Peninsula" for "birthdays, anniversaries or graduation dinners."

Cheesecake Factory, The ◑   16 | 16 | 15 | $25

Westfield Shoppingtown Valley Fair, 3041 Stevens Creek Blvd. (bet. S. Redwood Ave. & Winchester Blvd.), San Jose, 408-246-0092; www.thecheesecakefactory.com
See review in City of San Francisco Directory.

Chef Chu's   20 | 14 | 18 | $25

1067 N. San Antonio Rd. (El Camino Real), Los Altos, 650-948-2696; www.chefchu.com
"Longevity is an indicator of the appeal" of this Los Altos Mandarin "mainstay" that chewers (including "geeks", "'80s celebs" and "ex-presidents") choose for its "old-fashioned fancy Chinese" fare; "Larry Chu or his son" are "always on-site" ensuring "personalized service", but "DIYers" can also "buy the cookbook" or attend the "excellent cooking school" on the premises; aesthetes assert even if its popularity "hasn't changed in 20 years", the "dated" interior "should have."

CHEZ TJ ☒   25 | 24 | 25 | $76

938 Villa St. (bet. Castro St. & Shoreline Blvd.), Mountain View, 650-964-7466; www.cheztj.com
For a "special-occasion treat", this "intimate" multiroomed New French in a "beautiful restored" 1890 Victorian has long been the go-to place in Mountain View, provided "you're made of money"; it's been known for "pampering" service and pricey prix fixe dinners, and admirers assert the young chef's "enlightened tasters' menus with matching wines" (a "U.S. version of kaiseki") have "brought the establishment to new heights" – even if the old guard is still getting used to the "tiniest of portions" and "weird ice creams."

Club XIX   ▽ 22 | 24 | 22 | $66

The Lodge at Pebble Beach, 17 Mile Dr. (Hwy. 1), Pebble Beach, 831-625-8519; www.pebblebeach.com
After a day on the links, "it doesn't get much better" than this "classic" "country-club"-like "golfer's mecca" where Iron Johns dining on their "corporate cards" "sit near the outdoor fireplaces" and refuel; as "professional" staffers provision them, "everyone" takes in the "great views of the ocean and 18th hole of Pebble Beach" "instead of noticing" the Cal-French fare, which discriminating duffers deem "good but not great" ("a little stodgy") and too "pricey"; N.B. jackets suggested.

Cool Café   22 | 20 | 14 | $19

Stanford Univ. Cantor Arts Ctr., 328 Lomita Dr. (Museum Way), Palo Alto, 650-725-4758; www.cooleatz.com
"The best lunch on Stanford's campus by a country mile" (plus unpublicized "don't-miss Thursday dinners") can be

found at this Cantor Arts Center Californian cafe where "sustainable"-food "doyenne" Jesse Cool (Flea St. Café) presents an array of "terrific" organic (and "expensive") sandwiches, soups, salads and even beers; although the "cafeteria-style" interior is "a tight squeeze", the patio has a "magnificent location by the Rodin Sculpture Garden", making it many surveyors' "favorite exhibit at the museum."

Dish Dash 🖼   22 15 18 $23
190 S. Murphy Ave. (Washington Ave.), Sunnyvale, 408-774-1889; www.dishdash.net
Rising above Silicon Valley's mishmash of falafel stands and gyro joints, this a-mezzing "high-class" yet "economical" Middle Eastern in Downtown Sunnyvale offers a panoply of "tasty" "traditional" eats with a dash of "true gourmet flair"; speed eaters should note, however, that the "courteous servers" get "very slow" and the restaurant "terribly noisy" once it's "overrun by techies" on their lunch break.

Duarte's Tavern   20 12 18 $25
202 Stage Rd. (Pescadero Rd.), Pescadero, 650-879-0464; www.duartestavern.com
"As comfortable as an old sweatshirt", this "downscale" Pescadero "former stagecoach stop" (founded 1894) serves up Traditional American eats ("awesome" cream of green chile and cream of artichoke soups, "legendary olallieberry pie" in season) with a heapin' helpin' of "rural charm"; day-trippers declare "order these three things and forget the rest", though residents crowd the "cowboy bar" for the famous cioppino and surprisingly good "local wine list"; N.B. pronounced *doo-arts*.

Duck Club, The   20 20 20 $43
Stanford Park Hotel, 100 El Camino Real (Sand Hill Rd.), Menlo Park, 650-330-2790; www.stanfordparkhotel.com
Monterey Plaza Hotel & Spa, 400 Cannery Row (Wave St.), Monterey, 831-646-1700; www.woodsidehotels.com
See review in East of San Francisco Directory.

E&O Trading Company   19 21 17 $34
96 S. First St. (San Fernando St.), San Jose, 408-938-4100; www.eotrading.com
See review in City of San Francisco Directory.

Ecco Restaurant 🖼   24 20 22 $41
322 Lorton Ave. (Burlingame Ave.), Burlingame, 650-342-7355; www.eccorestaurant.com
Ecco-friendly epicures echo the sentiment that this Cal-Continental in Burlingame is "a little-known marvel" that's "all-around good" for an "impressive dinner with a date, clients" or even "foodies"; its "gorgeous, delicious" and "innovative" fare ("I almost took the pastry chef hostage to get the ice-cream recipe") and "outstanding wine list" are all "professionally" proffered in an "unpretentious",

"surprisingly quiet" room; N.B. there's a five-course tasting menu for $50.

Emile's ⊠   24 | 19 | 23 | $54 |
545 S. Second St. (bet. Reed & William Sts.), San Jose, 408-289-1960; www.emiles.com

San Jose's high-end, "high-ante" Franco-Swiss soufflé stalwart provides "classic fine dining" at its finest, offering build-your-own tasting menus of its "excellently executed" eats plus 450 wines in a mercifully "quiet, grown-up" environment where you can actually "talk and be heard"; service is "warm" and "Emile himself" "makes the rounds", so the "aging clientele" doesn't seem to mind the "1970s throwback" decor, but trendier types tsk-tsk it "needs freshening up" to ensure its "good name" endures.

Eulipia Restaurant & Bar   21 | 19 | 20 | $41 |
374 S. First St. (bet. San Carlos & San Salvador Sts.), San Jose, 408-280-6161; www.eulipia.com

Thanks to its "perfect location", this sprawling "Downtown San Jose institution" remains a pre-performance hit among the "thespian set", especially given its proximity to the recently reopened California Theatre; most reviewers applaud the "dependable" yet "still interesting" New American fare but those seeking something a bit more avant-garde say it's "getting a little tired" – not unlike some servers, who "can be quite slow" before curtain time.

EVVIA   26 | 23 | 22 | $45 |
420 Emerson St. (bet. Lytton & University Aves.), Palo Alto, 650-326-0983; www.evvia.net

The tragedy of Palo Alto's "hectic" Greek-Med temple is that it's so "hard to get in"; apparently everyone wants to partake of the "hearty", "savory", "ambrosial" offerings (the "sublime" "lamb chops are the standard by which others are measured") and be ministered to by the "indulgent yet not overbearing" servers who navigate the "lively, warm, inviting" (and tight) room; "brace yourself for the bill", though, because paying it can be a Herculean task.

Fandango   22 | 21 | 21 | $43 |
223 17th St. (Lighthouse Ave.), Pacific Grove, 831-372-3456; www.fandangorestaurant.com

Monterey Peninsula "locals and tourists dance into" this Pacific Grove Med with a "French cottage atmosphere"; even though the menu is "nothing earth-shattering", the "dependable" food has a "delectable extra something", the "great" 1,500-label wine list blends a slew of "old-world selections" with area bottlings, and the "homey feel" and "old-fashioned hospitality" make this a "wonderful place to relax and unwind"; "several dining areas" – from the "light and bright" main room to the "cozier" alcoves – mean "a different experience every time."

Flea St. Café
23 | 18 | 20 | $42

3607 Alameda de las Pulgas (Avy Ave.), Menlo Park, 650-854-1226; www.cooleatz.com

Jesse Cool's "trademark" "inventive", "delicious" Cal–New American dishes ("featuring locally grown peak-of-season and organic ingredients"), along with the "delightful woman" herself and her "caring" staff, appear in full regalia at her 23-year-old "high-end" Menlo Park mother ship; "reinvigorated" thanks to "a recent remodel", it "returns" to the "top tier of Peninsula restaurants", attracting Silicon Valley luminaries for "quiet, romantic" dinners and "stealth brunches on Sunday."

Flying Fish Grill
24 | 17 | 21 | $38

Carmel Plaza, Mission St. (bet. Ocean & 7th Aves.), Carmel, 831-625-1962

This Japanese-Californian in Carmel is "flying high" on the ratings scale because of "amazing and delicious" "fresh fish" prepared with a "light touch" and "creative" fusion "flair"; the "warm and friendly" personnel "make you feel right at home" in the "cozy" "basement" setting, though critics carp that for these prices they'd prefer it weren't so "dark and crowded."

Fook Yuen Seafood
22 | 12 | 14 | $27

195 El Camino Real (Victoria Ave.), Millbrae, 650-692-8600

"Wait, I'm still in Millbrae?" wonder won ton wanters who "feel like they're in Hong Kong" at this South Bay outpost of a chain with other links in Singapore and Australia; the "delicious" daily dim sum, "generous portions" of "fresh seafood" and Peking duck "like we had in China" are all far more memorable than the "shabby", "uninspired cavern of a room" and service that is "brisk" at best and even "obnoxious at times."

Fresh Cream
26 | 22 | 23 | $62

Heritage Harbor, 99 Pacific St. (bet. Artillery & Scott Sts.), Monterey, 831-375-9798; www.freshcream.com

The cream of the crop, Monterey's "intimate" "special-night-out restaurant" remains "as fabulous as ever"; the "sublime" "high-end" French-Continental food is a "big splurge, but worth it", say most, given the "breathtaking" "open views" of the "beautiful Bay" and the "elegant service" that come with it; those few who find it a "bit stiff" sniff "they should change the name to Sour Cream."

Fuki Sushi
22 | 18 | 19 | $37

4119 El Camino Real (bet. Arastradero & Page Mill Rds.), Palo Alto, 650-494-9383; www.fukisushi.com

"Reliable", "quiet and relaxing", this Palo Alto sushi spot is "perfect for a date or impressing a client" ("especially if you reserve a tatami room") thanks to "unbelievably buttery raw fish", "fresh, unique rolls", "adventurous appetizers" and 20 varieties of sake; bring "your corporate card" and "be ready to take your time", because service by the "kimono-clad waitresses" can be "painfully slow."

Gabriella Café   ▽ 21 | 19 | 18 | $30

910 Cedar St. (bet. Church & Locust Sts.), Santa Cruz, 831-457-1677; www.gabriellacafe.com

"Tucked away" in Santa Cruz, this "pretty", "intimate" bungalow is a "perfect date spot", whether you sit in the "dimly lit", art-filled dining room or the tiny "outdoor alley courtyard"; what warms the hearts of foodies most, though, is the "excellent" seasonal Cal-Ital cuisine that's "prepared only with organic ingredients" and complemented by "sophisticated" wines of the same regions; "service can be spotty", but gourmets gab the grub is "worth the wait."

Gayle's Bakery & Rosticceria   24 | 12 | 16 | $17

504 Bay Ave. (Capitola Ave.), Capitola, 831-462-1200; www.gaylesbakery.com

When "driving south down the coast, stop in" to Capitola's "best rotisserie and bakery" for an "abundance" of "savory" Traditional American "blue-plate specials, decadent desserts, artisanal breads and creative sandwiches", all served by a counter staff that "handles the load well"; despite its "kitschy" decor ("rarely visible" because of the "hordes of people") and "nice outdoor area", veterans advise "get everything to go and have a picnic" or "enjoy it in your own cozy home."

Gaylord India   19 | 17 | 19 | $33

1706 El Camino Real (Encinal Ave.), Menlo Park, 650-326-8761; www.gaylords.com

See review in City of San Francisco Directory.

Grasing's Coastal Cuisine   23 | 18 | 20 | $47

Sixth St. (Mission St.), Carmel, 831-624-6562; www.grasings.com

Grazers groove on the "varied menu" of "fresh and creative" Californian cuisine at this "idyllic" Carmel "retreat" owned by chef Kurt Grasing and NorCal food celeb Narsai David, where the cookery is matched by some "hidden gems" on the wine list; a "wonderful staff makes you comfortable" in the "lovely courtyard" assert admirers, yet "underwhelmed" detractors dis service that's "pretty vacuous" and decor that seems "dreary."

Happy Cafe Restaurant ⬧   ▽ 20 | 3 | 13 | $13

250 S. B St. (bet. 2nd & 3rd Aves.), San Mateo, 650-340-7138

The hungry get happy at this "cheap-eats" champ, a "small" San Matean that looks like an "archetypal" dump but comes across at lunchtime with dynamite dim sum, "excellent Shanghainese street food" and "Taiwanese home cooking" at "a steal of a price"; as a result, "be prepared to wait", "especially on weekends"; N.B. serves dinner Wednesday only.

Hong Kong Flower Lounge   21 16 15 $28
51 Millbrae Ave. (El Camino Real), Millbrae, 650-692-6666;
www.flowerlounge.net
"For the closest thing to a real Hong Kong restaurant"
"without the 14-hour flight", Peninsula potsticker partisans
head to this "two-story", high-end yet "tacky" Sino in
Millbrae with "a million Chinese people in line" and an
equally large "variety of live fish" in tanks; during the day
"excellent dim sum" rolls through and at night there are
"delicious" "Asian-style banquets" – but if you want
decent service from the "dispassionate" staff "it helps if
you speak Mandarin."

Hunan Home's Restaurant   21 11 17 $21
4880 El Camino Real (Showers Dr.), Los Altos, 650-965-8888
See review in City of San Francisco Directory.

Iberia   20 19 16 $42
1026 Alma St. (bet. Oak Grove & Ravenswood Aves.),
Menlo Park, 650-325-9981; www.iberiarestaurant.com
An "evening spent sipping Rioja while sampling tapas will
make you think you're in" Madrid instead of Menlo Park
at this "inconspicuous" Spanish where the "authentic"
comida, "European (slow) service" and charming "dog-
friendly" patio all further the fantasy; if what you seek is a
"fun night of small plates and vino, head straight for the
bar" as only traditional appetizers and entrees are served
in the Med-style main dining room.

IL FORNAIO   18 20 18 $35
327 Lorton Ave. (bet. Burlingame Ave. & California Dr.),
Burlingame, 650-375-8000
The Pine Inn, Ocean Ave. (Monte Verde St.), Carmel, 831-622-5100
Garden Court Hotel, 520 Cowper St. (bet. Hamilton &
University Aves.), Palo Alto, 650-853-3888
Hyatt Sainte Claire, 302 S. Market St. (San Carlos St.), San Jose,
408-271-3366
www.ilfornaio.com
See review in City of San Francisco Directory.

Izzy's Steaks & Chops   20 16 18 $37
525 Skyway Rd. (off Hwy. 101), San Carlos, 650-654-2822;
www.izzyssteaksandchops.com
See review in City of San Francisco Directory.

John Bentley's ⊠   25 20 23 $49
2991 Woodside Rd. (bet. Cañada & Whiskey Hill Rds.),
Woodside, 650-851-4988
2915 El Camino Real (bet. Dumberton Ave. & Selby Ln.),
Redwood City, 650-365-7777
www.johnbentleys.com
Now that there are two locations on the Peninsula where
John Bentley's "succulent" New American fare is served

"attentively" and "unpretentiously", "getting a reservation has gone from almost impossible to almost reasonable"; the "cozy", rustic original in Woodside still fills up with the "older" "BMW and Mercedes set" celebrating "special occasions" and business bigwigs "on company expense accounts", while the "sleek", "snazzy" "new Redwood City location" attracts a hipper cocktailing crowd that doesn't mind the "noise."

Juban   20 | 17 | 18 | $29
1204 Broadway (bet. California Dr. & El Camino Real), Burlingame, 650-347-2300
712 Santa Cruz Ave. (El Camino Real), Menlo Park, 650-473-6458
www.jubanrestaurant.com
These "GIY (grill-it-yourself)" *yakiniku* houses in Burlingame and Menlo Park – where "attentive" servers supply an "extensive selection" of "very fresh" meats and marinades, and then diners "do all the work" – are a "fun" "interactive" "place to take the kids", though "the Kobe beef may be wasted on their palates"; meanwhile, the frugal fret it's "counterintuitive to have to pay so much" just to "barbecue indoors"; N.B. there's also a branch in SF's Japantown.

jZcool   18 | 10 | 12 | $17
827 Santa Cruz Ave. (bet. Crane St. & University Dr.), Menlo Park, 650-325-3665; www.cooleatz.com
For "Flea St. Café–quality food on the go" conscientious customers come to this "gourmet counter" in Menlo Park, the "third element of the Jesse Cool empire"; expect "tasty", "creative" Californian "homestyle" fare, and if it seems "a bit pricey" given the "cafeteria-esque" service and "cavernous", "utilitarian" setting, "at least you know for sure" that the food "couldn't be more organic if it still had dirt on it"; N.B. closes at 3 PM Sundays and Mondays.

Kaygetsu   ∇ 27 | 21 | 25 | $71
Sharon Hts. Shopping Ctr., 325 Sharon Park Dr. (Sand Hill Rd.), Menlo Park, 650-234-1084; www.kaygetsu.com
Chef/co-owner Toshi Sakuma (ex Toshi's Sushiya) "puts his heart and soul" into this "calm, beautiful" Japanese "jewel" in a Menlo Park mall; he offers an à la carte menu with the "best sushi this side of Tokyo", but the "foodie must-have experience" here is the "exquisite" kaiseki dinner, a "relaxing" "two- to three-hour" "affair" demonstrating "much attention to detail and harmony with the seasons" that delighted diners deem "truly worthy of the high price."

Kingfish   19 | 20 | 16 | $35
201 S. B St. (2nd Ave.), San Mateo, 650-343-1226;
www.kingfish.net
The good times certainly do roll at this "loud and boisterous" tri-level Creole-influenced Eclectic, a "funky" yet "classy" spot that's "as hip as you can get in San Mateo"; "decent"

bayou cookery can be had here alongside "surprisingly great sushi" and "excellent wines", and though some scold service as the "slowest around", softhearted sorts sympathize with "the poor staffers who have to climb stairs all day and night"; N.B. the SF location near SBC Park opened post-*Survey*.

Koi Palace
24 17 12 $31

Serramonte Plaza, 365 Gellert Blvd. (bet. Hickey & Serramonte Blvds.), Daly City, 650-992-9000; www.koipalace.com

During the day at Daly City's dim sum darling "the crowd surges and sniffs appreciatively as waitresses trundle by with carts of dumplings and buns", and at dinnertime the fresh fish "flops straight from the tank onto your plate"; consequently koi-noisseurs continue coming to this Sino seafooder despite its "chaotic banquet-hall ambiance" and service "of the clattering plate, elbow-in-your-face variety"; on weekends "mayhem" may "overwhelm" the hostess, so be prepared for an "excruciating wait."

Kuleto's
20 18 19 $39

1095 Rollins Rd. (Broadway), Burlingame, 650-342-4922; www.kuletostrattoria.com

See review in City of San Francisco Directory.

Kurt's Carmel Chop House
– – – E

Fifth Ave. & San Carlos St., Carmel, 831-625-1199; www.carmelchophouse.com

Filling the primal need for prime rib in the Carmel area, Kurt Grasing (of nearby Grasing's) brings his cooking chops to bear at this sophisticated, art-filled, white-tablecloth venue where traditional steakhouse offerings (22-oz. porterhouses, beef filets) share the menu with such specialties as Assyrian lamb chops marinated in pomegranate juice; the dishes can be paired with stellar Central Coast wines from the restaurant's 500-label cellar, many from co-owner and culinary personality Narsai David's private stash.

La Cumbre Taqueria
21 8 13 $10

28 N. B St. (bet. 1st & Tilton Aves.), San Mateo, 650-344-8989

See review in City of San Francisco Directory.

La Forêt
25 25 25 $57

21747 Bertram Rd. (Almaden Rd.), San Jose, 408-997-3458; www.laforetrestaurant.com

A "remote", woodsy "hideaway" that's "out in the country" yet "just 20 minutes from Downtown" San Jose, this "creekside" Classic French is "perfect for romancing someone" if you "want to take it real slow" ("dining in a Barry White mentality"); along with loving the location, regulars appreciate the "gracious" service, 400-label wine list, "awesome wild game" and "great" Sunday brunches, though modernists balk at the "stuffy" scene and steep prices; N.B. jackets suggested for gents.

La Strada   – | – | – | M |
335 University Ave. (bet. Bryant & Waverly Sts.), Palo Alto, 650-324-8300; www.lastradapaloalto.com
"At long last, an Italian restaurant on the Peninsula" that's "actually interesting" announce *amici* who appreciate its "authentic" Bergamo *cucina* ("not your usual pile of noodles with red sauce"), including ethereal cured meats and "savory" wood-fired thin-crust pizzas; whether you're sitting "in front of the open kitchen", at the bar or "on the patio for people-watching", this "handsome" and "friendly" Palo Alto trattoria offers a slice of la dolce vita at prices that aren't strada-spheric.

La Taqueria 🚫🚭   24 | 8 | 13 | $11 |
15 S. First St. (Santa Clara Ave.), San Jose, 408-287-1542
See review in City of San Francisco Directory.

L'Auberge Carmel   ∇ 26 | 24 | 25 | $85 |
Monte Verde St. (7th Ave.), Carmel, 831-624-8578; www.laubergecarmel.com
"Nice table, if you can get it" report the lucky few who've nabbed one of the 12 at this elegant and extraordinarily expensive eatery located in the newly restored Carmel inn of the same name; chef Walter Manzke (also of Bouchée) and his "knowledgeable" staff present "ambitious" Cal tasting menus matched with "wonderful wines" (from a 500-label cellar), and prognosticators predict this "could be the [next] French Laundry" "if the kitchen could just put out the food" "in a timely manner" – as it is, budget "four hours to finish"; N.B. the adjacent salon offers a scaled-down bistro slate.

Lavanda   – | – | – | E |
185 University Ave. (bet. Emerson & High Sts.), Palo Alto, 650-321-3514; www.lavandarestaurant.com
An "imaginative" Mediterranean menu of "delectable" seasonal large and small plates plus an enormous, "enticing wine list" deftly navigated by "knowledgeable", "attentive" staffers make this "posh" Palo Alto restaurant and enoteca "one of the top dining spots in the South Bay Peninsula area" according to its satisfied supporters; in fact, at Thursday's "tasting events" featuring "local and international" vintners, "even experienced collectors learn something."

LEFT BANK   18 | 20 | 17 | $37 |
635 Santa Cruz Ave. (Doyle St.), Menlo Park, 650-473-6543
377 Santana Row (S. Winchester Blvd.), San Jose, 408-984-3500
Bay Meadows, 100 Park Pl. (Saratoga Dr.), San Mateo, 650-345-2250
www.leftbank.com
See review in North of San Francisco Directory.

LE PAPILLON   27 | 23 | 26 | $67
410 Saratoga Ave. (Kiely Blvd.), San Jose, 408-296-3730;
www.lepapillon.com

It may be "adjacent to a strip mall" but "when you walk into
this" "quiet, elegant", almost-30-year-old San Jose French,
"you'll think you've entered the Ritz"; longtime lepidopterists
have "nothing but the highest praise" for the "phenomenal"
"special tasting menus" and "increasingly interesting wine
pairings"; very proper yet "accommodating" staffers "often
surprise diners with a treat, compliments of the chef", but
the cash-conscious caution "break that piggy bank before
you go" 'cause this butterfly sure ain't free.

Lion & Compass ☒   19 | 18 | 20 | $39
1023 N. Fair Oaks Ave. (Weddell Dr.), Sunnyvale, 408-745-1260;
www.lionandcompass.com

Even post-boom this "longtime" "high-class" "Silicon Valley
power-lunch institution" in Sunnyvale continues to attract
"the VC" vanguard and an "older crowd" in search of the
newest "hot deal" ("I never saw so many suits in one
place"); the "tropical"-colonial look remains "unique" and
"service is friendly and prompt", so although a drop in Food
score suggests "it's past its glory days", its "reliable" New
American fare makes it "nice for business entertaining."

MacArthur Park   16 | 18 | 17 | $36
27 University Ave. (El Camino Real), Palo Alto, 650-321-9990;
www.spectrumfoods.com

See review in City of San Francisco Directory.

Maddalena's & Café Fino ☒   21 | 21 | 23 | $42
544 Emerson St. (bet. Hamilton & University Aves.), Palo Alto,
650-326-6082; www.maddalenasrestaurant.com

The "elegant" main room at this bipartite Palo Alto veteran
attracts "an older crowd" that appreciates the "delicious"
Continental standards and "excellent service" in "quiet",
"sumptuous", "Al Capone surroundings"; young 'uns opt
for Cafe Fino, the adjacent "jazz bar" where you get the
same food plus "fabulous" ambiance, "killer martinis" and,
with luck, owner Freddy Maddalena, who'll "greet you or
invite you to dance with him" "between the tables."

MANRESA   28 | 24 | 25 | $87
320 Village Ln. (bet. N. Santa Cruz & University Aves.), Los Gatos,
408-354-4330; www.manresarestaurant.com

At his "foodie paradise" in Los Gatos, David Kinch ("half
ingredient-driven chef and half mad scientist") concocts
"far and away the most remarkable fare in Silicon Valley";
his "fearlessly innovative" New American–New French
tasting menus served in a "contemporary, sexy" room keep
a "sophisticated clientele" "guessing" for "three hours
of bliss"; though many maintain the sometimes "superb"
service "still has room to improve" and oenophiles whine

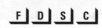
the *carte du vin* "falls short of the standard set by the cuisine", overall this evening of "food entertainment" is "worth every dime."

MARCHÉ 🗷   27 | 25 | 25 | $64

898 Santa Cruz Ave. (University Dr.), Menlo Park, 650-324-9092
As "Menlo Park's answer to fine dining in the city" ("without the traffic or parking problems"), this "elegant yet modern" New French is "increasingly the choice" of "billionaire VCs" for celebrating and "deal-making"; its *marché*-driven tasting menus ("inventive combinations") "compete with an equally fabulous à la carte" selection, while a "gracious" staff "suggests the perfect wine pairing"; wage slaves warn it helps "if you have a corporate credit card", because "in light of the dot-com bust", mere mortals find it "overpriced."

Marigold Indian   – | – | – | I

448 University Ave. (Kipling St.), Palo Alto, 650-327-3455;
www.marigoldcuisine.com
Though little known, this subcontinental storefront in Palo Alto is no wallflower, with its bright marigold-yellow walls, bold paintings and collection of curries, tandooris and biryanis whose "vivid flavors compare to other Indian restaurants' like oil painting to pastels" say supporters; it's tended by software engineer–turned-restaurateur Satish Sandadi, who now entices other Silicon Valley techies with all-you-can-eat lunch buffets and à la carte dinners served until 10 PM.

MARINUS   27 | 26 | 27 | $83

Bernardus Lodge, 415 Carmel Valley Rd. (Laureles Grade Rd.),
Carmel, 831-658-3500; www.bernardus.com
For the "best meal between Gary Danko and Los Angeles", "bring a compass" and navigate east to this "remote" retreat at Bernardus Lodge that "puts Carmel Valley on the culinary map"; "settle in" near the limestone fireplace, let the "expert" staff present "extraordinary" "French-style" creations "adapted to the New World" and "trust the sommelier" to steer you through the "outstanding wine" list (1,850 labels); though a few opine it's "overpriced", most mariners maintain the meal was "worth it."

Max's   16 | 13 | 16 | $23

1250 Old Bayshore Hwy. (Broadway), Burlingame, 650-342-6297
711 Stanford Shopping Ctr. (Sand Hill Rd.), Palo Alto, 650-323-6297
1001 El Camino Real (James Ave.), Redwood City, 650-365-6297
www.maxsworld.com
See review in City of San Francisco Directory.

Mezza Luna   21 | 18 | 21 | $34

459 Prospect Way (Capistrano Rd.), Princeton by the Sea,
650-728-8108; www.mezzalunabythesea.com
Surveyors say stepping into this "sunny" trattoria on Half Moon Bay with its "solid", "down-to-earth" Southern Italian

cucina makes you "feel like you're in North Beach" where "mama's in back cooking it herself"; with its "great location near Princeton Harbor" ("go for the view at sunset"), "balanced" staff and "value" pricing, it's "pleasant" for a "moonlit" dinner "after a day on the coast."

Mistral
20 | 19 | 18 | $36

370-6 Bridge Pkwy. (Marine World Pkwy.), Redwood Shores, 650-802-9222; www.mistraldining.com

"Fresh, tasty" and "reliable" French-Italian fare "keeps them coming back" to this "out-of-the-way" spot in Redwood Shores, aka the place "where Oracle eats" (it's located near the company's HQ); boasting a "wonderful" lagoon view, the "romantic" heated patio is preferred to the borderline "boring" interior, but in both places, service is said to be "uneven"; meanwhile, the "lively" and "noisy" bar is a "popular" "after-work hangout."

Montrio Bistro
22 | 20 | 21 | $42

414 Calle Principal (Franklin St.), Monterey, 831-648-8880; www.montrio.com

"Imagination and execution" are the hallmarks of the "inventive" Cal-Italian cuisine turned out by the open kitchen at this "stylish" Monterey "firehouse" bistro and served up by "friendly", "attentive" staffers; consequently it's "a very pleasant respite" from the tourist "hubbub" but "can get crowded" itself at times – blame the temptingly "diverse drink menu" at its "excellent bar."

NAVIO
24 | 27 | 24 | $68

Ritz-Carlton Hotel, 1 Miramontes Point Rd. (Hwy. 1), Half Moon Bay, 650-712-7000; www.ritzcarlton.com

If "price is no object" coastal day-trippers and hotel guests recommend this tony Half Moon Bay resort restaurant known for its "gorgeous setting" ("incredible views" of the Pacific and the golf course), "great" California-style seafood and "gracious" "Ritz-Carlton service"; those who come to "share an anniversary, engagement" or, at the very least, an "exquisite Sunday brunch" followed by "a stroll" on the bluffs report "life doesn't get any better than that."

Nepenthe
14 | 24 | 16 | $33

Hwy. 1 (¼ mi. south of Ventana Inn & Spa), Big Sur, 831-667-2345; www.nepenthebigsur.com

With a "glorious" 180-degree ocean view that makes it seem "you can see all the way to Baja", this historic "hippie haven" perched over Big Sur attracts its share of loyal locals along with out-of-towners; tip: "duck the tourists" and "head for the outdoor deck" to "linger as long as possible" over "really nice local wines" and "dangle your feet off the cliffs" while you carefully "ignore" the "snotty, incompetent service" and the "unremarkable", "overpriced" Traditional American eats.

North Beach Pizza ◗   18 | 9 | 14 | $16
240 E. Third Ave. (B St.), San Mateo, 650-344-5000;
www.northbeachpizza.com
See review in City of San Francisco Directory.

Oak City Bar & Grill   20 | 19 | 19 | $36
1029 El Camino Real (Ravenswood Ave.), Menlo Park,
650-321-6882; www.oakcitybarandgrill.com
With "ample" portions of "straightforward" New American
staples (e.g."hearty" mac 'n' cheese), a "casual" yet
"attractive" setting and "consistent" service, this "upscale
family spot" in Menlo Park has become "a great midweek
neighborhood place" ("perfect for lunch"); connoisseurs
of cutting-edge cuisine, however, contend the "solid" fare
is "well prepared" but "not very innovative."

O'mei   24 | 16 | 18 | $27
2316 Mission St. (King St.), Santa Cruz, 831-425-8458;
www.omeifood.com
Supporters of this Sino standby state it offers "the ultimate
designer-Chinese-food experience", via its "unique" and
"fantastic selection of regional dishes with a distinct
California twist" that's just "perfect for the taste buds of
Santa Cruz"; still, some say this stalwart has "hit its glass
ceiling" and won't break through till it fixes shortcomings
in the "drab" decor and "distracted service."

Original Joe's ◗   17 | 13 | 17 | $26
(aka Joe's, OJ's)
301 S. First St. (San Carlos St.), San Jose, 408-292-7030;
www.originaljoes.com
See review in City of San Francisco Directory.

Osteria ☒   22 | 15 | 19 | $32
247 Hamilton Ave. (Ramona St.), Palo Alto, 650-328-5700
Since 1971 Palo Alto locals have liked this "nothing-fancy"
Northern Italian for its "fresh, hot pasta" and "melt-in-
your-mouth calamari" served with a "no-fuss" attitude; ok,
the decor is "slightly meager", the scene can be "chaotic"
and too-close tables "make dining a squeeze", but no
matter – "they book up every single night" because "what
they do, they do well."

Oswald's   ∇ 25 | 18 | 23 | $43
1547 Pacific Ave. (Cedar St.), Santa Cruz, 831-423-7427
"San Francisco–quality" "fancy food" plus a "fabulous
wine list" and "enthusiastic", "competent service" – all
three "rare in Santa Cruz" – make this "intimate", art-filled
bistro a "jewel"; the ever-changing Californian fare is
"eclectic, organic" and "consistently great", so devoted
diners don't mind paying prices "on the high side" for
portions "on the small side" – in fact, given its following,
"reservations are a must."

PACIFIC'S EDGE   25 | 28 | 24 | $71
Highlands Inn, 120 Highlands Dr. (Hwy. 1), Carmel, 831-620-1234;
www.highlandsinn.hyatt.com
"Only if you are God" do you get a "better view" than the
"incomparable" seascape seen from Carmel's ritziest
resort restaurant, but here "location, location, location" is
just one of the attractions: the French–New American food
is "tremendous" (prix fixes with pairings are "not to be
missed"), the 1,700-label wine list is "more like a wine
book" and the "solicitous" staff's "*très* elegant"; sure, the
experience is "not inexpensive" but "those sunsets are
worth every penny."

Pancho Villa Taqueria   23 | 9 | 15 | $11
365 S. B St. (bet. 3rd & 4th Aves.), San Mateo, 650-343-4123
See review in City of San Francisco Directory.

Parcel 104   24 | 22 | 22 | $52
Santa Clara Marriott, 2700 Mission College Blvd.
(Great America Pkwy.), Santa Clara, 408-970-6104;
www.parcel104.com
One of Santa Clara's most "ambitious" all-day fine-dining
establishments, this "tasteful" Bradley Ogden production
serves "simple but imaginative" – and "excellent" – New
American cuisine made with locally grown ingredients,
plus some 500 wines; many comment that it's "odd to find
such a top-notch restaurant in a Marriott" and that it must
be "geared to those with large expense accounts"; that
said, "for the price" they feel the "slow" service and
"atmosphere lack energy."

Passage to India   20 | 13 | 15 | $21
1991 W. El Camino Real (Clark Ave.), Mountain View,
650-969-9990; www.passagetoindia.net
Variety isn't the only spice of life at this subcontinental
"buffet heaven" in Mountain View, particularly at the
"plentiful", "consistent" all-you-can-eat lunch and weekend
dinner smorgasbords; "clearly the profits go into the food" –
both the Indian and "Desi Chinese" (to be "experienced at
least once") – since "the interior looks like it hasn't been
redone" in years and "there are too few servers for the large
space"; N.B. vegetarian buffet dinner offered on Tuesdays.

Passionfish   25 | 18 | 23 | $40
701 Lighthouse Ave. (Congress Ave.), Pacific Grove,
831-655-3311; www.passionfish.net
Afishionados are hooked on this Californian pescatorium,
Pacific Grove's "best-kept secret, because it showcases an
ocean's worth of "sustainable seafood" in "mouthwatering"
preparations and its "extensive", "justifiably famous"
wine list won't sink you thanks to "minimal markup"; the
"modest, quiet atmosphere" may "disappoint tourists" but
locals know that with its "welcoming staff" and tabs far

smaller than what "you expect to pay" for "big-city" fare, you shouldn't let this one get away.

Pasta Moon   22 | 17 | 19 | $36
315 Main St. (Mills St.), Half Moon Bay, 650-726-5125; www.pastamoon.com
Convenient for refueling after "shopping on Main Street" or spending a day at the coast, this "reliable" Half Moon Bay trattoria "maintains the beach-town feel" with its "cozy", "friendly atmosphere"; "per the name", this "mainstay" excels at "perfectly prepared pasta" and has a "great" Italian-only wine list to boot, but critics howl that service "can be slow", the digs are "crowded" and the fare "waaaaay too pricey" ("it's noodles boiled in water, for Pete's sake").

Pasta Pomodoro   15 | 13 | 16 | $18
Evergreen Mkt., 4898 San Felipe Rd. (Yerba Buena Blvd.), San Jose, 408-532-0271; www.pastapomodoro.com
See review in City of San Francisco Directory.

Pearl Alley Bistro   ▽ 19 | 17 | 19 | $37
110 Pearl Alley (bet. Lincoln & Walnut Sts.), Santa Cruz, 831-429-8070; www.pearlalley.com
"You never know what will be on the menu" at this slightly "eccentric" Santa Cruz "getaway" "but you do know you'll end up talking about it for days"; the Eclectic menu moves monthly through "cuisines around the world" (the do-it-yourself Mongolian BBQ is always available, though), and the "cozy" interior is "reminiscent of European bistros"; a "sophisticated wine list" and "nice sunset views in the rear" are other attractions.

Pho Hoa-Hiep II   ▽ 20 | 7 | 12 | $11
85 Southgate Ave. (bet. Palmcrest & Park Plaza Drs.), Daly City, 650-992-3814
See review in East of San Francisco Directory.

Piatti   17 | 18 | 18 | $34
Sixth Ave. (Junipero St.), Carmel, 831-625-1766
3905 Rivermark Plaza (Montague Expwy.), Santa Clara, 408-330-9212
www.piatti.com
See review in East of San Francisco Directory.

Pisces ⌧   23 | 19 | 21 | $51
1190 California Dr. (Broadway), Burlingame, 650-401-7500; www.piscesrestaurant.com
Pleased Pisceans find the "innovative", "mouthwatering" California-style seafood right on track at this "charming", "crowded" Burlingame special-occasion spot set in a "nifty revamped railroad station" and staffed by "courteous" servers; however, a vocal minority of dissenters rails at the "narrow and loud" dining room that "rattles" "every time a

train goes by" and huffs the recently overhauled menu is "uninspired" ("try a new astrological sign").

Pizza Antica   21 | 17 | 17 | $23
334 Santana Row (Stevens Creek Blvd.), San Jose,
408-557-8373; www.pizzaantica.com
"Thanks for coming to San Jose, Gordon" grin gourmands grateful for the "four-star chef" making "genuinely stunning" "thin-crust pizza straight out of Italy" piled "with gourmet toppings" straight out of Cali; his "crackling" haute pies and "delicious", "unusual salads" – served in this Santana Row "beehive" and in a recently opened Lafayette branch – draw an "antic crowd of families with kids" who'll tolerate the "long wait" ("no reservations", "slow service") for the sake of the "high-caliber" "payoff."

Plumed Horse 🖼   23 | 21 | 24 | $56
14555 Big Basin Way (4th St.), Saratoga, 408-867-4711;
www.plumedhorse.com
A "perennial favorite" (though perhaps "not for the Waters/Keller crowd"), this "dark", wood-beamed South Bay "mainstay" changes its menu of "reliable" but "not very challenging" Cal-French standards each month but retains an "outstanding" wine list of more than 750 labels; that acclaimed cellar, plus the "attentive but not obtrusive" service, appeals to a "retired-with-money crowd" that happily trots in to hear the weekend jazz trio.

Rio Grill   20 | 17 | 19 | $37
Crossroads Shopping Ctr., 101 Crossroads Blvd. (Rio Rd.),
Carmel, 831-625-5436; www.riogrill.com
"Some things never change" and this "lively", "welcoming" Carmel veteran "falls into that category"; an ersatz adobe "where the locals go to trade gossip over guacamole", it serves "great Californian fare with a Southwestern twist" and "super wines", and the "noisy" "bar scene" is still "hoppin'" despite a "distracting shopping-mall location"; however, regulars report the food and "dated" decor "isn't as fun" or "innovative" "as it was 20 years ago" ("then again, I'm not either").

Ristorante Capellini   20 | 20 | 19 | $34
310 Baldwin Ave. (B St.), San Mateo, 650-348-2296;
www.capellinis.com
"You'll never get a bad meal" at this "tried-and-true" San Mateo Northern Italian where the "classy" Pat Kuleto interiors – featuring an open kitchen with wood-burning pizza oven – and "friendly" service "make you feel you are in Tuscany"; the "great bar" attracts revelers with "generous pours and cheerful bartenders" but the hard-of-hearing harp it also helps make the place "awfully loud", while some even suggest the "nothing-spectacular" menu "is getting stale."

Robert's Whitehouse　　▽ 21　19　20　$45
649 Lighthouse Ave. (19th St.), Pacific Grove, 831-375-9626;
www.robertswhitehouse.com
Voters register their approval of this little-known white
house in Pacific Grove, the current bully pulpit for chef-
owner Robert Kincaid (ex Fresh Cream); in this "elegant
Victorian" with "intimate", recently refurbished dining
rooms, "seasoned guests" savor his "lush, full-flavored"
French cuisine (including "fine prix fixe dinners that will
not send you into Chapter 11"), though a party of critics
vetoes the vittles and the "inattentive" service.

ROY'S AT PEBBLE BEACH　　23　25　22　$52
The Inn at Spanish Bay, 2700 17 Mile Dr. (Congress Rd.),
Pebble Beach, 831-647-7423; www.pebblebeach.com
Duffers and diners alike dig the "out-of-this-world location"
at Pebble Beach's Inn at Spanish Bay – featuring "million-
dollar views of the Pacific" and the famed golf greens –
that makes this "one of the best" in Roy Yamaguchi's chain
of Hawaiian Regional hot spots; luckily, most maintain the
"imaginative" cuisine (with its "exquisite architectural"
presentations) and "staff willing to make accommodations
without a pout" live up to the landscape, though a few do
fuss the food is "more flash than finesse."

Sardine Factory　　20　21　20　$51
701 Wave St. (Prescott Ave.), Monterey, 831-373-3775;
www.sardinefactory.com
Monterey's "aging dowager of Cannery Row" "still packs
'em in" like, yes, sardines with the help of "respectful"
staffers who proffer hard-to-find "fresh abalone" and "sand
dabs in season" and guide you through the "incredible
wine list"; opinions about decor depend on whether "you
like the classic, old-style look" that "hasn't changed since
Clint Eastwood hung out here in *Play Misty for Me*", but
most agree "factory is the right word" for the "standard"
seafood that's "lost its edge."

Scott's of Palo Alto　　–　–　–　E
#1 Town & Country Village (Embarcadero Rd.), Palo Alto,
650-323-1555; www.scottsseafood.com
Scott's of San Jose
185 Park Avenue (Almaden Blvd.), San Jose, 408-971-1700;
www.scottsseafoodsj.com
See review in East of San Francisco Directory.

Sent Sovi　　▽ 23　21　25　$59
14583 Big Basin Way (5th St.), Saratoga, 408-867-3110;
www.sentsovi.com
The "warm and welcoming staff" "treats you like a queen
or king" at this "pleasant", "romantic" Downtown Saratoga
spot, where the new "owners are trying to keep up the
standards" previously established here; supporters swear

the French-inspired Californian cuisine and wines "from the Santa Cruz mountains" are "solid and satisfying", but dissenters deem the "hit-or-miss" food more "conservative" than before; other gourmands just groove on the gestalt: "sometimes it's more about the experience than the taste."

Seven Restaurant & Lounge ☒   22 | 20 | 18 | $43 |
754 The Alameda (Bush St.), San Jose, 408-280-1644;
www.7restaurant.us
Oh-"so-chic for 408", this "happening" sophomore looks like a "NYC nightclub" – down to the "flashy cars parked outside" – even though it's set "in a dowdy part of San Jose" ("convenient to HP Pavilion" and Downtown theaters); "thirtysomethings" flock for cocktails and "enjoyable", "beautifully presented" French–New American fare, but boomers burned by "amateur" service and deafening "noise" are inclined to count this place out.

71 Saint Peter ☒   23 | 18 | 21 | $40 |
71 N. San Pedro St. (bet. Santa Clara & St. John Sts.), San Jose,
408-971-8523; www.71saintpeter.com
It may not be "sexy, exciting or trendy", but for a business lunch, a "pre-theater" bite or a date, surveyors say this "intimate" brick-and-tile "standard" in Downtown San Jose is as "welcoming" as its heavenly namesake, thanks to "professional", "attentive" staffers and a "nice patio"; connoisseurs confide the five-course tasting menu – which pairs "innovative", "seasonal" Cal-Med fare with "interesting wines" for a "bargain"-priced $45 – is "one of the South Bay's best-kept secrets."

SHADOWBROOK   20 | 26 | 22 | $39 |
1750 Wharf Rd. (Capitola Rd.), Capitola, 831-475-1511;
www.shadowbrook-capitola.com
"Just try to find a more romantic restaurant in the Bay Area" dare devotees of this "sprawling hillside" "destination" "overlooking Capitola"; loyalists love to "amble through terraced gardens", then take the tram to the entrance and have drinks or dine in the "intimate", "labyrinthine" interior; "personable" "surfers in bow ties" provide "polite" service, and as of early 2005, respondents report a "new chef has brought a more playful touch" to what had been an "embarrassingly boring" Continental–New American menu.

SIERRA MAR   27 | 29 | 26 | $72 |
Post Ranch Inn, Post Ranch/Hwy. 1 (30 mi. south of Carmel),
Big Sur, 831-667-2800
Perched 1,200 feet up "on the cliffs of Big Sur", the "all-glass dining room" at the Post Ranch Inn provides a "God's-eye view" of the Pacific Ocean that earns it the No. 1 ranking for Decor in this *Survey*; aside from the "incomparable" seascape, admirers also adore this "secluded" aerie for its "irresistible", internationally inflected Californian cuisine,

a 4,000-label wine list allowing for "wonderful pairings" and service that's "just right", all of which add up to a "profoundly peaceful" and "unforgettable" experience.

Spago Palo Alto 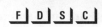 | 22 | 22 | 22 | $54 |
265 Lytton Ave. (bet. Bryant & Ramona Sts.), Palo Alto, 650-833-1000; www.wolfgangpuck.com
"Featuring all the Puck accoutrements" – "architectural" Cal-Med food, "haute pizzas" and "gorgeous" decor" (yes, that "actually is a Rauschenberg on the wall") – Palo Alto's "high rollers' restaurant" is still the place for "power diners" and Stanford students hoping to "impress their parents" with a sighting of "Wolfgang at the stove"; still, some wonder "isn't the self-bestowed importance a little passé" "since the Internet bubble popped"?

St. Michael's Alley | 23 | 19 | 21 | $36 |
806 Emerson St. (Homer Ave.), Palo Alto, 650-326-2530; www.stmikes.com
Saints and sinners alike (not to mention the Clintons) partake of "divine" brunches and "delicious", ever-changing dinners "prepared with TLC" at this "hippie-ish" Palo Alto Californian bistro, where the "accommodating proprietor wants you to leave happy"; founded in 1959, it's spent the past 10 years at this "out-of-the-way" location gathering a faithful following; nevertheless, the "unimpressed" damn this cloister as "overhyped" and confess "I'd like this a lot better at half the price."

Stokes Restaurant & Bar | 23 | 20 | 22 | $42 |
500 Hartnell St. (bet. Madison & Polk Sts.), Monterey, 831-373-1110; www.stokesrestaurant.com
Filled with "ghosts" of yore, this "beautiful" "hacienda" is a "piece of old Monterey", but surveyors are totally stoked that it dares to serve "innovative" Cal-Med meals "with panache" (instead of the "usual touristy fare in a vacation city") plus "late-night snacks and tapas" at the "great bar" till 10 PM; the "cozy rooms" with a plethora of fireplaces populated by "personable staffers who love the food they serve" make meals here a "real treat."

STRAITS CAFE | 21 | 20 | 17 | $34 |
1100 Burlingame Ave. (Highland Ave.), Burlingame, 650-373-7883
3295 El Camino Real (Lambert Ave.), Palo Alto, 650-494-7168
333 Santana Row (bet. Olin Ave. & Tatum Ln.), San Jose, 408-246-6320
www.straitsrestaurants.com
See review in City of San Francisco Directory.

TAMARINE | 25 | 24 | 21 | $41 |
Hotel Griffon, 546 University Ave. (Tasso St.), Palo Alto, 650-325-8500; www.tamarinerestaurant.com
Decorated in a "sumptuous" Asian style ("gorgeous original art", "nifty tableware, bowls and chopsticks"), Palo Alto's

hidden "haute Vietnamese" at the Hotel Griffon exudes an "über-cool" vibe that's compounded by its "scintillating" Eastern small plates and "attentive" staff; despite phos who cry "all fluff, no stuff" ("rice is supposed to come in bowls, not thimbles"), it's found "early success" so "book ahead", sit at the communal table or join the "VC's and SV types" at the "happening bar."

Tarpy's Roadhouse   21 21 19 $38
2999 Monterey-Salinas Hwy. (Canyon Del Rey Blvd.), Monterey, 831-647-1444; www.tarpys.com
True, it's a stone "house at the roadside", but 'roadhouse' is "not an ideal word to describe this gem" gripe grammarians who groove on this vintage venue specializing in "hearty portions" of "good, old-fashioned" American cookery and local wines; ok, it's "nothing to drive out of your way for", but "hungry tourists" consider it a "nice respite on the way to Monterey" and enjoy sitting on the "pleasant" patio to watch "jets land at the airport."

Taste Cafe & Bistro   ▽ 21 15 22 $34
1199 Forest Ave. (Prescott Ln.), Pacific Grove, 831-655-0324; www.tastecafebistro.com
"Far from the maddening crowds", this "cheery, yellow" European-style bistro in a Pacific Grove "strip mall" appeals to locals attracted to its "fun-loving atmosphere"; "naked cherubs oversee your every bite" of the "consistent" and "surprisingly innovative" Continental cuisine (including "wonderful desserts"), while the ministrations of "pleasant and knowledgeable servers" and "live jazz" Thursdays–Saturdays make it an "outstanding value."

Three Seasons   23 20 19 $34
518 Bryant St. (University Ave.), Palo Alto, 650-838-0353; www.threeseasonsrestaurant.com
See review in City of San Francisco Directory.

Trader Vic's   16 21 17 $43
Dina's Garden Hotel, 4269 El Camino Real (bet. Charleston & San Antonio Rds.), Palo Alto, 650-849-9800; www.tradervicspaloalto.com
See review in East of San Francisco Directory.

Turmerik   ▽ 22 18 19 $28
141 S. Murphy St. (bet. Evelyn & Washington Aves.), Sunnyvale, 408-617-9100; www.turmerik.com
"If you like your food spicy hot, this is the place" state sahibs who swear by this Sunnyvale subcontinental; its "low-priced, all-you-can-eat lunch buffet" with "lots of variety" "pulls in overflow crowds Monday–Friday", and a pleasant dining room that's earth-toned and comparatively "upscale" (featuring a full bar and "nice" tableware) constitutes a "great environment for a business" meal or dinner date.

231 Ellsworth 🅩   24 | 20 | 23 | $57 |
231 S. Ellsworth Ave. (bet. 2nd & 3rd Aves.), San Mateo,
650-347-7231; www.231ellsworth.com
In an "unseemly location" – the "culinary wasteland" of
San Mateo – this "clubby" "high-class" haunt for the "older
Peninsula crowd" combines a "luxurious" New American
menu (featuring a slew of "satisfying" prix fixe options), an
"exceptional" 800-entry wine list and a "professional" staff;
proponents praise the "quiet", "sophisticated setting", but
doubters declare the "spartan" room "needs to get in touch
with its feminine side" and charge the "extremely pricey"
place is "living on a great reputation, but not living up to it."

Udupi Palace   19 | 8 | 14 | $14 |
976 E. El Camino Real (Poplar Ave.), Sunnyvale, 408-830-9600;
www.udupipalace.net
See review in East of San Francisco Directory.

Village Pub, The   24 | 23 | 23 | $54 |
2967 Woodside Rd. (Whiskey Hill Rd.), Woodside, 650-851-9888;
www.thevillagepub.net
"Only tony Woodside could consider this place a pub"
chuckle surveyors "when in fact" the "high-end" New
American "comfort food" ("burgers and filets are side by
side on the menu"), "huge wine selection" and seamless,
"cheerful" service are "on par with SF's best restaurants";
"for sport, try to pick out the anonymous SV billionaires" in
the "plush" yet "simple" dining room or in the adjacent bar,
or just sit on the patio "and watch the exotic cars roll in."

Viognier   24 | 21 | 22 | $52 |
Draeger's Mktpl., 222 E. Fourth Ave. (bet. B St. & Ellsworth Ave.),
San Mateo, 650-685-3727; www.viognierrestaurant.com
Sure, it's "convenient", but this "swank restaurant" on the
"second floor of a San Mateo supermarket" has even more
going for it: "amazing" Californian tasting menus and an
"outstanding" list of "unique boutique wines", all served
by a "delightful" crew; "half the fun is going in through
gorgeous Draeger's Marketplace and the cooking school to
get there" but some Peninsulites complain the upstairs has
gone too upmarket, saying "prices have crept upwards" too.

Yankee Pier   18 | 15 | 17 | $30 |
378 Santana Row (S. Winchester Ave.), San Jose, 408-244-1244
San Francisco Int'l Airport, United Domestic Departure Terminal,
South San Francisco, 650-821-8938
www.yankeepier.com
See review in North of San Francisco Directory.

Zao Noodle Bar   14 | 12 | 13 | $16 |
261 University Ave. (bet. Bryant & Ramona Sts.), Palo Alto,
650-328-1988; www.zao.com
See review in City of San Francisco Directory.

Zibibbo　　　　　　　　　　　20 | 20 | 18 | $39 |

430 Kipling St. (bet. Lytton & University Aves.), Palo Alto, 650-328-6722; www.restaurantlulu.com

The atmosphere is "inviting" and "vibrant" at this "spendy but fun" Palo Alto sister of SF's Restaurant LuLu, a "longtime favorite" for its "hearty", "rustic" Mediterranean small plates; commenders call the "airy", multiroomed eatery a "great place to bring business associates" because its "unmatched wine-by-the-glass program" and family-style service "guarantee a lively dinner when dining with a group" – by the same token, though, the space is "loud" and dissenters deem service "uneven."

Zucca Ristorante　　　　　19 | 19 | 19 | $32 |

186 Castro St. (bet. Central & Villa Sts.), Mountain View, 650-864-9940; www.zuccaristorante.com

Though this Mountain View brasserie has "a small-town feel", its menu meanders around the Mediterranean, passing through Italy, France, Greece, Spain and Turkey to provide "something for everyone" ("well-prepared" small plates, "zesty, zingy" entrees, "innovative combos"), delivered to table by a "gregarious" and "knowledgeable" crew; participants particularly praise the "quaint outdoor patio" for dinner on "warm nights."

Indexes

CUISINES
LOCATIONS
SPECIAL FEATURES

Places outside of San Francisco are marked as follows:
E=East of SF; N=North; and S=South.

CUISINES

Afghan
Helmand, The

American
Alfred's Steak
A. Sabella's
Bing Crosby's/E
Bungalow 44/N
Burger Joint
Cafe Divine
Garden Court
Giordano Bros.
Home
Max's
MoMo's
Oola

American (New)
Alexis Baking Co./N
Arcadia/S
bacar
Basin/S
Beach Chalet
Bendean/E
Big 4
Bistro Ralph/N
Blue Plate
Boonville Hotel/N
Boulette's Larder
Boulevard
Cafe Esin/E
Cafe La Haye/N
Celadon/N
Central Park Bistro/S
Chenery Park
Chow/Park Chow
Chow/Park Chow/E
Cindy's Backstreet/N
Cosmopolitan
Cozmo's Corner
Deuce/N
Dottie's True Blue
Dry Creek Kitchen/N
Duck Club/E/N/S
Eulipia/S
Flea St. Café/S
Fog City Diner
French Laundry/N
Frisson
Fumé Bistro/N
Gary Danko
Indigo

John Bentley's/S
Kenwood/N
Lion & Compass/S
Luna Park
Madrona Manor/N
Manresa/S
Martini House/N
Mecca
Mendo Bistro/N
Michael Mina
Mirepoix/N
Moose's
Mustards Grill/N
Myth
955 Ukiah/N
Oak City B&G/S
One Market
Pacific's Edge/S
Parcel 104/S
Park Chalet
Park Grill
Postrio
Rest. Budo/N
rnm
Rotunda
Sauce
Seven/S
Shadowbrook/S
Slow Club
Street
Tablespoon
Terra/N
Town Hall
Town's End
2223
231 Ellsworth/S
Universal Cafe
Village Pub/S
Washington Sq. B & G
Winterland
Woodward's Garden
XYZ
zazu/N
Zin/N
Zinsvalley/N

American (Regional)
Maverick

American (Traditional)
Ahwahnee Din. Rm./E
Balboa Cafe

Cuisines

Balboa Cafe/E
Bette's Oceanview/E
Bistro Boudin
BIX
Blackberry Bistro/E
Brannan's Grill/N
Brazen Head
Buckeye Roadhouse/N
Cafe Cacao/E
Carnelian Room
Casa Orinda/E
Chapter & Moon/N
Cheesecake Factory
Cheesecake Factory/S
Chloe's Cafe
Dipsea Cafe/N
Duarte's Tavern/S
Ella's
Gayle's Bakery/S
Gordon's/N
Hard Rock Cafe
Kitchen at 868 Grant/N
Lark Creek/E
Lark Creek Inn/N
Liberty Cafe
MacArthur Park
MacArthur Park/S
Mama's Wash. Sq.
Mama's Royal Cafe/E
Market/N
Miss Millie's
Mo's
Nepenthe/S
Original Joe's
Original Joe's/S
Pork Store Café
Press/N
Red's Java House
Rick & Ann's/E
Rosamunde Grill
Rutherford Grill/N
Scott's/S/E
Tarpy's Roadhouse/S
Taylor's Automatic
Taylor's Automatic/N

Argentinean
Boca/N
El Raigon

Asian
Alexander's Steak/S
Asia de Cuba
Azie
Betelnut Pejiu Wu
butterfly embarcadero

Circolo
Hawthorne Lane
Lüx
Ponzu
Saigon Sandwiches
Watergate

Asian Fusion
AsiaSF
Blupointe
Bridges/E
CAFÉ KATi
Eos Rest./Wine Bar
Flying Fish Grill/S
House
Koo
Limón
Silks
SUMI

Bakeries
Alexis Baking Co./N
Bistro Boudin
Boulange Cole/Polk
Citizen Cake
Downtown Bakery/N
Gayle's Bakery/S
Il Fornaio
Il Fornaio/E/N/S
Liberty Cafe
Mama's Wash. Sq.
Model Bakery/N
Tartine Bakery
Town's End

Barbecue
Bo's Barbecue/E
Brother-in-Law BBQ
Buckeye Roadhouse/N
Everett & Jones/E
Foothill Cafe/N
Memphis Minnie's
Q

Belgian
Frjtz Fries

Brazilian
Espetus Churrascaria
Mangarosa

Burmese
Burma Super Star
Mandalay
Nan Yang/E

Cajun
Elite Cafe

Californian
Adagia/E
Ahwahnee Din. Rm./E
Albany Bistro/E
Albion River Inn/N
Alexander Valley/N
All Season's Cafe/N
Americano
Anton & Michel/S
Applewood Inn/N
Aqua
Asqew Grill
Asqew Grill/E
A Tavola/S
Bay Wolf/E
Bistro Aix
Bistro Elan/S
Bistro Ralph/N
Blackhawk Grille/E
Boonville Hotel/N
Bouchée/S
Bridges/E
Brix/N
Bucci's/E
butterfly embarcadero
Cafe Beaujolais/N
Cafe La Haye/N
Caffé Verbena/E
Canteen
Caprice/N
Carneros/N
Chez Panisse/E
Chez Panisse Café/E
Cindy's Backstreet/N
Citron/E
Cliff House Bistro
Club XIX/S
Coco 500
Cool Café/S
Desiree Café
Domaine Chandon/N
downtown/E
Ecco/S
Eliza's
Enrico's Sidewalk
Eos Rest./Wine Bar
Erna's Elderberry Hse./E
Farmhouse Inn/N
1550 Hyde Café
Firecracker
Flea St. Café/S

Flying Fish Grill/S
Foreign Cinema
Fork/N
Fournou's Ovens
Frascati
Gabriella Café/S
Garibaldis
Garibaldis/E
Globe
Grand Cafe
Grasing's Coastal/S
Hawthorne Lane
Hurley's/N
Jack Falstaff
Jardinière
Jimmy Bean's/E
John Ash & Co./N
Jordan's/E
Julia's Kitchen/N
jZcool/S
Lalime's/E
La Rose Bistro/E
La Scene Café
L'Auberge Carmel/S
Ledford House/N
Little River Inn/N
Lucy's /N
MacCallum House/N
Manka's Inverness/N
Meadowood Grill/N
Mezze/E
Montrio Bistro/S
Moosse Cafe/N
Napa Valley Grille/N
Napa Wine Train/N
Navio/S
Nectar Wine
Olema Inn/N
Osake/N
Oswald's/S
Pacific
Pangaea/N
Passionfish/S
Pearl/N
Pilar/N
Pinot Blanc/N
Pisces/S
Plumed Horse/S
PlumpJack Cafe
PlumpJack Cafe/E
Public
Ravenous Cafe/N
Rio Grill/S
Rivoli/E

Cuisines

Rubicon
Rue Saint Jacques
Santé/N
Sea Ranch Lodge/N
Seasons
Seaweed Café/N
Sent Sovi/S
71 Saint Peter/S
Sierra Mar/S
Silks
Soizic/E
Spago Palo Alto/S
Stokes/S
Stomp/N
St. Orres/N
Sutro's at Cliff Hse.
Syrah/N
Townhouse B&G/E
2223
Venus/E
Viognier/S
Watercress
Waterfront
Wente Vineyards/E
Wine Spectator/N
Zaré/N
Zax Tavern/E

Cambodian

Angkor Borei
Angkor Wat
Battambang/E

Caribbean

Cha Cha Cha
Charanga

Central American

Platanos

Cheese Steaks

Jay's Cheesesteak

Chinese

* dim sum specialist)
Alice's
Brandy Ho's
Chef Chu's/S
Dragon Well
Eliza's
Eric's
Firecracker
ook Yuen Seafood/S*
ary Chu's/N

Great China/E
Great Eastern*
Happy Cafe/S*
Harbor Village*
Henry's Hunan
Hong Kong Flower/S*
House of Nanking
Hunan Home's
Hunan Home's/S
Jade Villa/E*
Jai Yun
Koi Palace/S*
Mandarin
Mayflower*
O'mei/S
R & G Lounge
Rest. Peony/E*
Shanghai 1930
Shen Hua/E
Taiwan
Taiwan/E
Tommy Toy's
Ton Kiang*
Yank Sing*
Yuet Lee

Coffee Shops/Diners

Bette's Oceanview/E
FatApple's/E
Jimmy Bean's/E
Mel's Drive-In
Sears Fine Food
Taylor's Automatic

Continental

Adrian's/S
Anton & Michel/S
Caprice/N
Chantilly/S
Ecco/S
El Paseo/N
Fresh Cream/S
Maddalena's/S
Shadowbrook/S
Taste Cafe/S

Creole

Kingfish
Kingfish/S
PJ's Oyster Bed

Cuban

Cafe Lo Cubano
Habana
Los Flamingos

Delis
Jimtown Store/N
Max's
Max's/E/N/S
Saul's Rest./Deli/E

Dessert
Boulange Cole/Polk
Cafe Cacao/E
Café Tiramisu
Cheesecake Factory
Cheesecake Factory/S
Citizen Cake
Downtown Bakery/N
Emporio Rulli
Emporio Rulli/N
Fenton's Creamery/E
Tartine Bakery

Eclectic
Albany Bistro/E
Andalu
Barndiva/N
Celadon/N
Delancey St.
Firefly
Flavor/N
Harmony Club/N
Kingfish
Kingfish/S
Levende
Lime
Louka/E
Maria Manso's/N
Olivia/E
Pearl Alley Bistro/S
Picco/N
Pomelo
Ravenous Cafe/N
Sydney's
Va de Vi/E
Wappo Bar/N
Willi's Wine Bar/N
Willow Wood Mkt./N

English
Lovejoy's Tea Rm.

Eritrean
Massawa

Ethiopian
Axum Cafe
Blue Nile/E
Massawa

French
À Côté/E
Alexander Valley/N
Angèle/N
Aqua
Auberge du Soleil/N
Baraka
Bella Vista/S
Bistro V/N
BIX
Boulange Cole/Polk
Boulevard
Brannan's Grill/N
Cafe Beaujolais/N
Café Fanny/E
Cafe Jacqueline
Café Marcella/S
Campton Place
Casanova/S
Chez Spencer
Club XIX/S
El Paseo/N
Emile's/S
fig cafe & winebar/N
Fleur de Lys
French Laundry/N
Fresh Cream/S
Gregoire/E
Isa
Jardinière
Julia's Kitchen/N
Kenwood/N
La Folie
La Forêt/S
La Note/Café Clem/E
La Toque/N
Le Cheval/Le Petit Cheval/E
Le Papillon/S
Luna Park
Mistral/S
Monte Cristo Cafe
Nizza La Bella/E
Pacific's Edge/S
Pangaea/N
Père Jeanty/N
Pinot Blanc/N
Plouf
Plumed Horse/S
Robert's Whitehouse/S
Scala's Bistro
Seasons
Seaweed Café/N
Seven/S
Soizic/E

Sonoma Meritage/N
Tallula
Tao Cafe
Watercress
Watergate

French (Bistro)

Alamo Square
Anjou
Baker St. Bistro
Bistro Aix
Bistro Clovis
Bistro Elan/S
Bistro Jeanty/N
Bistro Liaison/E
Bistro Vida/S
Blupointe
Bouchon/N
Brigitte's/S
Butler & Chef Cafe
Cafe Bastille
Café Claude
Café Rouge/E
Chapeau!
Charcuterie/N
Chez Maman
Chez Papa Bistrot
Chou Chou
Christophe/N
Clémentine
Cote Sud
El Dorado Kitchen/N
Florio
Fringale
Galette
girl & the fig/N
Grand Cafe
Hyde St. Bistro
Jeanty at Jack's
Jojo/E
K&L Bistro/N
La Note/Café Clem/E
La Rose Bistro/E
Le Central Bistro
Le Charm Bistro
Le Petit Robert
Le Zinc
Dola
Rue Lepic
Rue Saint Jacques
Cent Sovi/S
South Park Cafe
Syrah/N
i Couz

Water St. Bistro/N
Zazie

French (Brasserie)

Absinthe
La Suite
Left Bank/E/N/S

French (New)

Ana Mandara
Azie
Cafe Cacao/E
Chaya Brasserie
Chez TJ/S
Citron/E
Cyrus/N
Erna's Elderberry Hse./E
Fifth Floor
Fork/N
Julius' Castle
Le Colonial
Manresa/S
Marché/S
Marché aux Fleurs/N
Marinus/S
Masa's
955 Ukiah/N
Quince
Rendezvous Inn/N
Rigolo
Ritz-Carlton Din. Rm.
Rubicon
SUMI

German

Suppenküche
Walzwerk

Greek

Evvia/S
Kokkari Estiatorio

Hamburgers

Balboa Cafe
Balboa Cafe/E
Barney's
Barney's/E/N
Burger Joint
Burger Joint/S
FatApple's/E
Joe's Cable Car
Mel's Drive-In
Mo's
Taylor's Automatic
Taylor's Automatic/N

Cuisines

Hawaiian
Moki's Sushi
Tita's hale 'aina

Hawaiian Regional
Roy's
Roy's Pebble Beach/S

Hot Dogs
Caspers Hot Dogs/E

Indian
Ajanta/E
Amber India/S
Breads of India/E
Gaylord India
Gaylord India/S
Indian Oven
Lotus of India/N
Marigold Indian/S
Mela Tandoori
Naan 'n Curry
Naan 'n Curry/E
Passage to India/S
Rotee
Shalimar
Shalimar/E
Tallula
Turmerik/S
Udupi Palace/E/S
Vik's Chaat Corner/E
Zante

Italian
(N=Northern; S=Southern)
Acquerello
Albona Rist. (N)
Alioto's (S)
Americano
Amici E. Coast Pizza
Amici E. Coast Pizza/N/S
Antica Trattoria (N)
Aperto
A 16 (S)
A Tavola/S
Bella Trattoria (S)
Bella Vista/S
Bistro Don Giovanni/N
Bistro V/N
Brindisi Cucina (S)
Buca di Beppo
Buca di Beppo/S
Cafe Citti/N (N)
Café Tiramisu (N)

Caffe Delle Stelle (N)
Caffe Macaroni
Caffè Museo
Caffé Verbena/E
Casanova/S (N)
Cook St. Helena/N (N)
Cork/N
Cucina Paradiso/N (S)
Cucina Rest./Wine Bar/N
Delfina (N)
Della Santina's/N (N)
Dopo/E
E'Angelo
Eccolo/E (N)
Emmy's Spaghetti
Emporio Rulli
Emporio Rulli/N
Florio
Frantoio/N (N)
Gabriella Café/S (N)
Gira Polli (S)
Gira Polli/N (S)
Globe
Il Davide/N (N)
Il Fornaio
Il Fornaio/E/N/S
Incanto (N)
Jackson Fillmore
Julius' Castle
Kuleto's (N)
Kuleto's/S (N)
La Ginestra/N (S)
La Strada/S
Last Supper Club (S)
Lo Coco's/E (S)
L'Osteria del Forno (N)
Mangarosa
Mario's Bohemian (N)
Mescolanza (N)
Mezza Luna/S (S)
Mistral/S
Montrio Bistro/S
Nizza La Bella/E
Nob Hill Café (N)
North Bch. Rest. (N)
Oliveto/E
Original Joe's
Original Joe's/S
Osteria/S (N)
Palio D'Asti
Pane e Vino (N)
Parma
Pasta Moon/S
Pasta Pomodoro

222
subscribe to zagat.com

Cuisines

Pasta Pomodoro/E/S
Pazzia
Pesce (N)
Phoenix Next Door/E
Piatti/E/N/S
Piazza D'Angelo/N
Pizza Antica/E/S
Pizzaiolo/E
Pizza Rustica/E
Pizzeria Picco/N (S)
Pizzeria Tra Vigne/N
Poggio/N
Postino/E
Prima/E
Quince
Rist. Bacco
Rist. Capellini/S (N)
Rist. Fabrizio/N (N)
Rist. Ideale
Rist. Milano (N)
Rist. Umbria (N)
Rose Pistola (N)
Rose's Cafe (N)
Rustico/N
Santi/N (N)
Scala's Bistro (N)
Scoma's/N
Sharon's By Sea/N
Sociale
Sonoma Meritage/N (N)
Tommaso's (S)
Tratt. Contadina
Tratt. La Siciliana/E (S)
Tra Vigne/N (N)
Uva Trattoria/N (S)
Venezia/E
Venticello (N)
Victorian Gardens/N (N)
Vivande Porta Via
Washington Sq. B & G
zazu/N (N)
Zuppa (S)

Japanese
(* sushi specialist)
Ace Wasabi's*
Anzu*
Blowfish Sushi*
Blowfish Sushi/S*
Buca di Beppo/S
Chaya Brasserie*
Deep Sushi*
Ebisu*
Flying Fish Grill/S

Fuki Sushi/S*
Godzila Sushi*
Grandeho Kamekyo*
Grasshopper/E
Hamano Sushi*
Hana Japanese/N*
Hotei*
Juban
Juban/S
Kabuto*
Kaygetsu/S*
Kirala/E*
Koo*
Kyo-Ya*
Maki
Mifune
Moki's Sushi*
O Chamé/E
Osake/N*
Ozumo*
Robata Grill/N*
Sanraku*
Shabu-Sen
Sushi Groove*
Sushi Ran/N*
Takara*
Ten-Ichi*
Tokyo Go Go*
Tsunami Sushi*
Uzen/E*
Yoshi's/E*
Zushi Puzzle*

Jewish
Saul's Rest./Deli/E

Korean
(* barbecue specialist)
Brother's Korean*
Koryo BBQ/E*

Mediterranean
Absinthe
À Côté/E
Auberge du Soleil/N
bacar
Baraka
Bay Wolf/E
Brigitte's/S
Bucci's/E
Cafe Esin/E
Cafe Gibraltar/S
Café Marcella/S
Café Rouge/E

Caffè Museo
Campton Place
Cetrella Bistro/S
Chez Nous
Chez Panisse/E
Chez Panisse Café/E
Coco 500
Cortez
downtown/E
El Dorado Kitchen/N
Enrico's Sidewalk
Evvia/S
Fandango/S
1550 Hyde Café
Foreign Cinema
Fournou's Ovens
Frascati
Garibaldis
Garibaldis/E
Hurley's/N
Insalata's /N
Lalime's/E
La Scene Café
Lavanda/S
Ledford House/N
Lucy's /N
Luella
Lüx
Manzanita/N
MarketBar
Mezze/E
Monti's Rotisserie/N
Olema Inn/N
Olivia/E
paul k
PlumpJack Cafe
PlumpJack Cafe/E
Public
Rest. at Stevenswood/N
Rest. LuLu
Ritz-Carlton Terrace
Rivoli/E
Savor
71 Saint Peter/S
Spago Palo Alto/S
Stokes/S
Truly Mediterranean
Underwood Bar/N
U Street Lounge
Wente Vineyards/E
Willow Wood Mkt./N
Zaré/N
Zatar/E
Zax Tavern/E

Zibibbo/S
Zucca/S
Zuni Café

Mexican
Cactus Taqueria/E
Colibrí Mexican Bistro
Doña Tomás/E
El Balazo
El Metate
Fuentes Tapas/N
Guaymas/N
Impala
Joe's Taco Lounge/N
Juan's Place/E
La Cumbre Taqueria
La Cumbre Taqueria/S
Las Camelias/N
La Taqueria
La Taqueria/S
Los Flamingos
Maya
Mi Casa/N
Mijita
Nick's Crispy Tacos
Pancho Villa
Pancho Villa/S
Picante Cocina/E
Puerto Alegre
Tacubaya/E
Taqueria Can-Cun

Middle Eastern
Dish Dash/S
Goood Frikin' Chicken
Kan Zaman
La Méditerranée
La Méditerranée/E
Truly Mediterranean
YaYa
Yumma's

Moroccan
Aziza

Nepalese
Little Nepal

Noodle Shops
Citizen Thai
Citrus Club
Hotei
Mifune
Osha Thai Noodles
So

Zao Noodle
Zao Noodle/E/S

Nuevo Latino
Asia de Cuba
Circolo
Destino
Platanos
Tamal

Pacific Rim
Jordan's/E
Pacific
Pacific Catch

Pakistani
Mela Tandoori
Naan 'n Curry
Naan 'n Curry/E
Pakwan
Pakwan/E
Rotee
Shalimar
Shalimar/E

Pan-Asian
AsiaSF
Bambuddha
Betelnut Pejiu Wu
Citrus Club
General Café/N
Grasshopper/E
Ponzu
RoHan Lounge
Straits Cafe
Straits Cafe/S
Tonga Room
Zao Noodle
Zao Noodle/E/S

Pan-Latin
Cascal/S
Charanga
Fonda Solana/E

Persian/Iranian
Maykadeh

Peruvian
Destino
Fresca
Limón
Mochica

Pizza
Amici E. Coast Pizza
Amici E. Coast Pizza/N/S

Bistro Boudin
Giorgio's Pizzeria
Goat Hill Pizza
La Ginestra/N
Lo Coco's/E
Manzanita/N
North Beach Pizza
North Beach Pizza/E/S
Palio D'Asti
Pauline's Pizza
Pazzia
Pizza Antica/E/S
Pizza Azzurro/N
Pizzaiolo/E
Pizza Rustica/E
Pizzeria Delfina
Pizzeria Picco/N
Pizzeria Tra Vigne/N
Pizzetta 211
Postrio
Tommaso's
Zachary's Pizza/E
Zante

Polynesian
Trader Vic's
Trader Vic's/E/S

Portuguese
LaSalette/N

Russian
Katia's Tea Rm.

Sandwiches
Cafe Divine
Caffe Centro
Citizen Cake
Downtown Bakery/N
Gayle's Bakery/S
Giordano Bros.
Jimtown Store/N
Mario's Bohemian
Max's
Max's/E/N/S
Model Bakery/N
Saigon Sandwiches

Seafood
Alamo Square
Alioto's
Aqua
A. Sabella's
Barbara Fishtrap/S

Blupointe
Catch
Farallon
Fish/N
Flying Fish Grill/S
Fook Yuen Seafood/S
Great Eastern
Guaymas/N
Hayes St. Grill
Hog Island Oyster
Koi Palace/S
Marica/E
Mayflower
McCormick & Kuleto
Monte Cristo Cafe
Navio/S
Pacific Café
Pacific Catch
Passionfish/S
Pearl Oyster Bar/E
Pesce
Pisces/S
PJ's Oyster Bed
Plouf
Sam's Grill
Sardine Factory/S
Scoma's
Scoma's/N
Scott's/S/E
Sea Ranch Lodge/N
Sea Salt/E
Sharon's By Sea/N
Swan Oyster Depot
Tadich Grill
Waterfront
Willi's Seafood/N
Yabbies Coastal
Yankee Pier/N/S
Yuet Lee

Charanga
Chez Nous
Citizen Thai
Cortez
E&O Trading Co.
Eos Rest./Wine Bar
Fonda Solana/E
Fork/N
General Café/N
Grasshopper/E
Harmony Club/N
Isa
Levende
Lime
Louka/E
Luella
Lüx
Medjool
Pearl Oyster Bar/E
Pesce
Picco/N
Ponzu
rnm
RoHan Lounge
Soi Four/E
Stokes/S
Stomp/N
Straits Cafe
Straits Cafe/S
Tamarine/S
Three Seasons
Three Seasons/S
Underwood Bar/N
Va de Vi/E
Willi's Seafood/N
Willi's Wine Bar/N
Wine Garden Food/N
Zibibbo/S
Zucca/S

Singaporean
Straits Cafe/S

Small Plates
À Côté/E
Andalu
AsiaSF
Baraka
Barndiva/N
Betelnut Pejiu Wu
Blanca Cafe
Cascal/S
César/E
Cha Cha Cha

Soul Food
Powell's Place

Southeast Asian
E&O Trading Co.
E&O Trading Co./S

Southern
Biscuits and Blues
Blue Jay Cafe
Brother-in-Law BBQ
Everett & Jones/E
Kate's Kitchen
Powell's Place

Spanish
(* tapas specialist)
Alegrias*
Basque Cultural Ctr./S
B44
Blanca Cafe*
Bocadillos*
Cafe Lo Cubano
César/E*
Esperpento*
Iberia/S*
Iluna Basque*
Picaro*
Pilar/N
Piperade
Ramblas*
Sabor of Spain/N*
Zarzuela*
Zuzu/N*

Steakhouses
Acme Chophouse
Alexander's Steak/S
Alfred's Steak
Anzu
A.P. Stump's/S
Boca/N
C & L Steak
Cole's Chop House/N
El Raigon
Espetus Churrascaria
Harris'
House of Prime Rib
Izzy's Steak
Izzy's Steak/N/S
Kurt's Carmel Chop House/S
Morton's Steak
Père Jeanty/N
Press/N
Ruth's Chris Steak
Vic Stewart's/E

Swiss
Emile's/S
Matterhorn Swiss

Taiwanese
Taiwan
Taiwan/E

Tearooms
Lovejoy's Tea Rm.

Thai
Bambuddha
Basil Thai
Cha Am Thai
Cha Am Thai/E
Citizen Thai
Khan Toke
King of Thai
Koh Samui
Manora's Thai
Marnee Thai
Osha Thai Noodles
Plearn Thai/E
Royal Thai/N
Soi Four/E
Thai House
Thep Phanom Thai

Turkish
A La Turca

Vegetarian
(* vegan)
Fleur de Lys
French Laundry/N
Geranium*
Greens
Herbivore*
Millennium*
Udupi Palace/E/S

Vietnamese
Ana Mandara
Bambuddha
Bodega Bistro
Crustacean
Le Cheval/Le Petit Cheval/E
Le Colonial
Le Soleil
Pho 84/E
Pho Hoa-Hiep II
Pho Hoa-Hiep II/E/S
Slanted Door
Tamarine/S
Tao Cafe
Thanh Long
Three Seasons
Three Seasons/E/S
Tu Lan

LOCATIONS

CITY OF SAN FRANCISCO

Bernal Heights
Angkor Borei
Blue Plate
Chez Maman
Emmy's Spaghetti
Geranium
Liberty Cafe
Little Nepal
Moki's Sushi
Taqueria Can-Cun
Zante

Castro
Asqew Grill
Catch
Chow/Park Chow
Cote Sud
Destino
Home
La Méditerranée
Lime
Los Flamingos
Pasta Pomodoro
SUMI
Tallula
Thai House
Tita's hale 'aina
2223

Chinatown
Brandy Ho's
Great Eastern
House of Nanking
Hunan Home's
Jai Yun
R & G Lounge
Yuet Lee

Cow Hollow
Amici E. Coast Pizza
Balboa Cafe
Betelnut Pejiu Wu
Brazen Head
Pane e Vino
Pasta Pomodoro
PlumpJack Cafe
U Street Lounge
YaYa

Downtown
Alfred's Steak
Anjou
Anzu
Aqua
Asia de Cuba
B44
Biscuits and Blues
BIX
Blupointe
Bocadillos
Brindisi Cucina
Cafe Bastille
Café Claude
Café Tiramisu
Campton Place
Canteen
Carnelian Room
Cheesecake Factory
Citizen Cake
Colibrí Mexican Bistro
Cortez
E&O Trading Co.
Emporio Rulli
Farallon
Frisson
Garden Court
Globe
Grand Cafe
Henry's Hunan
Jeanty at Jack's
King of Thai
Kokkari Estiatorio
Kuleto's
Kyo-Ya
La Scene Café
Le Central Bistro
Le Colonial
MacArthur Park
Masa's
Max's
Michael Mina
Millennium
Morton's Steak
Myth
Pacific
Palio D'Asti
Park Grill
Piperade
Plouf
Ponzu
Postrio

Rotunda
Rubicon
Sam's Grill
Sanraku
Scala's Bistro
Sears Fine Food
Seasons
Silks
Tadich Grill
Taqueria Can-Cun
Tommy Toy's
Trader Vic's
Yank Sing

Embarcadero

Americano
Boulette's Larder
Boulevard
butterfly embarcadero
Chaya Brasserie
Fog City Diner
Gaylord India
Harbor Village
Hog Island Oyster
Il Fornaio
La Suite
MarketBar
Mijita
Monte Cristo Cafe
North Beach Pizza
One Market
Ozumo
Red's Java House
Shanghai 1930
Slanted Door
Taylor's Automatic
Town's End
Waterfront

Excelsior

Joe's Cable Car
North Beach Pizza

Fisherman's Wharf

Alioto's
Ana Mandara
A. Sabella's
Bistro Boudin
Coco 500
Gary Danko
Grandeho Kamekyo
Hard Rock Cafe
Mandarin
McCormick & Kuleto
Scoma's

Glen Park

Chenery Park

Haight-Ashbury/ Cole Valley

Asqew Grill
Boulange Cole/Polk
Cha Cha Cha
Citrus Club
El Balazo
Eos Rest./Wine Bar
Grandeho Kamekyo
Kan Zaman
Massawa
North Beach Pizza
Pork Store Café
Zazie

Hayes Valley/Civic Center

Absinthe
Bistro Clovis
Caffe Delle Stelle
Citizen Cake
Espetus Churrascaria
Frjtz Fries
Hayes St. Grill
Indigo
Jardinière
Max's
Mel's Drive-In
paul k
Sauce
Suppenküche
Zuni Café

Inner Richmond

Angkor Wat
Bella Trattoria
Brother's Korean
Burma Super Star
Chapeau!
Clémentine
Giorgio's Pizzeria
Katia's Tea Rm.
King of Thai
Le Soleil
Mandalay
Mel's Drive-In
Q
RoHan Lounge
Straits Cafe
Taiwan

Inner Sunset

Chou Chou
Chow/Park Chow

Ebisu
Hotei
Koo
Marnee Thai
Naan 'n Curry
PJ's Oyster Bed
Pomelo
Yumma's

Japantown
CAFÉ KATi
Juban
Maki
Mifune
Pasta Pomodoro
Shabu-Sen
Takara
Winterland

Lower Haight
Axum Cafe
Burger Joint
Indian Oven
Kate's Kitchen
Memphis Minnie's
rnm
Rosamunde Grill
Rotee
Thep Phanom Thai

Marina
Ace Wasabi's
Alegrias
A 16
Asqew Grill
Baker St. Bistro
Barney's
Bistro Aix
Cozmo's Corner
Desiree Café
Dragon Well
E'Angelo
Emporio Rulli
Greens
Home
Isa
Izzy's Steak
Lüx
Mel's Drive-In
Nectar Wine
Pacific Catch
Parma
Three Seasons
Zushi Puzzle

Mission District
Andalu
Blowfish Sushi
Burger Joint
Cha Cha Cha
Charanga
Chez Spencer
Circolo
Delfina
El Metate
Esperpento
Firecracker
Foreign Cinema
Goood Frikin' Chicken
Herbivore
Jay's Cheesesteak
La Cumbre Taqueria
Last Supper Club
La Taqueria
Levende
Limón
Luna Park
Maverick
Medjool
Osha Thai Noodles
Pakwan
Pancho Villa
Pauline's Pizza
Picaro
Pizzeria Delfina
Platanos
Pork Store Café
Puerto Alegre
Ramblas
Slow Club
Tao Cafe
Taqueria Can-Cun
Tartine Bakery
Ti Couz
Tokyo Go Go
Truly Mediterranean
Universal Cafe
Walzwerk
Watercress
Woodward's Garden

Nob Hill
Acquerello
Big 4
C & L Steak
Crustacean
Fleur de Lys
Fournou's Ovens
Nob Hill Café

Ritz-Carlton Din. Rm.
Ritz-Carlton Terrace
Rue Lepic
Rue Saint Jacques
Ruth's Chris Steak
Shalimar
Swan Oyster Depot
Tonga Room
Venticello
Watergate

Noe Valley
Alice's
Barney's
Chloe's Cafe
Deep Sushi
Eric's
Firefly
Fresca
Hamano Sushi
Incanto
Le Zinc
Lovejoy's Tea Rm.
Miss Millie's
Pasta Pomodoro
Pomelo
Rist. Bacco
Savor

North Beach
Albona Rist.
Blanca Cafe
Cafe Divine
Cafe Jacqueline
Caffe Macaroni
Citizen Thai
El Raigon
Enrico's Sidewalk
Giordano Bros.
Gira Polli
Helmand, The
House
Iluna Basque
Impala
Julius' Castle
L'Osteria del Forno
Mama's Wash. Sq.
Mangarosa
Mario's Bohemian
Maykadeh
Moose's
Mo's
Naan 'n Curry
North Beach Pizza

North Bch. Rest.
Pasta Pomodoro
Rist. Ideale
Rose Pistola
Tommaso's
Tratt. Contadina
Washington Sq. B & G

Outer Richmond
Aziza
Cliff House Bistro
Kabuto
Khan Toke
King of Thai
Mayflower
Mescolanza
Pacific Café
Pizzetta 211
Sutro's at Cliff Hse.
Ton Kiang

Outer Sunset
Beach Chalet
King of Thai
Marnee Thai
Park Chalet
Pasta Pomodoro
Pho Hoa-Hiep II
So
Thanh Long

Pacific Heights
Chez Nous
Eliza's
Florio
Galette
Godzila Sushi
Quince
Rose's Cafe
Vivande Porta Via

Potrero Hill
Aperto
Baraka
Chez Maman
Chez Papa Bistrot
Eliza's
Goat Hill Pizza

Presidio Heights
Cafe Lo Cubano
Ella's
Garibaldis
Rigolo

Sociale
Sydney's

Russian Hill
Antica Trattoria
Boulange Cole/Polk
1550 Hyde Café
Frascati
Habana
Harris'
House of Prime Rib
Hyde St. Bistro
La Folie
Le Petit Robert
Luella
Matterhorn Swiss
Nick's Crispy Tacos
Pesce
Rist. Milano
Street
Sushi Groove
Tablespoon
Yabbies Coastal
Zarzuela

SBC Park/South Beach
Acme Chophouse
Amici E. Coast Pizza
Delancey St.
Kingfish
MoMo's

SoMa
AsiaSF
Azie
bacar
Basil Thai
Buca di Beppo
Butler & Chef Cafe
Caffe Centro
Caffè Museo
Cha Am Thai
Cosmopolitan
Fifth Floor
Fringale
Goat Hill Pizza
Hawthorne Lane
Henry's Hunan
Jack Falstaff
Koh Samui
Le Charm Bistro
Manora's Thai
Maya
Mel's Drive-In

Mochica
Mo's
Oola
Pazzia
Public
Rest. LuLu
Rist. Umbria
Roy's
Sanraku
South Park Cafe
Sushi Groove
Tamal
Town Hall
Tu Lan
XYZ
Zuppa

Tenderloin
A La Turca
Bambuddha
Bodega Bistro
Dottie's True Blue
Mela Tandoori
Naan 'n Curry
Original Joe's
Osha Thai Noodles
Pakwan
Saigon Sandwiches
Shalimar
Thai House

Twin Peaks/West Portal
Fresca

Upper Fillmore
Elite Cafe
Fresca
Jackson Fillmore
La Méditerranée
Powell's Place
Ten-Ichi
Zao Noodle

Upper Market/ Church Street
Mecca

Western Addition
Alamo Square
Blue Jay Cafe
Brother-in-Law BBQ
Herbivore
Jay's Cheesesteak
Tsunami Sushi

EAST OF SAN FRANCISCO

Albany
Albany Bistro
Caspers Hot Dogs
Fonda Solana
Nizza La Bella

Berkeley
Adagia
Ajanta
Barney's
Bendean
Bette's Oceanview
Bistro Liaison
Blue Nile
Breads of India
Cactus Taqueria
Cafe Cacao
Café Fanny
Café Rouge
César
Cha Am Thai
Chez Panisse
Chez Panisse Café
downtown
Eccolo
FatApple's
Great China
Gregoire
Jimmy Bean's
Jordan's
Juan's Place
Kirala
Lalime's
La Méditerranée
La Note/Café Clem
La Rose Bistro
Le Petit Cheval
Lo Coco's
Naan 'n Curry
North Beach Pizza
O Chamé
Olivia
Phoenix Next Door
Picante Cocina
Pizzaiolo
Plearn Thai
Rick & Ann's
Rivoli
Saul's Rest./Deli
Sea Salt
Shen Hua
Tacubaya

Taiwan
Tratt. La Siciliana
Udupi Palace
Venezia
Venus
Vik's Chaat Corner
Zachary's Pizza
Zatar
Zax Tavern

Danville
Blackhawk Grille
Bridges
Louka
Piatti

Dublin
Caspers Hot Dogs

El Cerrito
FatApple's

Emeryville
Asqew Grill
Bucci's
Pasta Pomodoro
Townhouse B&G
Trader Vic's
Zao Noodle

Fremont
Shalimar

Hayward
Caspers Hot Dogs
Everett & Jones
Pakwan

Lafayette
Bo's Barbecue
Chow/Park Chow
Duck Club
Pizza Antica
Postino

Lake Tahoe/
Olympic Valley
Balboa Cafe
PlumpJack Cafe

Livermore
Udupi Palace
Wente Vineyards

Locations

Oakland
À Côté
Barney's
Battambang
Bay Wolf
Blackberry Bistro
Cactus Taqueria
Caffé Verbena
Citron
Doña Tomás
Dopo
Everett & Jones
Fenton's Creamery
Garibaldis
Grasshopper
Jade Villa
Jojo
Koryo BBQ
Le Cheval
Lo Coco's
Mama's Royal Cafe
Marica
Max's
Mezze
Nan Yang
Oliveto
Pasta Pomodoro
Pearl Oyster Bar
Pho 84
Pho Hoa-Hiep II
Pizza Rustica
Rest. Peony
Scott's

Soi Four
Soizic
Uzen
Yoshi's
Zachary's Pizza

Orinda
Casa Orinda

Pleasant Hill
Caspers Hot Dogs
Left Bank

Richmond
Caspers Hot Dogs

San Ramon
Cafe Esin

Walnut Creek
Bing Crosby's
Breads of India
Caspers Hot Dogs
Il Fornaio
Lark Creek
Prima
Scott's
Three Seasons
Va de Vi
Vic Stewart's

Yosemite-Oakhurst
Ahwahnee Din. Rm.
Erna's Elderberry Hse.

NORTH OF SAN FRANCISCO

Bodega/Bodega Bay
Duck Club
Seaweed Café

Calistoga
All Season's Cafe
Brannan's Grill
Fuentes Tapas
Stomp
Wappo Bar

Corte Madera
Il Fornaio
Izzy's Steak
Max's

Forestville
Farmhouse Inn

Geyserville
Alexander Valley
Santi

Glen Ellen/Kenwood
Cafe Citti
fig cafe & winebar
Kenwood

Guerneville
Applewood Inn

Healdsburg/Windsor
Barndiva
Bistro Ralph
Charcuterie
Cyrus
Downtown Bakery

Locations

Dry Creek Kitchen
Jimtown Store
Madrona Manor
Manzanita
Mirepoix
Ravenous Cafe
Willi's Seafood
Zin

Larkspur
Emporio Rulli
Lark Creek Inn
Left Bank
Picco
Pizzeria Picco
Rist. Fabrizio
Yankee Pier

Mendocino County
Albion River Inn
Boonville Hotel
Cafe Beaujolais
Chapter & Moon
Ledford House
Little River Inn
MacCallum House
Mendo Bistro
Moosse Cafe
955 Ukiah
Pangaea
Rendezvous Inn
Rest. at Stevenswood
Sea Ranch Lodge
Sharon's By Sea
St. Orres
Victorian Gardens

Mill Valley
Buckeye Roadhouse
Bungalow 44
Dipsea Cafe
El Paseo
Frantoio
Gira Polli
Joe's Taco Lounge
La Ginestra
Mi Casa
Piatti
Piazza D'Angelo
Robata Grill

Napa
Alexis Baking Co.
Angèle
Bistro Don Giovanni

Celadon
Cole's Chop House
Foothill Cafe
Fumé Bistro
General Café
Julia's Kitchen
Mustards Grill
Napa Wine Train
Pearl
Pilar
Pizza Azzurro
Rest. Budo
Uva Trattoria
Zaré
Zinsvalley
Zuzu

Novato
Boca
Kitchen at 868 Grant

Petaluma
Cucina Paradiso
Water St. Bistro

Ross
Marché aux Fleurs

Rutherford
Auberge du Soleil
La Toque
Rutherford Grill

San Anselmo
Cucina Rest./Wine Bar
Fork
Insalata's

San Rafael
Amici E. Coast Pizza
Barney's
Dipsea Cafe
Il Davide
Las Camelias
Lotus of India
Maria Manso's
Royal Thai
Sabor of Spain

Santa Rosa/Rohnert Park
Flavor
Gary Chu's
Hana Japanese
John Ash & Co.
Monti's Rotisserie
Osake
Syrah

Willi's Wine Bar
zazu

Sausalito
Christophe
Cork
Fish
Poggio
Rustico
Scoma's
Sushi Ran

Sebastopol/Graton
Bistro V
K&L Bistro
Lucy's
Underwood Bar
Willow Wood Mkt.

Sonoma
Cafe La Haye
Carneros
Della Santina's
Deuce
El Dorado Kitchen
girl & the fig
Harmony Club
LaSalette
Santé
Sonoma Meritage

St. Helena
Cindy's Backstreet
Cook St. Helena

Market
Martini House
Meadowood Grill
Model Bakery
Pinot Blanc
Pizzeria Tra Vigne
Press
Taylor's Automatic
Terra
Tra Vigne
Wine Spectator

Tiburon
Caprice
Guaymas

West Marin/Olema
Manka's Inverness
Olema Inn

Yountville
Bistro Jeanty
Bouchon
Brix
Domaine Chandon
French Laundry
Gordon's
Hurley's
Napa Valley Grille
Père Jeanty
Wine Garden Food

SOUTH OF SAN FRANCISCO

Big Sur
Nepenthe
Sierra Mar

Burlingame
Ecco
Il Fornaio
Juban
Kuleto's
Max's
Pisces
Straits Cafe

Campbell
Buca di Beppo

Carmel/Monterey Peninsula
Adrian's
Anton & Michel

Bouchée
Casanova
Club XIX
Duck Club
Fandango
Flying Fish Grill
Fresh Cream
Grasing's Coastal
Il Fornaio
Kurt's Carmel Chop House
L'Auberge Carmel
Marinus
Montrio Bistro
Pacific's Edge
Passionfish
Piatti
Rio Grill
Robert's Whitehouse

Locations

Roy's Pebble Beach
Sardine Factory
Stokes
Tarpy's Roadhouse
Taste Cafe

Cupertino
Alexander's Steak

Half Moon Bay/Coast
Barbara Fishtrap
Cafe Gibraltar
Cetrella Bistro
Duarte's Tavern
Mezza Luna
Navio
Pasta Moon

Los Altos
Chef Chu's
Hunan Home's

Los Gatos
Café Marcella
Manresa

Menlo Park
Bistro Vida
Duck Club
Flea St. Café
Gaylord India
Iberia
Juban
jZcool
Kaygetsu
Left Bank
Marché
Oak City B&G

Millbrae
Fook Yuen Seafood
Hong Kong Flower

Mountain View
Amber India
Amici E. Coast Pizza
Cascal
Chez TJ
Passage to India
Zucca

Palo Alto
Bistro Elan
Buca di Beppo
Cool Café
Evvia

Fuki Sushi
Il Fornaio
La Strada
Lavanda
MacArthur Park
Maddalena's
Marigold Indian
Max's
Osteria
Scott's
Spago Palo Alto
St. Michael's
Straits Cafe
Tamarine
Three Seasons
Trader Vic's
Zao Noodle
Zibibbo

Redwood City
A Tavola
Chantilly
John Bentley's
Max's

Redwood Shores
Amici E. Coast Pizza
Mistral

San Carlos
Izzy's Steak

San Jose
Amber India
A.P. Stump's
Arcadia
Blowfish Sushi
Buca di Beppo
Cheesecake Factory
E&O Trading Co.
Emile's
Eulipia
Il Fornaio
La Forêt
La Taqueria
Left Bank
Le Papillon
Original Joe's
Pasta Pomodoro
Pizza Antica
Scott's
Seven
71 Saint Peter
Straits Cafe
Yankee Pier

Locations

San Mateo
Amici E. Coast Pizza
Central Park Bistro
Happy Cafe
Kingfish
La Cumbre Taqueria
Left Bank
North Beach Pizza
Pancho Villa
Rist. Capellini
231 Ellsworth
Viognier

Santa Clara
Brigitte's
Parcel 104
Piatti

Santa Cruz/
Aptos/Capitola
Gabriella Café
Gayle's Bakery
O'mei
Oswald's
Pearl Alley Bistro
Shadowbrook

Saratoga
Basin
Plumed Horse
Sent Sovi

South San Francisco/
Daly City
Basque Cultural Ctr.
Burger Joint
Koi Palace
Pho Hoa-Hiep II
Yankee Pier

Sunnyvale
Dish Dash
Lion & Compass
Turmerik
Udupi Palace

Woodside
Bella Vista
John Bentley's
Village Pub

SPECIAL FEATURES

(Indexes list the best in each category. Multi-location restaurants' features may vary by branch.)

Breakfast
(See also Hotel Dining)
Adagia/E
Adrian's/S
Alexis Baking Co./N
Bette's Oceanview/E
Blackberry Bistro/E
Boulange Cole/Polk
Boulette's Larder
Bucci's/E
Butler & Chef Cafe
Cafe Cacao/E
Café Fanny/E
Cafe Lo Cubano
Caffe Centro
Chloe's Cafe
Chou Chou
Desiree Café
Dipsea Cafe/N
Dottie's True Blue
Downtown Bakery/N
Ella's
Emporio Rulli
FatApple's/E
Galette
Gayle's Bakery/S
General Café/N
Gordon's/N
Il Fornaio
Il Fornaio/N/S
Jimmy Bean's/E
Jimtown Store/N
Kate's Kitchen
Koi Palace/S
La Note/Café Clem/E
Mama's Wash. Sq.
Mama's Royal Cafe/E
Mel's Drive-In
Model Bakery/N
Mo's
Oliveto/E
Poggio/N
Pork Store Café
Red's Java House
Rick & Ann's/E
Rigolo
Rose's Cafe
Savor

Sears Fine Food
Tartine Bakery
Town's End
Venus/E
Water St. Bistro/N
Willow Wood Mkt./N
Zazie

Brunch
Absinthe
Adagia/E
Ahwahnee Din. Rm./E
Albany Bistro/E
Alexander's Steak/S
Alexander Valley/N
Alexis Baking Co./N
Americano
Anzu
Baker St. Bistro
Balboa Cafe
Beach Chalet
Bistro Liaison/E
Bistro V/N
Bistro Vida/S
Blackberry Bistro/E
Blackhawk Grille/E
Blue Jay Cafe
Brix/N
Buckeye Roadhouse/N
Cafe Cacao/E
Campton Place
Canteen
Carnelian Room
Catch
Cetrella Bistro/S
Chez Maman
Chloe's Cafe
Chow/Park Chow
Chow/Park Chow/E
Citizen Cake
Cozmo's Corner
Delancey St.
Desiree Café
Dipsea Cafe/N
Dottie's True Blue
Duck Club/E/S
Elite Cafe
Ella's

Erna's Elderberry Hse./E
Fandango/S
fig cafe & winebar/N
Flea St. Café/S
Foreign Cinema
Fresca
Gabriella Café/S
Garden Court
Garibaldis/E
Gayle's Bakery/S
Geranium
girl & the fig/N
Gordon's/N
Grand Cafe
Greens
Harbor Village
Home
Il Davide/N
Insalata's /N
John Ash & Co./N
Jordan's/E
Kate's Kitchen
La Forêt/S
La Note/Café Clem/E
Lark Creek/E
Lark Creek Inn/N
Last Supper Club
Le Petit Robert
Levende
Le Zinc
Liberty Cafe
Luna Park
Mama's Royal Cafe/E
Mayflower
Memphis Minnie's
Mezze/E
Miss Millie's
MoMo's
Moose's
Navio/S
Nob Hill Café
Park Chalet
Pesce
Piazza D'Angelo/N
Picante Cocina/E
PJ's Oyster Bed
Q
Rest. LuLu
Rick & Ann's/E
Rio Grill/S
Ritz-Carlton Terrace
Rose's Cafe
Santi/N
Savor

Scott's/E
Seasons
Seaweed Café/N
Shadowbrook/S
Sharon's By Sea/N
Slow Club
St. Michael's/S
Sydney's
Taiwan/E
Tarpy's Roadhouse/S
Tita's hale 'aina
Ton Kiang
Town's End
Trader Vic's/E
2223
Universal Cafe
Venus/E
Viognier/S
Washington Sq. B & G
Wente Vineyards/E
Willow Wood Mkt./N
Yank Sing
Zazie
Zibibbo/S
Zucca/S
Zuni Café

Business Dining

Acme Chophouse
Alexander's Steak/S
Alfred's Steak
Amber India/S
Americano
Anzu
A.P. Stump's/S
Aqua
Azie
bacar
Basin/S
Big 4
Bing Crosby's/E
Bistro V/N
Boca/N
Boulevard
Caffé Verbena/E
Campton Place
C & L Steak
Carnelian Room
Cha Am Thai
Chantilly/S
Chaya Brasserie
Chef Chu's/S
Coco 500
Cole's Chop House/N

Special Features

Colibrí Mexican Bistro
Cool Café/S
Cosmopolitan
Duck Club/S
E&O Trading Co./S
Emile's/S
Evvia/S
Farallon
Flea St. Café/S
Fournou's Ovens
Fresh Cream/S
Fuki Sushi/S
Gaylord India
Gaylord India/S
Grand Cafe
Harris'
Hawthorne Lane
House of Prime Rib
Iberia/S
Il Fornaio
Il Fornaio/E/N/S
Izzy's Steak
Jack Falstaff
Jeanty at Jack's
Kaygetsu/S
Kokkari Estiatorio
Kuleto's
Kuleto's/S
Kyo-Ya
La Forêt/S
La Suite
Lavanda/S
Le Central Bistro
Le Papillon/S
Lion & Compass/S
MacArthur Park/S
Mandarin
Marinus/S
MarketBar
Masa's
Max's/E
Meadowood Grill/N
Mijita
Mistral/S
MoMo's
Monte Cristo Cafe
Moose's
Morton's Steak
Myth
Oak City B&G/S
One Market
Osteria/S
Ozumo
Pacific

Palio D'Asti
Park Grill
Pazzia
Picco/N
Piperade
Poggio/N
Ponzu
Postrio
Press/N
Rest. LuLu
Rist. Umbria
Ritz-Carlton Din. Rm.
Roy's
Rubicon
Ruth's Chris Steak
Sam's Grill
Sanraku
Seasons
71 Saint Peter/S
Shanghai 1930
Silks
South Park Cafe
Spago Palo Alto/S
St. Michael's/S
Tadich Grill
Tommy Toy's
Townhouse B&G/E
231 Ellsworth/S
Viognier/S
Waterfront
Yank Sing
Zibibbo/S
Zuni Café
Zuppa

Catering

Absinthe
Acquerello
Adagia/E
Adrian's/S
Alexis Baking Co./N
All Season's Cafe/N
Americano
Aqua
AsiaSF
Asqew Grill
Asqew Grill/E
Azie
Bambuddha
Barndiva/N
Bendean/E
Betelnut Pejiu Wu
B44
Bistro Liaison/E

Bistro V/N
BIX
Blackhawk Grille/E
Blowfish Sushi
Blowfish Sushi/S
Bocadillos
Boonville Hotel/N
Bouchée/S
Buckeye Roadhouse/N
Cafe Cacao/E
Cafe Esin/E
CAFÉ KATi
Caffé Verbena/E
Central Park Bistro/S
César/E
Cetrella Bistro/S
Cha Cha Cha
Charanga
Chaya Brasserie
Chef Chu's/S
Chenery Park
Chez Nous
Chez Papa Bistrot
Chez Spencer
Citron/E
Coco 500
Colibrí Mexican Bistro
Cool Café/S
Cucina Paradiso/N
Della Santina's/N
Desiree Café
Destino
downtown/E
Ebisu
Emile's/S
Emporio Rulli
Emporio Rulli/N
Eos Rest./Wine Bar
Evvia/S
Farallon
fig cafe & winebar/N
Florio
Frascati
Fresca
Fringale
Gabriella Café/S
Gayle's Bakery/S
General Café/N
Globe
Grasing's Coastal/S
Greens
Hana Japanese/N
Harbor Village
Iberia/S

Il Davide/N
Il Fornaio/S
Insalata's /N
Jack Falstaff
Jimtown Store/N
Julia's Kitchen/N
jZcool/S
Kingfish
Kingfish/S
Kokkari Estiatorio
La Méditerranée
La Méditerranée/E
La Strada/S
Lavanda/S
Left Bank/E/N/S
Manresa/S
Manzanita/N
Marché/S
Marinus/S
Max's
Memphis Minnie's
Mendo Bistro/N
Mi Casa/N
Millennium
Mochica
Moki's Sushi
Monti's Rotisserie/N
Nick's Crispy Tacos
Ozumo
Pangaea/N
Pearl/N
Père Jeanty/N
Pesce
Piatti/E/N/S
Piazza D'Angelo/N
Picante Cocina/E
Pilar/N
Pizza Antica/E
Pizza Rustica/E
PJ's Oyster Bed
Platanos
Pomelo
Q
Rest. LuLu
Rick & Ann's/E
Rose Pistola
Rose's Cafe
Roy's
Sabor of Spain/N
Santi/N
Saul's Rest./Deli/E
Seaweed Café/N
Shalimar
Shalimar/E

Slanted Door
Sociale
Spago Palo Alto/S
St. Michael's/S
Stokes/S
Straits Cafe
Straits Cafe/S
Sydney's
Tacubaya/E
Tallula
Town Hall
Town's End
Tratt. La Siciliana/E
Tra Vigne/N
Truly Mediterranean
2223
Victorian Gardens/N
Vik's Chaat Corner/E
Village Pub/S
Vivande Porta Via
Wappo Bar/N
Washington Sq. B & G
Wente Vineyards/E
Willi's Seafood/N
Willi's Wine Bar/N
Willow Wood Mkt./N
Winterland
Woodward's Garden
Yabbies Coastal
Yank Sing
YaYa
Yumma's
Zao Noodle
Zao Noodle/E/S
Zatar/E
zazu/N
Zibibbo/S
Zin/N
Zuppa

Celebrity Chefs

Acme Chophouse, *Traci Des Jardins*
Aqua, *Laurent Manrique*
Arcadia/S, *Michael Mina*
bacar, *Arnold Eric Wong*
Bistro Jeanty/N, *Philippe Jeanty*
Boca/N, *George Morrone*
Bocadillos, *Gerald Hirigoyen*
Bouchée/S, *Walter Manzke*
Bouchon/N, *Thomas Keller*
Boulevard, *Nancy Oakes*
Campton Place, *Daniel Humm*

C & L Steak, *Laurent Manrique*
Chef Chu's/S, *Lawrence Chu*
Chez Panisse/E, *Alice Waters*
Cindy's Backstreet/N, *Cindy Pawlcyn*
Citizen Cake, *Elizabeth Falkner*
Coco 500, *Loretta Keller*
Cool Café/S, *Jesse Cool*
Cyrus/N, *Douglas Keane*
Delfina, *Craig Stoll*
Dry Creek Kitchen/N, *Charles Palmer*
Eos Rest., *Arnold Eric Wong*
Farallon, *Mark Franz*
Fifth Floor, *Melissa Perello*
Flea St. Café/S, *Jesse Cool*
Fleur de Lys, *Hubert Keller*
French Laundry/N, *Thomas Keller*
Gary Danko, *Gary Danko*
Jack Falstaff, *James Ormsby*
Jardinière, *Traci Des Jardins*
Jeanty at Jack's, *Philippe Jeanty*
La Folie, *Roland Passot*
Lark Creek Inn/N, *Bradley Ogden*
La Toque/N, *Ken Frank*
L'Auberge Carmel/S, *Walter Manzke*
Left Bank/E/N/S, *Roland Passot*
Market/N, *Douglas Keane*
Martini Hse./N, *Todd Humphries*
Masa's, *Gregory Short*
Michael Mina, *Michael Mina*
Mijita, *Traci Des Jardins*
Mustards Grill/N, *Cindy Pawlcyn*
Oliveto/E, *Paul Bertolli*
Parcel 104/S, *Bradley Ogden*
Père Jeanty/N, *Philippe Jeanty*
Picco/N, *Bruce Hill*
Pilar/N, *Pilar Sanchez*
Pinot Blanc/N, *Joachim Splichal*
Piperade, *Gerald Hirigoyen*
Pizzeria Delfina, *Craig Stoll*
Pizzeria Picco/N, *Bruce Hill*
PlumpJack Cafe, *James Ormsby*
Poggio/N, *Chris Fernandez*
Postrio, *Wolfgang Puck*
Press/N, *Keith Luce*
Rest. Budo/N, *James McDevitt*
Ritz-Carlton Din. Rm., *Ron Siegel*
Roy's, *Roy Yamaguchi*
Roy's Pebble Beach/S, *Roy Yamaguchi*

Rubicon, *Stuart Brioza*
Slanted Door, *Charles Phan*
Spago Palo Alto/S, *Wolfgang Puck*
Terra/N, *Hiro Sone*
Town Hall, *Steven and Mitchell Rosenthal*
Yankee Pier/S, *Bradley Ogden*
Zuni Café, *Judy Rodgers*

Child-Friendly

(Alternatives to the usual fast-food places; * children's menu available)
Acme Chophouse
Adagia/E
Adrian's/S*
Ahwahnee Din. Rm./E*
Alexis Baking Co./N
Alice's
Alioto's*
Amici E. Coast Pizza*
Amici E. Coast Pizza/N/S*
Aperto*
Arcadia/S*
A. Sabella's*
Asqew Grill*
Asqew Grill/E*
Barbara Fishtrap/S*
Barney's*
Barney's/E/N*
Basque Cultural Ctr./S*
Beach Chalet*
Bella Trattoria
Bendean/E
Bette's Oceanview/E
Bistro Boudin
Boulange Cole/Polk
Brandy Ho's
Brannan's Grill/N
Brigitte's/S
Buca di Beppo*
Buca di Beppo/S
Bucci's/E
Buckeye Roadhouse/N*
Bungalow 44/N*
Burger Joint
Burma Super Star
Cactus Taqueria/E*
Cafe Cacao/E
Cafe Citti/N
Cafe Lo Cubano
Caffe Delle Stelle
Caffe Macaroni

Caffè Museo
Casa Orinda/E
Caspers Hot Dogs/E
Cetrella Bistro/S*
Cha Am Thai
Cha Am Thai/E
Cheesecake Factory
Cheesecake Factory/S
Chenery Park*
Chez Spencer
Chow/Park Chow*
Chow/Park Chow/E*
Cindy's Backstreet/N
Citrus Club
Cliff House Bistro
Cook St. Helena/N
Cool Café/S
Delancey St.
Dipsea Cafe/N*
Dottie's True Blue
Downtown Bakery/N
Duarte's Tavern/S*
El Balazo*
Eliza's
Ella's
Emmy's Spaghetti
Emporio Rulli
Emporio Rulli/N
Enrico's Sidewalk
Eric's
Everett & Jones/E
FatApple's/E*
Fenton's Creamery/E*
Fish/N
Fog City Diner*
Fook Yuen Seafood/S
Foothill Cafe/N
Gayle's Bakery/S*
General Café/N
Geranium*
Giordano Bros.
Giorgio's Pizzeria
Gira Polli
Gira Polli/N
Goat Hill Pizza
Goood Frikin' Chicken
Great China/E
Great Eastern
Guaymas/N
Harbor Village
Hard Rock Cafe*
Henry's Hunan
Home
Hong Kong Flower/S

Hunan Home's
Hunan Home's/S
Hurley's/N*
Il Fornaio*
Il Fornaio/E/N/S*
Insalata's /N*
Jade Villa/E
Jay's Cheesesteak
Jimmy Bean's/E*
Jimtown Store/N*
Joe's Cable Car
Joe's Taco Lounge/N
Juan's Place/E
Juban
Juban/S
jZcool/S*
King of Thai
Koi Palace/S
Koryo BBQ/E
Kuleto's
Kuleto's/S
La Cumbre Taqueria
La Cumbre Taqueria/S*
La Méditerranée*
La Méditerranée/E
Lark Creek/E*
Left Bank/E/N/S*
Lo Coco's/E*
Lovejoy's Tea Rm.*
Lucy's /N
Mama's Wash. Sq.*
Market/N
Max's*
Max's/E/N/S*
Mel's Drive-In*
Memphis Minnie's
Mi Casa/N*
Mifune
Model Bakery/N
Mo's*
Napa Valley Grille/N*
Nepenthe/S*
Nick's Crispy Tacos
North Beach Pizza
North Beach Pizza/E/S
North Bch. Rest.
O'mei/S
Original Joe's
Original Joe's/S*
Pancho Villa
Pancho Villa/S
Parcel 104/S*
Park Chalet*

Pasta Pomodoro*
Pasta Pomodoro/E/S*
Pauline's Pizza
Piatti/E/N/S*
Picante Cocina/E*
Pizza Antica/E/S*
Pizza Azzurro/N
Pizza Rustica/E
Pizzeria Picco/N
Pizzeria Tra Vigne/N*
Pork Store Café
Powell's Place*
Q
R & G Lounge
Rest. Peony/E
Rick & Ann's/E*
Rigolo*
Robata Grill/N
Saul's Rest./Deli/E*
Savor*
Scoma's*
Scoma's/N*
Sears Fine Food
Sharon's By Sea/N*
Shen Hua/E
Sydney's*
Taiwan
Taiwan/E
Taqueria Can-Cun
Tarpy's Roadhouse/S*
Taylor's Automatic
Taylor's Automatic/N
Tita's hale 'aina
Tommaso's
Ton Kiang
Venezia/E*
Waterfront
Willow Wood Mkt./N
Wine Garden Food/N*
Yankee Pier/N/S*
Yank Sing
Yumma's
Zachary's Pizza/E
Zao Noodle*
Zao Noodle/E/S*

Critic-Proof
(Gets lots of business
despite so-so food)
Beach Chalet
Buca di Beppo
Buca di Beppo/S
Mel's Drive-In
Nepenthe/S

Zao Noodle
Zao Noodle/E/S

Dancing
AsiaSF
Bambuddha
Frisson
Jordan's/E
Kan Zaman
Levende
Maddalena's/S
Monte Cristo Cafe
Plumed Horse/S
Shanghai 1930
Straits Cafe/S
Tonga Room
XYZ

Delivery
Absinthe
Adrian's/S
Ajanta/E
Alexis Baking Co./N
Amici E. Coast Pizza
Amici E. Coast Pizza/N/S
Angkor Borei
Angkor Wat
Asqew Grill
Asqew Grill/E
A Tavola/S
Barney's
Barney's/E/N
Basil Thai
Bendean/E
Blanca Cafe
Brandy Ho's
Buca di Beppo/S
Cha Cha Cha
Cortez
Desiree Café
Dish Dash/S
Emporio Rulli
Fuki Sushi/S
Gary Chu's/N
General Café/N
Giordano Bros.
Gira Polli
Goat Hill Pizza
Henry's Hunan
Insalata's /N
Jimtown Store/N
Joe's Cable Car
Kaygetsu/S
King of Thai

La Méditerranée
La Méditerranée/E
Las Camelias/N
Le Cheval/E
Lotus of India/N
Mandalay
Max's
Max's/E/N
Mela Tandoori
Mescolanza
Mistral/S
Montrio Bistro/S
North Beach Pizza
North Beach Pizza/E/S
Pakwan/E
Pho Hoa-Hiep II/E
Piatti/S
Pizza Antica/S
Pizza Rustica/E
Pork Store Café
Powell's Place
Rio Grill/S
Seven/S
Swan Oyster Depot
Ton Kiang
Tra Vigne/N
Turmerik/S
Vivande Porta Via
Yank Sing
Zante
Zatar/E

Dining Alone
(Other than hotels and places
with counter service)
Absinthe
Ace Wasabi's
Acme Chophouse
Andalu
Asqew Grill
bacar
Barney's/N
Bette's Oceanview/E
Bistro Jeanty/N
Bistro Ralph/N
Blanca Cafe
Blowfish Sushi
Blue Jay Cafe
Bocadillos
Bodega Bistro
Bouchon/N
Boulevard
Buckeye Roadhouse/N
Bungalow 44/N

Burger Joint
Cafe Bastille
Cafe Citti/N
Café Claude
Cafe Lo Cubano
Café Rouge/E
Cascal/S
César/E
Cetrella Bistro/S
Cha Cha Cha
Chez Maman
Chez Papa Bistrot
Chou Chou
Citizen Cake
Coco 500
Cook St. Helena/N
Cork/N
Dish Dash/S
Duarte's Tavern/S
E&O Trading Co./S
Ebisu
Emporio Rulli/N
Enrico's Sidewalk
Eos Rest./Wine Bar
Evvia/S
FatApple's/E
1550 Hyde Café
Firefly
Fog City Diner
Fringale
Frjtz Fries
Fuentes Tapas/N
Galette
General Café/N
Godzila Sushi
Grandeho Kamekyo
Hamano Sushi
Hog Island Oyster
Hurley's/N
Jack Falstaff
Kabuto
Kaygetsu/S
King of Thai
Kirala/E
Koo
La Note/Café Clem/E
Last Supper Club
La Suite
Left Bank/E/S
Le Petit Robert
Le Zinc
Lüx
Mario's Bohemian
MarketBar

Matterhorn Swiss
Maverick
Medjool
Mel's Drive-In
Mustards Grill/N
Myth
Nizza La Bella/E
Pasta Pomodoro
Pasta Pomodoro/E
Pearl Oyster Bar/E
Père Jeanty/N
Pho Hoa-Hiep II
Pho Hoa-Hiep II/E
Piperade
Pizza Antica/E/S
Poggio/N
Powell's Place
rnm
Robata Grill/N
Shabu-Sen
So
Sonoma Meritage/N
Suppenküche
Sushi Ran/N
Swan Oyster Depot
Sydney's
Tablespoon
Taqueria Can-Cun
Thai House
Ti Couz
Tokyo Go Go
Tommaso's
Town Hall
Tra Vigne/N
Tsunami Sushi
Viognier/S
Vivande Porta Via
Willi's Seafood/N
Wine Garden Food/N
Winterland
Yank Sing
Yoshi's/E
Zatar/E
Zazie
Zibibbo/S
Zuni Café
Zushi Puzzle

Entertainment
(Call for days and times of performances)
Ahwahnee Din. Rm./E (piano)
Albion River Inn/N (piano)
Ana Mandara (jazz)

Special Features

Anzu (jazz)
Asia de Cuba (Latin house)
AsiaSF (gender illusionists)
Aziza (belly dancer)
bacar (jazz)
Bambuddha (DJ)
Beach Chalet (jazz)
Big 4 (piano)
Bing Crosby's/E (piano)
Biscuits and Blues (blues)
Bistro Liaison/E (jazz)
BIX (jazz)
Blowfish Sushi/S (DJ)
Blue Jay Cafe (DJ)
Blupointe (DJ)
butterfly embarcadero (DJ/jazz)
Cafe Bastille (jazz)
Café Claude (jazz)
Carneros/N (bands)
Cascal/S (Spanish band)
Catch (piano)
Central Park Bistro/S (jazz)
Cetrella Bistro/S (jazz)
Chaya Brasserie (jazz)
Chez Spencer (piano)
Circolo (DJ)
Cosmopolitan (piano/vocals)
Cozmo's Corner (DJ)
Deep Sushi (DJ)
Destino (varies)
downtown/E (jazz)
Duck Club/S (piano)
E&O Trading Co. (varies)
Emmy's Spaghetti (DJ)
Enrico's Sidewalk (jazz)
Erna's Elderberry Hse./E (jazz)
Everett & Jones/E (varies)
Foreign Cinema (movies)
Frisson (DJ)
Frjtz Fries (DJ)
Galette (jazz)
Garden Court (harp/jazz)
Giordano Bros. (varies)
Hard Rock Cafe (pop/rock)
Harmony Club/N (piano)
Harris' (jazz/piano)
Impala (DJ)
Jardinière (jazz)
Jordan's/E (jazz)
Kan Zaman (belly dancing)
Katia's Tea Rm. (accordion)
La Note/E (accordion)
Ledford House/N (jazz)

Left Bank/N (jazz)
Levende (bands/DJ)
Lime (DJ)
Maddalena's/S (jazz)
Marinus/S (jazz)
Max's (singing waiters)
Max's/S (singing waiters)
Mecca (DJ)
Moose's (jazz)
Napa Wine Train/N (piano)
Navio/S (jazz)
Olema Inn/N (varies)
Pacific (piano)
Park Chalet (varies)
Pearl/N (live music)
Pinot Blanc/N (jazz)
Plumed Horse/S (jazz/piano)
Powell's Place (gospel)
Prima/E (jazz)
Puerto Alegre (mariachi trio)
Ramblas (flamenco guitar)
Ravenous Cafe/N (live music)
Ritz-Carlton Din. Rm. (harp)
RoHan Lounge (DJ)
Rose Pistola (jazz)
Rose's Cafe (guitar)
Santé/N (piano)
Sardine Factory/S (piano)
Scott's/E (jazz/piano)
Seasons (piano)
Shadowbrook/S (jazz)
Shanghai 1930 (jazz)
Slanted Door (DJ)
Stomp/N (live music)
Straits Cafe/S (DJ/jazz)
Sushi Groove (DJ)
Tallula (piano)
Tonga Room (bands)
Townhouse B&G/E (jazz)
Trader Vic's/S (varies)
U Street Lounge (DJ)
Uva Trattoria/N (piano)
Vic Stewart's/E (piano)
Wappo Bar/N (jazz)
Washington Sq. B & G (jazz)
Wine Garden Food/N (piano)
XYZ (DJ)
Yoshi's/E (jazz)
Zaré/N (jazz)
Zuni Café (piano)

Fireplaces
Adagia/E
Albion River Inn/N

Special Features

Alexander Valley/N
Anton & Michel/S
Applewood Inn/N
A. Sabella's
Auberge du Soleil/N
Barney's/E
Bella Vista/S
Betelnut Pejiu Wu
Big 4
Bistro Don Giovanni/N
Bistro Jeanty/N
Boca/N
Boonville Hotel/N
Bouchée/S
Boulange Cole/Polk
Brannan's Grill/N
Cafe Citti/N
Caprice/N
Casanova/S
Casa Orinda/E
Catch
Cetrella Bistro/S
Chantilly/S
Chez TJ/S
Chow/Park Chow
Chow/Park Chow/E
Della Santina's/N
Dipsea Cafe/N
Domaine Chandon/N
Duck Club/E/N/S
El Paseo/N
Erna's Elderberry Hse./E
Evvia/S
Fandango/S
Farmhouse Inn/N
Fleur de Lys
Flying Fish Grill/S
Foreign Cinema
French Laundry/N
Fresh Cream/S
Gaylord India/S
Guaymas/N
Harmony Club/N
Harris'
Home
House of Prime Rib
Hurley's/N
Iberia/S
Il Fornaio/E/N/S
John Ash & Co./N
Kenwood/N
Kokkari Estiatorio
Kuleto's

Lark Creek Inn/N
La Toque/N
Ledford House/N
Left Bank/N
Lion & Compass/S
Lüx
MacArthur Park
MacArthur Park/S
MacCallum House/N
Madrona Manor/N
Manka's Inverness/N
Marinus/S
Martini House/N
Mezza Luna/S
Mi Casa/N
Mistral/S
Moosse Cafe/N
Navio/S
Nepenthe/S
Oliveto/E
Olivia/E
Pacific
Pacific's Edge/S
Parcel 104/S
Piatti/E/N/S
Piazza D'Angelo/N
Pinot Blanc/N
Plouf
Plumed Horse/S
PlumpJack Cafe/E
Postino/E
Press/N
Prima/E
Ravenous Cafe/N
Rendezvous Inn/N
Rest. at Stevenswood/N
Rio Grill/S
Robert's Whitehouse/S
Rutherford Grill/N
Santé/N
Santi/N
Sardine Factory/S
Sea Ranch Lodge/N
Seasons
Seaweed Café/N
Shadowbrook/S
Shanghai 1930
Sharon's By Sea/N
Sierra Mar/S
Spago Palo Alto/S
Stokes/S
St. Orres/N
Tarpy's Roadhouse/S

Townhouse B&G/E
Vic Stewart's/E
Victorian Gardens/N
Village Pub/S
Viognier/S
Wine Spectator/N
Zibibbo/S
Zinsvalley/N

Historic Places

(Year opened; * building)
1800 Cote Sud*
1829 Cindy's Backstreet/N*
1844 Celadon/N*
1848 La Forêt/S*
1849 Tadich Grill
1853 Little River Inn/N*
1860 Pizza Antica/E*
1863 Cliff House Bistro
1864 Jeanty at Jack's*
1864 Pisces/S*
1866 Cole's Chop House/N*
1867 Sam's Grill
1868 General Café/N*
1875 Gordon's/N*
1875 La Note/E*
1876 Olema Inn/N*
1879 Il Fornaio/S*
1880 Deuce/N*
1881 Madrona Manor/N*
1882 MacCallum House/N*
1884 Terra/N*
1886 Willi's Wine Bar/N*
1889 Lark Creek Inn/N*
1889 Pacific Café*
1890 Chez TJ/S*
1890 Scoma's/N*
1893 Cafe Beaujolais/N*
1893 Jimtown Store/N*
1894 Duarte's Tavern/S*
1894 Fenton's Creamery/E
1897 Rendezvous Inn/N*
1900 Cha Cha Cha*
1900 French Laundry/N*
1900 La Ginestra/N*
1900 MacArthur Park*
1915 MacArthur Park/S*
1900 Pauline's Pizza*
1902 Santi/N*
1904 Moosse Cafe/N*
1904 Victorian Gardens/N*
1905 Model Bakery/N*
1905 Postino/E*
1905 Public*

1905 Tamal*
1906 Coco 500*
1906 Pork Store Café*
1907 Town Hall*
1908 Geranium*
1909 Mendo Bistro/N*
1909 Miss Millie's*
1910 Campton Place*
1910 Catch*
1910 Harris'*
1912 Swan Oyster Depot
1913 Balboa Cafe
1913 Zuni Café*
1914 Red's Java House*
1915 Jordan's/E*
1915 Napa Wine Train/N*
1917 Manka's Inverness/N*
1917 Pacific's Edge/S*
1917 Tarpy's Roadhouse/S*
1919 Sauce*
1920 A. Sabella's
1920 Kingfish/S*
1920 Rist. Capellini/S*
1922 Hawthorne Lane*
1922 Julius' Castle*
1923 Martini House/N*
1925 Adagia/E*
1925 Alioto's
1925 John Bentley's/S*
1927 Ahwahnee Din. Rm./E
1927 Townhouse B&G/E*
1928 Alfred's Steak
1929 L'Auberge Carmel/S*
1930 Caprice/N*
1930 Foreign Cinema*
1930 Lalime's/E*
1930 Lo Coco's/E*
1930 Original Joe's*
1932 Casa Orinda/E*
1934 Caspers Hot Dogs/E
1934 Trader Vic's/E
1935 Tommaso's
1937 Buckeye Roadhouse/N
1938 Sears Fine Food
1940 Rue Lepic
1945 Tonga Room
1947 Shadowbrook/S
1949 House of Prime Rib
1949 Nepenthe/S
1949 Taylor's Automatic/N
1950 Axum Cafe*
1951 Trader Vic's
1952 Plumed Horse/S
1955 Breads of India/E*

Special Features

Hotel Dining

Adagio Hotel
  Cortez
Ahwahnee Hotel
  Ahwahnee Din. Rm./E
Auberge du Soleil
  Auberge du Soleil/N
Bernardus Lodge
  Marinus/S
Blue Heron Inn
  Moosse Cafe/N
Blue Rock Inn
  Left Bank/N
Boonville Hotel
  Boonville Hotel/N
Campton Place Hotel
  Campton Place
Claremont Resort & Spa
  Jordan's/E
Clift Hotel
  Asia de Cuba
Commodore Hotel
  Canteen
Dina's Garden Hotel
  Trader Vic's/S
Doubletree Plaza
  Hana Japanese/N
El Dorado Hotel
  El Dorado Kitchen/N
Fairmont Hotel
  Tonga Room
Fairmont Sonoma Mission
  Santé/N
Farmhouse Inn
  Farmhouse Inn/N
Four Seasons Hotel
  Seasons
Garden Court Hotel
  Il Fornaio/S
Highlands Inn
  Pacific's Edge/S
Hill House Inn
  Sharon's By Sea/N
Hotel Griffon
  Tamarine/S
Hotel Healdsburg
  Dry Creek Kitchen/N
Hotel Monaco
  Grand Cafe
Hotel Nikko
  Anzu
Hotel Palomar
  Fifth Floor

Hotel Vintage Ct.
  Masa's
Hotel Vitale
  Americano
Huntington Hotel
  Big 4
Hyatt Sainte Claire
  Il Fornaio/S
Inn at Southbridge
  Pizzeria Tra Vigne/N
Inn at Spanish Bay
  Roy's Pebble Beach/S
Inn at Victorian Gardens
  Victorian Gardens/N
Lafayette Park Hotel & Spa
  Duck Club/E
Ledson Hotel
  Harmony Club/N
Les Mars Hotel
  Cyrus/N
Little River Inn
  Little River Inn/N
Lodge at Pebble Beach
  Club XIX/S
Lodge at Sonoma
  Carneros/N
MacCallum House Inn
  MacCallum House/N
Madrona Manor
  Madrona Manor/N
Mandarin Oriental Hotel
  Silks
Meadowood Resort
  Meadowood Grill/N
Monterey Plaza Hotel & Spa
  Duck Club/S
Mount View Hotel
  Stomp/N
Olema Inn
  Olema Inn/N
Palace Hotel
  Garden Court
  Kyo-Ya
Pan Pacific Hotel
  Pacific
Park Hyatt Hotel
  Park Grill
Phoenix Hotel
  Bambuddha
Pine Inn, The
  Il Fornaio/S
PlumpJack Squaw Valley Inn
  PlumpJack Cafe/E

Post Ranch Inn
  Sierra Mar/S
Prescott Hotel
  Postrio
Rancho Caymus Inn
  La Toque/N
Renaissance Stanford Ct.
  Fournou's Ovens
Ritz-Carlton Hotel
  Navio/S
  Ritz-Carlton Din. Rm.
  Ritz-Carlton Terrace
San Jose Marriott
  Arcadia/S
Santa Clara Marriott
  Parcel 104/S
Savoy Hotel
  Millennium
Sea Ranch Lodge
  Sea Ranch Lodge/N
Serrano Hotel
  Ponzu
Sir Francis Drake Hotel
  Scala's Bistro
Stanford Park Hotel
  Duck Club/S
Stevenswood Lodge
  Rest. at Stevenswood/N
Villa Florence Hotel
  Kuleto's
Vintners Inn
  John Ash & Co./N
Warwick Regis
  La Scene Café
Westin St. Francis
  Michael Mina
W Hotel
  XYZ

Jacket Required

Ahwahnee Din. Rm./E
Fleur de Lys
French Laundry/N
Masa's
Tommy Toy's

Late Dining

(Weekday closing hour)
Absinthe (12 AM)
Blanca Cafe (12 AM)
Bouchon/N (12:30 AM)
Brazen Head (1 AM)
Brother's Korean (varies)
Cafe Lo Cubano (12 AM)

Caspers Hot Dogs/E (varies)
Everett & Jones/E (varies)
Fonda Solana/E (12:30 AM)
Globe (1 AM)
Great Eastern (1 AM)
King of Thai (varies)
Koryo BBQ/E (12 AM)
Lime (varies)
Mel's Drive-In (varies)
Naan 'n Curry (varies)
North Beach Pizza (varies)
North Beach Pizza/E/S (varies)
Oola (1 AM)
Original Joe's/S (varies)
Osha Thai Noodles (varies)
Pancho Villa (varies)
RoHan Lounge (12 AM)
Sauce (12 AM)
Scala's Bistro (12 AM)
Taqueria Can-Cun (varies)
Thai House (varies)
Tsunami Sushi (12 AM)
Zuni Café (12 AM)

Meet for a Drink

Absinthe
Alexander's Steak/S
Americano
Ana Mandara
Andalu
AsiaSF
Azie
bacar
Balboa Cafe
Bambuddha
Barndiva/N
Beach Chalet
Betelnut Pejiu Wu
Big 4
Bing Crosby's/E
Bistro Clovis
Bistro Don Giovanni/N
Bistro V/N
Bistro Vida/S
BIX
Blanca Cafe
Blowfish Sushi
Blupointe
Bouchon/N
Boulevard
Brazen Head
Buckeye Roadhouse/N
Bungalow 44/N
butterfly embarcadero
Cafe Bastille

Special Features

Café Claude
Café Rouge/E
Carnelian Room
Cascal/S
Catch
Celadon/N
César/E
Cetrella Bistro/S
Cha Cha Cha
Chaya Brasserie
Citizen Thai
Cliff House Bistro
Colibrí Mexican Bistro
Cool Café/S
Cork/N
Cortez
Cosmopolitan
Cozmo's Corner
Cyrus/N
Delfina
Doña Tomás/E
E&O Trading Co.
E&O Trading Co./S
Elite Cafe
Enrico's Sidewalk
Eos Rest./Wine Bar
Farallon
1550 Hyde Café
fig cafe & winebar/N
Florio
Fonda Solana/E
Foreign Cinema
Frisson
Garibaldis
Garibaldis/E
Grasshopper/E
Guaymas/N
Harmony Club/N
Home
Hurley's/N
Iberia/S
Incanto
Jack Falstaff
Jardinière
Kan Zaman
Kingfish/S
Kokkari Estiatorio
Last Supper Club
La Suite
Lavanda/S
Le Colonial
Left Bank/N/S
Le Petit Robert
Levende

Le Zinc
Lime
Luna Park
MacArthur Park/S
Maddalena's/S
Manzanita/N
MarketBar
Martini House/N
Maverick
Mecca
Medjool
Michael Mina
MoMo's
Monte Cristo Cafe
Montrio Bistro/S
Moose's
Mustards Grill/N
Myth
Nepenthe/S
Nizza La Bella/E
Oliveto/E
One Market
Ozumo
Palio D'Asti
Pangaea/N
Park Chalet
paul k
Pearl Alley Bistro/S
Père Jeanty/N
Picaro
Picco/N
Plouf
Plumed Horse/S
Ponzu
Public
Puerto Alegre
Ramblas
Rest. LuLu
RoHan Lounge
Rose Pistola
Rose's Cafe
Roy's
Sardine Factory/S
Sea Salt/E
Shanghai 1930
Slow Club
Sonoma Meritage/N
Spago Palo Alto/S
Stomp/N
Suppenküche
Sushi Groove
Tablespoon
Tallula
Tamarine/S

Tokyo Go Go
Tonga Room
Town Hall
Townhouse B&G/E
Trader Vic's/E
Tra Vigne/N
2223
Underwood Bar/N
U Street Lounge
Va de Vi/E
Washington Sq. B & G
Waterfront
Willi's Seafood/N
Wine Garden Food/N
Wine Spectator/N
Winterland
Zax Tavern/E
Zibibbo/S
Zin/N
Zuni Café
Zuppa
Zuzu/N

Noteworthy Newcomers

Americano
Barndiva/N
Bendean/E
Bing Crosby's/E
Boca/N
Bungalow 44/N
C & L Steak
Canteen
Cascal/S
Coco 500
Cyrus/N
Fuentes Tapas/N
Jack Falstaff
Kitchen at 868 Grant/N
La Suite
L'Auberge Carmel/S
Luella
Maria Manso's/N
Maverick
Medjool
Mijita
Myth
Oola
Powell's Place
Rest. Budo/N
Stomp/N
Sutro's at Cliff Hse.
Tamal
Trader Vic's
U Street Lounge
Wine Garden Food/N

Winterland
YaYa

Offbeat

Ace Wasabi's
Albona Rist.
Angkor Wat
AsiaSF
Aziza
Bambuddha
Barndiva/N
Basque Cultural Ctr./S
Blowfish Sushi
Blue Nile/E
Buca di Beppo
Buca di Beppo/S
Buckeye Roadhouse/N
Caffe Macaroni
Casa Orinda/E
Caspers Hot Dogs/E
Cha Cha Cha
Destino
Duarte's Tavern/S
Fish/N
Flying Fish Grill/S
Frjtz Fries
Helmand, The
Jimtown Store/N
Joe's Cable Car
Kan Zaman
Katia's Tea Rm.
Khan Toke
Lovejoy's Tea Rm.
Martini House/N
Matterhorn Swiss
Maykadeh
Millennium
Nick's Crispy Tacos
Puerto Alegre
Red's Java House
RoHan Lounge
St. Orres/N
Straits Cafe
Tonga Room
Trader Vic's/E
Venezia/E
Yoshi's/E
Zante

Outdoor Dining

(G=garden; P=patio;
S=sidewalk; T=terrace;
W=waterside)
Absinthe (S)
À Côté/E (P)

Special Features

Adagia/E (P)
Adrian's/S (P,S)
Alexander Valley/N (P)
Alexis Baking Co./N (S)
Angèle/N (P,W)
Anton & Michel/S (P)
Aperto (S)
Applewood Inn/N (G,T)
A.P. Stump's/S (P)
A Tavola/S (S)
Auberge du Soleil/N (T)
Baker St. Bistro (S)
Bambuddha (W)
Barbara Fishtrap/S (P,S,W)
Barndiva/N (G,P)
Barney's (P)
Barney's/E/N (P)
Basin/S (P)
Bay Wolf/E (T)
Beach Chalet (W)
Betelnut Pejiu Wu (S)
B44 (S)
Bistro Aix (P)
Bistro Boudin (P)
Bistro Don Giovanni/N (P,T)
Bistro Elan/S (P)
Bistro Jeanty/N (P)
Bistro Liaison/E (P)
Bistro Vida/S (S)
Blackhawk Grille/E (P,T,W)
Blue Plate (G,P)
Blupointe (P)
Boca/N (P)
Bo's Barbecue/E (G)
Bouchon/N (P)
Boulange Cole/Polk (S)
Bridges/E (P)
Brindisi Cucina (S)
Brix/N (P)
Bucci's/E (P)
Buckeye Roadhouse/N (P)
Bungalow 44/N (P)
Cactus Taqueria/E (S)
Cafe Bastille (S,T)
Cafe Citti/N (P)
Café Claude (S)
Café Fanny/E (P)
Café Rouge/E (P)
Café Tiramisu (S)
Caffe Centro (S)
Caffè Museo (S)
Casanova/S (P)
Cascal/S (P)
Catch (P,S)

Celadon/N (P)
Central Park Bistro/S (S)
César/E (P)
Cha Am Thai/E (P)
Charanga (P)
Chaya Brasserie (P,S)
Cheesecake Factory (P,T)
Chez Maman (S)
Chez Papa Bistrot (S)
Chez Spencer (G,P)
Chez TJ/S (T)
Chloe's Cafe (S)
Chow/Park Chow (P,S,T)
Chow/Park Chow/E (P)
Cindy's Backstreet/N (P)
Citron/E (P)
Club XIX/S (P,W)
Cole's Chop House/N (T,W)
Cool Café/S (P)
Cork/N (P)
Cote Sud (P)
Cucina Paradiso/N (P,W)
Delancey St. (P,S)
Delfina (P)
Della Santina's/N (G,P)
Deuce/N (G,P)
Dipsea Cafe/N (G)
Domaine Chandon/N (P,T,W)
Doña Tomás/E (G,P)
Dopo/E (S)
Dry Creek Kitchen/N (S)
Duck Club/S (P)
E&O Trading Co./S (S)
Eccolo/E (P)
El Dorado Kitchen/N (S)
El Paseo/N (P)
Emporio Rulli (P)
Emporio Rulli/N (S)
Enrico's Sidewalk (P)
Everett & Jones/E (P,S)
Farmhouse Inn/N (T)
Fenton's Creamery/E (P)
Fish/N (W)
Flavor/N (P)
Flea St. Café/S (P)
Fog City Diner (S)
Fonda Solana/E (S)
Foreign Cinema (G,P)
Frantoio/N (G,P)
Frjtz Fries (P)
Fumé Bistro/N (P)
Gabriella Café/S (P)
Galette (P)
Garibaldis/E (S)

Gayle's Bakery/S (P)
General Café/N (T,W)
girl & the fig/N (P)
Grasing's Coastal/S (P)
Gregoire/E (S)
Guaymas/N (P,T,W)
Harmony Club/N (S)
Hog Island Oyster (P,W)
Home (P)
Hurley's/N (P)
Hyde St. Bistro (S)
Iberia/S (P)
Il Davide/N (P)
Il Fornaio (P)
Il Fornaio/E/N/S (P)
Impala (P)
Incanto (S)
Isa (P)
Jack Falstaff (P)
Jimmy Bean's/E (S)
Jimtown Store/N (P)
John Ash & Co./N (P)
Julia's Kitchen/N (G)
Kenwood/N (G)
Kingfish (S)
La Note/E (P)
Lark Creek/E (P)
Lark Creek Inn/N (P)
LaSalette/N (P)
La Strada/S (T)
La Suite (P)
Le Charm Bistro (P)
Le Colonial (P)
Left Bank/E/N/S (P,S)
Le Zinc (G)
Lion & Compass/S (P)
Louka/E (P)
Lucy's /N (P)
MacCallum House/N (T)
Madrona Manor/N (T)
Marché aux Fleurs/N (P)
Maria Manso's/N (P)
Marinus/S (T)
MarketBar (P)
Martini House/N (G,P)
Meadowood Grill/N (T)
Mezze/E (S)
Mi Casa/N (P)
Miss Millie's (G,P)
Mistral/S (P,W)
MoMo's (T)
Monti's Rotisserie/N (P)
Moosse Cafe/N (T)
Mo's (P)

Napa Valley Grille/N (P)
Nepenthe/S (P,W)
Nizza La Bella/E (S)
O Chamé/E (P)
Olema Inn/N (G)
Oliveto/E (S)
Pangaea/N (T)
Parcel 104/S (P)
Park Chalet (P,T,W)
Pasta Moon/S (P)
Pazzia (P)
Père Jeanty/N (P)
Piatti/E/N/S (P,W)
Piazza D'Angelo/N (P)
Picante Cocina/E (P)
Pinot Blanc/N (P)
Piperade (P)
Pizza Antica/E/S (P)
Pizzeria Tra Vigne/N (P)
Pizzetta 211 (S)
Plouf (S)
PlumpJack Cafe/E (P)
Poggio/N (S)
Postino/E (P)
Press/N (P)
Prima/E (P)
Ravenous Cafe/N (P)
Red's Java House (P,W)
Rendezvous Inn/N (T)
Rest. Budo/N (P)
Rick & Ann's/E (P)
Ritz-Carlton Terrace (T)
Rose Pistola (S)
Rose's Cafe (S)
Roy's Pebble Beach/S (P)
Rutherford Grill/N (P)
Santi/N (P)
Savor (G,P)
Scoma's/N (P,W)
Sea Salt/E (P)
Seaweed Café/N (P,S)
Seven/S (S)
71 Saint Peter/S (P)
Sharon's By Sea/N (P,W)
Sierra Mar/S (T,W)
Slow Club (S)
Sociale (P)
Sonoma Meritage/N (G,P)
South Park Cafe (S)
Spago Palo Alto/S (G,P)
St. Michael's/S (S)
Straits Cafe/S (P)
Sushi Ran/N (P)
Tarpy's Roadhouse/S (P)

Tartine Bakery (S)
Taylor's Automatic (P)
Taylor's Automatic/N (G,P)
Ti Couz (S)
Townhouse B&G/E (P)
Town's End (P)
Trader Vic's/S (T)
Tra Vigne/N (G)
Underwood Bar/N (P)
Universal Cafe (P)
Va de Vi/E (S,T)
Wappo Bar/N (P)
Waterfront (P,W)
Water St. Bistro/N (P)
Wente Vineyards/E (P)
Willi's Seafood/N (P)
Willi's Wine Bar/N (P)
Wine Spectator/N (T)
Yankee Pier/N/S (P)
Yumma's (G)
Zaré/N (P)
Zazie (G)
Zibibbo/S (G,P)
Zinsvalley/N (P)
Zucca/S (S)
Zuni Café (S)

People-Watching

Absinthe
Ace Wasabi's
À Côté/E
Ana Mandara
Asia de Cuba
AsiaSF
Balboa Cafe
Bambuddha
Barndiva/N
Betelnut Pejiu Wu
Bing Crosby's/E
Bistro Don Giovanni/N
Bistro Jeanty/N
BIX
Blowfish Sushi
Bouchon/N
Boulevard
Bungalow 44/N
Cafe Bastille
Café Claude
Caffe Centro
Cascal/S
Catch
César/E
Cha Cha Cha
Chaya Brasserie

Chez Panisse Café/E
Circolo
Cozmo's Corner
downtown/E
Downtown Bakery/N
Enrico's Sidewalk
Evvia/S
Flea St. Café/S
Foreign Cinema
Frisson
Grasshopper/E
Harmony Club/N
Jack Falstaff
Jardinière
Julia's Kitchen/N
Last Supper Club
La Suite
Left Bank/N
Levende
Lime
Mario's Bohemian
MarketBar
Martini House/N
Maverick
Mecca
Medjool
Mijita
Moose's
Mustards Grill/N
Myth
Nectar Wine
Pasta Pomodoro
Père Jeanty/N
Picco/N
Poggio/N
Postrio
Public
Rest. Budo/N
Rest. LuLu
Rose Pistola
Rose's Cafe
Scala's Bistro
Spago Palo Alto/S
Sushi Groove
Tallula
Tamarine/S
Tokyo Go Go
Town Hall
Tra Vigne/N
Tsunami Sushi
2223
U Street Lounge
Village Pub/S
Viognier/S

Winterland
Zibibbo/S
Zuni Café
Zuppa

Power Scenes
Alexander's Steak/S
Ana Mandara
Aqua
Arcadia/S
Asia de Cuba
Auberge du Soleil/N
bacar
Big 4
Blackhawk Grille/E
Bouchon/N
Boulevard
C & L Steak
Chaya Brasserie
Chef Chu's/S
downtown/E
Evvia/S
Fifth Floor
Fleur de Lys
Gary Danko
Hawthorne Lane
Il Fornaio/S
Jack Falstaff
Jardinière
Jeanty at Jack's
Kokkari Estiatorio
Le Central Bistro
Le Colonial
Lion & Compass/S
Martini House/N
Masa's
Michael Mina
Mistral/S
Moose's
Myth
One Market
Ozumo
Parcel 104/S
Park Grill
Pisces/S
Plumed Horse/S
Postrio
Press/N
Rest. Budo/N
Ritz-Carlton Din. Rm.
Rubicon
Sam's Grill
Sanraku
Silks

Spago Palo Alto/S
Tadich Grill
Tommy Toy's
Town Hall
Village Pub/S
Viognier/S
Zuni Café

Pre-Theater Dining
(Call for prices and times)
Central Park Bistro/S
Chapeau!
Clémentine
Grand Cafe
Hyde St. Bistro
Indigo
La Scene Café
Postrio
Rue Saint Jacques
Venus/E

Private Rooms
(Call for capacity)
Absinthe
Acme Chophouse
À Côté/E
Acquerello
Adagia/E
Albany Bistro/E
Alegrias
Alexander's Steak/S
Alfred's Steak
Americano
Ana Mandara
Andalu
Angèle/N
Anton & Michel/S
A.P. Stump's/S
Arcadia/S
Auberge du Soleil/N
Aziza
bacar
Baraka
Barndiva/N
Basin/S
Bay Wolf/E
Bella Vista/S
Betelnut Pejiu Wu
Big 4
Bing Crosby's/E
Bistro Aix
Bistro Liaison/E
Blackhawk Grille/E
Blanca Cafe

Blue Plate
Boca/N
Boonville Hotel/N
Boulevard
Bridges/E
Brix/N
Buca di Beppo/S
Buckeye Roadhouse/N
butterfly embarcadero
CAFÉ KATi
Café Rouge/E
Campton Place
C & L Steak
Caprice/N
Carnelian Room
Carneros/N
Casanova/S
Central Park Bistro/S
Cetrella Bistro/S
Cha Cha Cha
Chantilly/S
Chaya Brasserie
Chef Chu's/S
Chez TJ/S
Cindy's Backstreet/N
Citizen Thai
Citron/E
Cliff House Bistro
Club XIX/S
Cortez
Cosmopolitan
Cucina Rest./Wine Bar/N
Cyrus/N
downtown/E
Dry Creek Kitchen/N
El Paseo/N
Emile's/S
Eos Rest./Wine Bar
Erna's Elderberry Hse./E
Eulipia/S
Fandango/S
Farallon
Farmhouse Inn/N
Fifth Floor
Flea St. Café/S
Fleur de Lys
Florio
Foreign Cinema
Frantoio/N
French Laundry/N
Frisson
Garibaldis/E
Gary Chu's/N
Gary Danko

girl & the fig/N
Grand Cafe
Grasing's Coastal/S
Great Eastern
Habana
Harbor Village
Harris'
Hawthorne Lane
Hurley's/N
Iberia/S
Il Davide/N
Il Fornaio
Il Fornaio/S
Incanto
Indigo
Insalata's /N
Jardinière
Jeanty at Jack's
John Ash & Co./N
John Bentley's/S
Julia's Kitchen/N
Kenwood/N
Khan Toke
Kokkari Estiatorio
Kurt's Carmel Chop House/S
La Folie
La Forêt/S
Lalime's/E
Lark Creek Inn/N
La Strada/S
Last Supper Club
La Suite
La Toque/N
L'Auberge Carmel/S
Lavanda/S
Le Colonial
Ledford House/N
Left Bank/E/N/S
Le Papillon/S
Lion & Compass/S
Little River Inn/N
Louka/E
MacCallum House/N
Maddalena's/S
Madrona Manor/N
Manka's Inverness/N
Manresa/S
Manzanita/N
Marché/S
Marinus/S
Martini House/N
Masa's
Maya
Mecca

Mela Tandoori
Millennium
Montrio Bistro/S
Moose's
Morton's Steak
Myth
Navio/S
North Bch. Rest.
Olema Inn/N
Oliveto/E
One Market
Ozumo
Pacific
Pacific's Edge/S
Palio D'Asti
Parcel 104/S
Passionfish/S
Pauline's Pizza
Père Jeanty/N
Pesce
Piatti/N/S
Piazza D'Angelo/N
Pinot Blanc/N
PJ's Oyster Bed
Plumed Horse/S
PlumpJack Cafe
PlumpJack Cafe/E
Poggio/N
Ponzu
Postino/E
Postrio
Press/N
Prima/E
R & G Lounge
Rest. Budo/N
Rest. LuLu
Rio Grill/S
Rist. Ideale
Ritz-Carlton Din. Rm.
Robert's Whitehouse/S
Rose Pistola
Roy's
Rubicon
Ruth's Chris Steak
Santi/N
Sardine Factory/S
Sauce
Scala's Bistro
Scott's/E
Sea Ranch Lodge/N
Seasons
Sent Sovi/S
71 Saint Peter/S
Shadowbrook/S

Shanghai 1930
Silks
Slanted Door
Soi Four/E
Soizic/E
Spago Palo Alto/S
Stokes/S
Stomp/N
St. Orres/N
Straits Cafe/S
Sutro's at Cliff Hse.
Sydney's
Syrah/N
Tallula
Tamarine/S
Tarpy's Roadhouse/S
Terra/N
Ti Couz
Tommy Toy's
Town Hall
Townhouse B&G/E
Trader Vic's
Trader Vic's/E/S
Tratt. La Siciliana/E
Tra Vigne/N
2223
231 Ellsworth/S
Underwood Bar/N
Vic Stewart's/E
Village Pub/S
Viognier/S
Wappo Bar/N
Wente Vineyards/E
Wine Spectator/N
Yank Sing
Zarzuela
Zax Tavern/E
Zibibbo/S
Zinsvalley/N
Zuppa

Prix Fixe Menus
(Call for prices and times)
Absinthe
Acquerello
Ajanta/E
Alamo Square
Albany Bistro/E
Anjou
Aqua
Asia de Cuba
Auberge du Soleil/N
Aziza
Baker St. Bistro

Special Features

Barndiva/N
Bendean/E
Bistro Elan/S
Bistro Liaison/E
Bistro Ralph/N
BIX
Boonville Hotel/N
Bouchée/S
Brigitte's/S
Cafe Esin/E
Café Marcella/S
Campton Place
Carnelian Room
Carneros/N
Casanova/S
Cetrella Bistro/S
Chantilly/S
Chapeau!
Chaya Brasserie
Chez Panisse/E
Chez Panisse Café/E
Chez Spencer
Chez TJ/S
Christophe/N
Cindy's Backstreet/N
Citron/E
Cote Sud
Cyrus/N
Domaine Chandon/N
Dry Creek Kitchen/N
Duck Club/E
Ecco/S
Erna's Elderberry Hse./E
Espetus Churrascaria
Farallon
Firefly
Fleur de Lys
Florio
Fork/N
Fournou's Ovens
Frantoio/N
French Laundry/N
Gary Danko
Gaylord India/S
girl & the fig/N
Grand Cafe
Grasing's Coastal/S
Greens
Hana Japanese/N
Helmand, The
Hurley's/N
Indigo
Jardinière
Jordan's/E

Juban
Juban/S
Julia's Kitchen/N
Kyo-Ya
La Folie
La Forêt/S
Lark Creek Inn/N
La Scene Café
La Strada/S
La Toque/N
Le Charm Bistro
Ledford House/N
Left Bank/S
Le Papillon/S
Le Zinc
Lotus of India/N
Lovejoy's Tea Rm.
MacCallum House/N
Madrona Manor/N
Mandarin
Manka's Inverness/N
Manresa/S
Marché/S
Marica/E
Marinus/S
Market/N
Martini House/N
Masa's
Maya
Michael Mina
Millennium
Mirepoix/N
Moose's
Navio/S
Pacific
Pacific's Edge/S
Parcel 104/S
Pinot Blanc/N
Pisces/S
Ponzu
Postrio
Rendezvous Inn/N
Rest. Budo/N
Rist. Bacco
Ritz-Carlton Din. Rm.
rnm
Robert's Whitehouse/S
Roy's
Rubicon
Sanraku
Santé/N
Seasons
Sent Sovi/S
71 Saint Peter/S

Shanghai 1930
Sierra Mar/S
Silks
Slanted Door
Sociale
South Park Cafe
St. Orres/N
Syrah/N
Tallula
Tao Cafe
Tita's hale 'aina
Tommy Toy's
Ton Kiang
Town's End
Trader Vic's/S
Tratt. La Siciliana/E
2223
231 Ellsworth/S
Victorian Gardens/N
Viognier/S
Watergate
Wine Spectator/N
XYZ
Yabbies Coastal

Quiet Conversation

Acquerello
Alexander's Steak/S
Applewood Inn/N
Auberge du Soleil/N
Bay Wolf/E
Bella Vista/S
Cafe Jacqueline
Campton Place
C & L Steak
Casanova/S
Chantilly/S
Chez Panisse/E
Chez TJ/S
Cyrus/N
Duck Club/E/N/S
El Paseo/N
Farmhouse Inn/N
Fifth Floor
Fleur de Lys
Fournou's Ovens
Frisson
Gary Danko
Iberia/S
Julius' Castle
Lalime's/E
La Toque/N
L'Auberge Carmel/S
Louka/E

Lovejoy's Tea Rm.
Madrona Manor/N
Manresa/S
Marché aux Fleurs/N
Masa's
Michael Mina
O Chamé/E
Oswald's/S
Pacific's Edge/S
Park Grill
Picco/N
Postino/E
Quince
Rest. Budo/N
Seasons
Silks
St. Orres/N
SUMI
Victorian Gardens/N
Watergate

Raw Bars

Absinthe
Acme Chophouse
Angèle/N
A.P. Stump's/S
Aqua
bacar
Biscuits and Blues
Bistro Vida/S
Blowfish Sushi
Blowfish Sushi/S
Blupointe
Bouchon/N
Café Rouge/E
Elite Cafe
Farallon
Foreign Cinema
Fresca
Godzila Sushi
Hog Island Oyster
Kingfish
Kingfish/S
Left Bank/S
Monti's Rotisserie/N
Olema Inn/N
Osake/N
Ozumo
Parcel 104/S
Pearl Oyster Bar/E
Pesce
Rest. LuLu
Sea Salt/E
Seasons

Special Features

Sierra Mar/S
Sonoma Meritage/N
Sushi Ran/N
Swan Oyster Depot
Ti Couz
Watercress
Willi's Seafood/N
Yabbies Coastal
Yankee Pier/N/S
zazu/N
Zibibbo/S
Zucca/S
Zuni Café

Romantic Places

Acquerello
Ahwahnee Din. Rm./E
Albion River Inn/N
Alexander's Steak/S
Alexander Valley/N
Ana Mandara
Anton & Michel/S
Applewood Inn/N
Auberge du Soleil/N
Aziza
Barndiva/N
Bella Vista/S
Big 4
Bing Crosby's/E
Bistro Clovis
Bistro Elan/S
Bistro Vida/S
Blanca Cafe
Blue Nile/E
Boulevard
Cafe Beaujolais/N
Cafe Jacqueline
Caprice/N
Carnelian Room
Casanova/S
Chantilly/S
Chapeau!
Chez Panisse/E
Chez Spencer
Chez TJ/S
Christophe/N
Citron/E
Cool Café/S
Cyrus/N
Domaine Chandon/N
Duck Club/E/N/S
El Paseo/N
Emile's/S
Erna's Elderberry Hse./E

Farmhouse Inn/N
Fifth Floor
Flea St. Café/S
Fleur de Lys
French Laundry/N
Fresh Cream/S
Gabriella Café/S
Garden Court
Gary Danko
Incanto
Indigo
Jardinière
John Ash & Co./N
John Bentley's/S
Julius' Castle
Katia's Tea Rm.
Khan Toke
La Folie
La Forêt/S
Lalime's/E
La Note/E
Lark Creek Inn/N
La Toque/N
L'Auberge Carmel/S
Le Papillon/S
Little River Inn/N
MacCallum House/N
Maddalena's/S
Madrona Manor/N
Manka's Inverness/N
Marché aux Fleurs/N
Marinus/S
Martini House/N
Masa's
Matterhorn Swiss
Medjool
Michael Mina
Moosse Cafe/N
Napa Wine Train/N
O Chamé/E
Olema Inn/N
Pacific's Edge/S
Picco/N
Quince
Rest. at Stevenswood/N
Rest. Budo/N
Ritz-Carlton Din. Rm.
Ritz-Carlton Terrace
Robert's Whitehouse/S
Roy's Pebble Beach/S
Rue Saint Jacques
Sea Salt/E
Sent Sovi/S
71 Saint Peter/S

Shadowbrook/S
Sierra Mar/S
Silks
Slow Club
Soizic/E
St. Michael's/S
Stokes/S
St. Orres/N
Tallula
Terra/N
Venticello
Victorian Gardens/N
Viognier/S
Watergate
Wente Vineyards/E
Woodward's Garden
Zarzuela
Zax Tavern/E

Senior Appeal

Acme Chophouse
Acquerello
Alfred's Steak
Alioto's
Anton & Michel/S
Bella Vista/S
Big 4
Bing Crosby's/E
C & L Steak
Caprice/N
Chantilly/S
Christophe/N
Cole's Chop House/N
Cook St. Helena/N
Cyrus/N
Duck Club/E/N/S
Emile's/S
Eulipia/S
Fleur de Lys
Fournou's Ovens
Garden Court
Harris'
Hayes St. Grill
House of Prime Rib
Izzy's Steak
La Ginestra/N
Lalime's/E
Le Central Bistro
Masa's
Morton's Steak
North Bch. Rest.
Plumed Horse/S
Robert's Whitehouse/S
Rotunda

Sardine Factory/S
Scoma's
Sydney's
Tadich Grill
Vic Stewart's/E

Singles Scenes

Ace Wasabi's
Andalu
Asia de Cuba
Balboa Cafe
Bambuddha
Barndiva/N
Beach Chalet
Betelnut Pejiu Wu
BIX
Blowfish Sushi
Blue Plate
butterfly embarcadero
Cafe Bastille
Café Claude
Cascal/S
Catch
Cha Cha Cha
Circolo
Cosmopolitan
Cozmo's Corner
E&O Trading Co.
E&O Trading Co./S
Elite Cafe
Emmy's Spaghetti
Firecracker
Foreign Cinema
Frisson
Frjtz Fries
Guaymas/N
Home
Jack Falstaff
Kan Zaman
Kingfish/S
La Suite
Levende
Lime
Luna Park
Mecca
Medjool
MoMo's
Monte Cristo Cafe
Nectar Wine
Ozumo
Pearl Alley Bistro/S
PJ's Oyster Bed
Public
Puerto Alegre

Special Features

Ramblas
rnm
RoHan Lounge
Rose Pistola
Seven/S
Slow Club
Sushi Groove
Tallula
Ti Couz
Tokyo Go Go
Tsunami Sushi
2223
Universal Cafe
U Street Lounge
Winterland
Zibibbo/S
Zuni Café

Sleepers
(Good to excellent food, but little known)
A La Turca
Angkor Borei
Basin/S
Bodega Bistro
Boonville Hotel/N
Brindisi Cucina
Cafe Citti/N
Caffe Centro
Club XIX/S
Cook St. Helena/N
Cucina Paradiso/N
Cyrus/N
Desiree Café
Deuce/N
El Metate
fig cafe & winebar/N
Fuentes Tapas/N
Goood Frikin' Chicken
Happy Cafe/S
Harmony Club/N
Jai Yun
Joe's Cable Car
K&L Bistro/N
Katia's Tea Rm.
Kaygetsu/S
Kitchen at 868 Grant/N
Koo
La Rose Bistro/E
L'Auberge Carmel/S
Ledford House/N
Levende
Luella
MacCallum House/N

Mandalay
Mangarosa
Manka's Inverness/N
Maria Manso's/N
Massawa
Medjool
Mirepoix/N
Mochica
Monti's Rotisserie/N
Moosse Cafe/N
955 Ukiah/N
Olema Inn/N
Osake/N
Oswald's/S
Pangaea/N
Phoenix Next Door/E
Pho Hoa-Hiep II
Pho Hoa-Hiep II/E/S
Pizza Azzurro/N
Rendezvous Inn/N
Rest. at Stevenswood/N
Rest. Budo/N
Robert's Whitehouse/S
RoHan Lounge
Rotee
Santé/N
Seaweed Café/N
Sharon's By Sea/N
So
Sonoma Meritage/N
Stomp/N
St. Orres/N
Tamal
Tao Cafe
Taste Cafe/S
Turmerik/S
Uva Trattoria/N
Victorian Gardens/N
Water St. Bistro/N
Wine Garden Food/N
Woodward's Garden
Yumma's
Zatar/E
Zinsvalley/N
Zushi Puzzle

Tasting Menus
Acquerello
Aqua
Auberge du Soleil/N
Aziza
Bouchée/S
Cafe Esin/E
Campton Place

Carneros/N
Chantilly/S
Chapeau!
Chez Spencer
Citron/E
Cyrus/N
Domaine Chandon/N
Dry Creek Kitchen/N
Duck Club/E
Ecco/S
Fork/N
French Laundry/N
Gary Danko
Hana Japanese/N
Jardinière
Julia's Kitchen/N
Koi Palace/S
Kyo-Ya
La Folie
La Forêt/S
Lark Creek Inn/N
La Toque/N
L'Auberge Carmel/S
Le Papillon/S
MacCallum House/N
Madrona Manor/N
Manresa/S
Marché/S
Marinus/S
Martini House/N
Masa's
Michael Mina
Millennium
Mirepoix/N
Navio/S
Pacific
Pacific's Edge/S
Parcel 104/S
Pisces/S
Postrio
Rest. Budo/N
Ritz-Carlton Din. Rm.
Sanraku
Santé/N
Sea Ranch Lodge/N
Sent Sovi/S
71 Saint Peter/S
Shanghai 1930
Sonoma Meritage/N
Syrah/N
Tallula
Tommy Toy's
231 Ellsworth/S
XYZ

Teen Appeal

Barney's
Barney's/E/N
Beach Chalet
Buca di Beppo
Buca di Beppo/S
Burger Joint
Cactus Taqueria/E
Cheesecake Factory
Cheesecake Factory/S
FatApple's/E
Fenton's Creamery/E
Fog City Diner
Goat Hill Pizza
Hard Rock Cafe
Joe's Cable Car
MacArthur Park/S
Max's
Max's/E/N/S
Mel's Drive-In
Mo's
Park Chalet
Pauline's Pizza
Picante Cocina/E
Pizza Antica/E
Pizzeria Picco/N
Rutherford Grill/N
Sardine Factory/S
Shen Hua/E
Taylor's Automatic/N
Tonga Room

Theme Restaurants

Bing Crosby's/E
Buca di Beppo
Buca di Beppo/S
Hard Rock Cafe
Max's
Max's/E/N/S
Napa Wine Train/N

Trendy

Ace Wasabi's
À Côté/E
Aqua
Asia de Cuba
A 16
Azie
Balboa Cafe
Bambuddha
Barndiva/N
Betelnut Pejiu Wu
Bing Crosby's/E
Bistro Don Giovanni/N

Special Features

BIX
Blowfish Sushi
Blue Jay Cafe
Blue Plate
Bocadillos
Bouchon/N
Boulevard
Buckeye Roadhouse/N
Bungalow 44/N
Café Fanny/E
Café Rouge/E
Cascal/S
César/E
Cetrella Bistro/S
Cha Cha Cha
Charanga
Chez Nous
Chez Panisse Café/E
Chez Papa Bistrot
Cindy's Backstreet/N
Circolo
Deep Sushi
Delfina
Doña Tomás/E
downtown/E
Dry Creek Kitchen/N
Ebisu
Emmy's Spaghetti
Enrico's Sidewalk
Eos Rest./Wine Bar
Evvia/S
Farallon
Flea St. Café/S
Fonda Solana/E
Foreign Cinema
Fringale
Frisson
Garibaldis/E
girl & the fig/N
Globe
Iluna Basque
Isa
Jack Falstaff
Jardinière
Last Supper Club
La Suite
Levende
Lime
Limón
Luna Park
Martini House/N
Maverick
Mecca
Medjool

Moose's
Mustards Grill/N
Myth
Ozumo
Pearl Oyster Bar/E
Piazza D'Angelo/N
Picco/N
Piperade
Pizza Antica/S
Pizzeria Delfina
Pizzeria Picco/N
Plouf
PlumpJack Cafe
Poggio/N
Postino/E
Postrio
Press/N
Public
Rest. LuLu
rnm
Rose Pistola
Rose's Cafe
Santi/N
Slanted Door
Slow Club
Spago Palo Alto/S
Stomp/N
Sushi Groove
Tallula
Tamarine/S
Ti Couz
Tokyo Go Go
Town Hall
Trader Vic's/E/S
Tsunami Sushi
2223
Universal Cafe
U Street Lounge
Village Pub/S
Willi's Seafood/N
XYZ
Zibibbo/S
Zuni Café
Zuppa
Zuzu/N

Valet Parking
Absinthe
Acme Chophouse
Ahwahnee Din. Rm./E
Albona Rist.
Americano
Ana Mandara
Andalu

Antica Trattoria
Anzu
Aqua
Arcadia/S
Asia de Cuba
A 16
Auberge du Soleil/N
Azie
Aziza
bacar
Balboa Cafe
Big 4
Bing Crosby's/E
BIX
Blowfish Sushi/S
Boca/N
Boulette's Larder
Boulevard
Bridges/E
Buckeye Roadhouse/N
butterfly embarcadero
Campton Place
C & L Steak
Caprice/N
Casa Orinda/E
Chantilly/S
Chaya Brasserie
Cheesecake Factory/S
Citizen Cake
Club XIX/S
Coco 500
Cole's Chop House/N
Cortez
Crustacean
Delancey St.
Duck Club/E/S
Ecco/S
El Raigon
Emile's/S
Enrico's Sidewalk
Evvia/S
Farallon
Fifth Floor
Fleur de Lys
Foreign Cinema
Fournou's Ovens
Frisson
Garibaldis
Garibaldis/E
Gary Danko
Grand Cafe
Habana
Harris'
Hawthorne Lane

Hayes St. Grill
Home
Hong Kong Flower/S
House of Prime Rib
Il Fornaio
Il Fornaio/E/S
Impala
Insalata's /N
Jack Falstaff
Jardinière
Jeanty at Jack's
John Ash & Co./N
Jordan's/E
Julius' Castle
Kingfish
Kingfish/S
Kokkari Estiatorio
Kuleto's
Kuleto's/S
Kyo-Ya
La Folie
Lark Creek Inn/N
La Scene Café
La Suite
L'Auberge Carmel/S
Lavanda/S
Le Colonial
Left Bank/E/N
Le Petit Robert
Lion & Compass/S
Mangarosa
Marinus/S
Masa's
Matterhorn Swiss
Maykadeh
Mecca
Millennium
MoMo's
Moose's
Morton's Steak
Myth
Navio/S
Nob Hill Café
North Bch. Rest.
Oak City B&G/S
One Market
Pacific
Pacific's Edge/S
Parcel 104/S
Piazza D'Angelo/N
Picco/N
Pizzeria Picco/N
Plumed Horse/S
PlumpJack Cafe

Special Features

Poggio/N
Ponzu
Postino/E
Postrio
Prima/E
Quince
Rest. LuLu
Rist. Capellini/S
Rist. Milano
Ritz-Carlton Din. Rm.
Ritz-Carlton Terrace
rnm
Rose Pistola
Roy's Pebble Beach/S
Rubicon
Ruth's Chris Steak
Santé/N
Scoma's
Scott's/E
Seasons
Shanghai 1930
Sierra Mar/S
Silks
Slanted Door
Spago Palo Alto/S
Suppenküche
Thanh Long
Tokyo Go Go
Tommy Toy's
Townhouse B&G/E
Trader Vic's
Trader Vic's/E
231 Ellsworth/S
Venticello
Waterfront
Watergate
Wente Vineyards/E
Wine Spectator/N
Winterland
XYZ
Yankee Pier/N
YaYa
Zibibbo/S
Zuni Café

Views

Ahwahnee Din. Rm./E
Albion River Inn/N
Alexander Valley/N
Alioto's
Americano
Angèle/N
Applewood Inn/N
A. Sabella's

Auberge du Soleil/N
Barbara Fishtrap/S
Barndiva/N
Beach Chalet
Bella Vista/S
Bistro Boudin
Bistro Don Giovanni/N
Blackhawk Grille/E
Boulette's Larder
Brigitte's/S
Brix/N
Cafe Beaujolais/N
Cafe Gibraltar/S
Caprice/N
Carnelian Room
Chaya Brasserie
Cheesecake Factory
Chez TJ/S
Cliff House Bistro
Club XIX/S
Cool Café/S
Delancey St.
Domaine Chandon/N
Duck Club/E/N/S
Enrico's Sidewalk
Eos Rest./Wine Bar
Erna's Elderberry Hse./E
Fish/N
Fresh Cream/S
General Café/N
Greens
Guaymas/N
Hog Island Oyster
Il Fornaio/S
John Ash & Co./N
Jordan's/E
Julia's Kitchen/N
Julius' Castle
Kenwood/N
La Forêt/S
Lark Creek Inn/N
Ledford House/N
Little River Inn/N
Mandarin
McCormick & Kuleto
Meadowood Grill/N
Mijita
Mistral/S
Moosse Cafe/N
Napa Wine Train/N
Navio/S
Nepenthe/S
One Market
Ozumo

Pacific's Edge/S
Park Chalet
Pinot Blanc/N
Poggio/N
Press/N
Red's Java House
Rest. at Stevenswood/N
Rivoli/E
Rotunda
Roy's Pebble Beach/S
Scoma's
Scoma's/N
Scott's/E
Sea Ranch Lodge/N
Shadowbrook/S
Sharon's By Sea/N
Sierra Mar/S
Slanted Door
Sutro's at Cliff Hse.
Trader Vic's/E/S
Waterfront
Wente Vineyards/E
Wine Spectator/N
Zaré/N

Visitors on Expense Account

Acquerello
Alexander's Steak/S
Alexander Valley/N
Aqua
Auberge du Soleil/N
Azie
Boulevard
Campton Place
C & L Steak
Carnelian Room
Chez Panisse/E
Chez TJ/S
Club XIX/S
Cyrus/N
Dry Creek Kitchen/N
Erna's Elderberry Hse./E
Eulipia/S
Evvia/S
Fifth Floor
Flea St. Café/S
Fleur de Lys
French Laundry/N
Fresh Cream/S
Gary Danko
Greens
Harris'
Jack Falstaff

Jardinière
John Ash & Co./N
Julius' Castle
Kaygetsu/S
Kokkari Estiatorio
Kyo-Ya
La Folie
La Forêt/S
Lark Creek Inn/N
La Toque/N
L'Auberge Carmel/S
Mandarin
Manresa/S
Marinus/S
Masa's
McCormick & Kuleto
Michael Mina
Morton's Steak
Napa Wine Train/N
Oliveto/E
Pacific's Edge/S
Park Grill
Plumed Horse/S
Press/N
Rest. Budo/N
Ritz-Carlton Din. Rm.
Ritz-Carlton Terrace
Roy's
Roy's Pebble Beach/S
Santé/N
Sea Ranch Lodge/N
Seasons
Sent Sovi/S
71 Saint Peter/S
Shanghai 1930
Sierra Mar/S
Silks
Spago Palo Alto/S
Tommy Toy's
Village Pub/S

Wine Bars

bacar
Blanca Cafe
Bouchée/S
César/E
Cork/N
Cucina Paradiso/N
Cucina Rest./Wine Bar/N
Eos Rest./Wine Bar
1550 Hyde Café
fig cafe & winebar/N
Frascati
General Café/N

girl & the fig/N
Incanto
Kuleto's
La Toque/N
Le Zinc
Liberty Cafe
Millennium
Napa Wine Train/N
Nectar Wine
Pearl Alley Bistro/S
Prima/E
Rest. LuLu
Sabor of Spain/N
Sushi Ran/N
Tartine Bakery
Uva Trattoria/N
Va de Vi/E
Vivande Porta Via
Willi's Seafood/N
Willi's Wine Bar/N
Yabbies Coastal
Zibibbo/S
Zin/N

Winning Wine Lists

Absinthe
Acme Chophouse
À Côté/E
Acquerello
Albion River Inn/N
Alexander's Steak/S
Alexander Valley/N
Alioto's
All Season's Cafe/N
Angèle/N
Anton & Michel/S
A.P. Stump's/S
Aqua
A 16
Auberge du Soleil/N
Azie
bacar
Bay Wolf/E
Bella Vista/S
Bistro Aix
Bistro Clovis
Bistro Don Giovanni/N
Bistro Ralph/N
Blackhawk Grille/E
Blanca Cafe
Bocadillos
Bouchée/S
Bouchon/N
Boulevard

Bridges/E
Brix/N
CAFÉ KATi
Cafe La Haye/N
Campton Place
C & L Steak
Carnelian Room
Carneros/N
Casanova/S
Celadon/N
César/E
Cetrella Bistro/S
Chapeau!
Chez Panisse/E
Chez Panisse Café/E
Chez TJ/S
Citron/E
Club XIX/S
Cole's Chop House/N
Cork/N
Cote Sud
Cyrus/N
Deuce/N
Domaine Chandon/N
downtown/E
Dry Creek Kitchen/N
El Paseo/N
Emile's/S
Eos Rest./Wine Bar
Erna's Elderberry Hse./E
Fandango/S
Farallon
Farmhouse Inn/N
1550 Hyde Café
Fifth Floor
fig cafe & winebar/N
Flea St. Café/S
Fleur de Lys
Fournou's Ovens
French Laundry/N
Frisson
Gabriella Café/S
Gary Danko
girl & the fig/N
Gordon's/N
Grasing's Coastal/S
Greens
Hawthorne Lane
Incanto
Indigo
Jack Falstaff
Jardinière
Jeanty at Jack's
John Ash & Co./N

Julia's Kitchen/N
Julius' Castle
Kenwood/N
Kokkari Estiatorio
Kuleto's
Kuleto's/S
Kurt's Carmel Chop House/S
La Folie
La Forêt/S
Lark Creek Inn/N
LaSalette/N
La Toque/N
L'Auberge Carmel/S
Lavanda/S
Ledford House/N
Le Papillon/S
Liberty Cafe
Luella
Madrona Manor/N
Manresa/S
Manzanita/N
Marché/S
Marinus/S
Martini House/N
Masa's
Meadowood Grill/N
Mecca
Mendo Bistro/N
Michael Mina
Millennium
Monti's Rotisserie/N
Montrio Bistro/S
Moose's
Mustards Grill/N
Myth
Napa Valley Grille/N
Napa Wine Train/N
Navio/S
955 Ukiah/N
North Bch. Rest.
Oliveto/E
One Market
Oswald's/S
Pacific's Edge/S
Palio D'Asti
Pangaea/N
Park Grill
Passionfish/S
Pearl Alley Bistro/S
Père Jeanty/N
Picco/N
Pilar/N
Pinot Blanc/N
Piperade

Pisces/S
Plumed Horse/S
PlumpJack Cafe
PlumpJack Cafe/E
Poggio/N
Postrio
Prima/E
Quince
Rest. Budo/N
Rest. LuLu
Rio Grill/S
Ritz-Carlton Din. Rm.
Rivoli/E
Rose Pistola
Roy's
Roy's Pebble Beach/S
Rubicon
Sabor of Spain/N
Santé/N
Santi/N
Sardine Factory/S
Scala's Bistro
Sea Ranch Lodge/N
Seasons
Sent Sovi/S
Sierra Mar/S
Silks
Slanted Door
Spago Palo Alto/S
St. Michael's/S
Stomp/N
St. Orres/N
Sushi Groove
Sushi Ran/N
Syrah/N
Terra/N
Town Hall
Tra Vigne/N
231 Ellsworth/S
Va de Vi/E
Vic Stewart's/E
Village Pub/S
Viognier/S
Wappo Bar/N
Wente Vineyards/E
Willi's Seafood/N
Wine Garden Food/N
Wine Spectator/N
Yabbies Coastal
Zibibbo/S
Zin/N
Zinsvalley/N
Zuni Café

Worth a Trip

Albion
Albion River Inn/N
Ledford House/N

Berkeley
César/E
Chez Panisse/E
Chez Panisse Café/E
Eccolo/E
Lalime's/E
Rivoli/E
Zachary's Pizza/E

Big Sur
Sierra Mar/S

Boonville
Boonville Hotel/N

Carmel
Bouchée/S
Grasing's Coastal/S
L'Auberge Carmel/S
Marinus/S
Pacific's Edge/S

El Granada
Cafe Gibraltar/S

Forestville
Farmhouse Inn/N

Fort Bragg
Mendo Bistro/N
Rendezvous Inn/N

Geyserville
Alexander Valley/N
Santi/N

Graton
Underwood Bar/N

Gualala
St. Orres/N

Half Moon Bay
Cetrella Bistro/S
Navio/S

Healdsburg
Cyrus/N
Dry Creek Kitchen/N
Madrona Manor/N
Manzanita/N
Willi's Seafood/N

Inverness
Manka's Inverness/N

Kenwood
Kenwood/N

Larkspur
Emporio Rulli/N
Lark Creek Inn/N
Left Bank/N

Little River
Little River Inn/N

Livermore
Wente Vineyards/E

Los Gatos
Manresa/S

Manchester
Victorian Gardens/N

Mendocino
Cafe Beaujolais/N
MacCallum House/N

Menlo Park
Flea St. Café/S
Kaygetsu/S
Marché/S

Mill Valley
Buckeye Roadhouse/N

Monterey
Fresh Cream/S
Montrio Bistro/S
Stokes/S
Tarpy's Roadhouse/S

Mountain View
Chez TJ/S

Napa
Angèle/N
Celadon/N
Julia's Kitchen/N
Mustards Grill/N
Napa Wine Train/N
Pilar/N
Rest. Budo/N

Oakhurst
Erna's Elderberry Hse./E

Oakland
À Côté/E
Bay Wolf/E
Oliveto/E
Zachary's Pizza/E

Pacific Grove
Fandango/S

Palo Alto
Cool Café/S
Evvia/S
La Strada/S
Lavanda/S
Spago Palo Alto/S
Tamarine/S
Zibibbo/S

Pebble Beach
Club XIX/S
Roy's Pebble Beach/S

Pescadero
Duarte's Tavern/S

Special Features

Rohnert Park
  Hana Japanese/N
Rutherford
  Auberge du Soleil/N
  La Toque/N
San Anselmo
  Insalata's /N
San Jose
  A.P. Stump's/S
  Arcadia/S
  Emile's/S
  La Forêt/S
  Le Papillon/S
San Mateo
  Viognier/S
San Ramon
  Cafe Esin/E
Santa Rosa
  John Ash & Co./N
  Willi's Wine Bar/N
Saratoga
  Plumed Horse/S
Sausalito
  Sushi Ran/N

Sebastopol
  K&L Bistro/N
Sonoma
  Cafe La Haye/N
  Carneros/N
  girl & the fig/N
St. Helena
  Cindy's Backstreet/N
  Market/N
  Martini House/N
  Press/N
  Terra/N
  Tra Vigne/N
Woodside
  Bella Vista/S
  John Bentley's/S
  Village Pub/S
Yosemite Nat'l Park
  Ahwahnee Din. Rm./E
Yountville
  Bistro Jeanty/N
  Bouchon/N
  Domaine Chandon/N
  French Laundry/N

Alphabetical
Page Index

Places outside of San Francisco are marked as follows:
E=East of SF; N=North; and S=South.

vote at zagat.com   275

Alphabetical Page Index

Alphabetical Page Index

Alphabetical Page Index

Alphabetical Page Index

Wine Vintage Chart

This chart is designed to help you select wine to go with your meal. It is based on the same 0 to 30 scale used throughout this *Survey*. The ratings (prepared by our friend **Howard Stravitz,** a law professor at the University of South Carolina) reflect both the quality of the vintage and the wine's readiness for present consumption. Thus, if a wine is not fully mature or is over the hill, its rating has been reduced. We do not include 1987, 1991–1993 vintages because they are not especially recommended for most areas. A dash indicates that a wine is either past its peak or too young to rate.

	'85	'86	'88	'89	'90	'94	'95	'96	'97	'98	'99	'00	'01	'02	'03
WHITES															
French:															
Alsace	24	–	22	28	28	27	26	25	25	26	25	26	27	25	–
Burgundy	26	25	–	24	22	–	28	29	24	23	26	25	23	27	24
Loire Valley	–	–	–	–	24	–	20	23	22	–	24	25	23	27	26
Champagne	28	25	24	26	29	–	26	27	24	24	25	25	26	–	–
Sauternes	21	28	29	25	27	–	21	23	26	24	24	24	28	25	26
Germany	25	–	25	26	27	25	24	27	24	23	25	24	29	27	–
California (Napa, Sonoma, Mendocino):															
Chardonnay	–	–	–	–	–	–	–	24	26	25	25	24	27	29	–
Sauvignon Blanc/Semillon	–	–	–	–	–	–	–	–	–	25	25	23	27	28	26
REDS															
French:															
Bordeaux	24	25	24	26	29	22	26	25	23	25	24	28	26	23	24
Burgundy	23	–	21	24	26	–	26	28	25	22	28	22	24	27	–
Rhône	25	19	27	29	29	24	25	23	24	28	27	27	26	–	25
Beaujolais	–	–	–	–	–	–	–	–	–	–	23	24	–	25	28
California (Napa, Sonoma, Mendocino):															
Cab./Merlot	27	26	–	21	28	29	27	25	28	23	26	23	27	25	–
Pinot Noir	–	–	–	–	–	–	–	–	24	24	25	24	26	29	–
Zinfandel	–	–	–	–	–	–	–	–	–	–	–	–	26	26	–
Italian:															
Tuscany	–	–	–	–	25	22	25	20	29	24	28	26	25	–	–
Piedmont	–	–	–	27	28	–	23	27	27	25	25	28	23	–	–

subscribe to zagat.com